Toward Corporate IT Standardization Management:
Frameworks and Solutions

Robert van Wessel
Tilburg University, Netherlands

Information Science REFERENCE
INFORMATION SCIENCE REFERENCE
Hershey · New York

Director of Editorial Content:	Kristin Klinger
Director of Book Publications:	Julia Mosemann
Acquisitions Editor:	Lindsay Johnston
Development Editor:	Julia Mosemann
Publishing Assistant:	Devvin Earnest
Typesetter:	Michael Brehm
Quality control:	Jamie Snavely
Cover Design:	Lisa Tosheff
Printed at:	Yurchak Printing Inc.

Published in the United States of America by
Information Science Reference (an imprint of IGI Global)
701 E. Chocolate Avenue
Hershey PA 17033
Tel: 717-533-8845
Fax: 717-533-8661
E-mail: cust@igi-global.com
Web site: http://www.igi-global.com/reference

Library of Congress Cataloging-in-Publication Data

Van Wessel, Robert, 1965-
Toward corporate IT standardization management : frameworks and solutions / by Robert van Wessel.
p. cm.
Includes bibliographical references and index.
Summary: "Given the limitations and uncertainties in the field of IT standardization and standards, this book focuses on the effects of IT standardization and IT standards on a company"--Provided by publisher.
ISBN 978-1-61520-759-6 (hardcover) -- ISBN 978-1-61520-760-2 (ebook) 1. Information technology--Management. 2. Information technology--Standards. I. Title.

HD30.2.V366 2010
004.068--dc22

2009032618

British Cataloguing in Publication Data
A Cataloguing in Publication record for this book is available from the British Library.

Table of Contents

Foreword vii

Preface ix

Executive Summary xvi

Glossary xx

Acknowledgment xxvi

Section 1
Setting the Scene

Chapter 1
Introduction 1
Motivation of Research 1
Problem Definition 3
Scope and Research Approach 4
Summary 7
References 8
Endnotes 10

Section 2
Literature Review

Chapter 2
Standardization & Standards 12
Introduction 13
External Standardization Processes 15
IT Standardization in Organizations 28
Utilization of IT Standards in Organizations 34
Benefits and Risks of Standardization and Standards 37

Conclusions 41
Managerial Implications 41
References 42
Endnotes 48

Chapter 3
IT, Business Processes & Performance **50**
Introduction 50
The Value of IT 51
Business Process Performance 54
Some Elements of Process Performance 60
Conclusions 70
Managerial Implications 70
References 71
Endnotes 76

Section 3
Building a Conceptual Model

Chapter 4
Building the Conceptual Model **78**
Pilot Case Study 78
Managerial implications 86
Initial Conceptual Model 86
First Assessment and Further Research Outline 100
References 104
Endnotes 110

Section 4
Three In-Depth Case Studies

Chapter 5
Client/Server Standardization "Uniform Case" **112**
Introduction 112
Case Description 112
Case Analysis 119
Conclusions 129
Managerial Implications 130
References 131
Endnotes 131

Chapter 6
Software Development Standardization "CMM/DSDM Case"...... 133
Introduction...... 133
Case Description...... 134
Case Analysis...... 153
Conclusions...... 159
Managerial Implications...... 159
References...... 160
Endnotes...... 161

Chapter 7
HR IS Standardization "CHRISP Case"...... 162
Introduction...... 162
Case Description...... 164
Case Analysis...... 172
Conclusions...... 178
Managerial Implications...... 178
References...... 179
Endnotes...... 180

Section 5
A Reflection Upon the Case Studies:
Towards a Corporate IT Standadization Management Framework

Chapter 8
A Reflection Upon the Case Studies...... 182
Summary of the Cases...... 182
Cross Case Analysis...... 184
IT Governance...... 199
IT Management...... 205
Extended Conceptual Model...... 206
Managerial Implications...... 211
References...... 212
Endnotes...... 214

Section 6
A Fourth and Final Case Study to Test the Corporate IT Standadization Management Framework

Chapter 9
Information Security Management Standardization "ISO/IEC 17799 Case" 217
Introduction 217
Case Description 220
Case Analysis 231
Conclusions 239
Managerial Implications 239
References 240
Endnotes 242

Section 7
Conclusions, Discussion and Recommendations

Chapter 10
Conclusions, Discussion, Recommendations 245
Looking Back 246
Conclusions 247
Discussion 255
Looking Ahead 257
References 258
Endnotes 259

Summary 260

Appendix I: Case Study Questionnaire 263

Appendix II: List of Interviewees 269

About the Author 271

Index 272

Foreword

IT STANDARDISATION: THE HIDDEN ANSWER TO LOW PRODUCTIVITY GROWTH IN SERVICES?

In today's economy, productivity growth of services is a major societal issue. In the last decades, throughout the industrialized world, employment in services has grown to some two-third or more of the total work population, at the expense mainly of employment in the industrial sectors. So far, so good. We have a network society (Castells 1996), we have a post-industrial society (Bell 1973), we have a service economy, that is just fine. What is not fine at all is that, in those same last decades, productivity growth in the manufacturing sectors has mostly been around some 3%, whereas productivity growth in most sectors has been marginal at around 1-2%, or less, or zero, or even negative (Breitenfellner & Hildebrandt 2006). Productivity growth remains the "lubrication oil" of our modern economies: the mere fact that there is just a little bit more to divide amongst all of us makes many economic processes run smooth. No or minimal productivity growth, and our economies risk institutional sclerosis.

At the same time, it is not so that services have sacrificed productivity growth for an extreme customer orientation either. Again throughout the industrialized world, service have been noted to "stink" (Business week 2000), or, more academically formulated, "poor service prevails" (Gerstner & Libai 2007). In the Netherlands, two cable companies and one telco ranked the top-3 of most irritating companies, just ahead of the Dutch equivalent of the Internal Revenue Service. In a recent survey, less than 40% of customers saw banks and health care insurers as "customer-focussed", "open", "honest" or "reliable".

This forms an enigma. In the marketing literature, it is assumed that one major difference between manufacturing and services is that in manufacturing, higher quality means more standardization of the operational processes, but that in services the opposite is true. "In service delivery, the emphasis is on the perception of the customer and real-time customization to meet the needs of the customer. In other words, providing high-quality manufactured goods means standardizing as much as possible, but providing high-quality service means customizing as much as possible to whatever the individual customer desires" (Rust & Chung 2006, p.568). So, one could live with a world in which service did not reap the productivity benefits of standardization because they were more geared towards customized service delivery. However, it seems that neither productivity nor customer orientation are being achieved in most service sectors until now.

One potential solution to this enigma, and to the societal issue of low service productivity growth at the same time, is more and better IT standardization. IT supports work processes, but that does not mean that these processes have to be conducted in precisely the same way every time. The person providing the service can still mix and match the standardized components. However, the current state of the art in IT performance in the service sector is a far cry from such a setting. Service professionals have to work their way through a jungle of historically grown, often obscure and outdated IT systems on their way to serve their clients. Apparently, despite the many billions that companies in the service sectors have invested in information technology so far, better IT support is not so easy to achieve.

Clearly, IT standardization is very important and very difficult at the same time in services, and yet few executives will treat it with the priority it deserves in this line of reasoning. Hopefully, the present volume will be helpful in making changes in this situation. The author bases his recommendation on an in-depth understanding of what it really takes to achieve effective IT standardization in one of the most important service sectors, that of Banking. Its longitudinal perspective is rare in the academic literature, but precisely what we need to better understand the challenges in IT standardization, as these processes evolve over time.

Henk Akkermans
Tilburg, August 1, 2009

***Henk A. Akkermans** is full Professor Supply Network Dynamics at Tilburg University, Faculty of Economics and Business Administration, Information Management. He has an PhD in Technology Management at Eindhoven University of Technology, a Master in Information Management at Tilburg University and a Master in Japanese language and Culture at Leiden University. Henk Akkermans' research concerns decentralized inter-organisational supply chains and networks, in particular in the high-tech industries of electronics, telecom and aerospace. For his research, he develops system dynamics and agent-based models of real-world settings. His special interest is in the evolution of inter-organisational relationships and the interrelations between collaboration and performance.*

REFERENCES

Akkermans, H.A. and van der Horst, H. (2002): Managing IT Infrastructure Standardisation in the Networked Manufacturing Firm. *International Journal of Production Economics* 75(1) 213-228.

Breitenfellner, A. & Hildebrandt, A. (2006) High Employment with Low Productivity? The Service Sector as a Determinant of Economic Development. *Monetary Policy & the Economy* Q1/06, 1210-135.

Castells, M. (1996). *The Rise of the Network Society. Vol. I: The Information Age: Economy, Society and Culture*. Cambridge, MA; Oxford, UK: Blackwell

Bell, D (1973) *The coming of the Post-Industrial Society: A Venture in Social Forecasting*. Harper Colophon Books).

Brady, D (2000): Why Service Stinks. *Business Week*, October 23, 2000.

Baltesen, F. (2009) Klanten ontevreden over kwaliteit van zorgverzekeraar. ("Customers dissastisfied with quality of health care insurers", in Dutch) *NRC Handelsblad*, 3 april 2009.

Rust, RT & TS Chung (2006): Marketing Models of Service and Relationships. *Marketing Science* 25(6), 560–580.

Consumentenbond (2007) "Veel consumenten ergeren zich aan dienstverleners" (Many customers are annoyed by service providers", in Dutch) published on August 31, 2007 at www.consumentenbond.nl.

Preface

In day-to-day life, a lot of standardization initiatives are carried out within organizations. They aim to ensure quality and to reduce operational costs, to name but a few aims. Studies on the business impact of standards mostly focus on the consequences of product standards for market share (De Vries, 1999) whereas others looked into the balance between desires of entrepreneurs and the needs of society (Krechmer and Baskin, 2006). For information technology (IT), however, the side effects of standardization are not always taken into account–or even understood. Typically, in standardization there are significant uncertainties on the factual costs and benefits as well as on adequate planning and control strategies (Weitzel, 2003). One of the classic problems facing standardization and standards usage in companies is that of demonstrating its contribution to the company's total success (Hesser and Inklaar, 1997).

This problem is persistent and discussed by Lyytinen and King (2006) who argue that despite the importance of standardization, the IS field has not pursued research on it vigorously, considering that only roughly 2% of published journal papers dealt with IT standards during the last decade. Moreover, these papers, on the whole, focused on the content of new IT standards whereas studies on the impact of IT standards in companies were notably absent. In the *MIS Quarterly* Special Issue on Standard Making (August 2006), 2 of 7 of accepted papers dealt with the impact of IT standards. Although these studies focussed on using IT standards at the organizational level impact (Chen and Forman, 2006; Hanseth et al., 2006), examination of business performance efficiency and effectiveness remained unaddressed.

Given these limitations and uncertainties in the field of IT standardization and standards, this book focuses on the effects of company IT standardization and standards usage. We define a **company IT standard** as: "*The specification of an IT product or process to be repeatedly and consistently used in the company*." Company standards have, in general, the form of: 1) a reference to one ore more external standards (e.g. an international standard like ISO 17799 or a de-facto standard like Microsoft® Word®) officially adopted by the company; 2) a company modification of an external standard; 3) a subset of an external standard; 4) a standard reproduced from (part of) other external documents; or 5) a self-written standard (De Vries, 1999, p. 231).

Mintzberg (1984) considers standardization as a coordination mechanism for organizations. The organizational context and measures are important to the success of an IT company standard (Kayworth and Sambamurthy, 2000; Rada and Craparo, 2001; Hanseth and Braa, 2001) and Cargill (1989) argues that company standardization should be directed by an understanding of where an organization is going. Company IT standards provide long-term benefits to the enterprise as a whole, however business units may not observe a direct benefit from using the standards in the short term. Kayworth and Sambamurthy (2000) have shown that IT infrastructure standards can facilitate simultaneously localized exploitation and enterprise-wide integration that seems at first sight contradictory. In other words, this means that standards are able to facilitate flexibility. In this book, we will look into this quality aspect in detail.

Recent examples on the impact of company standards include survey research by Huang and Lee (2006) who investigated causal relationships in the four Balanced Scorecard (BSC) perspectives (Kaplan and Norton, 1992) of the information security management standard ISO/IEC 17799. In a survey research on the use of Enterprise Architecture (EA) IT standards, Boh and Yellin (2007) investigated to what extent the use of EA standards facilitate organizations to improve the sharing and integration of IT resources across the enterprise and how different governance mechanisms affect the use of EA standards.

Our main research objective is to investigate how organizations can realize the intended business benefits from IT standardization carried out in companies. In order to investigate this, we will also study what this standardization process entails and how the usage of the resulting standards impacts business performance. A number of research questions are formulated, including: how to effectively and efficiently deal with company IT standardization and company IT standards?; what are the effects of company IT standards, for facilitating business processes, on business performance?

In this book, we will create a conceptual model based on the scarce literature on company IT standards, complemented with insights gained from a pilot case study, to provide insight into the factors affecting performance of business processes. Using a number of case studies that were carried out at a large financial services company, this model will be further refined. To test the model empirically, the case study research method was used, because in a relative short timeframe in-depth knowledge can be gained and this method is suitable to explore and explain practical situations (Yin, 1994). Three case studies were carried out at a large financial services company and case selection was to ensure variability. In total, 23 interviews were held with 18 interviewees. The conceptual model will be tested from a cross case context and overarching themes will be discussed. The gained insight provides the basis for a Corporate IT Standardization Management Framework that contains the following constructs:

1. **Process of Standard Selection:** the way the company IT standard is chosen.
2. **Company Standard:** the specification of the IT product or process to be repeatedly and consistently used in the company.
3. **Implementation of Standard:** the way the company IT standard is put into operation.
4. **Use of Standard:** the way the company IT standard is operated.
5. **Process Performance:** the efficiency and effectiveness of the process as a result of using the company IT standard.
6. **Performance Measurement & Analysis:** the way in which efficiency and effectiveness of the company IT standard's use is assessed.
7. **Governance of Standard:** specifying the decision rights and accountability framework to encourage desirable behavior in the selection, implementation and use of the company IT in the organization.
8. **Management of Standard:** the decision-making efforts associated with planning, organizing, controlling, and directing the selection, implementation and use of the company IT in the organization.

This Corporate IT Standardization Management Framework was tested successfully in a fourth and final study. This framework turned out to be elementary in describing and explaining changes in process performance as a result of applying company IT standards, and consequently how organizations can realize the intended business benefits from company IT standardization.

STRUCTURE OF THE BOOK

This book is organized into ten chapters. A brief description of each of the chapters follows:

Chapter 1, *Introduction*, discusses the motivation to carry out the research on company IT standardization, the problem definition, the research scope and approach. It is an initial attempt to conceptualize and empirically understand the complex relationships between company IT standardization and its business benefits. It also details the research method chosen, which comprises both exploratory and explanatory case study research. This was considered the best way to complement theory in this underdeveloped domain of IS literature (Yin, 1994).

Chapter 2, *Standardization & Standards*, reviews literature on standardization and standards to identify key characteristics and benefits & risks with special focus on IT standardization and its effects on business performance in companies. Apart from a few exceptions, literature on how company IT standards impact business performance is notably absent. Current literature on IT standardization and standards mainly focuses on the standardization processes carried out in industry, by consortia and international standard setting organizations and on the effects of IT standards at a macro economic scale; literature on company standardization is scarce.

Chapter 3, *IT, Business Processes & Performance*, reviews literature on the value of IT related to business processes and performance. It also describes literature about IT investments and the impact of IT on the performance of the firm. The reason for this literature review is that effects of IT standards, which are an integral part of IT, will be investigated in several case studies. Supporting the case study analysis, a method will be adopted that is used to assess business performance from IT in general.

Chapter 4, *Building the Conceptual Model*, presents an initial conceptual model that should help in understanding the impact of company standards on business performance and focuses on the control of these standards. The conceptual model integrates aspects of standardization, standards usage and standards control and relates those to the impact of IT standards used in an organization on business process performance. Using this model, multiple in depth case studies will be carried out with the intention of gaining experience with the initial conceptual model and making generalization possible as part of the theory testing phase.

Chapter 5, *Client/Server Standardization "Uniform Case"*, describes a case study concerning company product standardization of both back-end and front-end of a desktop environment. This standardization project was carried out within a two-year timeframe, affecting 10,000 end users of a business unit. The main objectives of the standardization project, that included hardware and software of both front and back end, were 1) to reduce costs of development and support of both hardware and software; 2) to facilitate change flexibility. One of the core components of this program was application software rationalization, which ranged from desktop productivity tools to applications for complex financial transactions. The guiding principle in the application rationalization phase was that only one type of software was allowed, preferably the latest version, unless business functionality degraded considerably. The balance between functionality and support/license costs was the main criterion for putting an application on the list of standard software. The total number of client and server applications was downsized rigorously with approximately a factor 22 (from 6,000 to 265). This list of software products and C/S hardware constituted the set of company IT standards. In the application and control phases, heavy load applications that used to run on (midrange) desktops were migrated to high-end servers. This server based computing concept allowed running such applications on low-end desktops, which resulted in low overall hardware purchase and maintenance costs. In line with the observations by Rada and Craparo (2001), a technical review team carried out the verification of the specified IT product standards in projects. Strict conformity to the related service and project management processes were key ingredients in the successful usage of the set of IT standards. The team also reviewed any upgrades, replacements or patching needed. Standards were reviewed every 2 years and the review process resulted often in a new product that was incorporated in the set of IT standards, reflecting developments at both the technological and business environment.

Chapter 6, *Software Development Standardization "CMM/DSDM Case"*, describes a case study on company process standardization at a software development department. This standardization initiative was launched at the main software development department of the case company with the aim to bring about fundamental changes in the way business and IT developed software products. The goals of the program were to: 1) Improve quality; 2) Increase productivity and reduce costs; 3) Respond more rapidly to change; 4) Improve co-operation between business and IT; 5) Increase job satisfaction and attractiveness to staff. The company standards consisted of a combination of the Capability Maturity Model (CMM®) (Paulk, 1991) and the Dynamic System Development Method (DSDM™). DSDM was used to assist to reach CMM level 2. In the implementation phase, control of the separate CMM and DSDM projects was merged to increase staff acceptance and to deal with inefficiencies. These process standards were implemented accompanied with an organizational change process, which proved to be important for its success. The control on these process standards was considered as strict but one was allowed to deviate if certain aspects of the standard did not add value, under approval of a QA organization. A version for small projects was developed next to the possibility of tailoring. The idea was to first enforce the standards and accomplish discipline, than allow tuning and tailoring. A weakness in the implementation was the lack of alignment between business and IT that negatively impacted the whole program.

Chapter 7, *HR IS Standardization "CHRISP Case"*, describes a third in-depth case study on company IS product standardization, the ERP HR modules of PeopleSoft, which include the accompanying HR processes. A complete set of core HR processes, as part of an ERP HR suite, that were selected by the business as company standard, based on its Best-in-Class rating by the HR profession. This initiative included standardization of data (both syntax and semantics) which is known to be complicated (Boh and Yellin, 2007). The main driver was lack of consistency of HR management information in the HR information systems and the impossibility of proper analysis and reporting. The HR administration was based on dispersed spreadsheet-like tools often lacking historic data. The goals of the global HR IS were: 1) cost savings through empowerment of employees (self service) and consequently a reduction of HR headcount and reduced HR IS costs; 2) provision of quality services that enable the enterprise to improve its HR function; 3) comply globally with legal and fiscal requirements. The standardization process, especially of the data semantics, turned out to be ineffective, as roles and responsibilities between corporate and local HR units were not effectively assigned. This included 1) lack of mandate and decision rights from the corporate core, 2) the nature of advises (recommended in stead of mandatory), 3) lack of ownership of HR data elements. As a consequence, the data standardization process was limited to a relatively small set of entities. In the application phase, the HR business in some business units did not fully support the standard. To get buy in from local HR, therefore, no standard way of implementing the HR IS was enforced. The possibility of implementing optional features of the standard did not help to make this project an immediate success either. As the implementation took too long and the scope of the deliverables remained too narrow, a rigorous change in the way of implementing the standard was made which resulted in positive effects on the application of the company IT standard.

Chapter 8, *A Reflection Upon the Case Studies*, provides a cross case analysis using replication logic tactic (Yin, 1994). The case studies will be compared and the conceptual model will be reassessed. The gained insights result in the Corporate IT Standardization Management Framework. This framework includes the constructs governance and management of company IT standards that are key to influence the effects of company IT standards on business process performance. This framework will be tested in a fourth and final case study to increase validity of the framework and the case study research.

Chapter 9, *Information Security Management Standardization "ISO/IEC 17799 Case"*, describes the fourth and final in-depth case study using the Corporate IT Standardization Management Framework. This case study describes the positive effects of using an information security management standard on the risk profile, satisfying internal and external requirements. It is discussed how changes in governance and management of the standard could have resulted in potentially even better process performance of the information security function. This includes business-IT alignment, project management, and performance monitoring. Because collaboration with and input from the business was only marginal, the business benefits of the implemented measures, though substantial, remained sub-optimal.

Chapter 10, *Conclusions, Discussion, Recommendations*, provides a final discussion following the four in-depth case studies. The research questions will be answered and the business benefits identified in the case studies will be discussed, as well as whether these hold in a more general sense also. The contributions to theory and practice will be discussed including the generalizability of the findings and the limitations of this research. The chapter concludes with a number of recommendations.

In sum, no studies to date directly addressed the success factors of effective and efficient selection, implementing and usage of company IT standards on process performance. Only very limited research has been carried out on company IT standards, which holds especially for the empirical effects of using such standards in practice. An extended conceptual model has been developed and tested successfully which consists of constructs and variables that affect process performance. Furthermore, the case studies show that with company IT standardization business benefits are achieved. Overall results from the case studies show that service quality and flexibility increase when using standardized products or processes, and simultaneously costs go down. Customer satisfaction depends on the level of business participation in the selection and implementation phase. Last but not least, this book details how to realize intended business benefits from company IT standardization. It is demonstrated how governance and management of company IT standards, moderating selection, implementation and usage, affects process performance and thus contributes significantly to accomplish intended business benefits. To the best of our knowledge, the extended conceptual model relating selection, implementation and use of standards to process performance and moderated by governance and management did not exist until now.

With regard to the business impacts, it offers organizations the opportunity to enhance process performance when using company standards. It provides insight on how company IT standards affect business processes and it shows how to govern and manage such standards in practice. The implications of this research to organizations refer to design and decision making regarding selection, implementation and usage of standards by organizations. Companies may wish to reconsider how they are dealing with company IT standards.

TARGET AUDIENCE

The primary audiences of this book are scholars and lecturers with backgrounds in, for example, Information Systems, IT Management, Business Studies, and Economics. They will be typically interested in the full coverage of this book, including the research method, construction and test of the conceptual models created in this study.

However, this book will also be of interest to practitioners such as corporate IS managers who are in charge of planning the development and/or the adoption of standards-based systems within their organizations. To serve this latter group the following reading guide is provided:

Table 1. Reading guide for practitioners

Reader interested in	Chapter(s)	Section(s)
Background and rationale of this study	1.	Motivation of Research; Problem Definition
General concepts on Standardization & Standards	2.	External Standardization Processes
Company Standards	2.	IT Standardization in Organizations; Utilization of IT standards in Organizations
General concepts on IT, Business Processes & Performance	3.	The Value of IT; Business Process Performance
Governance of Company Standards	8.	IT Governance; IT Management; Extended Conceptual Model[1]
Case studies on Company Standards	5, 6, 7, 9.	All
Conclusions and recommendations on Company Standards	10.	All

In addition at the end of each chapter, a section is included with "Managerial Implications" that summarizes the main practical topics and ideas discussed.

REFERENCES

Boh, W.F., & Yellin, D. (2007). Using Enterprise Architecture Standards in Managing Information Technology. *Journal of Management Information Systems, 23*(3), 163–207.

Cargill, C.F. (1989). *Information Technology Standardization: Theory, Process, and Organizations.* Bedford, MA: Digital Press.

Chen, P., & Forman, C. (2006). Can Vendors Influence Switching Costs and Compatibility in an Environment with Open Standards? *MIS Quarterly, 30,* Special Issue, 541-562.

De Vries H. (1999). *Standardization: A Business Approach to the Role of National Standardization Organizations.* Boston: Kluwer Academic Publishers.

Hanseth, O., & Braa, K. (2001). Hunting for the treasure at the end of the Rainbow: Standardizing Corporate IT Infrastructure. *Computer Supported Cooperative Work, 10*, 261-292.

Hanseth, O., Jacucci, E., Grisot M., & Aanestad M. (2006). Reflexive Standardization: Side Effects and Complexity in Standard Making. *MIS Quarterly, 30,* Special Issue, 563-581.

Hesser, W., & Inklaar, A. (1997). *An introduction to standards and Standardization.* DIN-Normungskunde Band 36, Beuth Verlag GmbH, Berlin.

Huang, S.H., & Lee, C.L. (2006). Balancing performance measures for information security management. A balanced scorecard framework. *Industrial Management and Data Systems, 106*(2), 242-255.

Kaplan, R.S., & Norton, D.P. (1992). The Balanced Scorecard - Measures that Drive Performance. *Harvard Business Review, 70*(1), 71-79.

Kayworth, T., & Sambamurthy, V. (2000). Facilitating localized exploitation and enterprise-wide integration in the use of IT infrastructures: The role of PC/LAN infrastructure standard. *Database for Advances in Information Systems, 31*(4), 54-81.

Krechmer, K., & Baskin, E.J. (2006). The entrepreneur and standards. In *IEC, International Standardization as a Strategic Tool - Commended Papers from the IEC Centenary Challenge 2006, Geneva: International Electrotechnical Commission* (pp. 142-152).

Lyytinen, K., & King, J.L. (2006). Standard making: A critical research frontier for information systems research. *MIS Quarterly, 30*, Special Issue, 405-411.

Mintzberg, H. (1984). *Structures in Fives: Designing Effective Organizations*. Englewood Cliffs, NJ: Prentice-Hall.

Paulk, M.C., Curtis, B., & Chrissis, M.B. (1991, August). *Capability Maturity Model for Software* (Tech. Rep. CMU/SEI-91-TR24). Software Engineering Institute.

Rada, R., & Craparo, J.S. (2001). Standardizing Management of Software Engineering Projects, *Knowledge, Technology, & Policy, 14*(2), 67- 77.

Weitzel, T. (2003). A Network ROI, MISQ Special Issue Workshop Standard Making: A Critical Research Frontier for Information Systems. *Pre-Conference Workshop, International Conference on Information Systems, December 12-14, 2003, Seattle, Washington* (pp. 62-79).

Yin, R.K. (1994). *Case Study research, Design and Methods* (2nd ed.). Thousand Oaks, CA: Sage Publications Inc.

ENDNOTE

1 In Chapter 4 an initial conceptual model is created and subsequently tested in a number of case studies described in Chapters 5, 6 and 7. This model will be further detailed in Chapter 8 and will be tested in the case study as described in Chapter 9.

Executive Summary

INTRODUCTION

In organizations a variety of standardization initiatives are carried out. These initiatives are typically to ensure quality of products and services or to reduce operational costs, to name but a few goals. Studies on the business impact of standards mostly focus on the consequences of product standards for market share whereas others look, for example, at the needs of entrepreneur's vs. those of society. For information technology (IT), however, the effects especially of company-internal standardization are not normally taken into account, and neither are they properly understood. Typically, in standardization there are significant uncertainties on the factual costs and benefits as well as on adequate planning and control strategies. One of the classic problems facing standardization and standards usage in organizations is that of demonstrating its contribution to the company's total success. Given these limitations and uncertainties in the field of (corporate) IT standardization and standards, this book will be focusing on the effects of IT standardization and IT standards on a company.

OVERALL OBJECTIVE AND APPROACH

An in-depth analysis is provided of how organizations can derive the envisaged business benefits from company IT standardization, or in other words *how organizations can deliver the anticipated business benefits from company IT standardization.* This includes how company IT standards – and corporate standardization – should be managed. To answer the above question an initial framework has been created and tested in three case studies, as described in Chapters 5 to 7. The initial framework (Figure 1) was further detailed in Chapter 8 and was successfully validated in the case study as described in Chapter 9.

SELECTION, IMPLEMENTATION AND USE

A company IT standardization process is a process that is carried out by an organization with the objective of providing specifications for an IT product or process (which may include the accompanying data used in that process) to be repeatedly and consistently used in that company. Such products or processes are called **company IT standards**. The components of this process are the *selection* "the way the company IT standard is chosen", the *implementation* "the way the company IT standard is put into operation" and the *use* "the way the company IT standard is operated".

Figure 1. Framework for corporate IT standardization management

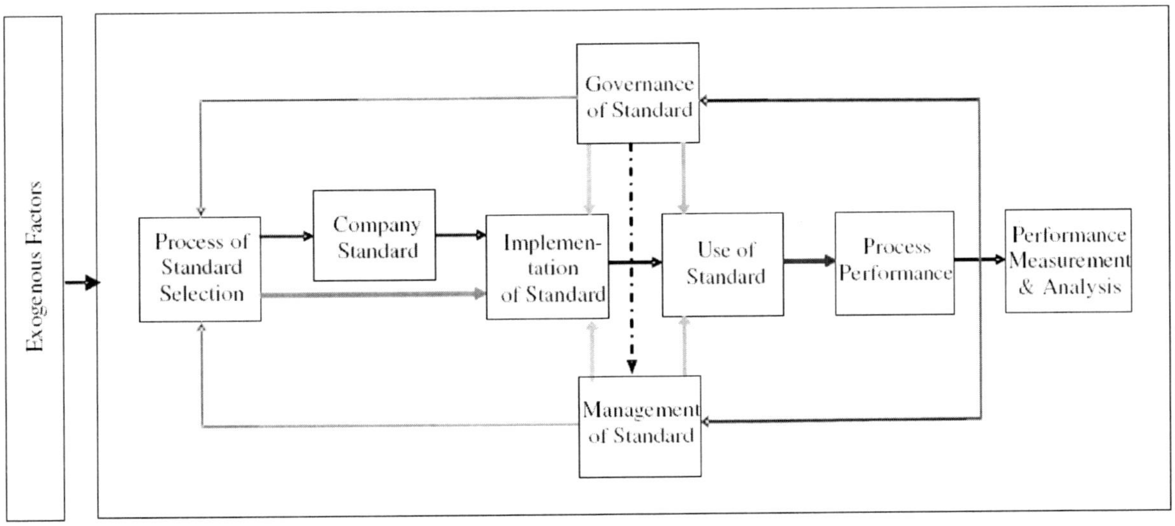

With respect to the process of company IT standard selection, the level of involvement and cooperation between Business and IT is important. Although business drivers for standardization such as cost reduction and quality improvement may be clear, the absence of proper business alignment can counteract the potential benefits of company standards. Regarding the implementation of the company IT standard, the quality of project management plays an important role. But of equal importance is to ensure that a prescribed set and/or standard way of implementation is pursued, especially for standards that are being implemented across organizational units (see *HRM* case study, Chapter 7). Failure to do so could result in incompatible instances of the standard, severely diminishing its benefits. As far as the use of the company IT standard is concerned, there are several important elements that determine whether such a standard is being used effectively. Important elements include: 1) processes and procedures that support the usage of the standard, such as the way exceptions are dealt with and whether these are integrated in the existing standard; 2) the type of standard, as process standards typically have more impact on the way staff work than product and data standards have; 3) the level of Management support of the standard from both IT and Business and the enforcement by the IT organization. For company IT standards with an enterprise wide reach, efficient usage becomes even more challenging, because what is perceived as beneficial by one unit does not necessarily hold good for another organizational unit.

An important observation, especially when implementing and using process standards, is that one can not change the way staff is working without giving careful attention to changes in behavior as well (see case studies in Chapters 6 and 7). So, an organizational change process accompanying the implementation of company IT process standards boosts its effectiveness. Another important observation is that the implementation sequence a) product, process vs. b) process, product impacts on the usage. In other words, to first agree on process standards, and only then on the supporting product standards pays off.

Variables that contribute to the effectiveness of company IT standards include: 1) the level of endorsement by Business and IT management; 2) the level of prescription and enforcement of related processes and procedures; 3) the level of collaboration between Business and IT. As part of the second item, so-called implementation standards are of importance. It constitutes a detailed description of how to implement a chosen company standard in order to prevent incompatible versions of the same standard. Such activities should be monitored by a central authority.

The case studies described in this book show that business benefits are accomplished by using the company IT standards and that the three components (selection, implementation and use) are essential elements in the process of company IT standardization. In addition, the case studies also show that two other components are essential to accomplish intended business benefits from company IT standardization: its respective governance and management.

GOVERNANCE AND MANAGEMENT

There are two components that constitute the company IT standardization management framework, which are governance and management of the company IT standards.

Governance of company IT standards relate to the decision rights specification and accountability (Weill and Ross, 2004). The elements of governance are to encourage desirable behavior in the selection, implementation and usage of IT standards within an organization. It deals with the capabilities and activities which should be standardized enterprise wide to support IT efficiencies, data integration and facilitating process standardization and integration, and which ones should be kept local. Another important aspect of this governance is whether to centralize or decentralize selection and implementation activities.

Management of company IT standards relate to the decision-making concerning planning, organizing, controlling, and directing the selection, implementation and usage of IT standards within an organization. As implementation of IT standards is typically carried out in projects, management of IT standards in this phase relates to Project Management, whereas in the operational phase (usage) this activity is related to IT Service Management. The selection of IT standards can be part of either of these two management activities.

The four case studies reveal that management and governance are dominant moderators for selection, implementation and usage of company IT standards. With management and governance one can affect process performance and thus contribute to the realization of the intended business benefits. Effects that influence selection, implementation and usage of company IT standards and thus indirectly process performance are:

As far as governance is concerned:

- The extent to which Business and IT were involved
- The extent of Business and IT alignment
- The level of agreed ownership of the standard and/or entities within this standard.

With respect to management, these include:

- The level of consideration paid to the business model and business drivers
- The level of endorsement by senior management
- The extent to which exception handling is carried out
- The level of restrictiveness of the standard

CONCLUSIONS

The primary value offered by company IT standards is to improve business performance that, either directly or indirectly, results in business benefits. Examples of intended business benefits are: 1) to cut costs of development and support of the IT infrastructure; 2) to improve customer satisfaction with the IT services offered; 3) to facilitate interoperability and quality of the information systems both intra- and inter-company; 4) to increase scalability and adaptability of IT systems.

In order to achieve the intended benefits from company IT standardization, it is essential a number of steps are taken. Foremost, determine what is to be standardized enterprise wide and what should remain specific to local needs. Then, based on the intended business benefits, determine which data from business processes (KPIs) have to be measured and ensure those data is collected one way or the other. Subsequently baseline these measurements to make comparisons at a later stage possible. Realization of expected business benefits is conditional to the way governance and management on selection, implementation and usage of company IT standards are carried out. The influence of governance and management have been presented in the case studies described in this book, which resulted in an overall improvement from a process performance perspective.

As far as governance is concerned, key factors for effective selection, implementation and usage of company IT standards and ultimately the intended business benefits are ownership and accountability. Ownership of the company standard should reside at the functional domain (such as IT, HR and Finance). These domain owners are accountable for the contents of the standard and make certain it reflects present-day business needs. Governance of the company IT standards should be an integral part of the overall IT governance of the company, as IT standards set specifications for (part of) the overall IT infrastructure. Paramount in the governance of company standards is that the correct stakeholders should be involved from both Business and (local) IT in the decision, implementation and use of company standards and that ownership has been assigned to the domain owners. Key contributors to effective management of company IT standards include endorsement by Senior Management and the way exceptions are being handled and thus how business requirements and the company standards remain aligned.

The overall conclusion is that company IT standards can positively affect process performance and thus provide Business benefits, provided adequate governance and management of selection, implementation and usage is set-up. In addition it should be recognized that the level of enterprise-wide company standardization depends on the level of diversification of the Businesses (i.e. the more diversification, the less the need for enterprise-wide company standardization).

With the application of IT product and/or process standards, considerable improvements on process performance can be gained. Significant positive effects were described at the financial, customer, internal and learning & growth perspectives. In other words, organizations can gain business benefits from IT standards. Furthermore this book provides an insight into significant aspects affecting process performance as a result of company IT standards.

It provides insight to the industry about how company IT standards affect business processes and provides examples and guidance on how to govern and manage such standards in practice. It allows managers to be fully aware of the potential of governance and management of company standards. Managers should be aware of the impact of allocation of decision rights and the setting of accountabilities related to company standardization. Finally, companies may wish to reconsider how they carry out selection, implementation and usage of company IT standards.

Glossary

Acronym	Description	FINCORP jargon
2FA	Two Factor Authentication	
AIM	FINCORP Instruction Manual	×
AIMS	Time registration tool	×
ANSI®	American National Standards Institute	
API	Application Programming Interface	
APS™	Advanced Photographic System	
ARBO	Working conditions, in Dutch “Arbeidsomstandigheden”	
ASCII	American Standard Code for Information Interchange	
ATM	Automated Teller Machine	
B2B	Business to Business	
BCDB	Business Contact Database	×
B-IT	Business-IT	
BMST	Benchmark Short Term	×
BPR	Business Process Redesign	
BREL	Benchmark Recommendations Long Term	×
BSC	Balanced Scorecard	
BSI	British Standards Institution	
BTPB	Business Technology Policy Board	×
BU	Business Unit	
C	A computer programming language	
C/S	Client/Server	
CAB	Change Advisory Board	
CART	Corporate Architecture Review Team	×
CAT	Corporate Architecture Team	×

Acronym	Description	FINCORP jargon
CBD	Component-Based Development	×
C-BUS	Communication BUS	×
CCM	Configuration & Change Manager	×
CDRAP	Cryptographic enhancement program	×
CHRISP	Common Human Resources Information System Program	×
CIA	Confidentiality, Integrity, Availability	
CIO	Chief Information Officer	
CMM®	Capability Maturity Model	
COBIT®	Control Objectives for Information and related Technology	
COO	Chief Operating Officer	
COTS	Commercial Of The Shelf	
CPU	Central Processing Unit	
CQO	Central Quality Officer	×
CRM	Customer Relationship Management	
CSPC	Corporate Standards and Policies Committee	×
DI	Device Interface	
DIN	Deutsches Institut für Normung	
DNB	De Nederlandsche Bank	
DNS	Domain Name System	
DQS	Domain Quality System	×
DSDM™	Dynamic Systems Development Method	
DVD	Digital Versatile Disk	
DWH	Data Wharehouse	
EA	Enterprise Architecture	
EITAF	Enterprise Information Technology Architecture Framework	×
EDI	Electronic Data Interchange	
EDIFACT	Electronic Data Interchange For Administration, Commerce, and Transport	
EFQM	European Foundation for Quality Management	
ERP	Enterprise Resource Planning	
FED	The Federal Reserve, the central bank of the United States	
FET	Full Expertise Teams	×
FIX	Financial Information Exchange	
FP	Function Point	

Acronym	Description	FINCORP jargon
FTE	Full Time Equivalent	
GART	Global Account Request Tool	✘
GLBA	Gramm-Leach-Bliley Act	
GSM	Global System for Mobile communications, originally from French: "Groupe Spécial Mobile"	
GSS	Group Shared Services	✘
GUI	Graphical User Interface	
HIPAA	Health Insurance Portability and Accountability Act	
HLAM	High-Level-Account Monitoring	✘
HP	Hewlett Packard®	
HR	Human Resources	
HRM	Human Resources Management	
HRMS	Human Resource Management System	
HRTP	Human Resources Transformation Programme	✘
HTML™	HyperText Markup Language	
HTTP	HyperText Transfer Protocol	
I/O	Input/Output	
IBM®	International Business Machines	
IDM	Infrastructure Delivery Managers	✘
IEC	International Electrotechnical Commission	
IEEE	Institute of Electrical and Electronics Engineers	
IETF	Internet Engineering Taskforce	
IFRS	International Financial Reporting Standard	
IFX	Interactive Financial Exchange	
IMS®	Integrated Management System	
IPR	Intellectual Property Right	
IQS	Integrated Quality System	✘
IRR	Internal Rate of Return	
IS	Information System	
ISM	Information Security Management	
ISO	International Organization for Standardization	
IT	Information Technology	
ITGI	IT Governance Institute	

Acronym	Description	FINCORP jargon
ITIL®	Information Technology Infrastructure Library	
ITU	International Telecommunication Union	
JAVA™	A technology developed by Sun® Microsystems for machine-independent software	
JTC1	ISO/IEC Joint Technical Committee 1	
JVM	JAVA™ Virtual Machine	
KCI	Key Control Indicators	
KPA	Key Process Area (CMM)	
KPI	Key Performance Indicator	
LAN	Local Area Network	
LCD	Liquid Crystal Display	
LCIRT	Local Computer Emergency Response Team	×
LINUX®	Operating system kernel used by a family of UNIX®-like operating systems	
MIS	Management Information System	
MoSCoW	MUST have, SHOULD have, COULD have, WON'T have (DSDM)	
MPEG	Motion Pictures Experts Group	
MSF	Microsoft® Solutions Framework	
NASA	National Aeronautics and Space Administration	
NESMA	Dutch user group of software metrics, in Dutch "Nederlandse Software Metrieken Gebruikers Associatie"	
NPV	Net Present Value	
NSO	National Standardization Organization	
NTSC	National Television System Committee	
OA	Development Architecture, in Dutch: "Ontwikkel Architectuur"	×
OFX	Open Financial Exchange	
ORAP	Operational Risk Approval Process	×
OSI	Open Systems Interconnection	
PA	Professional Attitude	×
PAS	Publicly Available Specifications	
PC	Personal Computer	
PCI	Peripheral Controller Interface	
PFM	Portfolio Manager	×
PIM	Process Improvement Manager	×
PIP	Process Improvement Plans	×

Acronym	Description	FINCORP jargon
POSIX®	Portable Operating System Interface	
PP	Payback Period	
PPI	Project Performance Indicators	×
PPM	Professionalize Project Management	×
PQAL	Project Quality Assurance Lead	×
PSP	Policies, Standards, Procedures	×
QA	Quality Assurance	
QM	Quality Management	
R&D	Research and Development	
RAD	Rapid Application Development	
RAS	FINCORP' remote access service (via Internet)	×
RBAC	Role Based Access Control	
RDBMS	Rational Database Management Systems	
RFP	Request for Proposal	
ROC	Regulation on Organization and Control	
ROI	Return on Investment	
ROM	Read Only Memory	
RSA	Risk Self Assessments	×
RUP®	Rational Unified Process	
SAP®	Systems, Applications and Products, in German "Systeme, Anwendungen und Produkte (in der Datenverarbeitung)"	
SBU	Strategic Business Unit	
SDO	Standards Development Organization	
SEI	Software Engineering Institute, Carnegie Mellon University	
SEPG	Software Engineering Process Group	
SGML	Standard Generalized Markup Language	
SI	International System of Units (abbreviated SI from the French Le Système International d'Unités)	
SLA	Service Level Management	
SME	Small and Medium-sized Enterprises	
SMTP	Simple Mail Transfer Protocol	
SOA	Service Oriented Architecture	
SOM	Standard Operating Model	×
SOMA	System development method, in Dutch "Systeem Ontwikkelings Methodiek"	×

Acronym	Description	FINCORP jargon
SOX	Sarbanes-Oxley Act	
SQS	Standard Quality System	×
SSL	Secure Socket Layer	
SSO	Single Sign On	
STE	Dutch securities exchange commission, in Dutch "Stichting Toezicht Effectenverkeer"	
SWIFT	Society for Worldwide Interbank Financial Telecommunication	
SWOT	Strengths, Weaknesses, Opportunities, and Threats	
TAM	Technology Acceptance Model	
TCO	Total Cost of Ownership	
TCP/IP	Transmission Control Protocol/Internet Protocol	
TOE	Technology-Organization-Environment	
TRAP	Technology Risk Accreditation Process	×
TRM	Technology Risk Management	×
UNIX®	Computer operating system developed by AT&T Bell Laboratories®	
USB	Universal Serial Bus	
UTP	Unshielded Twisted Pair	
VHS™	Video Home System	
W3C™	World Wide Web Consortium	
WINTEL	Concatenation of Windows® and Intel®	
WTO	World Trade Organisation	
XML™	Extensible Markup Language	

Acknowledgment

I would like to acknowledge the help of all involved in the creation of this book. First of all I would like to express my deep appreciation and gratitude to Prof. Dr. Piet Ribbers of Tilburg University, The Netherlands, for his deep insights, broad knowledge, intellectual challenges and stimulating conversations. The same is true for Dr. Henk de Vries of Rotterdam School of Management, Erasmus University, The Netherlands. Henk's suggestions and critiques were always very valuable, detailed and timely.

I would also like to thank all staff from the case company who assisted me in one way or the other and those who provided me with valuable insights as part of the case studies. Special thanks to Kay Jacobs and the publishing team at IGI Global, whose contributions throughout the publication process have been much valuable.

I want to thank my kids, family and friends for supporting me and special thanks to my cousin Ankie Jefferiss-Van Wessel who waded through the text of this book and has made it much better. Last but not least sincerest gratitude to my wife, Marian, for her unfailing support and encouragement when writing this book.

Robert M. van Wessel
The Hague, July, 2009

Section 1
Setting the Scene

This chapter discusses the motivation to carry out the research on company IT standardization, the problem definition, and the research scope and approach. This study is an initial attempt to conceptualize and empirically understand the complex relationships between company standardization and its business benefits. A conceptual model should help in understanding the impact of company standards on business performance and focuses on the control of these standards.

Chapter 1
Introduction

MOTIVATION OF RESEARCH

In today's competitive world it is essential to minimize the time required to deliver new business solutions to the market and to minimize the costs of the Information Technology (IT) systems supporting the business. Companies are increasingly confronted with cost cutting issues while the market demands an increasing flexibility towards the customer at the same time. This is certainly true for financial service companies as they are faced with costs of IT development and delivery that are continuously increasing. These costs are caused by necessary adaptations in IT as changes in the business environment are taking place all the time, such as globalization, regulatory requirements and more demanding customers.

One of the ways to break the trend of rising IT-costs is to introduce standardization of the IT infrastructure. IT infrastructure is defined as a shared set of capital resources that provide the foundation on which specific IT applications are built (Duncan, 1995; Broadbent and Weill, 1997). In general the IT infrastructure of a firm consists of several layers and standardization may concern any of these layers. Standardization simplifies interoperability and re-usability but may impact on, for example, the agility and responsiveness to adapt IT services to business changes. As there is an intuitive tension between standardization and flexibility (Hanseth et al., 1996) in some sort of way one has to "standardize for flexibility". In more general terms, the drawbacks and advantages of standardization and usage of standards

DOI: 10.4018/978-1-61520-759-6.ch001

Figure 1. The IT infrastructure (Adapted from Weill and Broadbent, 1998)

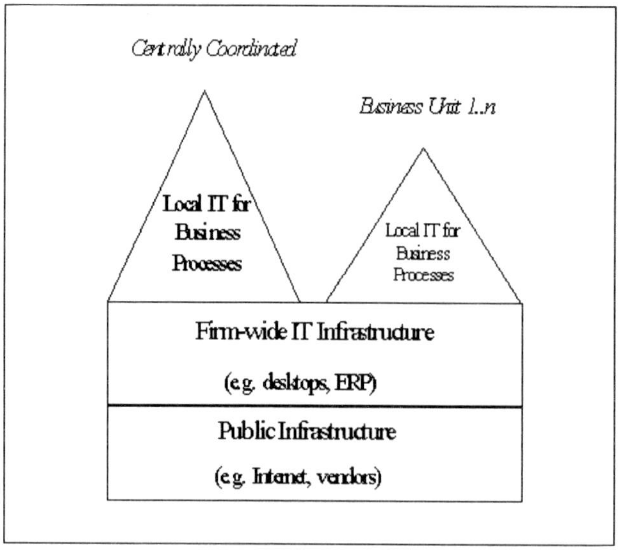

on business performance are unclear. The same is true on how to accomplish the intended benefits from standardization of the IT infrastructure.

Flexibility is just one of the aspects of effectiveness of business performance. In general, business performance can be expressed in terms of efficiency and effectiveness. Shafer and Byrd (2000) summarize anticipated improvements in business performance resulting from usage of IT and this study will investigate how such business benefits hold for the usage of IT standards as well:

- improved quality,
- reduced costs,
- increased flexibility,
- improved customer satisfaction,
- overall improvements in operations.

It is especially the combination of these five benefits which is the most challenging as organizations have to provide customized products and services in a timely and cost efficient fashion. Several concepts have been introduced addressing this, such as modularization (Pine, 1993) and virtual corporations (Davidow and Malone, 1992). *Modularization* is a concept for products and processes that have been designed as independent building blocks based on customer requirements and can be assembled relatively easily and inexpensively into specific forms. It has been the basis for what is called "mass customization". A *virtual corporation* is an arrangement where the product or service is created only after an order is placed. A supply chain of organizations is created for that purpose, and the product or service is tailored instantly in response to the customer requirements.

The main research objective of this book is to investigate how organizations can realize the intended business benefits from IT standardization. In order to investigate this, we will also study what this standardization process entails and how the usage of the resulting standards impacts business performance.

Although ultimately the interest lies in the business performance effectiveness and efficiency, for practical reasons, the focus of this study will be on its intermediate level: the performance of business processes.

The justification for carrying out this research, on how to ensure effective and efficient IT standardization and IT standard usage in a company, stems from the fact that this phenomenon has hardly been investigated in the academic literature and that results are not well understood in everyday practice. A globally operating financial services enterprise, FINCORP, will be used as a case company.

PROBLEM DEFINITION

What is the Research Problem?

Since the eighties, economists have paid a lot of attention to standardization, but their focus has mainly been limited to the consequences of product standards for market share (De Vries, 1999). One of the classic problems still facing standardization in companies is that of demonstrating its contribution to the company's total success (Hesser and Inklaar, 1997). IT standardization in companies results in one or more **company IT standards** that we define as:

"A specification of an IT product or process to be repeatedly and consistently used in the company."[1]

Typically, in standardization there are significant uncertainties about the actual costs and benefits as well as about adequate planning and control strategies (Weitzel, 2003, p. 64). West (2003, p. 315) even argues that although the organizational adoption of information technologies is at the center of the Information Systems (IS) domain, the role of standards in IT production and use is generally ignored. Research on the economic value or impact of standards has, by and large, been limited to the macro economic level (Swann, 2000; Temple and Williams, 2002; Blind, 2004; WTO, 2005). In addition, Turowski (2000) identified that there is a lack of fundamental research on what is the "right" flexibility and granularity of standards. The fact that flexibility is polymorphous[2] and standards and flexibility are multidimensional[3] concepts complicates the research. However, several examples show (Kayworth and Sambamurthy, 2000; Rada and Craparo, 2001; Herbold, 2002) that standardization in companies can have a positive impact on business performance in general and flexibility in particular.

A lot of research has been carried out on the Value of IT (e.g. Chan, 2000; Melville et al., 2004; Thatcher and Pingry, 2004). In these studies most researchers concluded that determining direct effects of IT on business performance turned out to be unfeasible and unrealistic as this impact is diluted by numerous other factors that contribute to the overall performance as well. Consequently it is not possible to pinpoint the contribution of IT to business performance. However, one abstraction level down - the business processes - it is possible to specifically pinpoint the contribution of IT (Davenport 1993, Hammer and Champy, 1993).

Boynton and Victor (1991, p. 65) identified in the early nineties of the twentieth century the contradictory requirements of simultaneous delivery of customized quality services, the reduction of operational costs and the quick delivery of products to the market. Customization of quality services is affiliated to *flexibility*, whereas reduction of operational costs is associated with *standardization*. This research will detail the complex relationship between the IT standardization process, the application of the IT

Table 1.

Detailed research questions in this respect are:
1. What is a company IT standardization process and which distinguishable components does it encompass?
2. How can business effects of IT standards be measured?
3. How do company IT standards affect business performance?
4. How can the intended application of company IT standards be assured?

standard and the resulting business performance. More specifically, we will focus on how to ensure that the expected business performance improvements from company IT standardization will be met. This is an area of research that has never been comprehensively analyzed before.

This brings us to the main research question and a number of detailed ones that focus on the anticipated benefits of company IT process and product standards.

Research Question

How can organizations realize intended business benefits from company IT standardization?

To gain more insight into company IT standardization and standards we formulated some additional questions on the process, on how to measure the advantages and disadvantages of company IT standards, and on how to make sure its intended application.

SCOPE AND RESEARCH APPROACH

Scope

The scope of this research is limited to IT product and process standardization and standards that are utilized in support processes of enterprises (i.e. domain of research). The unit of analysis is the Business Unit in which the IT process or product standard has been adopted, which can be a formal or informal standard or a specification of a proprietary process or product. Changes in business process performance, as a result of utilizing these standards, are analyzed using a case study approach at a financial services company. In particular, focus will be on how organizations can achieve intended benefits from company IT standardization.

The focus of this research on company IT standards in enterprises (2) is explained as follows. Research carried out on formal and informal external standardization and its macro-economic effects has been subject to much research (e.g. Cargill, 1989; Cusumano et al., 1992; Besen and Farell, 1994; Besen and Saloner, 1994; Rutkowski, 1995; Hesser and Inklaar, 1997; Rada, 2000; Swann, 2000; Blind, 2004). However, the positive and negative effects of using standards in companies have had little attention in academic literature (Hesser and Adolphi, 1994; Hesser and Hoops, 2001; De Vries, 2006a). This is especially true on how to realize the intended business benefits from company IT standardization. Furthermore, it is in the interest of the company in which the research project has been carried out to gain more knowledge about this subject.

Figure 2. Research scope

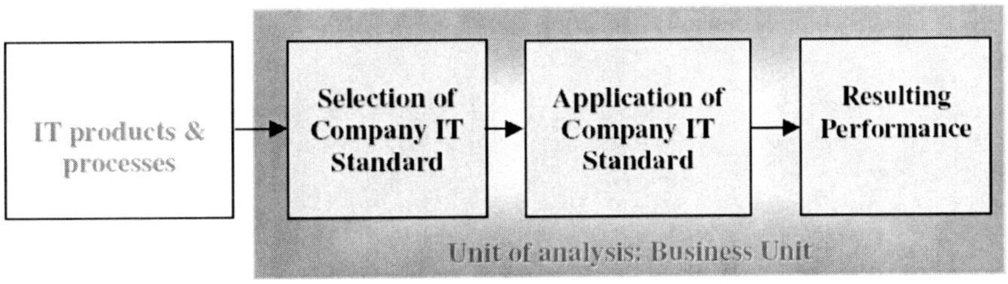

Why is it a Problem?

Standardization is a rather young academic discipline (De Vries, 2002) and there is still a lot we do not know about the ultimate effects of standards and the necessary preconditions for efficient and effective standardization (Hesser and Inklaar, 1997). Others even argue that research on IT standards is one of the most underestimated research domains (Jakobs, 2003). Traditionally, economic studies treat standardization as an endogenous factor in market development (e.g. David and Greenstein, 1990). Economists have tended to concentrate primarily upon the effects that standards have upon the behavior of buyers and sellers of technological products in the marketplace.

Naemura (1995) argues that little has been written on what happens to standards once they have been deployed. Generally, data were lacking concerning the utilization of standards. Turowski (2000) recognized that there is still a lack of fundamental research on the "right" flexibility and granularity of standards, especially from an economic point of view. Furthermore, it is not clear what the effects are of standardization on business performance and how to realize the intended benefits.

In order to ensure the quality of standardization projects and their output, there may be the need for new metrics to assess claims on the effectiveness of standards (Sherif 2003a). In addition, Spivak and Brenner (2001, p.142) point out that: "*the benefits of standardization are derived by the users of standards, not by standards developing organizations*". The goal of the research is, therefore, to investigate how to gain the intended business benefits and to provide insight into the effects of standardization on business process performance, that is expressed in terms of efficiency and effectiveness.

What is the Research Method?

To understand how to accomplish the expected benefits from company IT standardization and its effects on business performance the following approach has been taken. A literature study was carried out of standardization in general and for company standardization in particular, in order to assess the existing body of knowledge. Literature has also been reviewed on the value of IT and how to describe business performance.

In addition, a pilot case study has been executed at FINCORP. Interviews on the subject of company IT standardization were carried out with key informants at corporate and business unit level. Furthermore, several kinds of materials have been analyzed such as official documentation on policies and standards, newsletters, presentations and leaflets. Based on the literature review and the pilot case study, a conceptual model has been designed with constructs and propositions.

Figure 3. Research approach

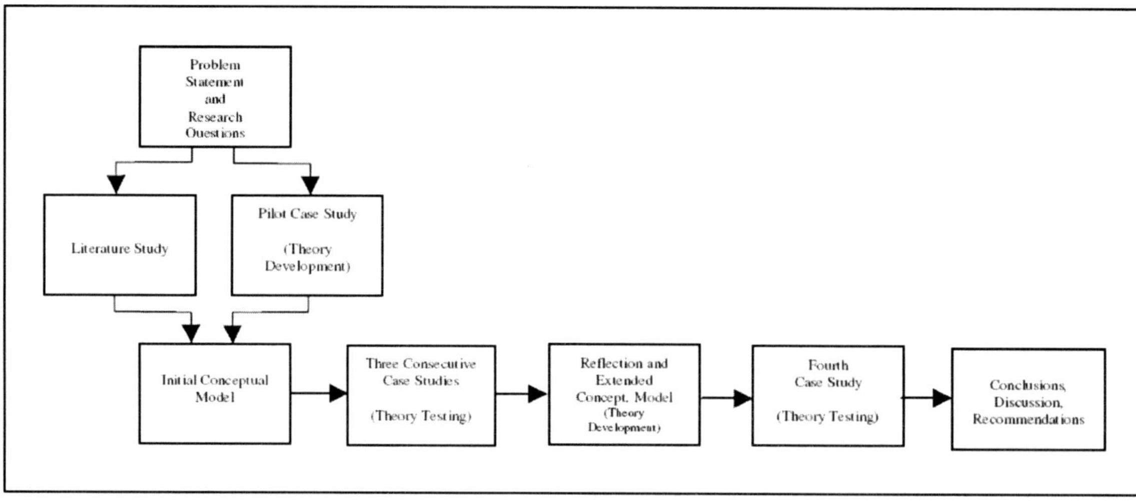

To gain experience with the conceptual model, in depth case studies were carried out. The first case study concerned IT product standardization, whereas the second case study was related to IT process standardization. The third case study concerned a company ERP standard, which basically is an IT product with predefined business processes. For the case studies (semi-)structured interviews were carried out and official company records and additional qualitative and quantitative data were used. Financial, organizational and technical objectives and results were evaluated. Effects on business process efficiency and effectiveness have been investigated using a Balanced Scorecard type measurement approach.

Comparative analyses of the case study data have been carried out, which resulted in theory refining, verification, and model amendments, focussing on how to realize intended benefits from company IT standardization. The three case studies were followed up with a forth and final case study on the application of an information security management process standard. This whole process is depicted in Figure 3.

Why this Method?

The focus has been on operational use and practical application of company IT standards. With a given process or product standard in the market place, how will selection, implementation and usage influence the business process effectiveness and efficiency? And how can companies influence and realize the intended benefits of these standards?

In order to examine these phenomena and gather empirical knowledge, a number of approaches are possible:

1. **Case study research:** carry out a number of in-depth case studies and identify relationships between a relatively large number of variables in a limited number of settings.
2. **Statistical research:** identify relationships between a relatively small number of variables that are studied in a large number of settings.

3. **Design-oriented research:** design, implement and execute a method and apply one or more experiments.

I have chosen for case study research, because in a relative short timeframe knowledge can be gained by making use of literal and theoretical replication (Yin, 1994, p.46). Furthermore, case study research is suitable to explore and explain practical situations without the requirement to have control over behavioral events such as in experiments (Yin, 1994, p.6). By having direct access to company data, in-depth case studies were considered to add more value to the theoretical body of knowledge on this research subject, than carrying out a large number of surveys at other companies. In Appendix I the case study questionnaire is listed. A reason for not choosing design-oriented research is its lengthy time span and inherently small focus and applicability whereas useful results are not guaranteed beforehand.

SUMMARY

This chapter has discussed the motivation to carry out the research and its problem definition, its scope and research approach and focused on the case study research method, including case study selection and research procedures. This study is an initial attempt to conceptualize and empirically understand the complex relationships between company standardization and business benefits. A conceptual model should help in understanding the impact of standards on business performance focusing on the control of these standards.

Research is to provide more insight into:

- How organizations can realize intended business benefits from company IT standardization.
- What a company IT standardization process is and which distinguishable components it encompasses.
- How company IT standards affect business performance.
- How business effects of IT standards can be measured.
- How the intended application of company IT standards can be assured.

The outline of this book is as follows. In the following two chapters, literature on standardization and business performance is reviewed, respectively. In chapter 4 a pilot case study on standardization of IT in our financial services case company, FINCORP, will be described and in combination with the literature reviews of chapters 2 and 3, a conceptual model will be introduced. This model is used in a number of case studies, described in chapters 5, 6 and 7, trying to answer the detailed research questions. Based on these in-depth case studies, a critical reflection leads to an enhanced conceptual model, as described in chapter 8. With this latest model, more in-depth case study research is executed as described in chapter 9, with the objective of adding theoretical knowledge to this research subject and at the same time extend practical value. In the final chapter 10, interpretation and discussion is provided and conclusions are drawn. Ideas and directions for future research are discussed as well to encourage further investigations into this subject.

REFERENCES

Besen, S. M., & Farrell, J. (1994). Choosing How to Compete: Strategies and Tactics in Standardization. *The Journal of Economic Perspectives*, *8*(2), 117–131.

Besen, S. M., & Saloner, G. (1994). Compatibility standards and market for telecommunications services. In T.J. Allen and Morton M.S. Scott (Eds.), Information technology and the corporation of the 1990s: research studies. New York: Oxford University Press.

Blind, K. (2004). *The economics of standards: theory, evidence, policy*. Cheltenham, UK: Elgar Publishers.

Boynton, A. C., & Victor, B. (1991). Beyond flexibility: building and managing the dynamically stable organization. *California Management Review*, *34*(1), 53–66.

Broadbent, M., & Weill, P. (1997). Management by Maxim: How Business and IT Managers Can Create IT Infrastructures. *Sloan Management Review*, *38*(3), 77–92.

Cargill, C. F. (1989). *Information Technology Standardization: Theory, Process, and Organizations*. Bedford, MA: Digital Press.

Chan, E. (2000). IT value: The great divide between qualitative and quantitative and individual and organizational measures. *Journal of Management Information Systems*, *16*(4), 225–261.

Cusumano, M., Mylonadis, Y., & Rosenbloom, R. (1992). Strategic maneuvering and mass-market dynamics: The triumph of VHS over Beta. *Business History Review*, *66*(1). doi:10.2307/3117053

Davenport, T. H. (1993). *Process Innovation: reengineering work through Information Technology*. Cambridge, MA: Harvard Business School Press.

David, P. A., & Greenstein, S. (1990). The Economics of compatibility standards: An introduction to recent research. *Economics of Innovation and New Technology*, *1*, 3–41. doi:10.1080/10438599000000002

Davidow, W. H., & Malone, M. S. (1992). *The virtual corporation: structuring and revitalizing the corporation for the 21st century*. New York: HarperBusiness.

de Vries, H. J. (1999). *Standardization: A Business Approach to the Role of National Standardization Organizations*. Boston, MA: Kluwer Academic Publishers.

de Vries, H. J. (2002). Standardization - Mapping a Field of Research. In Bolin, S. (Ed.), *The Standards Edge* (pp. 99–121). Ann Arbor, MI: Bolin Communications.

de Vries, H. J. (2006a). Best Practice in Company Standardization. *International Journal of IT Standards and Standardization Research*, *4*(1), 62–85.

Duncan, N. B. (1995). Capturing flexibility of Information Technology Infrastructure: A study of Resource Characteristics and their Measure. *Journal of Management Information Systems*, *12*(2), 37–57.

Hammer, M., & Champy, J. (1993). *Reengineering the corporation: a manifesto for business revolution*. New York: McGraw-Hill.

Hanseth, O., Monteiro, E., & Hatling, M. (1996). Developing Information Infrastructure: The tension Between Standardization and Flexibility. *Science, Technology & Human Values*, *21*(4), 407–426. doi:10.1177/016224399602100402

Herbold, R. J. (2002). Inside Microsoft: Balancing Creativity and Discipline. *Harvard Business Review*, *80*(1), 72–79.

Hesser, W., & Adolphi, H. (1994). *Economic Benefits of Company Standardization*. Hamburg, Federal Republic of Germany: Universität der Bundeswerh.

Hesser, W., & Hoops, L. (2001). Company Standardization as a Strategic Management Tool: The Influence of Standardization in the Construction Process on Competitive Strategies. In Standards, Compatibility and Infrastructure Development, proceedings of the 6th EURAS Workshop, June 2001 (pp. 137-146).

Hesser, W., & Inklaar, A. (1997). *An introduction to standards and Standardization. DIN-Normungskunde* (*Vol. 36*). Berlin: Beuth Verlag GmbH.

Jakobs, K. (2003). Preface. *International Journal of IT Standards and Standardization Research*, *1*(1), i.

Kayworth, T., & Sambamurthy, V. (2000). Facilitating localized exploitation and enterprise-wide integration in the use of IT infrastructures: The role of PC/LAN infrastructure standard. *The Data Base for Advances in Information Systems*, *31*(4), 54–81.

Melville, N., Kraemer, K., & Gurbaxani, V. (2004). Information Technology and Organizational Performance: Integrative Model Of IT Business Value. *Management Information Systems Quarterly*, *28*(2), 283–332.

Naemura, K. (1995). User involvement in the life cycles of information technology (IT) and telecommunication standards. In Hawkins, R., Mansell, R., & Skea, J. (Eds.), *Standards, Innovation and Competitiveness. The politics and economics of standards in Natural and Technical Environments*. Aldershot, UK: Edward Elgar Publishing Limited.

Pine, B. J. (1993). *Mass Customization: the new frontier in business competition*. Cambridge, MA: Harvard Business School Press.

Rada, R. (2000). Consensus Versus Speed. In Jakobs, K. (Ed.), *Information Technology Standards and Standardization: A Global Perspective* (pp. 19–34). Hershey, PA: Idea Group Publishing.

Rada, R., & Craparo, J. S. (2001). Standardizing Management of Software Engineering Projects. *Knowledge, Technology, &. Policy*, *14*(2), 67–77.

Rutkowski, A. M. (1995). Today's Cooperative Standards Environment and the Internet Standards-Making Model. In Kahn, B., & Abbate, J. (Eds.), *Standards Policy for Information Infrastructure (pp. Xiv, 653)*. Cambridge, MA: MIT Press.

Shafer, S. M., & Byrd, T. A. (2000). A framework for measuring the efficiency of organizational investments in information technology using data envelopment analysis. *Omega*, *28*, 125–141. doi:10.1016/S0305-0483(99)00039-0

Sherif, M. H. (2003b). When is standardization slow? *International Journal of IT Standards and Standardization Research, 1*(1), 19–32.

Spivak, S. M., & Brenner, F. C. (2001). *Standardization Essentials. Principles and Practice*. New York: Marcel Dekker Inc.

Swann, P. G. M. (2000). *The Economics of Standardization; Final Report for Standards and Technical Regulation Directorate Department of Trade and Industry*. UK: Manchester Business School, University of Manchester.

Temple, P., & Williams, G. (2002). *The Benefits of Standards: trading with and within Europe. European Committee for Standardization*. Brussels: CEN.

Thatcher, M., & Pingry, D. (2004). An Economic Model of Product Quality and IT Value. *Information Systems Research, 15*(3), 268–286. doi:10.1287/isre.1040.0029

Turowski, K. (2000). Establishing Standards for Business Components. In Jakobs, K. (Ed.), *Information Technology Standards and Standardization: A Global Perspective* (pp. 131–151). Hershey, PA: Idea Group Publishing.

Weill, P., & Broadbent, M. (1998). *Leveraging the new Infrastructure. How Market Leaders Capitalize on Information Technology*. Cambridge, MA: Harvard Business School Press.

Weitzel, T. *(2003). A Network ROI.* MISQ Special Issue Workshop Standard Making: A Critical Research Frontier for Information Systems. Pre-Conference Workshop, International Conference on Information Systems, December 12-14, 2003, Seattle, Washington *(pp. 62-79).*

West, J. (2003). The role of standards in the creation and uses of information systems. *MISQ Special Issue Workshop Standard Making: A Critical Research Frontier for Information Systems. Pre-Conference Workshop, International Conference on Information Systems, December 12-14, 2003, Seattle, Washington* (pp. 314-326).

WTO (World Trade Organization). (2005). World Trade Report 2005: Standards, 'offshoring' and air transport. Geneva.

Yin, R. K. (1994). *Case Study research, Design and Methods* (2nd ed.). Thousand Oaks, CA: Sage Publications Inc.

ENDNOTES

[1] It is defined as 'a' not as 'the' since not necessary all aspects, elements, etc need to be specified.
[2] Meaning of concept depends on context.
[3] Two or more independent variables are required to uniquely specify a concept.

Section 2
Literature Review

In this section academic literature will be reviewed on standardization, standards, to identify key characteristics and benefits & risks with special focus on IT standardization and its effects on business performance in companies.

Apart from a few exceptions, literature on how company IT standards impact business performance is notably absent. Current literature on IT standardization and standards mainly focuses on the standardization processes carried out in industry, by consortia and international standard setting organizations and on the effects of IT standards at a macro economic scale, literature on company standardization is scarce.

Also literature will be assessed on the value of IT related to business processes and performance. This section also describes literature about IT investments, and the impact of IT on the performance of the firm. The reason for this literature review is that effects of IT standards, which are an integral part of IT, will be investigated in several case studies. Supporting the case study analysis, a method will be adopted that is used to assess business performance from IT in general.

Chapter 2
Standardization & Standards

The inherently multidisciplinary process of standardization and its outcome, standards, are fascinating and complex subjects since it involves issues ranging from technological, organizational and economic to legal and sociological aspects (Hesser and Inklaar, 1997).

Standards have been with us for over 5000 years, starting with the first alphabets and measurement systems and centuries later by national coin-based currencies. In the 19th century there was an enormous struggle with dozens of railroad gauges throughout Europe and the USA, that cried out for standards. This was also an issue as regards electricity (voltages, net frequencies, etc). Only in 1865 the International Telegraph Union (which became the International Telecommunication Union (ITU) in 1932), founded by twenty countries, addressed this problem. And just after the Second World War in 1947, the International Organization for Standardization (ISO) was established (Hesser and Inklaar, 1997; Spivak and Brenner, 2001).

In the following section a literature study is presented on both standardization and standards to identify key characteristics and benefits & risks as far as relevant to this thesis. Basically three types of literature (journals and books) have been studied related to: 1) Information System (IS) management, 2) General management and 3) Standardization and standards. The first category included primary IS journals (MIS Quarterly; Journal of Management Information Systems; Communications of the ACM) and second-

DOI: 10.4018/978-1-61520-759-6.ch002

ary IS journals (including Computer Standards and Interfaces; Database for Advances in Information Systems; Knowledge, Technology & Policy) which were reviewed on the subject of IT standardization and IT standard usage. The second category consisted of top management journals such as Academy of Management Review, Harvard Business Review, Sloan Management Review and California Management Review whereas the third category included more popular journals (like Information and StandardView). 'Standard' books on this subject were included also, for instance the ones from Verman (1973), Cargil (1989) and De Vries (1999). Rationale was to determine the current "state of the art" on standardization with special focus on IT standardization and its effects on business performance in companies.

INTRODUCTION

Historically speaking, standardization was seen as a means of reducing costs by decreasing diversities to make economies of scale possible. By standardizing across technology (e.g. platforms, applications), data (syntaxis and semantics) and processes (e.g. billing, procurement, vendors) organizations can reduce the complexity of their operations. This can lead to higher *efficiency* because such standards can result in e.g. timesaving, enable reuse, or allow reduction in replications or support staff. But the "optimal" level of such standardization in organizations is dependent on a lot of factors that should be addressed by the management of those organizations.

Apart from these efficiency aspects there are the *effectiveness* gains too. Standardization can make organizations plan better for future changes with greater flexibility to support new functions and improved scalability of existing functions. Other effectiveness incentives include improving the quality of business processes or improving their competitiveness. Apart from to these benefits there are drawbacks such as switching costs when converting from one standard to the other.

Economics research on standards adoption and competition between standards, considers two main streams in which standards affect the usage of new technology:

- Network effects (Farrell and Saloner, 1985; Katz and Shapiro, 1985);
- Switching costs (Von Weizsäcker, 1984; Farrell and Shapiro, 1988).

Network effects[1] describe a positive correlation between the benefits of individual users and the usage of standards. Direct network effects include:

- Economies of scale (Chandler, 1990; David and Greenstein, 1990);
- Externality (Katz and Shapiro, 1985; David and Steinmueller, 1994; Liebowitz and Margolis, 1994);
- Compatibility (Katz and Steinmueller, 1994);
- Bandwagon effect (Farrell and Saloner, 1988; Frohlich and Westbrook, 2002);
- Path dependency (David, 1985; Arthur, 1989; Liebowitz and Margolis, 1995);
- Free riders (Weiss and Toyofuku, 1996; Schoechle, 2004).

Standards can result in variety reduction, thereby lowering production costs and creating *economies of scale*. This refers to the condition where the cost of producing an extra unit of a product decreases as the volume of output increases, in other words the variable costs go down. When the variable costs are low and the fixed costs are high, this may cause a significant entry barrier for competitors, which can prohibit new players from entering the market. When the fixed costs are reduced by an innovation this barrier could be removed. A network *externality* is a benefit granted to users of such a product by another's purchase of the product, i.e. every new user in the network increases the value of being connected to that network. A good example is the GSM standard for mobile telecommunication (Bekkers, 2001). Moreover, network effects arise when consumers value *compatibility* with others, creating economies of scope between different consumers' purchases. This behaviour often stems from the ability to take advantage of the same features of products and processes. The *bandwagon effect* occurs when first adopters make a unilateral public commitment to one standard. First adopters of a standard take the highest risk, but they also have the benefit of developing competence early. If others follow the lead they will be compatible at least with the first mover, and potentially with the followers. Bandwagon pressures are caused by the fear of non-adopters appearing different from adopters and possibly performing at a below-average level, if competitors substantially benefit from the standard. So organizations are pressured to adopt standards by the sheer number of adopting organizations in the market even when individual assessments of the merits of standard adoption are unclear. In other words there is a *path dependency* meaning that decisions by later adopters of a standard depend strongly on those by made by previous adopters. The stronger the network effects, the higher the probability that market mechanisms do not work as they should in selecting superior standards as this is influenced by historical events (e.g. QWERTY keyboard versus Dvorak Simplified Keyboard). Often companies are unwilling or unable to participate in, and contribute to standardization processes. The creation of standards involves costs, while the benefits are not exclusively for the participating members. All the same, they have access to the standard because many standards are publicly available on the Internet. This phenomenon is called the *free rider* problem.

Next to these direct effects, so-called indirect network effects are recognized. This is the case when adoption of a standard itself does not offer direct benefits on other users of the standard, but the adoption of the standard might ultimately benefit others. The distinction between direct and indirect refers to the source of benefit to participants in the network, not necessarily to the magnitude of the network effect. For example, greater adoption of Xbox® consoles should generate greater variety in Xbox 360™ game titles. Common adoption would allow producers to achieve scale more easily. Katz and Shapiro (1985) showed how an indirect network effect (i.e. the availability of software to support a hardware standard) made the more popular standard more attractive to future adopters (p. 424). Other consumers or producers are likely to adopt such benefits as well.

<u>Switching costs</u> refer to the costs associated with converting from one standard to the other. Among this second category on standards adoption and competition are the

- Installed base effects – Farrell and Saloner, 1986
- Lock-in effects – Arthur, 1989; Farrell, 1990; Liebowitz and Margolis, 1995

A group of users that use a standard is called the *installed base*. Once this installed base has been created, users tend to stick with one standard even when it has become old-fashioned or inferior compared to an alternative. The reason is that conversion has become too difficult and/or too costly, so users are *locked-in* into the old standard (Arthur, 1989). A classic example is the QWERTY keyboard layout (David 1985). Von Weizsäcker was one of the firsts to consider asymmetric switching costs. He elaborated how users consider the net present value of expected future switching costs. Vendors use such switching costs to build barriers to subsequent competitors. Klemperer (1987) grouped switching costs into three categories: transition costs (e.g. conversion), training costs (e.g. courses for end users) and contractual costs (e.g. contract ending fine).

The economic value or impact of standards has rarely been measured, as indicated in the Problem Definition. The few examples include assessments from a macro economic perspective (Swann, 2000; Temple and Williams, 2002; Blind, 2004; WTO, 2005) or the business perspective of SMEs participating in formal standardization (Schaap & De Vries, 2004). Another line of research focuses on the socio-economic effects of standards (e.g. Graham et al., 1995; Egyedi, 1996, Gerst et al., 2005).

The next sections of this Chapter are structured using Figure 2 from Chapter 1 that depicts the research scope. In Section "External Standardization Processes," formal and informal standardization processes will be described, including the end-result 'Standards'. Then in Section 'IT Standardization in Organizations," the process to come to IT standards and how these are being used in companies will be analyzed. Finally in Section "Utilization of IT Standards in Organizations," the usage of standards is discussed as described in current literature.

EXTERNAL STANDARDIZATION PROCESSES

The Process

Definition of Standardization

Standardization is a method to achieve standards that can be accomplished in a myriad of manners. The official ISO/IEC (2004) definition (No. 1.1) all National Standardization Organizations subscribe to, is:

The activity of establishing, with regard to actual or potential problems, Provisions for common and repeated use, aimed at the achievement of the optimum degree of order in a given context.

Notes:

1. In particular, the activity consists of the processes for formulating, issuing and implementing standards.
2. Important benefits of standardization are improvement of the suitability of products (including services) and processes for their intended purposes, prevention of barriers of trade and facilitation of technological co-operation.

This definition is limited in scope because it has a focus on the formal standardization organizations. Furthermore it is pretty vague *'a given context'* and imprecise *'optimum degree of order' (*De Vries, 1999, p. 138). In this book we also consider IT products and processes other than those created by formal standardization organizations (see Figure 2, Chapter 1). Therefore, de definition of standardization by De Vries (1999, p. 155) is more appropriate in this context. After considering a large number of definitions by standardization organizations, in dictionaries and from other sources, De Vries (1999, p. 155) arrives at the following:

"Standardization is the activity of establishing and recording a limited set of solutions to actual or potential matching problems[2], directed at benefits for the party or parties involved, balancing their needs and intending and expecting that these solutions will be repeatedly or continuously used, during a certain period, by a substantial number of the parties for whom they are meant."

Furthermore De Vries enumerates some general aims of standardization (p. 3):

- variety reduction;
- enabling communication;
- contributing to safety, health and the environment;
- contributing to the functioning of the global economy;
- protection of consumer and community interests.

Likewise, Jakobs et. al. (1996) enumerate the following main motivations for standardization:

- integration;
- internationalization;
- cooperation.

Although this section concerns external standardization processes, the general theme of this book is about IT standardization in companies and consequently we define a company (IT) standardization process as follows:

A company IT standardization process is a process carried out by an organization with the objective of providing specifications for an IT product or process to be repeatedly and consistently used in that company.

The definition by De Vries also holds for company IT standardization but our definition is more specific.

Classification

There are several ways to classify the process of standardization (De Vries, 1999, p.137). De Vries demonstrates that in general, standardization literature shows a lack of consistency regarding the classification of standards and many current standardization classifications mix "apples and oranges". However, a common distinction is made from the way in which standards are developed, which can be divided into 1) formal standardization processes, and 2) informal standardization processes.

1. *Formal* standardization processes, which are inherently open and public, are carried out by standards developing organizations (SDOs) such as ISO, ITU and IEC (international), ANSI, BSI and DIN (national). International standardization processes are often regarded as inefficient, because of their lengthy and expensive procedures. The creation of the OSI standard is a good example in this respect. Standards originating in formal processes are referred to by many as *de jure* standards (Jakobs, 2003).

Table 1. Characteristics of formal and informal standards development (Spivak and Brenner 2001, p.136)

	Informal standard development	Formal standard development
Type	De facto	De jure
Participants	Relatively homogeneous, single minded	Diversified, varied objectives
Procedures	Ignore or short cut traditional procedures; expediency; short-term results	Due process, open, consensus, public review, authorization
Communication	Difficult; often no formal structure, secretariat, or fixed address; often restricted distribution	Easy, fixed address; standards ready available

2. *Informal* standardization processes occur in many ways. Examples are industrial standardization processes carried out by consortia with the objective of achieving a large market share of the stakeholders. This process may result in multiple standards, which is for example the case for Java and UNIX. Other examples are standardization processes executed by scientific or professional societies like IEEE, Internet Engineering Taskforce (IETF) or the World Wide Web consortium (W3C).

A special category are *de facto* standards that originate from the free play of the market and "just emerge" when a product or technology achieves large acceptance through market mechanisms. Informal industrial consortia or a single company develop products or processes and generally bear the trademark of leading enterprises or business consortia. De facto standards are in many instances proprietary (i.e. single vendor) ones. Other firms may join by making compatible products to participate in the large market share and the standard becomes even wider spread. Examples are Philips'® Audio Compact Cassette, JVC's™ Video Home System (VHS™) and Microsoft's Windows® operating system.

Spivak and Brenner (2001) summarize general characteristics between informal and formal standard development:

They elaborate on de facto standards and identify three types:

However, De Vries (2006b) argues *de facto* standardization does not exist, since 'de facto' refers to the end-result of any standard development process (i.e the de facto standard). Furthermore, whether the Proprietary and Strategic de facto types are really distinct instances, or just another End-result de facto seems to be a matter of taste. But there are more issues with the categorization in de facto and de jure. He also points out that standardization processes and standards are being studied from a number of different disciplines and perspectives, which do not necessarily exclude each other. With research on standards and standardization being a relatively young discipline, almost inevitably, concepts and related terms used to describe IT standards are diverse and sometimes confusing. For instance, the distinction between de jure and de facto standards is inconsistent, as the first is related to organizations that develop the standards, whereas the latter is related to acceptance of the standard in the marketplace. De Vries (p.4) proposes, therefore, a classification based on the following definition of a standard: "*approved specification of a limited set of solutions to actual or potential matching problems, prepared for the benefits of the party or parties involved, balancing their needs, and intended and expected to be used repeatedly or continuously, during a certain period, by a substantial number of the parties for whom they are meant*".

Table 2. Categories of de facto standards (Spivak and Brenner, 2001, p.137)

Type	Description	Example
Proprietary de facto	A company strategically positions its products to expand market share and collects royalties by licensing intellectual property rights	Microsoft Windows
End-result de facto	Market forces designate one company's product as the standard among equally effective competitors	VHS; NTSC
Strategic de facto	Informal industrial consortia and occasionally users attempt to establish sufficient critical mass to define a standard in a particular field	Dolby Digital™; DVD+R; APS

This definition contains elements related to: a) the process of development, b) to subject matters and c) to its usage. As a standard can fulfill diverse functions for different stakeholders, a classification scheme based on its usage is not considered as feasible from a scientific point of view. Therefore, his twofold classification scheme looks like:

1. A classification based on the 'Organization that drives the process', for instance:
   - Governmental;
   - Formal;
   - Consortium;
   - Company.

The main issue with this classification is that current literature does not provide unambiguous definitions of these terms. Note that 'de facto' is not part of this class as this relates to the market acceptance and not the process of development.

2. A classification based on the 'Characteristics of the process', for instance:
   - Anticipatory, participatory, responsive;[3]
   - Open or closed;
   - Consensus or non-consensus.

He also discusses 'Actors that are interested or involved', but this does not result in unambiguous distinctions. These include functional classifications, such as: intrinsic, extrinsic (e.g. for interoperability) and subjective (e.g. cost reductions) or related to time, obligation, business model or Property Rights.

Evolving Process

Cargill (1989) provides a strategy for standards development. His view involves developing standards well in advance of the perceived technological and economic benefits. Cargill argues that standards should be seen as marketing tools that answer the planning needs of corporations to develop new markets and direct the growth instead of a mere set of technical specifications. The concept of technological maturity can been used to show the dilemma of when to standardize. On the one hand, early standardization guards against diversity, preventing incompatibility but hinders experimenting with alternatives. Premature standardization (anticipatory) leaves no time for the market to smooth out the kinks and separate the "nice-to-haves" from the "need-to-haves". On the other hand, late standardization (responsive) makes it more difficult to reach consensus and causes years of market confusion and the need to cope with a proliferation of versions that arise in the interim. To sum up, if technology matures before the market takes off, standardization can take place smoothly in the meantime (concurrent) and this is considered as the easiest case. A comprehensive discussion can be found in Simons and De Vries (2004, p. 135). Sherif (2003c) looked into innovation and standardization throughout the technology life cycle of public telecommunication networks. He discovered different time horizons for telecommunication equipment vendors and service providers on technology evolution. He argues that firms, regulators and standard development organizations should align development of marketing and standardization strategies to the evolution of a specific technology being used.

In general, IT standardization undergoes fundamental changes. The focus is shifting from standardization on technologies towards standardization on business practices. It has shifted from integration of information technologies to interoperability of information systems and business processes. In Table 3, trends are specified showing how standardization evolves or has already taken place.

Werle (2001) adds to this: from regulation to coordination and from intergovernmental and other official organizations to private forums and consortiums of standardization.

A shift in the creation of standards tends to take place from the formal standardization processes towards informal standardization processes (compare for example the *de facto* 'TCP/IP'[4] and the equivalent *consensus* 'OSI layer'). Rutkowski (1995) has proposed the following explanatory factors for the success of the (informal) Internet standards process:

- Individual participation
- Direct open participation by experts and innovators
- Output consists of demonstrated working standards
- Emphasis on meeting real user needs
- A well management development process
- Minimal institutional ossification
- Standards approved are via a robust expert review process
- Standards and related material are instantly and globally accessible
- Activities are network based
- Creating the right culture

Table 3. Trends in standard setting processes (Betancourt and Walsh, 1995)

Was	Is
Operational	Strategic
Technology driven	Business driven
Single issue / vertical	Complex issue / horizontal
Stand-alone product	Products are part of services
Single business involvement	Corporate involvement
Company standards (products)	Process standards
Market reactive	Market driven
Locally driven	Globally driven
Local manufacturing	Global manufacturing

Table 4. Prevailing institutional features of standard developing organizations (Werle, 2001, p.129)

1. Participation is within certain membership rules open to those who are "substantially interested."
2. The work is committee-based, cooperative and consensus-oriented. It follows formalized rules and procedures.
3. Organizations and working procedures are impartial, unsponsored and politically independent ("due process"). The organizations are non-profit organizations.
4. The work is based on technological knowledge and follows the principle of parsimony of standards. It is not remunerated (voluntary) and conceived of as superior to market selection of standards.
5. Standards are non-mandatory and public goods. However, they are not necessarily provided to the public completely free of charge.

Therefore the open source TCP standards "just emerged" and became de facto standards, whereas the equivalent one from the OSI 7-layered model[5] failed to get critical mass within the user community. The TCP/IP standard is relatively simple to implement, which is just what users want. But there are other reasons for this as well. During the Internet hype around the turn of the 21st century hundreds of billions of dollars were mobilized to build the Internet infrastructure in a few years. Under normal conditions this would probably have taken over a decade. To facilitate and participate in this hype, IT vendors and users had no choice but to collectively embrace the existing open standards of TCP/IP, HTML, Java, and XML (Mak and Ramaprasad, 2001).

Although informal standardization is perceived to be more efficient than standardization carried out by SDOs, Sherif (2003b) has two important comments. First of all, the company or group of informal consortia often bases its work on existing formal standards. For example HTML and XML, developed by W3C, are based on the open standard of the 'Standard Graphic Markup Language' (SGML) by ISO. Secondly SDOs have speeded up their process but this has not been widely acknowledged yet. Sherif mentions the ITU organization that is able to produce standards in an 18-month timeframe. Therefore the perceived slowness of SDOs may have some political and ideological motivations (e.g. market mechanism, privatization and deregulation) after all. Moreover, Egyedi (2003) argues there is a dominant rhetoric that underestimates the openness of standardization carried out by industry consortia and overestimates the democratic process in formal standardization organizations.

The participation of suppliers and end users in standard-setting movements has been recognized as a critical success factor for a long time (Poppel and Goldstein, 1987). Fomin and Keil (2000) propose for example that CIOs should become participants of standardization committees because they know the needs of the user communities they represent. One should make sure that only aligned user requirements are fed into the process of standardization and mechanisms are provided to enable continuous input of requirements.

Werle (2001) specifies prevailing features of the formal SDOs, however, many of which are shared by the private organizations as well.

De Vries (1999, p. 69) sketched the wishes of several customers of National Standard Organizations (NSOs, such as the British Standards Institution and Deutsches Institut für Normung) concerning the use of standards. These customers come from four distinct areas: Companies, Customer Organizations, Governments, and Standards Development Organizations. In general their wishes include:

Several proposals for improvement of the standardization process date from decades ago but have not yet been implemented. This illustrates the difficulty in changing the formal standardization processes. It appears to be difficult for SDO customers to express their needs concerning standards and standardization. In general, they do not go further than the level of *'processes should be speeded up'* (p.131). Rada (2000) treats the dilemma of how to reach standards that are created in a speedy way as well as

Table 5. Wishes of customers of national standard organizations

NSO customers wishes	NSO meet criteria?
Editorial conditions should be met concerning e.g. format, numbering, pictures, abbreviations and references to other standards.	Yes
Standards should be accurate, without contradictions, simple to understand for qualified people, corresponding to the state of technology and should not hinder future technological developments.	To certain extent
Scope and field of application should be described unambiguously.	To certain extent
Set of standards should be coherent	To certain extent
In general, national and regional standards should be based on international standards.	To certain extent
Electronic devices should be used, such as the Internet and means for advanced text processing	To certain extent
Information to facilitate their use should be added to standards, including lists of differences with preceding standards	No

Table 6. Standardization: consensus versus speed (Rada, 2000)

Consen-sus	**Yes**	*ISO*	*IETF*
	No	-	*W3C*
		Low	**High**
		Speed	

accepted by all participants. Because IT standards will continue to change quickly, traditional standards development organizations are now trying to anticipate these new needs. Other organizations can create standards within a few months, but consensus is not guaranteed. In general, the matrix of Table 6 can be drawn up for consensus standardization. He provides some examples of both formal and informal standardization organizations:

- The formal IT standardization processes[6] are by many characterized by its time-consuming and arduous work. Therefore ISO/IEC is modifying its approach by evolving their standardization process into a set of concurrent ones trying to speed up the whole process. However ISO/IEC is not in a position to force industry to use their standards and ISO standards do not always result in market acceptance either (compare OSI standards)[7].
- The World Wide Web Consortium (W3C), founded in October 1994, is to support the advancement of IT technology through (informal) standardization in the field of networking, graphics and user interfaces for the Internet. W3C is a consortium dominated by industry members and has more than 500 member organizations participating. They create products, for example the HTTP standard, which are freely available to all without charge. The entire standardization process can occur in a matter of weeks. The director of W3C is the sole approver of the standards, which is one of the reasons of rapid standards deliveries. However consensus is not guaranteed and the influence of major vendors taking part in the process is a particular point of concern.
- The Internet Engineering Task Force (IETF) is a large, open and international community. It is the key organization for (informal) Internet standardization and consists of network designers, operators, vendors and researchers. Draft standards are publicly created by working groups and

must have multiple, independent implementations. With relatively little bureaucracy these draft standards pass from one stage to the next and typically reach permanent status within a year. Furthermore IETF only accepts implemented standards, whereas ISO for example accepts hypothetical standards as well.

The variety in processes and organizations can be attributed to, for example, different intentions, different scopes and different approaches to protection of intellectual property rights. Rada (2000) discusses some shortcuts in the formal process of standards development, such as the Publicly Available Specifications (PAS) process (see also De Vries, 1999). The shortcuts include the development of *informal* standards by efficient organizations like IETF being turned into *formal* standards by the international standards organizations afterwards. A special case is the 'fast track' approach in which standards developed by JTC1 members (typically national standard bodies or associated organizations) are submitted for approval and converted into ISO/IEC standards. A recent example is ISO/IEC 38500:2008, a standard for IT Governance, that is based on its Australian predecessor AS8015:2005[8] which took less than two years to complete.

It can be concluded that there is no consensus on the classification of standardization processes, although the classification based on the organization that drives and the characteristics of the process seems to be the most unambiguous one. Furthermore, the general perception is that both informal and formal standardization processes tend to become speedier and in some cases this even occurs because of a fruitful combination of the two.

The Process Deliverable

In this section the end result of the process of standard development will be discussed: the standard itself; the definition, classification and structure of standards will be discussed.

Spivak and Brenner (2001) show that standardization results in standards of many forms. Particular applications may be but are not necessary limited to:

1. Physical standards or units of measure;
2. Terms, definitions, classes, grades, ratings or symbols;
3. Test methods, recommended practices, guides to application of products and processes;
4. Standards for systems and services, e.g. to allow interoperability, variety reduction and increase quality;
5. Standards for health, safety, consumers and the environment.

Definition of Standard

The word *standard* originates from the Latin 'extendere' (to stretch) but oddly enough in other European languages, variants of the Latin 'norma' (guideline, directive) are used for standard, e.g.

Dutch – norm
French – norme
German – Norm
Italian – normale

Spanish – norma

In the section on classification of standardization processes we gave an overview of standardization and the problems with its categorization. Likewise, with standards, there is no generally agreed categorization and definition of what constitutes a standard. Webster's New Universal Unabridged Dictionary defines a standard as *"An authoritative principle or rule that usually implies a model or pattern for guidance, by comparison with which the quantity, excellence, correctness etc. Of other things may be determined."*David and Greenstein (1990, p.4) define (technological) standards as *"a set of technical specifications adhered to by a producer, either tacitly or as a result of a formal agreement"*. Alternatively, in ISO/IEC (2004) the definition of a standard is as follows:

A document, established by consensus and approved by a recognized body, that provides, for common and repeated use, rules, guidelines or characteristics for activities or their results, aimed at the achievement of the optimum degree of order in a given context. Note: Standards should be based on the consolidated results of science, technology and experience, and aimed at the promotion of optimum community benefits.

Like the ISO/IEC standardization definition, this one (No. 3.2) is mainly restricted to the formal standard development organizations (e.g. established by consensus and a document only). It excludes specifications that evolved in the market place and that established themselves as de facto standards. In many cases, these were never approved by any recognized body. In addition it excludes specifications that have been adopted by forums or private consortia (for example IETF and W3C respectively) even though these institutions are generally committed to consensus.

Brunsson and Jacobson (2000) refer to *standards*, as 'explicit rules issued without reference'. Apart from standards they identified *directives* 'mandatory rules' and *norms* 'rules that are not mandatory'. However, it is often impossible to distinguish between these three types of rules. They argue, some of these 'rules' may turn op as a norm in some settings and as a directive or standard in others. For example (p.14), *"a standard clause used in an agreement form, perhaps between a buyer and a seller, becomes a directive for the parties to the agreement"*.

Despite this lack of agreement on what seems to be a lock-in of the research community (De Vries, 2006b, p.18) on the definition of a standard, in this book we focus on <u>company IT standards</u> that were defined in the problem definition section: "A specification of an IT product or process to be repeatedly and consistently used in the company".

Classification

Regarding classification of standards there is no agreement either, which at least is consistent with the issues already identified. Standards can also be classified in a variety of ways, for example according to 1) the standard setting mechanism, 2) legal obligations, or 3) characteristics of a process or product.

A classical distinction is made by Verman (1973) who differentiates into subject, aspect and level that are represented on three axes in this so-called standardization space. Two axes (the aspect and subject axis) are nominal ones, whereas the level axis is a sort of ordinal one. Although this is a way to classify standards its practical use is limited.

The type of standard that emerges when standardization is carried out depends on the aspects of the subject. Which of the aspects in Table 7 are applicable depends on the nature of the subject. An example that would fit into this space is standardization in financial management (Subject: commerce; Aspect: forms; Level: international). The financial reporting in conformance to the International Financial Reporting Standard (IFRS) is a well-known example. Another example is given by Spivak and Brenner (2001) on the interchangeability of railway track gauges (Subject: transport; Aspect: specifications; Level: national):

William Jessop invented metal rails for transportation around 1795 and laid them at the same distance as the cartwheel ruts of the English Roads that were probably unchanged for centuries. In fact this turned out to be the same distance of wheel tracks found in Pompeii: 4 ft 8 ½ in (1.44 m). However narrow-minded judgment and reasoning resulted in a proliferation of "dozens " of railway gauges. In the mid 19th century in the US alone 33. This lack of standardization resulted in significant inefficiencies like unloading and reloading and unnecessary investments in additional locomotives and other rolling stock.

As indicated earlier, De Vries (1999) showed that there is - contradictory to the subject itself[9] - no standard way of categorizing standardization and thus its resulting standards. Nevertheless, there are logical and sound ones, such as the classic classification by David and Greenstein (1990). They distinguish three categories of standards:

1. Reference standards
2. (Minimum) quality standards
3. Interface or compatibility standards

The first two categories of standards cover processes or products that match certain defined characteristics on content whereas the last category describes inputs and outputs of processes and products in order to successfully incorporate them into a larger entity[10].

As far as process standards are concerned, Davenport (2005) classifies those into three types: 1) process activity and flow standards, 2) process performance standards, 3) process management standards. Examples in these categories include: for the first category the Supply Chain Operations Reference model, for the second category a benchmark model on efficiency of staff requirements by the internal HR function and in the last category standards like CMM, ISO 9001 and ISO/IEC 17799.

Using De Vries' definition of what constitutes a standard, he divides a classification scheme based on subject matters, into three main groups De Vries (2006b, p.19):

Table 7. The three dimensions of Lal Verman's standardization space (Verman, 1973)

Axis	Value
Subject	Engineering, Transport, Housing/Building, Food, Agriculture, Forestry, Chemicals, Commerce, Science, Education
Aspect	Nomenclature, Symbols; Specification; Sampling & Inspection, Test & Analysis, Grading & Classification, Simplification, Rationalization, Code of Practice, Bylaws, Packaging & Labeling, Forms & Contracts
Level	Individual, Company, Association, National, International

1. A *basic standard* is of general importance and not designed for e.g. some sort of industry.
2. A *requiring standard* sets prerequisites to entities or relations between entities. These can be performance standards, that set operational criteria without specifying how these should be met, and standards that describe solutions. In horizontal standards all entities can be of the same kind.
3. A *measurement standard* describes methods to check whether criteria set in a requiring standard are met.

These are listed in Table 8. In this classification scheme, the ones used by David and Greenstein map to the first two classes: the classic and requiring standards.

He also discusses classification of standards related to differences in entities, but this does not result into clear and distinguishable categories.

We can conclude that in this domain there is no consensus on definition and categorization either. However, in this research I will focus on company IT standards of the class called "requiring standards" (Table 8) because economic aspects for this category are of more importance given the research scope.

Structure and Function

Jakobs et. al. (1996) recognizes the tension between a standard's inherent goal of catering for generic functionality and the need for maintaining flexibility to deal with local variability. However, the use of standards does not necessarily mean hindrance to effective usage. Entities or combinations of entities can be considered as modules in a larger system, with a related structure of different standards. De Vries (1999, p31) writes:

'A standards structure preferably corresponds to a layer structure and, when applicable, to modules within layers. A basic standard can describe the structure. Other standards set requirements or provide test methods for entities, groups of entities, or interfaces between entities. In a good standards structure, a standard can be changed without affecting too many other ones. In a stable standards structure, interface specifications are kept unchanged during a long period. This can be reached when the modules or layers each provide different functions. A functional analysis of entities and standards related to these

Table 8. Classification of standards (De Vries, 1999, 2006b)

Class (subject)	Sub class	Type	Example
1. Basic standard	-	Unit standard	SI system
		Reference standard	OSI model
2. Requiring standard	Performance-based standard	Interference standards	Electromagnetic compatibility
		Quality standard	Fire mitigation
	Design-based standard	Interference standards	Diesel particle filter
		Horizontal compatibility standard	Power cables, A4 paper format
		Vertical compatibility standard	Bluetooth, USB
		Quality standard	CMM
3. Measurement standard	-		Breathalyzer

entities can be of help in designing an entity architecture and a related standards architecture that are stable in time.'

When used as a method of standardization, the results are building blocks with different degrees of abstraction. To make them interoperate or interconnect, clearly defined and separable interfaces have to be defined. The definition and standardization of interfaces within a modular system is an elementary component of modularization. In Chapter 3 the concept of modularization will be further discussed.

Standards also evolve over time. For example, they mature or are a result of market competition when a firm has the power to set de facto standards and industries may settle on these standards even though they are inferior to others. Gosain (2003), therefore, proposes the following strategies in dealing with evolving standards:

- The dependencies across components are continually bridged through intermediary layers as and when standardization regime changes. Protocol converters, also known as 'gateway technologies' should be used.
- The dependencies across components are minimized through loose coupling so that standardization regime changes in any layer have a minimal impact on other layers. Modularity should be used.
- The impacted components are rapidly reconfigured when standardization regime changes.

Young (1996) argues that the economic significance of standards (and the preceding standardization) is to reduce transaction (and production) costs. This is true for standards referring to for example accounting rules and legal contacts. It is less costly to fill in the blanks on standard contacts than to create them from scratch. Likewise, Akkermans and Van der Horst (2002) enumerate three main reasons why to create standards in the first place:

1. Standards allow variety reduction to enable economies of scale, resulting in reduction of transaction costs and other cost efficiencies;
2. Standards allow effective communication at both the organization and IT level. It facilitates connectivity, interfacing and interoperability;
3. Standards facilitate changes (portability, flexibility) because they reduce diversity.

Tassey (1995) identified in addition:

4. Standards provide accepted methods of producing information (e.g. test and measurement data);
5. Standards prescribe accepted levels of performance (e.g. min quality, safety).

De Vries (1999, p.25) discusses that the use of standards contributes to efficiency, because:

- One makes use of the expertise of others, one doesn't have to develop a standard oneself and the existing standard can be employed immediately;
- Procurement costs decrease due to quantity rebates, reduction of stocking costs, price competition between suppliers and lower maintenance costs due to routine work/procedures.

Table 9. Motives of stakeholders in open standards (Krechmer, 2006)

Stakeholder	Driven by	Perspective
Creator	Market development and control issues	A standard is considered to be open if the creation of the standard follows the tenets of open meeting, consensus and due process.
Implementer	Production, implementation and distribution cost efficiencies	A standard is considered to be open when it serves the market they wish, it is without cost to them, does not preclude further innovation by them, does not obsolete their prior implementations, and does not favor a competitor.
User	Efficiency improvements	A standard is considered to be open when multiple implementations of the standard from different sources are available, when the implementation functions in all locations needed, when the implementation is supported over the user-planned service life, and when new implementations desired by the user are backward compatible to previously purchased implementations.

Cargill (1995) argues that standards should be user-requirement driven and not primarily focussed on technology. Therefore, the challenge is to identity user requirements, since users in general do not care about technology or standards; they want solutions. All too often there is a lack of business rationale for standards as well. It is important for companies to know how standards are created and established in order to value, for example, their usefulness or interdependence on suppliers. Standards in the market place are often commercially motivated only. Nevertheless, David (1995, p.18) argues that standardization and homogenization can bring efficiency gains only at the cost of suppressing some idiosyncratic sources of consumer satisfaction.

A special kind of standards that support both creators and users are the so-called open standards, which will be discussed in, the next section.

Open Standards

A key characteristic of open standards is that they are not owned by anybody, nor can a single firm or consortium change them. This is in contrast to proprietary specifications of products or services that are typically owned and controlled by a single firm and which producers of complementary or competing products or services can use only if they license it. Bird (1996) defines open standards as: "*a publicly available specification that is developed and maintained by an open, public consensus process and that is consistent with international* (formal) *standards, where relevant.*"

The purpose of open standards is to support common agreements that enable communications open to all (Krechmer, 2005). Therefore, open standards are to reduce vendor power over buyers, typically as a result of multi-vendor competition between implementations of the standard (West, 2004). Krechmer (2006) identifies three categories of stakeholders in open standards: Creators, Implementers and Users. Each category is driven by specific economic needs such as market development or cost efficiency (Table 9).

It is as yet unclear whether open standards are superior to others (Aggarwal et al., 2006). Although theoretically, open standards seem to be preferable to single firm proprietary specifications (that may evolve into de facto standards), open standards can result into multiple implementations from multiple vendors, and thus into incompatibility and vendor lock-in. In this respect, Egyedi (2005) distinguishes benevolent and malevolent deviations of open standards. With benevolent deviations, standard-compliant but incompatible products and services are created unintentionally or for other valid reasons, for example, certain features of the open standards may be unnecessary for its intended use. With malevolent deviations vendors introduce changes to open standards to hinder development and adoption of competitive products and in that way locking users into their specific version by implementing:

1. additional functionalities to the open standard (embrace-and-extend strategy);
2. only parts of the open standard (embrace-and-omit strategy);
3. adaptations to the open standard (embrace-and-adapt).

In all three situations the integrity of a standard is compromised. Indeed several examples exist of open standard implementations (embrace-and-extend strategy) that resulted in incompatible versions of for example UNIX "*While the trademarked "Unix" was all derived from AT&T's IPR, the "open systems" evolved into multiple independent implementations—including several "open source" implementations—each compliant with the accepted POSIX specification* (West, 2003a, p.1263)." Another example is provided by Chen and Forman (2006) who showed that vendors were able to influence switching costs to their advantage in the market for routers and switches in spite of the presence of open standards in the industry, such as Ethernet® and TCP/IP.

IT STANDARDIZATION IN ORGANIZATIONS

Introduction

Following the definition in the problem definition, company IT standardization is the process to agree on a specification of an IT product or process to be repeatedly and consistently used in that company. Cargill (1989) argues that company standardization should be directed by an understanding where a company is going (p. 63) and can gain the most by standardization of products and processes that require a great deal of expertise to create.

These company standards have, in general, the form of: 1) a reference to one ore more external standards officially adopted by the company; 2) a company modification of an external standard; 3) a subset of an external standard; 4) a standard reproduced from (part of) other external ones; or 5) a self-written standard (De Vries, 1999, p. 231). Integrally linked to these company standards, there is the process that takes place within companies when selecting these company standards[11]. This section deals with some general issues and discusses standardization of interfaces and IT architectures.

Jakobs (2002) gives an overview of standardization possibilities from the *business transaction* point of view (Figure 1). Five levels are identified and each of these levels is suitable for standardization.

At the highest level special care must be taken because companies may gain or lose competitive advantage when using standardized instances of business processes.

Weill and Ross (2004, p.170) discuss that enterprises try to accomplish three types of IT standardization:

1. Technology – to generate economies of scale with shared services;
2. Data – to facilitate process integration with e.g. standardized customer, supplier or product data;
3. Processes – to facilitate process excellence and organizational learning.

Figure 1. Standardization may concern several levels (Adapted from Jakobs, 2002)

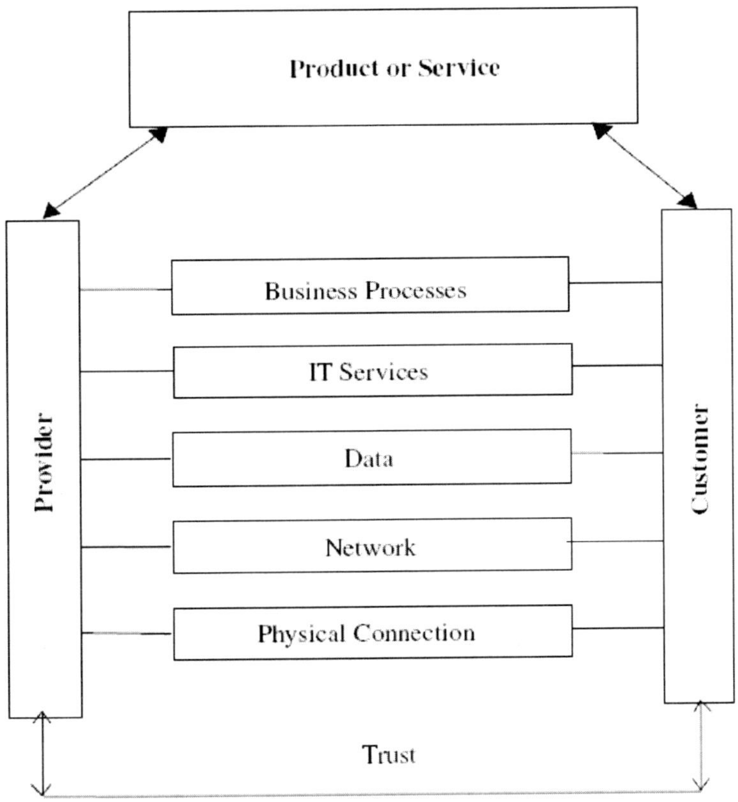

Table 10. Standardization levels

Level	Examples	Type
Business process	Profit and loss reporting of Business Units	Functionality
IT Service	SWIFT, Reuters 3000, MS Office 2000	Functionality, user interface
Data	EDIFACT, XML	Interface
Network	TCP/IP	Interface
Physical	UTP	Interface

They found that enterprises promoting business unit autonomy usually focus on shared technology and infrastructure services only, whereas enterprises seeking more synergies between the business units gradually work towards data and process standardization as well.

From an organizational design point of view, Mintzberg (1984) sees standardization as a coordination mechanism for organizations. He distinguishes several types of coordination mechanisms like standardization of work processes or process in/outputs. Furthermore he specifies standardization of skills and norms. When one standardizes on skills, the result is that knowledge or background of staff is standardized instead of work or outputs. When one standardizes on norms, staff will share a common set of beliefs and achieve coordination based on that. Mowshowitz (1997) introduces a concept called metamanagement that could be used to compose and manage a virtual organization. Metamanagement requires a standardized organizational structure and processes to achieve interchangeability and compatibility. Modularity is a means to accomplish this by the use of standardization and interchangeability.

As argued earlier, standardization can take place at the product (technology & data), process and even the organizational level. Akkermans and Van der Horst (2002) state that one should not standardize during the early stages of organizational maturity where business processes tend to change frequently. Referring to the five levels of the Capability Maturity Model (CMM), in stages 2 and 3 one should apply collaborative standards whereas in stages 4 and 5 the use of coercive standards is to be enforced.

Scott (1990) addresses the importance of standardization at the process level. Process improvement initiatives are beneficial as long as two or more organizations agree to work together on a long-term basis, i.e., they set mutual flexible standards for working together. Boynton, et al. (1994) also argue that, in order to take advantage of IT in general, emphasis should be on (standardized) IT management processes. Variety reduction of infrastructure technologies is key to the costs-effective deployment and operation of an infrastructure. From a standardization point of view one should focus on three other aspects of IT control:

1) Minimize technological churn
2) Remove obsolete technologies
3) Avoid redundant or duplicate technologies

An important question that can be asked is the following: "Is it necessary for distinct divisions within enterprises to carry out a separate standardization process and do they result in different standards?"[12]. A mapping may be made between the type of standardization and the value propositions as defined by Treacy and Wiersema (1995). Their model deals with the value propositions companies have to offer and the following standardization incentives can be identified:

- The first incentive covers the *product leadership* value proposition of firms like Sony®. Companies that strive for effectiveness in producing new products or services could build their processes using standard IT infrastructure components. As this offers reusability and interoperability of technology they can introduce new products or services relatively fast and easy.
- The second incentive relates to the *customer intimacy* value proposition Tracy and Wiersema define. The information and IT requirements of these firms center on understanding and serving customers. They often strive for a single view of the customer, which requires standardized data definitions (both syntax and semantics). Standards must be created in such a way that they are flexible, i.e. scalable and extensible. Only in that way is it possible to answer the specific needs of customers.
- The last incentive is the most traditional one and links to the *operational excellence* value proposition of firms like Ford® and McDonalds®. These companies are process driven and tend to have centralized management structures designing standardized enterprise-wide data definitions and processes to minimize coordination costs. The advantage of standardization is clearly seen from the low-cost, high-volumes perspective.

In the financial services industry, for example, these standardization incentives relate to the following market segments respectively:

1. The highly volatile and demanding markets of Investment Banking
2. The niche markets of Private banking and Asset Management
3. The volume markets of Consumer and Commercial Banking

For the financial services sector, the use of the Internet has encouraged development of many standards for financial data exchange, like FIX, OFX and IFX, all based on the Extensible Markup Language XML. It enables exchange of structured data between multiple internal and/or external systems for immediate updating of records. This clearly relates to the second incentive of standardization.

A same line of thought can be found in Weill and Ross (2004, p. 175). They found that the demand for synergies (at the technology, data and processes level) aligns to a certain extent with that of the value disciplines. Product leadership only requires technology synergies, customer intimate firms also seek shared data whereas enterprises pursuing operational excellence strive for all three types of standardization activities.

There has been a substantial amount of research on the organizational adoption of information systems. Much of the research on organizational adoption of information systems draws on two frameworks: the Technology Acceptance Model (TAM) and the Technology-Organization-Environment (TOE) framework. The TAM (Davis, 1989) is based on the theory of reasoned action from social psychology and predicts an individual's acceptance behavior towards a new technology. This model has proven to be robust and has been cited as the most widely applied theoretical model in the IS field (Lee et al., 2003). The TAM is useful for understanding why individuals accept particular technologies, however, the model is less suited for investigation of organizational-level acceptance of technologies as these adoption decisions (such as the introduction of a new company IT standard) are strategic level concerns (Lippert and Govindarajulu, 2006).

The TOE framework (Depietro et al., 1990, p.153) has originally been developed to study the adoption of innovations and has been adapted by many IS researchers to investigate the organizational acceptance of new technologies (Zhu and Kraemer, 2005). The TOE framework identifies three key components that influence an organization's information systems adoption decision: the technological (technologies in use and new ones relevant to the organization), organizational (measures such as scope, size and amount of resources) and environmental context (the area in which the organization operates such as competitors and regulatory requirements). Despite the importance of IT standards, the role of such standards in the adoption decisions by organizations has been rarely considered (Dedrick and West, 2003, p.238).

Interfaces

Akkermans and Van der Horst (2002) consider interfaces from the point of view of processes and technological products. At the process level, inputs as well as outputs can be standardized. This is typically interface standardization. Even the whole process as such is an option. At the technology level they argue that standardization works best for applications that are integral and stable over a long period. Nevertheless at the organizational level standardization can also take place, which is not discussed in that article.

In Bonino and Spring (1991) the interface concept is discussed, enabling technical interoperability and interconnection, which is clarified in Table 11 that lists three interface categories.

Stegwee and Rukanavo (2003) extend their view on communication and interfacing beyond that of pure technical systems to those between socio-technical systems (i.e. human, process and technical entities). Their framework contains three types, as specified Table 12.

Turowski (2000) discusses standardization and interfaces related to markets (vendor-buyer relationships). He identifies two modeling layers, a business domain layer and a technical layer and standardization may occur at both these layers. At the business domain layer, standards can be set for example for business data interchange formats (data exchange) and at the technical layer for middleware and basic techniques like XML. He proposes relatively fine-grained core standards at both layers with built-in extensibility to anticipate on changes in the dynamic area of business domains (planning and control, purchase, procurements, etc). In other words, he defines standards that are flexible[13] to some extent.

Table 11. Three categories of technical interfaces

Interface category	Application	Interoperability enabling
Graphical user interface (GUI)	Communication	Determines effective usage of applications. A user interface, consisting of the set of dials, knobs, operating system commands, graphical display formats, and other devices provided by a computer or a program to allow the user to communicate and use the computer or program. (A GUI can be split up into: Application screen layout; keyboard; help facilities; character set; operating system)
Application program interface (API)	Functioning	A programming interface, consisting of the set of statements, functions, options, and other ways of expressing program instructions and data provided by a program or language for a programmer to use.
Device interface (DI)	Connection	Centers on matters relating to storage, output and communication devices. The physical and logical arrangement supporting the attachment of any device to a connector or to another device.

Table 12. Three hierarchies of interfaces or compatibility (Stegwee and Rukanavo, 2003, p.167)

Type	Purpose	Level	Human	Process	Technical
Interoperability	Enables entities to operate as one	Use information at a *pragmatic,* process control and application level	Behavioral scenarios and procedures	Providing for external controls on process behavior	Interaction standards like SMTP
Interchangeability	Enables entities to exchange information	Use information at a *semantic,* input/output and presentation level	Language systems like natural languages and vocabularies	Displaying the same behavior in terms of I/O	Data representation standards like ASCII or HTML
Interconnection	Enables entities to communicate	Exchange information at a *syntactic,* process flow and network level	Communication systems like speech and writing	Provisioning for external inputs and outputs	Communication standards like TCP/IP

Table 13. Key elements of the four successive IT architecture competencies (Ross, 2003)

	Application Silo architecture stage	Standardized Technology architecture stage	Rationalized Data architecture stage	Modular architecture stage
Strategic Implications	Local/Functional Optimization	IT Efficiency	Process Optimization	Customization and flexibility
IT Capability	Applications serve isolated needs	Firm-wide technology standards	IT focussed on wiring core business processes	Modules enable business model extensions
Business Case for IT	ROI of applications	Reduced IT costs; interoperability	Improved business performance; integration	Time to market; strategic agility
Key Characteristics	Isolated applications	Standardization and centralization of technology components	Standardization of data and business processes; embedding core processes in the IT infra	Loosely coupled applications, data and technology components
Benefits	Encourages innovation	Economies of scale; Reduction of complexities	Single face to the customer, Platform positioned for innovation	Greater efficiencies while allowing local customization
Risks	Expensive and difficult to maintain; Interoperability cumbersome	Managerial resistance to both concept and enforced approach	Management challenges; requires disciplined processes and strong central organization	Difficult to accomplish and master.

IT Architecture

Weill and Ross (2004, p.30) define IT architecture as "the organizing logic for data, applications, and infrastructure, captured in a set of policies, relationships, and technical choices to achieve desired business and technical standardization and integration".

Ross (2003) describes a process to reach a standardized enterprise IT architecture with as final stage a modular architecture. In accomplishing standardized enterprise architectures, Ross' (2003) architecture model describes four stages when and where standardization efforts should take place. Given the basic *'application silo architecture stage'* of individual applications serving isolated business needs, efforts should be directed at enterprise-wide IT technology standardization first. In this *'standardized technology architecture stage'* IT resources are put in a shared infrastructure allowing cost savings e.g. by a significant reduction in the number of vendor packages that offer similar functionalities. It also increases IT maintainability, reliability and security. Lead times range from 2 to 6 years. Following that, companies are to focus on standardizing their business processes and related data to overcome the application silo problem of application-specific data in order to reach the *'rationalized data architecture stage'*. Appropriately defining the core processes is essential for creating an effective rationalized architecture. Several tools are available that support data rationalization such as ERP and CRM systems and middleware. Finally, the *'modular architecture stage'* is about reuse and preserving global standards while enabling customization and local differences. It allows the quick implementation of core products, alternative channels and interfaces to back-end processes through re-use or use of locally developed front-end modules. The four stages and its key elements are listed in Table 13.

As business requirements continuously change, the enterprise IT architecture is to facilitate flexibility. This can be achieved by building a firm-wide technical shared infrastructure (e.g. servers and desktops) and by standardizing firm-wide used data (e.g. by ERP systems). The shared infrastructure and data provide the base for all other applications that are needed to support the business processes. Weill and

Ross argue that the distinction between infrastructure on the one hand and business specific applications on the other hand, allows enterprises to profit from economies of scale while retaining flexibility. By doing so one can create specified, reliable and modular services (p.34).

Although technology, data and process standardization are the defining characteristics of enterprise architecture, the reach and range of such standardization depends on the value disciplines of the company. More diversified businesses typically have fewer needs for firm-wide standardization and this could be limited to the shared infrastructure, which facilitates common objectives such as security and IT procurement. In other words indiscriminately standardizing all technology, data and business processes across the enterprise obviously is not the answer to realize the intended business benefits from company IT standardization as the level of standardization depends on the type of company, its business and whether we are dealing with core or supporting processes.

The three-tier standardization hierarchy (technology, data and processes) as identified by Weill and Ross will have special attention in this research, because of its relevance for company IT standardization and usage. This includes the level of BU autonomy related to reach and range of IT standardization.

UTILIZATION OF IT STANDARDS IN ORGANIZATIONS

This section deals with the case when a company selects and uses IT standards that are already available on the market. In other words, the company selects existing standards for direct usage. Some of the scarce examples available in the IS literature are discussed and we show that the effective usage of such standards depends, among others, on the level of formalization and prescription of relationships in companies.

Vlaar (2006b) poses that formalization in (inter)organizational relationships may concern both process (input, output and behavior) and process outcomes (policies, regulations, contacts, etc). He identifies three attributes of formalization: 1) the degree of formalization; 2) the subject of formalization and 3) the intention behind formalization. The degree of formalization in organizational relationships ranges from low to high whereas the subject concerns the extent to which formalization applies to inputs, outputs and or process as a whole. The intention of formalization in organizational relationships deals with the nature of the formalization, which may vary from enabling to enforcing. Arguments for the coordination function of formalization can be found in March and Simon's theory of organizational behavior (March and Simon, 1958). They argue that formalization gives rise to clear expectations and common understanding of participants in organizational relationships which simplifies problem solving and decision-making. As company standardization concerns intra-organizational relationships, these aspects should be considered when dealing with this subject.

Cargill (1989, p. 63) identifies three methods by which a company can bring about internal/company standardization: regulatory style, laissez faire, or a combination of these two. Through a regulatory style, standards are made mandatory and this style is more suited to a mature business. Cargill argues that for matters that are regulatory in nature or deal with safety regulations, this style is to be preferred. For industries where stringent quality is essential this method also works well. A disadvantage of this style when carried out rigorously, it may cause any standard to become an end in itself, forgetting why the standard was imposed in the first place. The second style allows the developer or user to ignore the use of the standard, effectively making the whole standards program utterly useless. Cargill explains that the third style is probably the most difficult to impose since every potential standard requires evaluation for its return and impact on the company and customers. He also stresses the active participation of management in this governance process. Cargill (1989, p. 61) also comments on the selection of IT standards within a company "*A standards group should begin by determining what its own purpose will be. While this necessity is so obvious as to be axiomatic, it is neglected by many internal standards groups*".

Infrastructure standards provide long-term benefits to the enterprise as a whole, however business units may not see a direct benefit from using the standards in the short term. Kayworth and Sambamurthy (2000) show that infrastructure standards can simultaneously facilitate localized exploitation and enterprise-wide integration, which seems contradictory at first sight. They argue that the firms can simultaneously facilitate PC-LAN infrastructure responsiveness to localized exploitation and firm-wide integration by implementing standards of moderate complexity and strict restrictiveness along with high levels of enforcement. Localized exploitation is defined as the ability to respond to individual business unit needs and opportunities. Enterprise-wide integration is defined as the use of IT capabilities for process and information integration across business units. In other words this means that standards can facilitate flexibility. Their research was limited to the role of the design and enforcement of corporate level PC-LAN infrastructure standards. They identified three attributes of these infrastructure standards:

1. Comprehensiveness (degree of prescription or the extent to which rules and procedures have been instituted);
2. Restrictiveness[14] (freedom of choice within the standard);
3. Enforcement (level of education, monitoring or sanctioning).

Motivation for these attributes was as follows:

- Experience and knowledge can be condensed in comprehensive standards, making technical choices more efficient;
- Standards should be designed with the right mix of restrictiveness and pliability (Duncan, 1995);
- Proper enforcement of standards is needed otherwise they will be ignored (Costly, 1995).

The appropriate level of enforcement depends on the organization in which they are employed. These practices could include random inspections or monitoring software checking for non-conformities. Sanctions range from refusal of the non-standard technology to connection to the network, to deliberately charging high costs of support.

Kayworth and Sambamurthy (2000) show that the organizational context in which these standards are being used is an important factor for the effectiveness of IT infrastructure standards and thus the success to satisfy specific local needs and enterprise wide integration. They identified the following main components of this organizational context:

- Corporate IS/Business Unit collaboration
- Information sharing
- Rationality of decisions
- Local IT expertise
- Perceived complexity of standards.

They conclude that the best results are obtained when these standards are implemented using a moderate degree of comprehensiveness and high levels of restrictiveness and enforcement. Furthermore, these standards must be implemented in the environment of an active collaboration between Corporate IS and local Business Units.

Rada and Craparo (2001) provide an example of management of IT standards. They presented a 'software management standards' case on IT software development projects within an enterprise. The company started the standardization of the software development process with a strict division-wide approach, but evolved into a loose one that hindered productivity. Rada and Craparo (2001, p.72) observed that: *"... several units were annoyed at the intervention by the corporate headquarters in the way of working of the unit and felt that working to MSF[15] as a standard would be a bureaucratic nuisance rather than a productivity enhancer. Those who were opposed to working with MSF understood the corporate plan but were able to proceed with management methods largely as prior to the corporate standardization effort. No formal compliance organization per se existed, and there were few repercussions for not following the directive to adopt the MSF team and process model."*

Therefore, special measures were taken that ranged from monitoring and advising staff to ensure compliance with the standard, to awareness training and continual refinement and development of the standard. The enhanced standard selection and management initiative resulted in:

- Formalized control by a dedicated technical review team on projects and associated standards.
- Proactive involvement and alignment of business and IT management.
- Significantly more projects completed on time, on target and within budget.

The importance of the alignment between Business and IT for company standards was also recognized by Monteiro and Hanseth (1999) who describe a case of company wide rationalization of a Lotus Notes® infrastructure. They called this process 'continuous re-appropriation' in order to seize opportunities and improvise in response to changes as they occur. Next, Hanseth and Braa (2001) discussed the problems when implementing a standardized corporate IT infrastructure. Their case study indicates that decisions about implementing and using IT standards were made through constant realignment of interest among the staff involved and were not based on a rational process. This resulted in failure as different and incompatible implementations of the standard materialized.

Herbold (2002) showed that company standardization initiatives can really pay off, provided some drastic measures are imposed from the top. These included standardization of data definitions and business templates, using off-the shelf products where possible, trimming system development efforts, and refraining from linking legacy systems and processes to new ones. Consequently, significant efficiency gains were accomplished in the finance, procurement and HR areas without sacrifices to innovation and creativity. Robert et al. (1998) also described the importance of management support for standardization, which concerned a software development methodology in their case.

Doniger and Goodwin (1996) give another example of achieving costs savings through the use of standards. Overall costs at an oil and gas firm decreased by around 30%, due to reduced repetition of work and more collaboration between operators, suppliers and design contractors. They describe a specification of software built by a software corporation that includes:

- Standard way for user interface
- Standards for hardware and system software

- Standard way of defining data structures and definitions
- Standard way to connect applications

Weill and Broadbent (1998, p. 266) identified "Standards Management" in a cluster of infrastructure services. Standards management should at least encompass:

- Recommendation of at least one standard component in the IT architecture (e.g. hardware, operating systems, data, communications);
- Enforcement of IT architecture and standards.

This cluster of infrastructure management services was based on several companies they worked with.

To conclude this section, an important aspect of the usage of company standards is discussed: the exception process to IT standards to enable organizational leaning in this respect. Weill and Ross (2004, p.99) argue that technology standards are critical to both business and IT efficiency. However, the occasional exceptions to IT standards are not only appropriate but are even necessary. Without a practical exception process one tends to ignore the standards and implement exceptions without any approval. The occasional exceptions to enterprise standards can be facilitated with the architecture exception process. This process allows development teams to sidestep the enterprise architecture standards and in many cases the architecture teams have the responsibility of granting these exceptions. Best practice processes resolve most issues at the operational level, while quickly escalating any potentially strategic exception requests to the CIO, COO and business unit heads. A rapid exception escalation process reinforces the enterprise architecture and new requirements are expected to be incorporated into the IT architecture standards (p.76).

In the case study research, the three designated styles by Cargill (1989) will be scrutinized, especially from the point of view of influence on business performance. This will include, but is not limited to the architecture exception process, prescription and enforcement level in usage of standards, participation of stakeholders and alignment with business requirements. The link between standardization and flexibility, as discussed in Kayworth and Sambamurthy (2000), will also get special attention. Possible effects will be investigated from a larger perspective, including the influence of the organizational context.

BENEFITS AND RISKS OF STANDARDIZATION AND STANDARDS

Standards can be both enabling and inhibiting at the same time. Enabling, as economies of scale can be exploited (network effects) and technological progress can unfold. Inhibiting, because changes may require large switching costs (lock-in, path dependency) or otherwise hamper technological progress.

Advantages

Several authors (e.g. Bonino and Spring, 1991; David, 1995; Tassey, 1995; Hesser and Inklaar, 1997; Bird, 1998; Succi et al., 1998, De Vries, 1999; Brunsson and Jacobson, 2000; Schaap and De Vries, 2004) identified advantages of formal and informal standardization.

From the manufacturers/suppliers point of view, standardization:

1. Gives an enlarged market in which to sell or gives rise to new markets and strategies.
2. Allows introduction of new products without having to create a complete vertically or horizontally integrated system.
3. Results in fewer varieties of products that have to be kept in stock, maintained or serviced.
4. Improves the productivity by diminishing inefficiencies associated with trial and error processes.
5. Increases efficiency with respect to e.g. internal control, reporting and procurement.
6. Creates added value product features to win new customers rather that porting or resolving differences between products.
7. Leads, through competition, to potential new alliances and/or new standards.

From the customer/user perspective:

1. Increased flexibility, allows communication among heterogeneous products; e.g. the ability to move applications and data from one system to the next.
2. Freedom of choice, allows moving complementary parts from one product to the other and mixing components from several brands to build systems best satisfying one's needs; e.g. buy the best solution from the best supplier at any given time and have all of the parts interoperate.
3. Lower costs of integration, because components are built on common, open specifications and have been proved to interoperate. In addition, reduced testing and reduction of user training when products change.
4. Decreases prices, due to increased competition among manufacturers and suppliers and larger second-hand markets.
5. Easier purchase because the benefit from having a set of standards merged into a product standard, results in significant time and costs savings and attention can focus on the business-specific aspects of the purchase.

Other benefits include economies of scale / network externalities, lower transactional costs, lower operational risk, improved process efficiency, and adhered performance in terms of quality, environment or safety.

Disadvantages

David and Greenstein (1990, p.12) argue that standards reduce entry costs and risks for new firms leading to increased price competition and reduced profits. This affects the ability to sustain investments in improving the quality of products and services. Crawford (1991) specifies a number of other disadvantages:

- New standards often do not indicate the differences with its predecessors leaving it up to the user to determine these differences on their own.
- Because of the large number of different standards, users find it difficult to find the right ones especially because some standards lack clear definition of its scope
- Standards occasionally favor certain companies over others or alternatively, (political) consensus has been achieved in making standards less explicit that result in weak standards.

- Standards may raise barriers to new competitors, especially for those from less developed countries, when unusual or high level of performance criteria are specified.

Besen and Farrell (1994) point out that for competition to become the (de facto) standard it may also delay market growth by encouraging customers to wait and see which standards emerge, i.e. what others will do. Additionally, when a de facto standard has emerged better products, processes or services that arrive later on the market may be unable to displace poorer but earlier standards. This is because compatibility with the installed base[16] is required. A company may encounter too high switching costs when it wants to choose the other and better standard. Effectively, this results in maintaining the current and less favorable one. These so-called "lock-in effects" (Farell and Saloner, 1986; Arthur, 1989) are well known disadvantages of standards. A classic example is the case of the VHS video technology (Cusumano et al., 1992).

Kayworth and Sambamurthy (2000, p. 56) note that aversion to standardization may manifest itself in, for example, job estrangement and feelings of inability to innovative and to be motivated for one's tasks. Generally one can say that formalized rules should not be applied to non-routine tasks because they may be perceived to be coercive restricting individual flexibility.

Mähönen (2000), Wakid and Radack (1997) cite some other disadvantages when using standards in general and for IT in particular. According to them, it is difficult to develop timely, precise and easily implementable standards (for IT) because:

1. The decision making process, including the typical jargon, is difficult to understand. Public awareness should be emphasized more.
2. It has been claimed that the standardization committees have produced too little, too late.
3. The specifications often contain ambiguities and uncertainties, due to poor writing, and can therefore be interpreted in different ways. The texts are often unnecessarily complicated or detailed and as a consequence the results are far less than perfect.
4. Technical specifications often include many options ("may-be" bits) that can be implemented in different ways messing up the interoperability goal.
5. Rapid change in the development and use of information technology make standards for IT less useful and attractive.
6. Standardization is sometimes considered by the IT-industry as a danger to the Intellectual Property Rights (conflicting with patents, copyrights, trademarks and trade secrets).

Earlier, Bonino and Spring (1991) addressed this third disadvantage as well. Because of the rapidly changing nature of IT, these standards are outdated quickly. Therefore they no longer provide a general and long-lasting solution to problems. This motivates to standardize on the process domain and possibly organizational domain first, and in the IT domain last. The fourth disadvantage was identified by Arnold (1994) as well and he enlarges on other risks of using (de facto and consensus) standards. Within ISO the process of developing a formal standard used to be long with an average time of 7 years (Brunsson and Jacobson (2000) but it was brought down to 2.8 years in 2006 (ISO, 2006). Many technical decisions are taken as a result of compromises like introducing additional functionality. In practice this means accepting variations by allowing implementation dependencies. Disadvantages, related to de facto standards may include: 1) being tied to a single manufacturer and 2) choosing a product that is incompatible with other standards. Note that these two items are examples of "lock-in effects".

In addition, Brunsson and Jacobson (2000, p.171) add the following "*Many of the objections to standards and standardization are similar to the objections to rules and regulation in general. Standardization is often seen as an unwelcome, unnecessary and harmful intrusion*" because:

1. it impedes individualism - becoming more alike is often seen as undesirable;
2. it may hinder innovation[17];
3. the honest intentions of standardization organizations are questionable;
4. it may result in poor solutions;
5. it might be better to let markets decide on products and services;
6. it is considered to be too weak a form of regulation.

This section is concluded with an example (Table 14) of an enumeration of the advantages and disadvantages of the use of consensus standards and the use of proprietary Application Program Interfaces (APIs) in the financial services industry (Nybo, 2002). In this same article Nybo gives an estimate of an industry standard for fixed-income electronic trading systems (FIX) which has been developed and introduced several years ago. Financial services companies would have saved around $4 billion from 1998 to 2002. This relates to one of the benefits of standards in general: lower integration costs (user advantage no. 3). Financial institutions spent over 70% of their software development effort on building and maintaining system interfaces in 1999 (TowerGroup, 021:37S, December 1999).

In Chapter 4 a conceptual model will be described based on the little literature available on the subject of IT standards selection, application and control and its consequences for business process performance. Also the results from a pilot case study, which has been carried out at group level of a large financial services company, will be included in this model. But first, in Chapter 3 a literature review will be described on the subject of IT value and business performance.

Table 14. Advantages and disadvantages between API and industry standard (Nybo, 2002)

	Disadvantage	Advantage
Industry Standard	• An industry standard needs to be managed by a centralized body. Modifications to the standard can be delayed. • Implementation of the standard has been delayed and it may be too late for rapid adoption. • Systems deploying the standard face expensive conversions and costs of supporting two protocols. • Specialized market sectors with disparate trading conventions may not be able to fully embrace the standard.	• Economies of scale are associated with deploying the same protocol across multiple client installations. • An industry standard or protocol facilitates electronic trading and order routing. • Implementing new connections to clients is cheaper. • Small firms can afford implementation of protocol. • An industry standard enables desk-to-desk communications. • A standard facilitates enhanced price discovery through indications of interests.
Proprietary API	• Extremely expensive to implement for new clients • Only makes sense to target resources for higher volume clients that justify the expense of developing the API • Integrating an API is time consuming and requires significant lead-time to test and deploy. • Creates barrier to entry for small firms without significant IT resources.	• Proprietary APIs are created and maintained by one organization and can quickly be modified to adapt to changing needs. • A proprietary API provides a competitive advantage to a firm that has extensive deployments and can serve to dissuade other systems from entering a particular market sector. • Expensive development is already "in the bag." There is little need to adopt, test, and implement a new standard. • A firm's proprietary system is designed for a particular market sector and takes into account trading conventions and special practices.

CONCLUSIONS

Current economic research on standardization and standards has focused on standardization processes and the macro-economic level rather than the company level and has hardly addressed the management perspective. The standardization processes can be divided roughly into formal and informal ones. The first category concerns official SDOs whereas the second category includes industrial and professional societies. The classification of standards is, rather hilariously, not standardized. Scholars categorize standards in multitudinous ways that are often inconsistent. Of the more relevant categorizations are the subject matters related one (e.g. quality and compatibility standards, see Table 8) and the one that differentiates standards according to the way these are developed (e.g. anticipatory, non-consensus and open standards). It was also discussed that it is still unclear whether open standards are superior to other standards.

MANAGERIAL IMPLICATIONS

Standardization in companies occurs in general at three levels: the technology level (e.g. to accomplish complexity reduction), the data level (e.g. to accomplish process integration) and the process level (e.g. to accomplish improved process control). These activities were defined as company IT standardization and are important in creating an enterprise architecture that facilitates flexibility to anticipate continuously changing business requirements. Although technology, data and process standardization are the defining characteristics of an enterprise architecture, the reach and range of such standardization depends on the value disciplines of the company. Product leadership only requires technology synergies, customer intimate firms also seek shared data whereas enterprises pursuing operational excellence strive for all three types of standardization activities.

The distinction between infrastructure on the one hand and business specific applications on the other hand, allows enterprises to profit from economies of scale while retaining flexibility. More diversified businesses typically have fewer needs for firm-wide standardization than enterprises seeking more synergies between the business units. Enterprises promoting business unit autonomy usually focus on shared technology and infrastructure services only, whereas enterprises seeking more synergies between the business units gradually work towards data and process standardization as well.

Finally we have seen that a number of control measures are key in order to effectively make use of company IT standards. These could include sanctions such as refusal of the non-standard technology connecting to the network and deliberately charging high costs of support for non-compliant technology. More supportive is to advising staff to ensure compliance with the standard and awareness training. Others include prescription and enforcement (otherwise they will be ignored), an exception/deviation processes (to enable organizational learning in this respect) and the participation of all relevant stakeholders in both Business and IT.

REFERENCES

Aggarwal, N., Dai, O., & Walden, E. A. (2006). Do Markets Prefer Open or Proprietary Standards for XML Standardization? An Event Study. *International Journal of Electronic Commerce*, *11*(1), 117–136. doi:10.2753/JEC1086-4415110105

Akkermans, H. A., & Van der Horst, H. (2002). Managing IT infrastructure standardisation in the networked manufacturing firm. *International Journal of Production Economics*, *75*(1-2), 213–228. doi:10.1016/S0925-5273(01)00201-8

Arnold, D. (1994). Conformance testing ICT Standards: Costly chore or valuable insurance? *StandardView*, *2*(4), 182–187. doi:10.1145/223282.223283

Arthur, W. B. (1989). Competing Technologies, Increasing Returns, and Lock-In by Historical Events. *The Economic Journal*, *99*(394), 116–131. doi:10.2307/2234208

Bekkers, R. (2001). *Mobile Telecommunications Standards*. Artech House.

Besen, S. M., & Farrell, J. (1994). Choosing How to Compete: Strategies and Tactics in Standardization. *The Journal of Economic Perspectives*, *8*(2), 117–131.

Betancourt, D., & Walsh, R. (1995). The evolution of Strategic Standardization Management. *StandardView*, *3*(3), 117–126. doi:10.1145/226191.226211

Bird, G. B. (1998). The Business benefit of Standards. *StandardView*, *6*(2), 76–80. doi:10.1145/301688.301691

Blind, K. (2004). *The economics of standards: theory, evidence, policy*. Cheltenham, UK: Elgar Publishers.

Bonino, M. J., & Spring, M. B. (1991). Standards as change agents in the information technology market. *Computer Standards & Interfaces*, *12*, 97–107. doi:10.1016/0920-5489(91)90059-9

Boynton, A. C., Zmud, R. W., & Jacobs, G. C. (1994). The influence of IT management practice on IT use in large organizations. *Management Information Systems Quarterly*, *18*(3), 299–318. doi:10.2307/249620

Brunsson, N., & Jacobson, B. (2000). *A World of standards*. New York: Oxford University Press Inc.

Cargill, C. F. (1989). *Information Technology Standardization: Theory, Process, and Organizations*. Bedford, MA: Digital Press.

Cargill, C. F. (1995). A five-segment model of standardization. In Kahin, B., & Abbate, J. (Eds.), *Standards Policy for Information Infrastructure*. Cambridge, MA: MIT Press.

Chandler, A. D. (1990). *Scale and Scope: The Dynamics of Industrial Capitalism*. Cambridge, MA: The Belknap Press of Harvard University Press.

Chen, P., & Forman, C. (2006). Can vendors influence switching costs and compatibility in an environment with open standards? *Management Information Systems Quarterly*, *30*, 541–562.

Costly, J.L. (1995, September 4). Take Control of PC Assets. *PC Week*, 96.

Crawford, W. (1991). *Technical Standards - An introduction for Librarians* (2nd ed.). Boston, MA: G.K. Hall & Co.

Cusumano, M., Mylonadis, Y., & Rosenbloom, R. (1992). Strategic maneuvering and mass-market dynamics: The triumph of VHS over Beta. *Business History Review*, *66*(1). doi:10.2307/3117053

Davenport, T. H. (2005). The coming commoditization of processes. *Harvard Business Review*, ▪▪▪, 100–108.

David, P. A. (1985). Clio and the Economics of QWERTY. *The American Economic Review*, *75*, 332–337.

David, P. A. (1995). Standardization policies for network technologies: the flux between freedom and order revisited. In Hawkins, R., Mansell, R., & Skea, J. (Eds.), *Standards, Innovation and Competitiveness. The politics and economics of standards in Natural and Technical Environments*. Aldershot, UK: Edward Elgar Publishing Limited.

David, P. A., & Greenstein, S. (1990). The Economics of compatibility standards: An introduction to recent research. *Economics of Innovation and New Technology*, *1*, 3–41. doi:10.1080/10438599000000002

David, P. A., & Steinmueller, W. E. (1994). Economics of Compatibility Standards and Competition in Telecommunication Networks. *Information Economics and Policy*, *6*(3-4), 217–241. doi:10.1016/0167-6245(94)90003-5

Davis, F. D. (1989). Perceived usefulness, perceived ease of use, and user acceptance of information technology. *Management Information Systems Quarterly*, *13*, 319–340. doi:10.2307/249008

de Vries, H. J. (1999). *Standardization: A Business Approach to the Role of National Standardization Organizations*. Boston: Kluwer Academic Publishers.

de Vries, H. J. (2006b). IT Standards Typology. In Jakobs, K. (Ed.), *Advanced Topics in IT Standards and Standardization Research*. Hershey, PA: Idea Group Inc.

Dedrick, J., & West, J. (2003). Why firms adopt open source platforms: A grounded theory of innovation and standards adoption. *MISQ Special Issue Workshop Standard Making: A Critical Research Frontier for Information Systems. Pre-Conference Workshop, International Conference on Information Systems, December 12-14, 2003, Seattle, Washington* (pp. 236-257).

Depietro, R., Wiarda, E., & Fleischer, M. (1990). The Context for Change: Organization, Technology and Environment. In Tornatzky, L. G., & Fleischer, M. (Eds.), *The processes of technological innovation* (pp. 151–175). Lexington, MA: Lexington Books.

Doniger, A., & Goodwin, N. (1996). Standards: What's in it for Me? *StandardView*, *4*(2), 108–113. doi:10.1145/234999.235006

Duncan, N. B. (1995). Capturing flexibility of Information Technology Infrastructure: A study of Resource Characteristics and their Measure. *Journal of Management Information Systems*, *12*(2), 37–57.

Egyedi, T. M. (1996). *Shaping Standardization: A study of standards processes and standards policies in the field of telematic services*. Delft University Press.

Egyedi, T. M. (2003). Consortium Problem Redefined: Negotiating 'Democracy' in the Actor Network on Standardization. *Journal of IT Standards & Standardization Research, 1*(2), 22–38.

Farrell, J. (1990). Economics of Standardization. In Berg, J. L., & Schumny, H. (Eds.), *An Analysis of the Information Technology Standardization Process*.

Farrell, J., & Saloner, G. (1985). Standardization, Compatibility, and Innovation. *The Rand Journal of Economics, 16*, 70–83. doi:10.2307/2555589

Farrell, J., & Saloner, G. (1986). Installed base and compatibility: innovation, product pre-announcements and predation. *The American Economic Review, 76*(5), 940–955.

Farrell, J., & Shapiro, C. (1988). Dynamic competition with switching costs. *The Rand Journal of Economics, 19*, 123–137. doi:10.2307/2555402

Fomin, V., & Keil, T. (2000). Standardization: Bridging the gap between economic and social theory. *International Conference on Information systems (ICIS), In proceedings of the 21st International Conference on Information Systems, Brisbane* (pp. 206-217).

Frohlich, M. T., & Westbrook, R. (2002). Demand chain management in manufacturing and services: web-based integration, drivers and performance. *Journal of Operations Management, 20*(6), 729–745. doi:10.1016/S0272-6963(02)00037-2

Gerst, M., Bunduchi, R., & Williams, R. (2005). Social shaping & standardization: a case study from auto industry. In *Proceedings of the 38th Hawaii International Conference on System Sciences, IEEE Computer Society, Los Alamitos, CA*.

Gosain, S. (2003). Realizing the vision for Web Services: strategies for dealing with imperfect standards. *MISQ Special Issue Workshop Standard Making: A Critical Research Frontier for Information Systems. Pre-Conference Workshop, International Conference on Information Systems, December 12-14, 2003, Seattle, Washington* (pp. 10-29).

Graham, I., Spinardi, G., Williams, R., & Webster, J. (1995). The Dynamics of EDI Standard Development. *Technology Analysis and Strategic Management, 7*(1), 3–20. doi:10.1080/09537329508524192

Hanseth, O., & Braa, K. (2001). Hunting for the treasure at the end of the Rainbow: Standardizing Corporate IT Infrastructure. *Computer Supported Cooperative Work, 10*, 261–292. doi:10.1023/A:1012637309336

Herbold, R. J. (2002). Inside Microsoft: Balancing Creativity and Discipline. *Harvard Business Review, 80*(1), 72–79.

Hesser, W., & Inklaar, A. (1997). *An introduction to standards and Standardization. DIN-Normungskunde* (*Vol. 36*). Berlin: Beuth Verlag GmbH.

ISO/IEC. (2004). *ISO/IEC Guide 2:2004. Standardization and related activities - General vocabulary*. Geneva, Switzerland: International Organization for Standardization / International Electrotechnical Commission.

Jakobs, K. (2002). *IT Normen und Standards - Grundlage der Informationsgesellschaft. Internal document.* RWTH Aachen, Informatik IV.

Jakobs, K., Procter, R., & Williams, R. (1996). Users and Standardization - Worlds Apart? The Example of Electronic Mail. *StandardView*, *4*(4), 183–191. doi:10.1145/243492.243495

Katz, M. L., & Shapiro, C. (1985). Network Externalities, Competition and Compatibility. *The American Economic Review*, *75*(3), 424–440.

Kayworth, T., & Sambamurthy, V. (2000). Facilitating localized exploitation and enterprise-wide integration in the use of IT infrastructures: The role of PC/LAN infrastructure standard. *The Data Base for Advances in Information Systems*, *31*(4), 54–81.

Klemperer, P. (1987). The Competitiveness of Markets with Switching Costs. *The Rand Journal of Economics*, *18*(1), 138–150. doi:10.2307/2555540

Krechmer, K. (2005). The meaning of open standards. In R. H. Sprague, Jr. (Ed.), *Proceedings of the 38th Hawaii International Conference on System Sciences*. Los Alamitos, CA: IEEE Computer Society Press.

Krechmer, K. (2006). Open standards requirements. In Jakobs, K. (Ed.), *Advanced topics in information technology: Standards and standardization research* (*Vol. 1*, pp. 27–48). Hershey, PA: Idea Group Inc.

Lee, Y., Kozar, K., & Larsen, K. (2003). The technology acceptance model: Past, present, and future. *Communication of the AIS*, *12*, 752–780.

Liebowitz, S. J., & Margolis, S. E. (1994). Network Externality: An Uncommon Tragedy. *The Journal of Economic Perspectives*, *8*(2), 133–150.

Liebowitz, S. J., & Margolis, S. E. (1995). Path Dependence, Lock-In, and History. *Journal of Law Economics and Organization*, *11*, 205–226.

Lippert, S. K., & Govindarajulu, C. G. (2006). Technological, Organizational, and Environmental Antecedents to Web Services Adoption. *Communications of the IIMA*, *6*(1), 146–158.

Mähönen, P. (2000). The Standardization Process in IT - Too Slow or Too Fast? In Jakobs, K. (Ed.), *Information Technology Standards and Standardization: A Global Perspective* (pp. 35–47). Hershey, PA: Idea Group Publishing.

Mak, K. T., & Ramaprasad, A. (2001). An Interpretation of the Changing IS/IT-Standard Game, Circa 2001. *Knowledge, Technology, &. Policy*, *14*(2), 20–30.

March, J. G., & Simon, H. A. (1958). *Organizations*. New York: John Wiley & Sons Inc.

Mintzberg, H. (1984). *Structures in Fives: Designing Effective Organizations*. Englewood Cliffs, NJ: Prentice-Hall.

Monteiro, E., & Hanseth, O. (1999). Developing corporate infrastructure: implications for international standardization? In K. Jakobs & R. Williams (Eds.), *1st IEEE Conference on Standardization and Innovation in Information Technology, Aachen, Germany, Sept. 15- 17*. IEEE Press.

Mowshowitz, A. (1997). On the theory of virtual organizations. *Systems Research and Behavioral Science, 14*(6), 373–384. doi:10.1002/(SICI)1099-1743(199711/12)14:6<373::AID-SRES131>3.0.CO;2-R

Nybo, A. (2002). A fixed-income protocol: too late or too early? TowerGroup, Needham MA, USA, research paper 030:03S.

Poppel, H., & Goldstein, B. (1987). *Information Technology: The Trillion-Dollar Opportunity* (p. 6). New York: McGraw-Hill.

Rada, R. (2000). Consensus Versus Speed. In Jakobs, K. (Ed.), *Information Technology Standards and Standardization: A Global Perspective* (pp. 19–34). Hershey, PA: Idea Group Publishing.

Rada, R., & Craparo, J. S. (2001). Standardizing Management of Software Engineering Projects. *Knowledge, Technology, &. Policy, 14*(2), 67–77.

Robert, T. L. Jr, Gibson, M. L., Fields, K. T., & Rainer, K. Jr. (1998). Factors that impact implementing a system development methodology. *IEEE Transactions on Software Engineering, 24*(8), 640–649. doi:10.1109/32.707699

Ross, J. W. (2003). Strategic IT architecture competency. *MIS Quarterly Executive, 2*(1), 31–43.

Rutkowski, A. M. (1995). Today's Cooperative Standards Environment and the Internet Standards-Making Model. In Kahn, B., & Abbate, J. (Eds.), *Standards Policy for Information Infrastructure*. Cambridge, MA: MIT Press.

Schaap, A., & de Vries, H. (2004). *Evaluatie van normalisatie-investeringen - Hoe MKB-bedrijven kunnen profiteren van deelname aan normalisatie*. Zoetermeer, The Netherlands: FME-CWM. (in Dutch)

Schoechle, T. D. (2004). *The privatization of standardization: Enclosure of knowledge and policy in the age of digital information*. Dissertation, University of Colorado, Boulder, Colorado, USA.

Scott, W. R. (1990). Technology and structure: an organizational-level perspective. In Goodman, P. S., & Sproull, L. S. (Eds.), *Technology and organizations*. San Francisco, CA: Jossey-Bass.

Sherif, M. H. (2003a). The role of JITSR in enhancing the management of ICT standards. *International Journal of IT Standards and Standardization Research, 1*(1), 62.

Sherif, M. H. (2003b). When is standardization slow? *International Journal of IT Standards and Standardization Research, 1*(1), 19–32.

Sherif, M. H. (2003c). Technology substitution and standardization in telecommunication services. *Standardization and Innovation of Information Technology (SIIT) 2003 Conference Proceedings* (pp. 241-252).

Simons, C. A. J., & de Vries, H. J. (2004). *Standaard of maatwerk. Bedrijfskeuzes tussen uniformiteit en verscheidenheid.* Schoonhoven, Academic Service. (in Dutch)

Spivak, S. M., & Brenner, F. C. (2001). *Standardization Essentials. Principles and Practice*. New York: Marcel Dekker Inc.

Stegwee, R. A., & Rukanova, B. D. (2003). Standard Making: A Critical Research Frontier for Information Systems. *MISQ Special Issue Workshop Standard Making: A Critical Research Frontier for Information Systems. Pre-Conference Workshop, International Conference on Information Systems, December 12-14, 2003, Seattle, Washington* (pp. 161-170).

Succi, G., Predonzeni, P., Valerio, A., & Vernazza, T. (1998). Representing compatibility and Standards: A case Study of Web Browsers. *StandardView*, *6*(2), 69–75. doi:10.1145/301688.301690

Swann, P. G. M. (2000). *The Economics of Standardization; Final Report for Standards and Technical Regulation Directorate Department of Trade and Industry*. UK: Manchester Business School, University of Manchester.

Tassey, G. (1995). The roles of standards as technology infrastructure. In Hawkins, R., Mansell, R., & Skea, J. (Eds.), *Standards, Innovation and Competitiveness. The politics and economics of standards in Natural and Technical Environments*. Aldershot, UK: Edward Elgar Publishing Limited.

Temple, P., & Williams, G. (2002). *The Benefits of Standards: trading with and within Europe. European Committee for Standardization*. Brussels: CEN.

Treacy, M., & Wiersema, F. (1995). *The discipline of Market leaders: Choose your Customers, Narrow Your Focus, Dominate Your Market*. UK Addison-Wesley Publishing Company.

Turowski, K. (2000). Establishing Standards for Business Components. In K. Jakobs (Ed.): in 'Information Technology Standards and Standardization: A Global Perspective (pp. 131-151)bs K., Idea Group Publishing, Hershey, PA, USA.

Verman, L. C. (1973). *Standardization - A new discipline*. Hamden, CT: Archon Books.

Vlaar, P. W. L. (2006). *Making Sense of Formalization in Interorganizational Relationships: Beyond Coordination and Control*. Doctoral Dissertation, ERIM Ph.D. Series Research in Management 75, Erasmus University Rotterdam, The Netherlands.

von Weizsäcker, C. (1984). The Costs of Substitution. *Econometrica*, *52*(5), 1085–1116. doi:10.2307/1910989

Wakid, S., & Radack, S. (1997). Measurement Based Standards for future Information Technology Systems. *StandardView*, *5*(1), 36–40. doi:10.1145/253452.253479

Weill, P., & Broadbent, M. (1998). *Leveraging the new Infrastructure. How Market Leaders Capitalize on Information Technology*. Boston, MA: Harvard Business School Press.

Weill, P., & Ross, J. (2004). *IT Governance - How Top Performers Manage IT Decision Rights for Superior Results*. Boston, MA: Harvard Business School Press.

Weiss, M., & Toyofuku, R. (1996). Free-ridership in the standards-setting process: the case of 10BaseT. *StandardView*, *4*(4), 205–212. doi:10.1145/243492.243508

Werle, R. (2001). Standards and Standards Organizations in the International Free Trade Regime. *Knowledge, Technology, &. Policy*, *14*(3), 127–140.

West, J. (2003a). How Open is Open Enough? Melding Proprietary and Open Source Platform Strategies. *Research Policy, 32*(7), 1259–1285. doi:10.1016/S0048-7333(03)00052-0

West, J. (2004). *What are Open Standards? Implications for Adoption, Competition and Policy.* Paper presented at the Standards and Public Policy Conference, Federal Reserve Bank of Chicago, May 13-14, 2004.

WTO (World Trade Organization). (2005). World Trade Report 2005: Standards, 'offshoring' and air transport. Geneva.

Young, H. P. (1996). The Economics of Convention. *The Journal of Economic Perspectives, 10*(2), 105–122.

Zhu, K., & Kraemer, K. L. (2005). Post-Adoption Variations in Usage and Value of E-Business by Organizations: Cross-Country Evidence from the Retail Industry. *Information Systems Research, 16*(1), 61–84. doi:10.1287/isre.1050.0045

ENDNOTES

1. Network effects are also known as network externalities. It describes the effect that each buyer of a technology receives additional benefits as the user network increases in size. Examples are mobile GSM phones and DVD+RW recorders.
2. Problem of interrelated **entities** that do not harmonize with one other. Solving it means determining one or more features of these entities in a way that they harmonize with one other, or of determining one or more features of an **entity** because of its relations(s) with one or more other **entities**. (An **entity** is any concrete or abstract thing that exists, did exist or might exist, including associations among these things. Example: a person, object, event, idea, process, etc.)
3. Denotes the synchronization between technological developments and its standards.
4. Other open source examples are LINUX, DNS, SMTP and 'C'.
5. The Open Systems Interconnection (OSI) transport and management protocols (ISO 7498) define logically separated generic data communication functions that are hierarchically layered.
6. IT standardization is carried out together by the International Organization for Standardization (ISO) and the International Electrotechnical Commission (IEC) in the ISO/IEC Joint Technical Committee 1 (ISO/IEC JTC1) "Information Technology"
7. The (anticipatory) OSI standard, failed because of attempts to satisfy all requirements of the parties involved (Sherif, 2003a). A pitfall of anticipatory standards is that they tend to become too complex.
8. http://www.incits.org/archive/2007/in070477/j1n8432.pdf (Retrieved on 2008-05-30)
9. ISO/IEC Guide 2 'General terms and their definitions concerning standardization and related activities' (ISO/IEC, 2004) claimed to be, but failed.
10. In the first decades of computing the vertical integration model was used, where complexities of interoperability were minimal. Technologies came from a single supplier and business activities were compartmentalized. With the emergence of client server computing in the 1980's and the

increasing integration of information systems, the need for the standards of the second category increased.

11 As this latter topic is an important subject of this book and there is only very little literature available on this subject we have carried out a pilot case study to get an insight into these processes with the objective of to explore this aspect in practical terms and to complement the scarce literature. This pilot case study can be found in Chapter 4.

12 See the detailed research questions in Chapter 1

13 Flexible, as far as the interface is concerned.

14. Originally called flexibility, but renamed here to avoid confusion with the definition in Chapter 3.

15 Microsoft Solutions Framework (MSF)

16 The number of users of a standard is called the installed base (Farell and Saloner, 1986)

17 This is a somewhat contradictory disadvantage related to compatibility, which in itself is seen as an advantage of standards. When one does not need to maintain compatibility with existing hardware and software, new generations of for example Intel's processor could have evolved at a much faster rate.

18 In fact this is just what de facto standards are all about.

Chapter 3
IT, Business Processes & Performance

This chapter describes literature about IT investments, and the impact of IT on the performance of a firm. The reason for this study is that effects of IT standards, which are an integral part of IT, will be investigated in several case studies. Supporting the case study analysis, a method will be adopted that is used to assess business performance from IT in general.

Business performance in general can be assessed from different angles, such as financial performance, process performance and transaction performance. Literature from various disciplines shows the complexity of and the disagreement as regards measurement and description of business performance. However, it is generally accepted that these impacts can be assessed best at the intermediate level: that of business processes. After the introduction, literature dealing with IT value and business performance will be discussed. Then a specific method, the Balanced Scorecard, will be dealt with and an explanation is given why we used it in this research. This chapter concludes with a look at the concept of flexibility, as part of business performance, and what it means in relation to IT standards.

INTRODUCTION

The link between IT as enabler, or at least as facilitator, for business processes was recognized in the early nineties of the last century. The importance and benefits of adopting process-oriented perspectives of business value have been recognized for a long time (Kauffman & Weill, 1989). It were Davenport &

DOI: 10.4018/978-1-61520-759-6.ch003

Short (1990) and Hammer & Champy (1993) who introduced a methodology, called Business Process Redesign or Business Process Reengineering (BPR) respectively, which focussed on business processes instead of on tasks.

A process is defined as a "specific ordering of work activities across time and place, with a beginning, an end, and clearly identified inputs and outputs: a structure for action" (Davenport 1993, p. 5). Davenport classifies business processes into 1) operational processes as part of the activities in the value chain of the organization and 2) management processes that are associated with resource control and administration. He elaborates on the relationship between processes and information systems: "Strategic objectives lead to process-related objectives, which lead to information systems-related objectives" (p. 215). Hammer & Champy discuss, for instance, a standard purchasing system for all divisions within Hewlett Packard that provided data to a corporate procurement database. This new purchasing process allowed them the benefits of both centralization (volume discounts) and decentralization (meeting needs locally) (p.95)

These authors urged organizations to reinvent themselves via radical change and not via incremental improvement. In BPR, IT is the key enabler to reorganize and optimize business processes in order to increase the organization's efficiency and effectiveness. As Davenport (1993, p. 318) argued, "... the notion that information technology could be a source of dramatic change and business improvement, that is, that information technology could provide competitive advantage". ERP systems, telecommunication networks and web based applications on the Internet, are examples that enable the reengineering of these business processes.

However, most companies did not take the revolutionary approach "Don't automate - Obliterate (Hammer, 1990)" of radical change. Because of resource, organizational and political constraints, most companies still took the incremental approach (Kettinger et al. 1997), probably severely limiting their potential. In fact, one of the major criticisms on BPR is that organizations fail to develop a change-oriented culture next to changing their business processes (Khoong, 1996; Guha et al., 1997; Speier et al., 1998). Brynjolfsson and Hitt (2000) also argue that the business value of IT is limited less by computational capability and more by the ability of managers to invest in new processes and organizational structures to leverage this capability.

THE VALUE OF IT

The task of measuring the real costs and benefits of IT and IT investments is a notoriously complex problem (Brynjolfsson and Hitt, 1998) as there are tangibles & intangibles and direct & indirect costs and benefits involved. In spite of a lot of research in this field, there is still no generally accepted framework. The majority of studies have focused on productivity as the measure of IT value, whereas others have used profit or have focused on the impact of IT on intermediate performance measures such as product quality and output levels as the measure of IT value (Thatcher and Pingry, 2004). Melville et al. (2004) developed a process-oriented model to assess the impact of IT on business activities.

Davern and Kauffman (2000, p.122) state that IT value measurements have been carried out at various levels of analysis, starting from the individual level, via the business process and firm level up to the macroeconomic level. But few scholars are satisfied, as there is general disagreement on both method and outcome. A basic model on the impact of IT on performance is provided by Bakos (1987) as depicted in Figure 1. IT impacts on organizational structures and processes, thereby affecting organizational per-

Figure 1. A basic model on the impact of IT on performance (Adapted from Bakos, 1987)

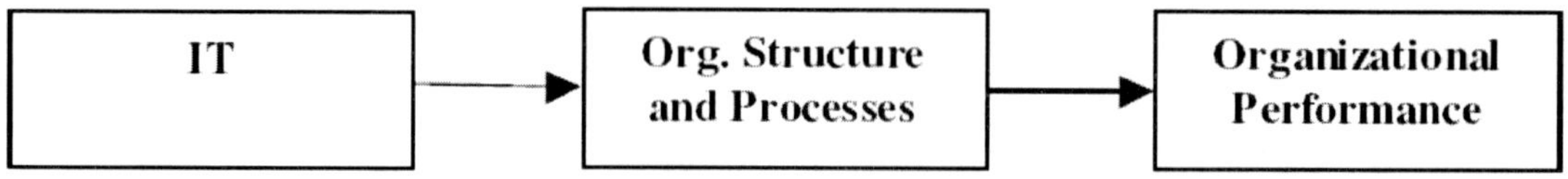

formance. Barua et al. (1995) also argue that the effects of IT on organizational performance (second order effects) can best be identified through measurements of first order effects.

Weill and Broadband (1998, p. 50) devised a four-level scheme to assess the impact of IT on Business Performance (Figure 2). At each level, variables that relate to efficiency and effectiveness are specified. The further one moves up the levels, the more difficult it becomes to actually determine the impact of IT on business performance. At the topmost level "Business Unit Financial Performance" the impact is diluted due to the fact that there are numerous factors that influence the performance. Furthermore they note that Business Value is strongly dependent on the firm's context and objectives.

Melville et al. (2004) list several theoretical paradigms that have been used to examine the performance impacts of IT. These include: 1) Microeconomics, 2) Industrial organization theory, 3) Sociology and socio-political paradigms and 4) Resource-based view of firms. They point out that the term performance is used in mainstream IS literature to denote both intermediate process-level measures and organizational measures. Moreover, researchers define performance in different ways: as efficiency and/or as effectiveness. As a catch all, they define IT business value as: "*the organizational performance impacts of information technology at both the intermediate process level and the organization-wide level, and comprising both efficiency impacts and competitive impacts*", p. 287. For our purposes, the impacts of IT standards, we will focus only on efficiency and effectiveness at the intermediate process level. With regard to performance they argue it comprises of *business process performance* as well as

Figure 2. Hierarchy of impact of IT standardization on business performance (Adapted from Weill and Broadbent, 1998, p.50)[1]

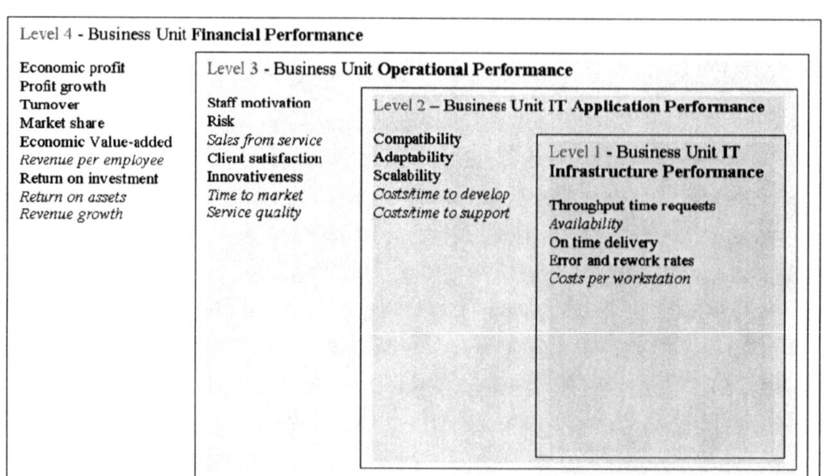

organizational performance. Business process performance is referred to as "measures which include quality, customer service, flexibility, information sharing, and inventory management" and to organizational performance as: "overall firm performance, including cost reduction, revenue enhancement, profitability, market value and competitive advantage". Business process performance is described in detail later on in this Chapter.

Melville et al. developed a descriptive model (Figure 3) of the IT business value generation process that is based on the resource-based view of firms (Wernerfelt, 1984), which combines the rationale of economics with the management perspective. It is a 3 layer model consisting of the firm, its competitive environment and its macro environment. It is also based on the work of Weill (1992) and Barua et al., (1995) that have modeled the impact of IT on firm performance mediated by intermediate processes. The layers of the model are:

1. The Local Firm - At the organizational level, application of IT and organizational resources impact on business processes which may ultimately impact on organizational performance (Brynjolfsson and Hitt 2000).
2. The Competitive Environment - When IT stretches beyond the boundaries of the firm, business processes and IT resources of trading partners and industry characteristics influence the IT business value generation of the firm.
3. The Marco Environment - National and international factors influence the application of IT and thus organizational performance.

Although the external factors 2) and 3) play a role in which IT business value can be generated and captured, we will not focus on those in order to confine the scope of this research, as described in Chapter 1.

Figure 3. IT Business value model (Adapted from Melville et al., 2004)

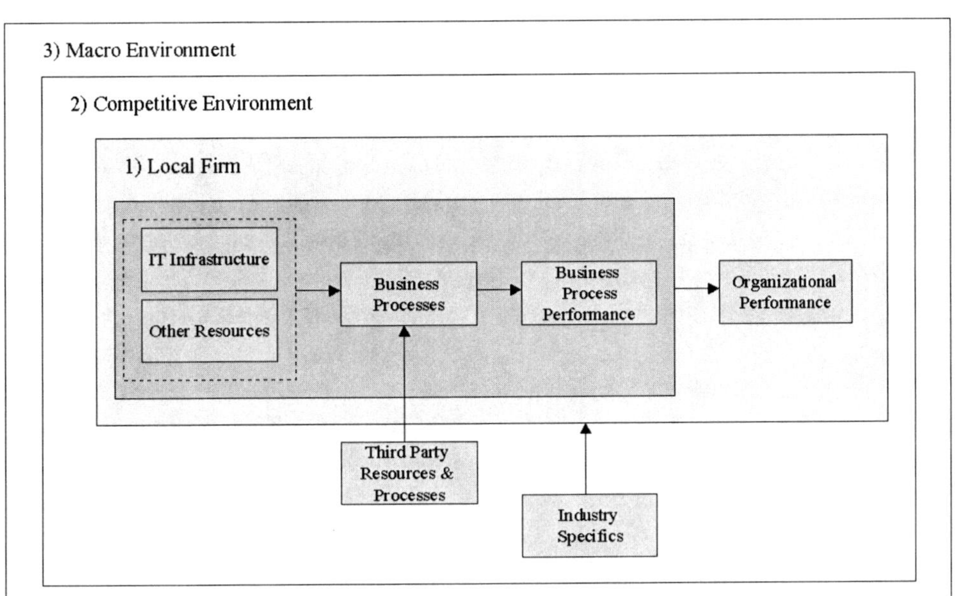

Boynton et al. (1994) introduce a conceptual model with key factors that affect the value of IT. It has the following constructs and variables:

- IT management climate (variables: planning; vision; control structures)
- Managerial IT knowledge (variables: information exchange, discuss problems and opportunities openly; common degree of understanding)
- IT management process effectiveness (variables: project management; service control; service planning; IT functional management; application development and maintenance)
- Level of IT use (variables: cost reduction; management support; strategic planning; competitive thrust)

The absence of a generally accepted theoretical framework on the relationship between IT investments and organizational performance, has led to a fractured research stream with many simultaneous but non-overlapping discussions. Based on a comprehensive review of IT value articles, Chan (2000, p.241) also argues that a more balanced perspective of IT value is required. A potential candidate is discussed further on.

The concepts and models described in this section will be used in the next chapter as a starting point to design an initial conceptual model, which will be used to ascertain the impact of IT standards on business process performance.

BUSINESS PROCESS PERFORMANCE

As discussed in the previous section, to directly assess the impact of IT on the performance of a firm seems to be an unreasonable abstraction. The problem with measuring business performance, particularly financial measures as a result of IT investments, is that outcomes are in most cases diluted and only visible as second or third order effects (Weill & Broadbent, 1998). IS literature suggests that the effects of IT are best recognized at the process level within a firm (Ray et al., 2005). Figure 4 shows the same 4 levels as in Figure 2 but now related to the respective IT standards.

Business process performance should reflect the objectives set by management (March and Simon, 1958; Bouma, 1968). It can be expressed in terms of efficiency and effectiveness. Efficiency is a relative concept, because values can be compared to others, whereas effectiveness has an absolute value related to achieving the objectives or not. Since business value from IT is derived through its impacts on intermediate business processes we, therefore, focus on those. Davenport and Beers (1995) argue that process performance can be a leading indicator of future financial performance. They show there are many possible measures of process performance, for example time, costs, quality and customer satisfaction (p.62).

Van Heck (1993, p.35), focusing on quality attributes of EDI systems related to users, groups efficiency (rapidity, user-friendliness, carefulness, workability) and 'effectivity' (availability, usefulness, support decision making /end-user) together with reliability (correctness, completeness, permissibility, timeliness) and continuity (organizational certainty, elasticity, repairablesness, degradation/turning possibilities), into dynamic quality attributes. Next to this, static quality attributes are listed (flexibility, maintainability, testability, portability, connectivity, re-usability, suitability).

Figure 4. Influence of IT standards on business performance

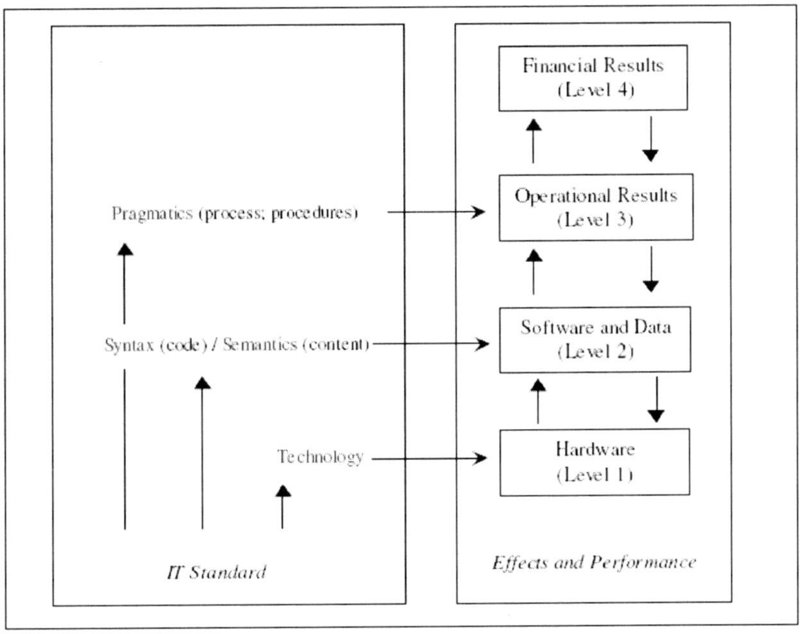

Toppen (1999, p.111) identified several key elements of process performance, divided into transaction oriented and process oriented performance criteria. The elements from the latter category are of interest in the research context and include: throughput time, reliability, quality, efficiency, costs (production and coordination costs), risks, controllability, flexibility, logistic performance.

Keung (2000) approaches business process performance from a stakeholder driven stance. He identified, based on the EFQM[2] management model, financial (i.e. investor), employee, customer and societal aspects. He adds the innovation aspect to satisfy the four stakeholder groups in the long term to accommodate business processes' continuous improvement. He reasons that performance indicators should be process-specific and are to be derived from both the strategic enterprise-wide goals and specific process goals.

Hatten and Rosenthal (2001, p.65) list other potentially important elements of business process performance such as legal constraints, community interests and even public opinion. In the financial services industry regulatory compliance and confidentiality, integrity and availability of data are yet other important elements. As an example at the process level (operational results), they list process capabilities objectives of a PC manufacturer/assembler (Table 1).

Following a literature review on the process orientation to measure IT business value, Davamanirajan et al. (2006) argue that identifying the impact on IT at the processes level is a first step towards better understanding of firms' performance and management practice. They split process performance into terms of productivity and quality, like the number of transactions per labor hour and the percentage of error-free processed transactions respectively.

Summarizing, one can conclude there is no consensus in IS literature on how to categorize process performance at a high abstraction level and that specific performance aspects are dependent on the specifics of a business process and the objectives set by management. However, process performance can

Table 1. Business process performance of a PC manufacturer (Hatten and Rosenthal, 2001, p.66)

Process	Process Capability Objective
New Product Development	Time to market, product failures, warranty costs, product/process advances, ramp-up costs
Order Acquisition	Number of calls required, consultative contacts, cross-selling rate
Order Fulfillment	Capacity, response rate, set-up time, lead time, rework costs, cost improvement, incomplete shipments, on-time delivery, warranty costs
Post-Sales Service	Number of calls required, complaint/complement ration, conversions of problems into opportunities.

be expressed in terms of efficiency (e.g. costs, time) and effectiveness (e.g. controllability, customer satisfaction, flexibility, quality, reliability, risks). As insight into the results of the usage of IT standards on business process performance is an important part of this research, some of these elements that play an important role in the financial services industry, will be discussed later on in this Chapter

Balanced Scorecard

One way to measure organizational performance is using the Balanced Scorecard (BSC) approach developed by Kaplan and Norton (1992). The organization's operations are assessed from multiple vantage points - financial, client satisfaction, internal business and learning & growth. The BSC is used to provide feedback at all levels - strategic, tactical or operational - on how well strategies and plans are being met. This performance information can be used to improve decision making within the organization, to enable proactive problem correction and to promote continuous improvement.

The Balanced Scorecard was originally presented by Kaplan and Norton (1992) as a measurement system to 'drive performance' for business. They argue that traditional financial accounting measures to evaluate firms, such as return on investment, are too restrictive and should be complemented with measurements of intangible business activities. The Balanced Scorecard includes the firm's current operating performance and in addition its future performance drivers by measuring and tracking business performance from four vantage points: financial, customer, internal business process, and learning & growth. Later on they expanded this concept into a strategic management tool for an organization as a whole (Kaplan and Norton, 1996) and permitted decomposition of the high-level (corporate) scorecard into business unit and functional scorecards (Kaplan and Norton, 2000). Recently they added elements for determining organizational alignment of human, information and organization capital with its strategy (Kaplan and Norton, 2004). To date, the BSC is well established in many firms (Abrana & Buglione, 2003, p. 341; Hu and Huang, 2005, p. 3). In any case, key to come to any BSC is to connect with the business goals and strategy of the organization as a whole (Martinsons et al., 1999, p. 72; Chand et al., 2005, p. 560).

The BSC should assist companies to ensure their strategies are recognized and communicated all through the organization and stresses the importance of non-financial measurements. The traditional dominant financial perspective is amended with the non-financial ones as listed in Table 2. In other words, it balances between short- and long-term objectives, between desired outcomes (lagging indicators) and performance drivers of these outcomes (leading indicators), and between qualitative/subjective and quantitative/objective measures (Papalexandris et al., 2005, p. 214). Its related performance measures must be linked back to the financial performance measures through cause-and-effect relationships. These form the crux to the successful implementation of this strategic management tool. It is important to note that the BSC was never intended to be a structured set of key metrics but "a management system to put strategy into action"

Kaplan and Norton (1996) stress the importance to build in cause-and-effect relationships and to include sufficient performance drivers in order to meet the targets set. They identified four hurdles in effective BSC implementation that have to be taken:

i. Vision and strategies are not actionable;
ii. Strategies that are not linked to department, team or individual goals;
iii. Strategies that are not linked to long- and short-term resource allocation;
iv. Feedback that is tactical, in stead of strategic.

As Hitt and Brynjolfsson (1996) discuss, it is essential to understand that assessing the contribution of IT to business performance is not a single question, but is composed of several related but quite distinct issues. They have split the question whether investments in IT 1) have improved business profitability, 2) have created value for customers and 3) have increased productivity. These questions can be linked to the Balanced Scorecard approach, see Table 2.

Hardjono and Bakker (2002, p.176) examine the BSC in relation to other models to control the strategy of an organization. They argue that since the BSC originates from measuring performance of an organization, it lacks certain elements that are characteristic to other management models. These are in particular: 1) the BSC has no feedback–loop and, as a consequence, cause and effects are only implicitly related; 2) results of performance measurements are not directly linked to management or organizational domains.

Nevertheless they discuss the benefits of using the BSC in conjunction with other management models, like the EFQM management model (European Foundation for Quality Management), as such combinations complement each other beneficially (see Figure 5).

For the BSC there are a number of strengths and weaknesses when using it for IT purposes (Milis and Mercken, 2004, p. 96). Among its strengths are:

1. The Balanced Scorecard forces management to take a broad view on IT investments.
2. Many different evaluation techniques can be integrated into the framework, ROI, NPV or any other (adjusted) capital investment appraisal techniques.
3. The framework can be used for feasibility evaluation and also for follow up and ex-post evaluation.

Table 2. Perspectives and some generic indicators in the Balanced Score Card (Kaplan & Norton, 1996, p.44)

Perspective	Possible Indicator
Financial	Return on investment, economic value-added
Customer	Customer satisfaction, retention, market, and account share
Internal	Quality, response time, cost, and new product introductions
Learning & Growth	Employee satisfaction and information system availability

Figure 5. Example of the BSC blended with another management model (Adapted from Hardjono and Bakker, 2002, p.177)

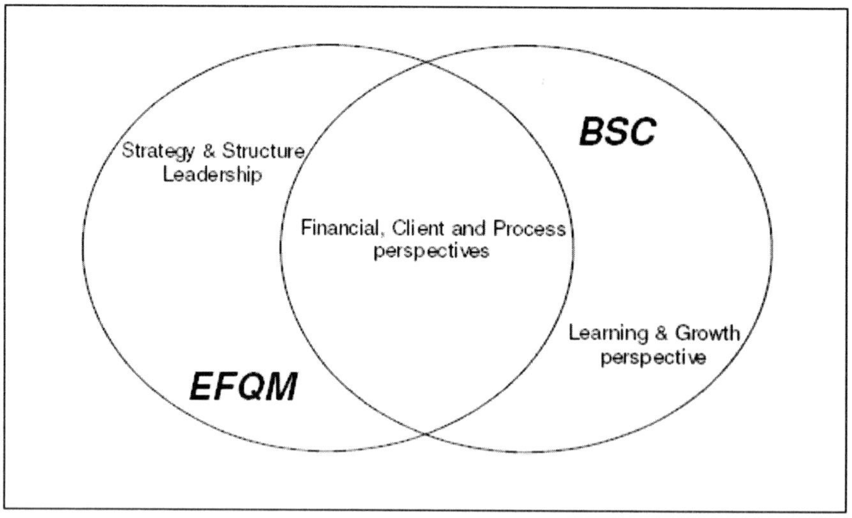

And among its weaknesses are:

1. As there are probably no generic IT measures, metrics must be tailored to fit a specific organization's goals, activities and customer base.
2. The customer perspective and the financial perspective might become too narrow when focusing on internal users and senior management only. This may jeopardize the strategic cohesion.

A major critic of the BSC is Nørreklit, who argues that "*the crux of the balanced scorecard is the linking together of the measures of the four areas in a causal chain which passes through all four perspectives*", Nørreklit (2000, p67). According to the author the core of the problem is that the business relations and causalities between the perspectives are problematic. He argues that there is no cause-and-effect chain but mere a logical relationship, which may lead to suboptimal or even faulty solutions. Furthermore, the BSC supposedly does not ensure any organizational rooting, which makes it less effective as strategic management tool. However, because of the practical applicability and relative fairness compared to other techniques it is still considered as an appropriate measurement tool in this research. In Chapter 4 we will explain in detail why the Balanced Scorecard was chosen as a measurement tool but first we will look into some traditional and more advanced performance measurement and evaluation methods.

IT Investment Appraisals

The concept of business performance can be assessed from various perspectives and a mixture of vantage points. As discussed in Sedera et al. (2001) many traditional measurement and evaluation methods (like Return on Investment, Net Present Value, Economical Value Added and Return on Capital Employed) only include tangible financial benefits and have failed to provide appropriate measurements of performance.

Hitt and Brynjolfsson (1996, p.139) argued that in general little correlation was found between IT investments and business profitability: "... *on average, firms are making the IT investments necessary to maintain comparative parity but are not able to gain competitive advantage*". This in contrast to client satisfaction and productivity that were indeed positively influenced by IT investments. However, later studies on the relationship between IT investment and productivity revealed positive linkages and have attributed this to improvements in business processes and metrics to assess intangibles of IT (Brynjolfsson and Hitt, 1998).

Milis and Mercken (2004) provide an overview of four IT investment appraisal techniques: 1) capital investment appraisal techniques, 2) its adjusted versions, 3) new evaluation techniques and 4) mixed methods for IT investment appraisals. Each technique has its own strengths and weaknesses and there is no overall best and generally accepted method available.

In the first category, among the most popular are: payback period (PP), return on investment (ROI), internal rate of return (IRR) and net present value (NPV). However it is because of too many conceptual and functional uncertainties, that it is not possible to use these techniques in an effective way. Some authors even argue that these methods are less appropriate to evaluate IT investments (Martinsons et al., 1999; Tiernan & Peppard, 2004) as it is difficult to assess costs and benefits and to incorporate risk levels objectively. Of the second category, adjusted traditional evaluation methods, such as adjusted capital investment-appraisal techniques and the discount rate sensitivity, could provide an alternative although these techniques are seldom used in practice.

New evaluation techniques, the third category, include Strategic Fit, Information Economics and the options model although none of these non-traditional techniques is generally accepted as yet. The first technique is based on the rationale that IT investments should be evaluated primarily in function of their contribution to a firm's competitive advantage. The second is a scoring technique that results in a weighted total score based on scores for capital investment and qualitative criteria (Parker, 1996). Among these qualitative criteria, De Haes & Van Grembergen (2005) list the following:

- Alignment with strategy;
- Competitive advantage/need;
- Legal or organizational necessity;
- Reduction of operational risk;
- Management support;
- Support of information architecture;
- Functional or technical uncertainty.

The core problem with this technique is that Information Economics relies entirely on consensus of subjective opinions. The options model is based on the financial products although the assumptions of microeconomic theory must be carefully assessed within each specific research context (Melville et al., 2004, p.288).

Finally, among the mixed methods there are the Multi-layer evaluation process and the Balanced Scorecard (BSC). The first method uses a combination of different techniques to overcome the weaknesses of one and benefit from the strength of the other. As discussed earlier, the BSC uses a combination of traditional financial evaluation techniques (the financial perspective) and metrics aligned with the company business aims and strategy (customer, internal and learning & growth perspectives). Milis and Mercken advocate the multi-layer evaluation process or an evaluation process derived from the BSC, for the appraisal of major IT investments.

As the BSC framework does not include techniques for consolidated individual perspectives, this has to be done subjectively, without the benefit of a formal quantitative representation. Therefore Abrana & Buglione (2003) propose a multidimensional performance measurement model (QEST)[3] to be used with an IT BSC that facilitates the above, although practical applicability has not yet been proven. Next to the BSC, Abrana & Buglione (2003) discuss mixed methods, such as the Intangible Asset Monitor the Skandia Navigator, the Performance Pyramid, the Performance Prism, the EFQM Excellence Model and the General Framework for Performance Measurement. Again, these methods have not been proven in practice either.

SOME ELEMENTS OF PROCESS PERFORMANCE

In this section some important elements of business process performance will be described, based on the list of Toppen (1999). These include *risk* related to legal and regulatory compliance, *reliability* and *controllability* related to data protection and *flexibility* related to IT. Compliance will be assessed from the legal and regulatory perspective and data protection as part of best practices in information security. Flexibility will be described in general terms and then specifically relating to IT and IT standards. Conclusions will be drawn in how to use this concept in the research.

Legal and Regulatory Compliance

In the financial services industry, legal and regulatory compliance is a very important subject. Examples are legal requirements from United States federal laws (such as Sarbanes-Oxley Act, Gramm-Leach-Bliley Act, Health Insurance Portability and Accountability Act) or regulatory requirements of the Basel Committee on Banking Supervision (Basel II). In Table 3 an overview is listed of these laws and regulations.

- As the business processes of most organizations are supported by IT, it is obvious that IT plays a vital role in internal control and mitigating the related risks. That is why a number of important IT topics should be addressed in which legal and regulatory compliance must be satisfied. To a certain extent there is overlap in the specific requirements of these laws and regulations, as indicated below. SOX requires that, as part of sections 302, 404 and 409, a number of information security controls should be implemented. This includes information security risk assessments, security incident management, intrusion prevention, vulnerability management and software application controls.
- GLBA requires that financial services companies have an information security plan in place guaranteeing that clients' nonpublic personal information is adequately protected. This plan includes carrying out regular information security risk assessments and having vulnerability management in place.

Table 3. Some international laws and regulations

Subject	Objective	Scope	Reference
Sarbanes-Oxley Act (SOX)	To help protect investors and restore investor confidence.	1. Regulate, inspect and discipline accounting firms in their roles as auditors of public companies; 2. Corporate governance and enhanced financial disclosure.	http://www.gao.gov
Gramm-Leach-Bliley Act (GLBA)	To strengthen competition among commercial and investment banks that allowed them to consolidate.	Design, implement and maintain safeguards to protect customers' personal financial information and perform risk analysis on business processes.	http://www.ftc.gov/privacy/gl-bact
Health Insurance Portability and Accountability Act (HIPAA)	To protect health insurance coverage for workers and their families when they change or lose their jobs.	Regulations for use and disclosure of Protected Health Information (health status, provision of health care, or payment for health care) linked to an individual; includes any part of a patient's medical record or payment history.	http://www.cms.hhs.gov/hipaa/
Basel II	To measure the adequacy of a bank's capital to promote consistency in risk management.	1. Ensure minimum capital requirements; 2. Separate operational risk from credit risk, and quantify both; 3. Align economic and regulatory capital more closely to reduce the scope for regulatory arbitrage.	http://www.bis.org/publ/bcbsca.htm

- HIPAA requires that, as part of sections 164.306, 164.308 and 164.312, security safeguards are satisfied at the organizational, process and technical level. Examples include designation of a privacy officer, role based access control, and encryption and corroboration.
- Basel II requires that financial services companies have established information security controls, rule base access control, have protected proprietary and confidential information and have vulnerability management and incident management processes in place.

Data Protection

The level of reliability and controllability of data are integrally linked to managing the risk related to legal and regulatory requirements. In a broader sense this is about ensuring the confidentiality, integrity and availability of data. To this end several international and industry best practice standards are available such as ISO/IEC 17799 and COBIT. Table 4 shows the 11 sections (that start at no.5) of the ISO/IEC 17799 standard and its control objectives with regard to the process of information security management.

The standard is written as a set of guidances that can be tailored to the specific risks and needs of an organization. By implementing a set of controls, consisting of policies, practices, procedures, organizational structures and software functions, the preservation of information related to confidentiality, integrity and availability is to be achieved. It is important to understand that performance criteria are not included in this ISO standard and it is up to the organization to set them for their specific needs (ISO/

Table 4. ISO/IEC 17799:2005 standard and its control sections

ISO/IEC 17799:2005 section	Control objectives regarding
5. **Security Policy**	• Information Security Policy
6. **Organizing Information Security**	• Internal organization • External parties
7. **Asset Management**	• Accountability for assets • Information classification
8. **Human Resource Security**	• Prior to employment • During employment • Termination or change of employment
9. **Physical and Environmental Security**	• Secure areas • Equipment security
10. **Communications and Operations Management**	• Operational procedures and responsibilities • Third party service delivery management • System planning and acceptance • Protection against malicious and mobile code • Backup • Network security management • Media handling • Exchange of information • Electronic commerce service • Monitoring
11. **Access Control**	• Business requirement for access control • User access management • User responsibilities • Network access control • Operating system access control • Applications and information access control • Mobile computing and networking
12. **Information Systems Acquisition, Development and Maintenance**	• Security requirements in information system • Correct processing in applications • Cryptographic controls • Security of system files • Security in development and support services • Technical vulnerability management
13. **Information Security Incident Management**	• Reporting information security events and weaknesses • Management of information security incidents and improvements
14. **Business Continuity Management**	• Information security aspects of business continuity management
15. **Compliance**	• Compliance with legal requirements • Compliance with security policy and standards • Information systems audit considerations

IEC 17799, 2005, p. XI). However, when the business process performance in these 11 sections is met, legal and regulatory requirements in IT are satisfied to a very large extent.

Flexibility

An important question has to be answered: "Be flexible for what?" Given the scope of this research and the research questions, the answer is: "Flexibility of IT for changes in the business environment". And to be more specific the question should be answered: "In what way do IT standards inhibit or facilitate such flexibility?" To address this issue, general aspects of flexibility will be discussed and then flexibility related to IT is addressed.

General Aspects of Flexibility

As indicated in the introduction of this book, flexibility is both a polymorphous and a multidimensional concept. Flexibility requirements for mechanical manufacturing (e.g. Koste and Malhotra, 1999) are totally different from the ones for business processes (e.g. Boynton and Victor, 1991) which exemplifies its polymorphous nature. An example of its multidimensional nature is expressed in the attributes of organizational flexibility: time and intention (Evans, 1991). There is no common operational definition for flexibility (Duncan, 1995) which is caused by the polymorphous nature of it. Different disciplines address different aspects of flexibility. Among these disciplines are contributions of (Evans, 1991):

- Economy
- Strategic management
- Military strategy
- Decision theory
- System analysis

In order to substantiate the complex nature of the flexibility concept, Evans (1991) states three capabilities and enumerates a dozen related terms: 1) adaptability; 2) agility; 3) corrigibility; 4) elasticity; 5) hedging; 6) liquidity; 7) malleability; 8) plasticity; 9) pliability; 10) resilience; 11) robustness; 12) versatility.

These capabilities are:

- Yielding to pressure (4, 8, 10, 11) - strength
- Capacity for new situations (1, 2, 12) - scaleable Susceptibility of modification (3, 5, 6, 7, 9) - extensible

which effectively corroborates the polymorphous nature of flexibility.

Some authors even argue that standardization is a precursor for flexibility and flexibility presupposes modularization (Hanseth et al., 1996). Crucial issues are at what level flexibility is desirable and at what level or which part standardization of IT infrastructure, data, processes or products could contribute. Egyedi (2002) characterizes so-called flexible standards: these should be simple, small, and 'lightly modularized'. However, the question which features these standards should have remains unanswered.

There are several ways to look at and classify flexibility. Larso (1998) classified flexibility into three main groups whereby all possible types of flexibility fall into one of these groups (Table 5). Strategies on aspects such as costs, quality, product variety and the responsiveness of the processes depend on the viewpoint and context. These aspects relate to a certain flexibility type and the importance of those aspects is stressed over others.

Larso does not list infrastructure flexibility but this could be part of all three flexibility categories. From an organizational point of view, Volberda (1992) identified similar kinds of flexibility related to processes and organizations and even adds a fourth one. These are listed in Table 6.

Table 5. Three categories of flexibility (Larso, 1998)

Flexibility category	Description	Flexibility type
Strategic flexibility	The ability to shift from one strategy to another; from one competitive priority to another	Economic, Organizational, Manufacturing, R&D, Marketing
Tactical flexibility	The ability to cope with changes in customers' demands	Volume, Product mix, Modification/New product, Delivery time
Operational flexibility	The ability to change processes (at plant level)	Capacity, Change over, Expansion, Machine, Operation, Process, Product, Production, Resource, Routing

Table 6. Four kinds of organizational flexibility (Volberda, 1992)

Type	Relates to
Operational flexibility	the input and output of organizational processes
Structural flexibility	the ability to modify processes to changes in the environment
Strategic flexibility	the ability to change organization goals and activities to changes in the environment
Meta flexibility	the degree in which an organization senses the environment and ascertains its consequences

Evans (1991) proposes a framework consisting of "time" and "intention" dimensions (Table 7)).

He argues that the need for flexibility of technology firms is needed in order to compete effectively. Therefore companies need to continuously tune their strategies and refocus their resources. Flexibility can even be seen as a strategic resource and potential source of sustainable competitive advantage (Duncan, 1995).

Alternatively to Evans' scheme, Avison et al. (1995) propose that flexibility is typically described in terms of the dimensions "time" (speed and response) and "range". In addition, Golden and Powell (2000) introduce a model consisting of four dimensions by adding the "focus" dimension to the three others that were already identified, as listed in Table 8. However, one can argue that the range and focus dimension introduced by the other authors are part of Evans' original scheme (time and intention respectively).

The lack of standardization in electronic interconnectivity and its negative influences on several strategic initiatives to improve services and reduce costs has been known for a long time now (Besen and Saloner, 1994). In order to be globally competitive, industries should adopt standardized IT technologies, enabling mutual linkages between existing heterogeneous systems.

But business processes also need to be more flexible in order to meet the customer's product and service requirements. It should be possible to quickly modify these processes or even replace them entirely in order to anticipate the fact that a product or service life cycle becomes shorter and shorter

Table 7. Flexibility framework, (Evans, 1991)

Intention	**Offense**	*Pre-emptive*	*Exploitive*
	Defense	*Protective*	*Corrective*
		Ex Ante	**Ex Post**
		Time	

Table 8. Organizational flexibility (Goldon and Powell, 2000)

Dimension of flexibility	Scope	Measure of flexibility	Example
Time	Operational (ex ante)	Efficiency	Investments
	Strategic (ex post)	Responsiveness	IT architecture
Range	Foreseen circumstances	Versatility	Planning
	Unforeseen circumstances	Robustness	Strategy change
Intention	Defensive	Reactiveness	Change control
	Offensive	Proactiveness	
Focus	Internal	Reliability	Manufacturing, HRM, organizational structures
	External		Outsourcing, supply chains

(Boynton and Victor, 1991). Finally, Boynton (1993) argues that flexibility is necessary because of the changing nature of the competition:

- Changes in competitive requirements: product demands on choice and customization are changing faster than ever and product life cycles are getting shorter and shorter.
- Changes in process technologies and know-how (human manufacturing, distribution, marketing, finances): build a stable base of process capabilities that are at the same time flexible, efficient and long lasting.

For organizations to become more responsive to changes in the market place, Boynton argues that IT systems of "knowing" should deliver information fast and efficiently.

Flexibility Related to IT

It has been recognized that IT infrastructure can influence a firm's ability to use IT strategically (Allen and Boynton 1991; Weill 1993, Davenport and Linder 1994, Duncan 1995, Ross et al. 1996, Armstrong and Sambamurthy 1999; Broadbent et al. 1999; Sambamurthy et al. 2003). The flexibility of an IT infrastructure is dependent on the extent to which a firm adopts standards for the components of its IT infrastructure, which includes standards for hardware, system software, data and applications (Broadbent and Weill 1997).

Golden and Powell (2000) argue that IT contributes both to technological and organizational flexibility and research should address both these areas. Duncan (1995) defines flexibility, related to IT infrastructures, as the degree to which resources are sharable and reusable. Given the scope of this research the flexibility definition given by Egyedi (2001, p.41) on changes (e.g. exchange and improvement) to IT infrastructure is the most appropriate and will be adopted:

System flexibility refers to a situation where a change can be introduced to a component or subsystem without losing the functionality of or investments in the adjacent component or subsystem.

Duncan (1995) enumerates three common factors that play a significant role in enabling flexibility of IT infrastructures:

- The alignment of IS plans to business objectives.
- The quality of information technology and architecture plans.
- The skills of the personnel involved.

These are critical conditions for an organization to be able to respond rapidly and effectively to emerging needs or opportunities. She argues that IT standards may be designed solely as cost controls, but they could be used to increase flexibility by ensuring characteristics such as compatibility and connectivity. By using compatibility tools such as middleware, firms can find the optimal modus between the restrictiveness of a single technology and the integration problems when using a variety of ones. In other words, the IT infrastructure should be designed in such a way that it is able to evolve with emerging technologies.

Duncan (1995) gives two reasons why infrastructure flexibility is so important for firms. First it affects the feasibility and costs of technology-based business innovations by reducing the time to market for new products. When new products can make use of an existing infrastructure, cost can be significantly lower than redesigning it from scratch. Secondly it affects a firm's ability to refine or reengineer business systems. As business processes evolve, the supporting infrastructure should be able to do so correspondingly. The ideal infrastructure is one that is designed to evolve itself by allowing support of continuously changing business processes. It is suggested to standardize at the interface level (e.g. network protocols or middleware). A framework for infrastructure evaluation regarding flexibility is introduced (Table 9).

In more general terms, and in relation to interface standardization this leads to: "building flexibility into the interface level of processes and technology by standardizing these interfaces".

In this context a very interesting concept is that of modularity. It is a promising example of a design concept that makes flexibility of IT possible. Products and processes are designed in such a way that they consist of independent modules that can be assembled relatively easily and inexpensively into different product or process forms, depending on customer requirements (Pine 1993, Baldwin and Clark 1997). Already in the late eighties Matutes and Regibeau (1988) pointed out that when firms make their products compatible, customers can mix and match components from different sources into tailored systems. The concept of modularity will be discussed in the next subsection.

Table 9. Infrastructure flexibility (adapted from Duncan, 1995)

Dimension of flexibility	Scope	Measure of flexibility	Example
Compatibility	Component characteristics	Portability, interfacing	Platform
Connectivity	IT practices	Number of protocols	Network
Modularity	IT capabilities	Sharable data and business processes	Data, application

Modularity

Modularity refers to the principle where products or processes are produced separately and used interchangeably in different configurations without compromising its integrity. This principle is not new as both Hesser and Inklaar (1997, p.28) and Spivak and Brenner (2001, p.10) point out, it was Eli Whitney who became the father of mass production for war purposes by introducing the principle of interchangeable parts of armament production in 1799.

The power of modular design lies in the possibility to allow flexible responses to change. As one might expect, like standards, modularity can be found in processes or products alike. In literature several examples can be found which typify processes and products as modular, ranging from aircraft to watches (Wolters, 2002). Fine (1998) even identifies a third category, supply chains, although in general no explicit distinguishing is made between intraorganizational and interorganizational processes. Wolters showed that concurrent design in all three dimensions leads to better results and performance in particular circumstances than a more asynchronous approach would do.

Wolters (p.108) defines modularity as:

A system is modular when it consists of distinct (autonomic) components, which are loosely coupled with each other, with a clear relationship between each component and its functions(s) are well-defined, standardized interface connecting the components, which require low levels of coordination.

Modularity in combination with IT was introduced by Pine (1993) and he states: '*The best method for achieving full mass-customization - for minimizing costs while maximizing individual customization - is by creating modular components that can be configured into a wide variety of end products and services, offering both economies of scale and economies of scope.*'

However, Baldwin and Clark (1997) claim that modular systems are much more difficult to design than comparable interconnected or integral systems. Furthermore, the modular systems designers must know a great deal about the inner workings of the overall product or process.

Baldwin and Clark (1999) show that the IT industry has changed dramatically because of the adoption of modularity (like the IBM-PC[4]). Modular designed computer systems consist of components that have standardized interfaces enabling interconnection and interoperability. Each module conforms to these interface rules and they are interchangeable. This in contrast with fully integrated systems. Egyedi (2001) also argues that standardized interfaces seem to enhance the flexibility between adjacent technical artifacts.

Product Modularity

Baldwin and Clark (1997) and Fine (1998) give the most essential features of product modularity:

- Modules are independent of each other
- Modules have a single functionality
- Modules are interchangeable

Module interfaces are standardized. This allows both producers and customers to mix-and-match modules, resulting in many variations of the end-product. Baldwin and Clark (1997), therefore, identify

Table 10. Product modularity types

Type	Description
Modular in production	Part of the product is standardized and produced independently before assembly into the end-product. These parts (e.g. tires) may be standardized.
Modular in design	Within an overall architecture, the modules are designed independently and interfaces are standardized. Than the modules are 'mixed-and-matched' to create the end-product.
Modular in use	Customers themselves mix-and-match components to create the end-product.

three types of product modularity: *modular-in-production, modular-in-design* and *modular-in-use* as listed in Table 10. The modularity decreases when one or more of these features is not met.

A specific implementation of modularity is the bus structure (Pine, 1993). It consists of a standardized structure to which several kinds of components can be attached. The standardized structure allows variation in type, number and location of the modules that can plug onto it. Another and more widely used implementation is the section structure that allows combination of components in arbitrary ways, as long as they are in conformance with a standardized interface (e.g. Lego® building blocks).

Process Modularity

A process can be modular as well. It can be set-up in such a way that there are only loose couplings between the process components that are in fact standardized interfaces between these processes. These interfaces could be contracts, transaction protocols, operating procedures, and input/output agreements (Wolters, p.115). Some authors (Sanchez, 1997) even argue that there are no principal differences between process modularity and product modularity.

That standardization and modularity are related but different concepts, is depicted in Figure 6.

A module is a sub-assembly that reduces complexity and implementation time, but does not necessarily have to comply with a standard. However, the interfaces between the modules are standardized by definition. Each module can be divided into sub-modules that can be standardized as well. So, modular design can be combined with (right-hand side of Figure 6) or without standardization (left-hand side) of (sub)processes or (sub)products.

Figure 6. Relationship between standardization and modularization. Key element in modularization are the standardized interfaces

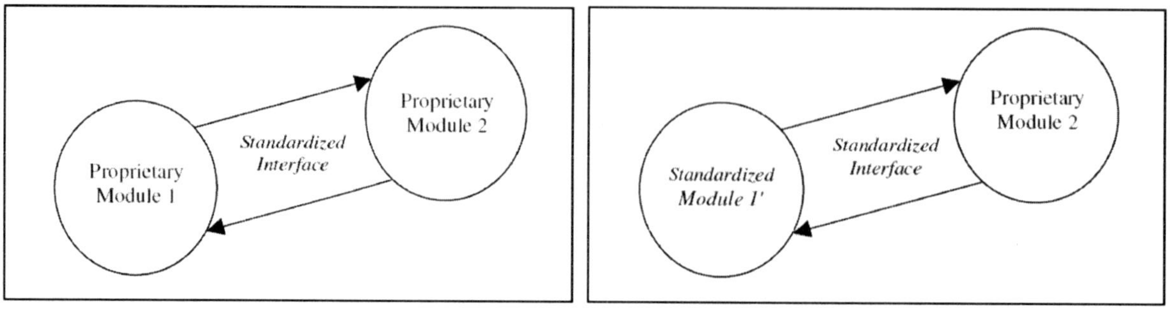

Example: Flexible Standards

This section describes some potentially flexible standards. However, when flexibility within a standard is not chosen at the right (interface) level, the implementation of it may result in a multitude of incompatible instances of that standard.

XML

Basic XML is a nice example of a flexible standard. W3C developed XML (see Chapter 2, Table 6) and is a meta-language providing the rules for defining tagged markup languages that can be used in B2B eCommerce applications. Its key attributes are listed in Table 11.

XML has the potential for enhanced document processing and validation. Unfortunately with respect to the XML semantics there is still a problem. In case of XML no single standard emerged but there are currently 3 competing ones in the market space, as listed in Table 12. These are not compatible because each is dependent on its own schema definitions. A schema is a formal specification of the grammar for one particular language. This inhibits efficient interoperation between these three instances of XML standards.

Other Standards

Another example of a flexible standard in digital multimedia is the Motion Pictures Experts Group, MPEG2. In this standard several areas (like stream filtering requirements, conditional access and the transport layer) have been left unspecified on purpose. The standardization process took place notably easier and resulted in implementation flexibility for the standard.

Table 11. Key Attributes of XML (Robertson, 2001)

Attribute	Significance
Open architecture	Enables platform and vendor-independence.
Extensibility	Permits user-defined business rules and syntax.
Multi-application functionality	Makes sharing possible among systems within the enterprise and between enterprises.
Data manipulation	Creates a content-based, usable data stream.
Validation	Verifies the structural validity of exchanged data.
Efficiency	Reduces redundancies and manual error.

Table 12. Three instances of the XML standard for B2B eCommerce

XML-oriented standard	Main sponsor
CXML	Ariba
CBL	Commerce One
Biztalk	Microsoft

However, some caution should be taken here as well. It is of the utmost importance to allow flexibility at a suitable interface level. The Financial Information Exchange (FIX) standard is seen as a flexible standard because it allows tailoring by a company to it's own needs. But just because of that it has resulted in an overabundance of versions and this fragmentation adversely affects its effectiveness.

Another unsuccessful example is the OSI model. In spite of the fact that it is an excellent example of hierarchical modularization, each OSI protocol is stuffed with so many features that implementation is quite difficult, let alone changing it (Hanseth et al., 1996). The difference between the Internet Protocol stack (IETF) and the OSI stack (ISO) is a nice example of a simple standard versus a very complex one. TCP/IP contains just a few modules and options for a network infrastructure and was able to grow in complexity when required. The OSI stack on the other hand includes protocols and options to these protocols, to satisfy every possible need.

From a perspective of modularity, there is no need for systems to use common standards internally because it is the interface level that counts. Mechanisms for adding new features should be defined, without changing the existing ones. This does not mean one has to define interfaces with countless options, but its structure should facilitate evolution as the environment changes. If flexibility is allowed within a standard the outcome is expected to be better. In other words: *standardize for flexibility*! This mindset has also been recognized by Gaynor and Bradner (2001, p.44).

CONCLUSIONS

Similar to standards, there is no common definition for flexibility. In the research context, flexibility is defined as the degree to which IT resources are *sharable and reusable*. But organizational flexibility will also have attention. Furthermore, several authors suggest that during the process to come to IT standards, flexibility should be taken into account. Therefore, the speed at which environments change, suggests to create (technology, data and process) standards that allow incorporation of benefits of future services by means of configurable interfaces defined as part of the standard.

Literature from various disciplines shows the complexity of and the disagreement as regards measurement and description of business performance. Business performance can be assessed from several perspectives and the importance and benefits of adopting a process-oriented perspective has long been recognized.

MANAGERIAL IMPLICATIONS

IT impacts processes, thereby affecting business performance. To directly assess the impact of IT on the performance of a firm seems to be an unreasonable abstraction. The process view can be used as a proxy, since business process performance should reflect the objectives set by management.

As one of the importance aspects of performance, system flexibility refers to a situation where a change can be introduced to a component or subsystem without losing the functionality of, or investments in the adjacent component or subsystem. IT infrastructure should be designed in such a way that it is able to evolve with emerging technologies and market changes. Therefore, it is suggested to standardize at the interface level of processes and technology.

The Balanced Scorecards has been selected as measurement tool, since this method includes financial as well as non-financial elements and has been widely accepted in industry. This allows us to assess the value of company IT standards on processes on a number of effectiveness criteria, that are related to intended business benefits such as organizational flexibility and information risk.

REFERENCES

Abrana, A., & Buglione, L. (2003). A multidimensional performance model for consolidating Balanced Scorecards. *Advances in Engineering Software*, *34*, 339–349. doi:10.1016/S0965-9978(03)00033-4

Allen, B. R., & Boynton, A. C. (1991). Information Architecture: In search of efficient flexibility. *Management Information Systems Quarterly*, *15*(4), 435–442. doi:10.2307/249447

Armstrong, C., & Sambamurthy, V. (1999). Information Technology Assimilation in Firms: The Influence of Senior Leadership and IT Infrastructures. *Information Systems Research*, *10*(4), 304–327. doi:10.1287/isre.10.4.304

Avison, D. E., Powell, P. L., Keen, J., Klein, J. H., & Ward, S. (1995). Addressing the need for flexibility in information systems. *J Mgmt Syst*, *7*(2), 43–60.

Bakos, J. (1987). Dependent variables for the study of firm and industry-level impacts of information technology. In *Proceedings of the Eighth International Conference on Information Systems, Pittsburgh, December 1987* (pp. 10-23).

Baldwin, C. Y., & Clark, K. B. (1997, Sep.-Oct.). Managing in an age of modularity. *Harvard Business Review*, 84–93.

Barua, A., Kriebel, C. H., & Mukhopadhyay, T. (1995). Information Technologies and Business Value: An Analytic and Empirical Investigation. *Information Systems Research*, *6*(1), 3–23. doi:10.1287/isre.6.1.3

Besen, S. M., & Saloner, G. (1994). Compatibility standards and market for telecommunications services. In Allen, T. J., & Scott Morton, M. S. (Eds.), *Information technology and the corporation of the 1990s: research studies*. New York: Oxford University Press.

Bouma, J. L. (1968). *Leerboek der bedrijfseconomie, Deel 1A Inleiding*. Den Haag, Netherlands: Delwel.

Boynton, A. C. (1993). Achieving dynamic stability through information technology. *California Management Review*, *35*(2), 58–77.

Boynton, A. C., & Victor, B. (1991). Beyond flexibility: building and managing the dynamically stable organization. *California Management Review*, *34*(1), 53–66.

Boynton, A. C., Zmud, R. W., & Jacobs, G. C. (1994). The influence of IT management practice on IT use in large organizations. *Management Information Systems Quarterly*, *18*(3), 299–318. doi:10.2307/249620

Broadbent, M., & Weill, P. (1997). Management by Maxim: How Business and IT Managers Can Create IT Infrastructures. *Sloan Management Review*, *38*(3), 77–92.

Broadbent, M., Weill, P., & Clair, D. (1999). The Implications of Information Technology Infrastructure for Business Process Redesign. *Management Information Systems Quarterly*, *32*(2), 159–182. doi:10.2307/249750

Brynjolfsson, E., & Hitt, L. (2000). Beyond Computation: Information Technology, Organizational Transformation and Business Performance. *The Journal of Economic Perspectives*, *14*(4), 23–48.

Brynjolfsson, E., & Hitt, L. M. (1998). Beyond the productivity paradox. *Communications of the ACM*, *41*(8), 49–55. doi:10.1145/280324.280332

Chan, E. (2000). IT value: The great divide between qualitative and quantitative and individual and organizational measures. *Journal of Management Information Systems*, *16*(4), 225–261.

Chand, D., Hachey, G., Hunton, J., Owhoso, V., & Vasudevan, S. (2005). A balanced scorecard based framework for assessing the strategic impacts of ERP systems. *Computers in Industry*, *56*, 558–572. doi:10.1016/j.compind.2005.02.011

Davamanirajan, P., Kauffman, R. J., Kriebel, C. H., & Mukhopadhyay, T. (2006). System design, Process Performance and Economic Outcomes. In *Proceedings of the 39th Hawaii International Conference on System Sciences.*

Davenport, T. H. (1993). *Process Innovation: reengineering work through Information Technology*. Boston: Harvard Business School Press.

Davenport, T. H., & Beers, M. C. (1995). Managing information about processes. *Journal of Management Information Systems*, *12*(1), 57–80.

Davenport, T. H., & Linder, J. (1994). Information Management Infrastructure: The new Competitive Weapon. In *Proceedings of the 27th Hawaii International Conference on System Sciences.*

Davenport, T. H., & Short, J. E. (1990). The New Industrial Engineering: Information Technology and Business Process Redesign. *Sloan Management Review*, 11–27.

Davern, M. J., & Kauffman, R. J. (2000). Discovering potential and realizing value from information technology investment. *Journal of Management Information Systems*, *16*(4), 121–143.

de Haes, S., & van Grembergen, W. (2005). IT Governance Structures, Processes and Relational Mechanisms. In *Proceedings of the 38th Hawaii International Conference on System Sciences.*

Duncan, N. B. (1995). Capturing flexibility of Information Technology Infrastructure: A study of Resource Characteristics and their Measure. *Journal of Management Information Systems*, *12*(2), 37–57.

Egyedi, T. (2001). Infrastructure Flexibility Created by Standardized Gateways: The Cases of XML and the ISO Container. *Knowledge, Technology, &. Policy*, *14*(3), 41–54.

Egyedi, T. (2002). *Standards enhance system, flexibility? Mapping compatibility strategies onto flexible objectives.* Contribution to Responsibility under Uncertainly: Science, Technology and accountability, EASST2002 Conference, Standardization Track, July 31st to August 3rd, University of York., UK

Evans, J. S. (1991). Strategic flexibility for high technology maneuvers: a conceptual framework. *Journal of Management Studies, 28*(1), 69–89. doi:10.1111/j.1467-6486.1991.tb00271.x

Fine, C. H. (1998). *Clockspeed - Winning Industry Control in the Age of Temporary Advantage*. Reading, MA: Perseus Books.

Gaynor, M., & Bradner, S. (2001). Using Real Options to Value Modularity in Standards. *Knowledge, Technology, &. Policy, 14*(2), 41–66.

Golden, W., & Powell, P. (2000). Towards a definition of flexibility: in search of the Holy Grail? *Omega, 28*, 373–384. doi:10.1016/S0305-0483(99)00057-2

Guha, S., Grover, V., Kettinger, W., & Teng, J. (1997). Business process change and organizational performance: exploring an antecedent model. *Journal of Management Information Systems, 14*(1), 119–154.

Hammer, M. (1990). *Reengineering Work: Don't automate - Obliterate. Harvard Business Review*. July/August.

Hammer, M., & Champy, J. (1993). *Reengineering the corporation: a manifesto for business revolution*. New York: McGraw-Hill.

Hanseth, O., Monteiro, E., & Hatling, M. (1996). Developing Information Infrastructure: The tension Between Standardization and Flexibility. *Science, Technology & Human Values, 21*(4), 407–426. doi:10.1177/016224399602100402

Hardjono, T. W., & Bakker, R. J. M. (2002). Management van processen - Identificeren, besturen, beheersen en vernieuwen. Kluwer / INK, Deventer / Zaltbommel, 2de druk (in Dutch).

Hatten, K.J., & Rosenthal, S.R. (2001). Why-and How- to systematize performance measurement. *Journal of Organizational Excellence*, Autumn, 59-73.

Hesser, W., & Inklaar, A. (1997). *An introduction to standards and Standardization. DIN-Normungskunde* (*Vol. 36*). Berlin: Beuth Verlag GmbH.

Hitt, L. M., & Brynjolfsson, E. (1996). Productivity, Business Profitability, and Consumer Surplus: Three Different Measures of Information Technology Value. *Management Information Systems Quarterly, 20*, 2. doi:10.2307/249475

Hu, Q., & Huang, C. D. (2005). Aligning IT with Firm Business Strategies Using the Balance Scorecard System. In *Proceedings of the 38th Hawaii International Conference on System Sciences*.

Kaplan, R. S., & Norton, D. P. (1992). The Balanced Scorecard - Measures that Drive Performance. *Harvard Business Review, 70*(1), 71–79.

Kaplan, R. S., & Norton, D. P. (1996). *The Balanced Scorecard: Translating Strategy into Action*. Boston: Harvard Business School Press.

Kaplan, R. S., & Norton, D. P. (2000). Having trouble with your strategy? Then map it. *Harvard Business Review, 78*, 167–176.

Kaplan, R. S., & Norton, D. P. (2004). Measuring the strategic readiness of intangible assets. *Harvard Business Review, 82*(2), 52–63.

Kauffman, R. J., & Weill, P. (1989). An Evaluative Framework for Research on the Performance Effects of Information Technology Investment. In J. I. DeGross, J. C. Henderson, and B. R. Konsynski (Eds.), *Proceedings of the Tenth International Conference on Information Systems, Boston, Massachusetts* (pp. 377-388).

Kettinger, W. J., Teng, J. T. C., & Guha, S. (1997). Business Process Change: A Study of Methodologies, Techniques and Tools. *Management Information Systems Quarterly*, (March): 55–80. doi:10.2307/249742

Keung, P. (2000). Process performance measurement system: a tool to support process-based organizations. *Total Quality Management, 11*(1), 67–85. doi:10.1080/0954412007035

Khoong, C. M. (1996). Culture-Sensitive, Strategy-Level Reengineering, Information Systems &. *Operations Research, 34*(1), 43–56.

Koste, L. L., & Malhotra, M. K. (1999). A theoretical framework for analyzing the dimensions of manufacturing flexibility. *Journal of Operations Management, 18*(1), 75–93. doi:10.1016/S0272-6963(99)00010-8

Larso, D. (1998). An investigation of the relationships between manufacturing flexibility and continuous improvement: a case study. In Migliore, H. (Ed.), *Flexible automation and intelligent manufacturing* (pp. 227–239). Oregon, USA: Portland State University.

March, J. G., & Simon, H. A. (1958). *Organizations*. New York: John Wiley & Sons Inc.

Martinsons, M., Davison, R., & Tse, D. (1999). The balanced scorecard: a foundation for strategic management of information systems. *Decision Support Systems, 25*(1), 71–88. doi:10.1016/S0167-9236(98)00086-4

Matutes, C., & Regibeau, P. (1988). Mix and Match: Product Compatibility without Network Externalities. *The Rand Journal of Economics, 19*, 221–234. doi:10.2307/2555701

Melville, N., Kraemer, K., & Gurbaxani, V. (2004). Information Technology and Organizational Performance: Integrative Model Of IT Business Value. *Management Information Systems Quarterly, 28*(2), 283–332.

Milis, K., & Mercken, R. (2004). The use of the balanced scorecard for the evaluation of Information and Communication Technology projects. *International Journal of Project Management, 22*, 87–97. doi:10.1016/S0263-7863(03)00060-7

Nørreklit, H. (2000). The balance on the balanced scorecard-a critical analysis of some of its assumptions. *Management Accounting Research, 11*, 65–88. doi:10.1006/mare.1999.0121

Papalexandris, A., Ioannou, G., Prastacos, G., & Soderquist, K. E. (2005). An Integrated Methodology for Putting the Balanced Scorecard into Action. *European Management Journal, 23*(2), 214–227. doi:10.1016/j.emj.2005.02.004

Parker, M. (1996). Strategic transformation and information technology. Upper Saddle River, NJ.

Pine, B. J. (1993). *Mass Customization: the new frontier in business competition.* Boston, MA: Harvard Business School Press.

Ray, G., Muhanna, W. A., & Barney, J. B. (2005). Information Technology and the Performance of the Customer Service Process: A Resource-Based Analysis. *Management Information Systems Quarterly, 29*(4).

Robertson, E. (2001). OFX and IFX: The Standards Challenge, TowerGroup, Needham MA, USA, research paper 028:61N.

Ross, J. W., Beath, C. M., & Goodhue, D. L. (1996). Developing long-term Competitiveness through IT Assets. *Sloan Management Review, 38*(1), 31–42.

Sambamurty, V., Bharadwaj, A., & Grover, V. (2003). Shaping Agility through Digital Options: Reconceptualizing the role of Information Technology in contemporary firms. *Management Information Systems Quarterly, 27*(2), 237–264.

Sanchez, R. (1997). Preparing for an Uncertain Future - Managing Organization for Strategic Flexibility. *International Studies of Management and Organization, 27*(2), 71–94.

Sedera, D., Gable, G., & Rosemann, M. (2001). A Balanced Scorecard Approach to Enterprise Systems Performance Measurement. In *Proceedings of the Twelfth Australasian Conference on Information Systems.*

Speier, C., Harvey, M., & Palmer, J. (1998). Implementing Intra-organizational Learning: An Infrastructure to Support Business Process Reengineering. *Knowledge and Process Management, 5*(2), 76–86. doi:10.1002/(SICI)1099-1441(199806)5:2<76::AID-KPM20>3.0.CO;2-7

Spivak, S. M., & Brenner, F. C. (2001). *Standardization Essentials. Principles and Practice.* New York: Marcel Dekker Inc.

Thatcher, M., & Pingry, D. (2004). An Economic Model of Product Quality and IT Value. *Information Systems Research, 15*(3), 268–286. doi:10.1287/isre.1040.0029

Tiernan, C., & Peppard, J. (2004). Information Technology: Of Value or a Vulture? *European Management Journal, 22*(6), 609–623. doi:10.1016/j.emj.2004.09.025

Toppen, R. (1999). *Improving the Performance of Electronic Business Networks - A research into Information Technology enabled redesign of market networks and processes in the financial sector.* Doctoral Thesis, Tilburg University, Tilburg, The Netherlands.

van Heck, H. W. G. M. (1993). *Design Management of Electronic Data Interchange Systems.* Doctoral Thesis, Landbouwuniversiteit Wageningen, The Netherlands.

Volberda, H. W. (1992). *Organizational Flexibility - Change and Preservation - A Flexible Audit & Redesign Method.* Doctoral Dissertation Rijksuniversiteit Groningen, Wolters Noordhoff.

Weill, P. (1992). The Relationship Between Investment in Information Technology and Firm Performance: A Study of the Valve Manufacturing Sector. *Information Systems Research, 3*(4), 307–331. doi:10.1287/isre.3.4.307

Weill, P. (1993). The role and value of information technology infrastructure: Some empirical observations. In Banker, R. A., Kauffmann, R. J., & Mahmood, M. A. (Eds.), *Strategic Technology Management: Perspectives on Organizational Growth and Competitive Advantage* (pp. 547–572). Hershey, PA: Idea Group Publishing.

Weill, P., & Broadbent, M. (1998). *Leveraging the new Infrastructure. How Market Leaders Capitalize on Information Technology*. Boston, MA: Harvard Business School Press.

Wernerfelt, B. (1984). A Resource-Based View of the Firm. *Strategic Management Journal*, *5*(2), 171–180. doi:10.1002/smj.4250050207

Wolters, M. J. J. (2002). *The Business of Modularity and the Modularity of Business*. Doctoral Dissertation Erasmus University Rotterdam, ERIM Ph.D. Series in Management 11, The Netherlands TRAIL Research School.

ENDNOTES

1. The variables in *Italics* denote the original ones from their schema, whereas we added the straight text.
2. European Foundation for Quality Management
3. Quality factor, Economic, Social and Technical dimensions (QEST) model
4. PCI slots and USB connections are successful examples of standard PC interfaces.

Section 3
Building a Conceptual Model

In this chapter the following two questions will be answered: a) What are relevant constructs derived from literature as discussed in the literature review of the pervious section; b) What are relevant propositions in that respect? With regard to the constructs that constitute the conceptual model, all literature reviewed dealt with IT systems or processes (standardized or not) or its investments and the effects on efficiency and effectiveness. Furthermore the reviewed literature is all part of the IS research domain. We will explain how these constructs and its operational referents (the variables) were developed. But first a pilot case study will be described that has been carried out to complement the scarce literature on the implementation and usage of IT products and process standards in companies.

Chapter 4
Building the Conceptual Model

It is difficult to isolate the business contribution of IT investments, and investments related to IT standardization are no exception, as discussed in the previous chapter. In Chapter 2 literature on standard setting processes and standards was described and in Chapter 3 literature was reviewed on the impact of IT on the process performance of a firm. In this chapter the choice for the research method, as part of the research approach depicted in Chapter 1, Figure 3, will be clarified and an initial conceptual model will be composed. The research method chosen comprises both exploratory and explanatory case study research as this was considered the best way to complement theory in this underdeveloped domain of IS literature (Yin, 1994). The conceptual model integrates aspects of standardization, standards application and standards control, and relates those to the impact of IT standards used in an organization on business process performance.

PILOT CASE STUDY

Introduction

Since little scientific literature exists on selection and control of usage of IT standards within organizations, a pilot case study was carried out to get insight into these processes with the objective of exploring

DOI: 10.4018/978-1-61520-759-6.ch004

this aspect in practice and complementing the scarce literature. It may provide some conceptual clarifications for the conceptual model later on. The pilot case study on IT Standardization was carried out at the Corporate Center and at a Strategic Business Unit (SBU) of FINCORP, a global financial services company. Interviews were held with experts in this field (see Appendix II, Table 1). Furthermore, a collection of materials was analyzed such as official documentation on policies and standards, newsletters, presentations and leaflets.

Corporate IT Standardization

Objectives of the Corporate IT standardization department are listed in one of the policy documents: 1) to save money, 2) to comply with rules from regulators such as the Dutch National Bank and 3) to design IT systems that can react quickly and robustly to changing business needs. In other words standards should:

- Decrease the total cost of ownership;
- Assure a secure environment;
- Comply with regulatory requirements;
- Increase interoperability;
- Increase flexibility.

In general the interviewees agree with these consequences, except for flexibility. Some stick to the popular belief of 'the more efficient the less flexible', referring to economies of scale, whereas others perceive standards as tools to enhance flexibility. These individuals mentioned for example that making use of interoperability software (like gateways and middleware) one can link all sorts of idiosyncratic application software. In addition, there was no consensus whether standards should be used as a control

Table 1. Selection criteria for IT Standards

Selection Criteria	Weighting Factor
Product/Service capability	10
Product Supportability	10
Commercial considerations, including Total Cost of Ownership (TCO)	10
Manufacturer or vendor track record	9
Existing installed base[2]	9
Implementation considerations	9
Product category coverage	8
Product Manageability	8
Manufacturer or vendor strategy	8
Global Supply model	7
Manufacturer or vendor partnerships	7
Market Research reports	7
Manufacturer or vendor references	6

tool or not. Nevertheless, what everybody agreed on, is that standards are to meet the business drivers, like cost reductions and to comfort the level of flexibility.

The IT Product Standardization policy of this financial services company consists of the following mandatory rules and is reviewed every two years, like any other policy and standards in this company:

1. Preferably open industry standards should be used to enable interaction with the bank's customers and business partners as well as to provide the means to ensure *interoperability* of IT systems bank-wide.
2. Preferably protocols/vendors/products with a wide market support should be adopted to guarantee ample available skills/resources and competitiveness in the market place.
3. Preferably IT systems should be based on standard protocols to mitigate the diversity of the bank's systems.
4. Preferably existing investments must be re-used and leveraged and new products must not be introduced where the required functionality is already available.

IT standards are designed and approved by so called Corporate Architecture (Review) Teams.

Corporate Architecture (Review) Team (CAT/CART) Funnel

For the design and review of Policy, Standard and Procedures (PSPs) the bank makes use of the CAT/CART funnel, which is an established structured approach. A Corporate Architecture Team (CAT) contains staff from specific (multiple) disciplines with in-depth knowledge about the subject for which the PSPs are to be established. The CAT will create a draft version, complete from the discipline standpoint but to be more broadly reviewed by the Corporate Architecture Review Team (CART) on inter-disciplinary and inter-unit aspects of the subject. The CART must have a clear context for its c onsideration of the proposed PSPs (with the focus on both the knowledge and representation part). Regarding IT aspects, an ICT Corporate Standards and Policies Committee (CSPC) will act as a pre-approval body. All PSPs approved by ICT CSPC must also be submitted and approved by the Business CSPC.

Corporate policies and standards are reviewed and approved by the CAT, CART and CSPC process. The resulting IT policies and standards are published as corporate policies of FINCORP. Key activities of the CAT-CART organization are:

- Co-ordination and facilitation of IT standardization across the SBUs
- Policy and Standard Initiation Process
- Standardization & Approval Process
- Exception Process
- Architecture methodology, training and support
- guiding principles, process model, organizational model, tools, documentation standards
- Endorsement of knowledge exchange

The CAT/CART is an international organization that decides on policy and development of IT standards for the entire FINCORP organization and was established in 1997. It consists of several CAT's that in essence is a working party of experts drawn from the bank's various IT departments. They discuss a specific IT theme and submit proposals for standards to the CART that reviews it from an overall IT perspective. The review process usually takes two months. The final decision and entry into the corporate policy and standard manual, in case of approval, is made by the CSPC that consists of representatives from the senior management of both Business and IT.

It is important to take note that CSPC approval is actually the very first instance at which the Business sees these IT standards. In other words, input at an early stage during the development of IT standards is not common practice. The reason is partly because of a general lack of interest at the Business side for IT and partly because of IT-monarchism (Weill and Ross, 2004).

Areas for group level standards are: Networking, Information Security (including data privacy), Messaging and GroupWare, Middleware & Enterprise Application integration, Platforms (Desktops & Enterprise Servers), System and Infrastructure Management. The development of new policies and standards is triggered from both within and outside the bank:

- FINCORP Business and its customers
- FINCORP Procurement
- The CSPC, CART or CATs teams
- (S)BU standardisation organisations
- Dutch central bank "*De Nederlandsche Bank*", e.g. Regulation on Organization and Control (ROC, articles 54 through 57)
- Dutch security authority "*Stichting Toezicht Effectenverkeer*", (STE)
- European Committee of Central Banks, e.g. Basel II
- US Government, e.g. The Sarbanes-Oxley Act (section 404)

Success of adoption of group level standards is heavily dependent on the active participation of the several IT units within the SBUs and the commitment of its management. Therefore, synchronization of the local standardization process (per SBU) and the Corporate CAT/CART process has the full attention of senior management at corporate level[1].

In the organization a mandatory exception process exists, applicable to all corporate and (S)BU specific policies and standards. Deviation requests from the policies must at least contain:

- A description of the deviation and possibly an alternative approach.
- The reason for the deviation that must clearly indicate the reasons for not being able to comply with the PSP.
- An assessment of the risks associated with non-compliance to the PSP, including all risk categories of the FINCORP Risk Framework.
- The request for deviation must formally be signed-off by senior management responsible for requesting the deviation.

Deviations from IT PSPs must be approved by the CSPC and are periodically reviewed (typically once a year) by the policy owner.

IT Standardization Approach at an SBU

Another approach to select IT standards was created by the Investment banking division because of the general attitude that corporate IT standards were not adding enough value to their business. The SBU's IT department used a set of selection criteria and weighting factors (Table 1) to determine (SBU specific) IT products standards, like those for Rational Database Management Systems (RDBMS) and middleware. Oddly enough, for this initiative there was no direct input from the business departments either.

Besides this method an improved Business-IT alignment is aimed at by making use of a "Technology Reference Map" (see Figure 1). This reference map helps to clarify the link between the technology used to support the business and the impact this technology has upon the business. Any product specification in this list that is to be promoted to company IT standard has to pass the "Technology Approval Commission" which consists of Business and IT directors and is subsequently ratified by the Business Technology Policy Board (BTPB). It was typical for this organization that this board had only minimal cooperation with any corporate initiative related to IT standardization.

One of the interviewed IT architects of this SBU elaborates that an IT architecture, that accommodates a number of IT standards, is to support the business unit's strategy and objectives. As objectives differ between SBUs, business performance criteria of a retail or investment bank differ, one can not standardize all of IT regardless. This comment is in accordance with the framework by Ross (2003). The IT architect argued: " *Strategy precedes architecture (the how) and architecture precedes standards (the what)* ".

Figure 1. Technology reference Map to improve business-IT alignment

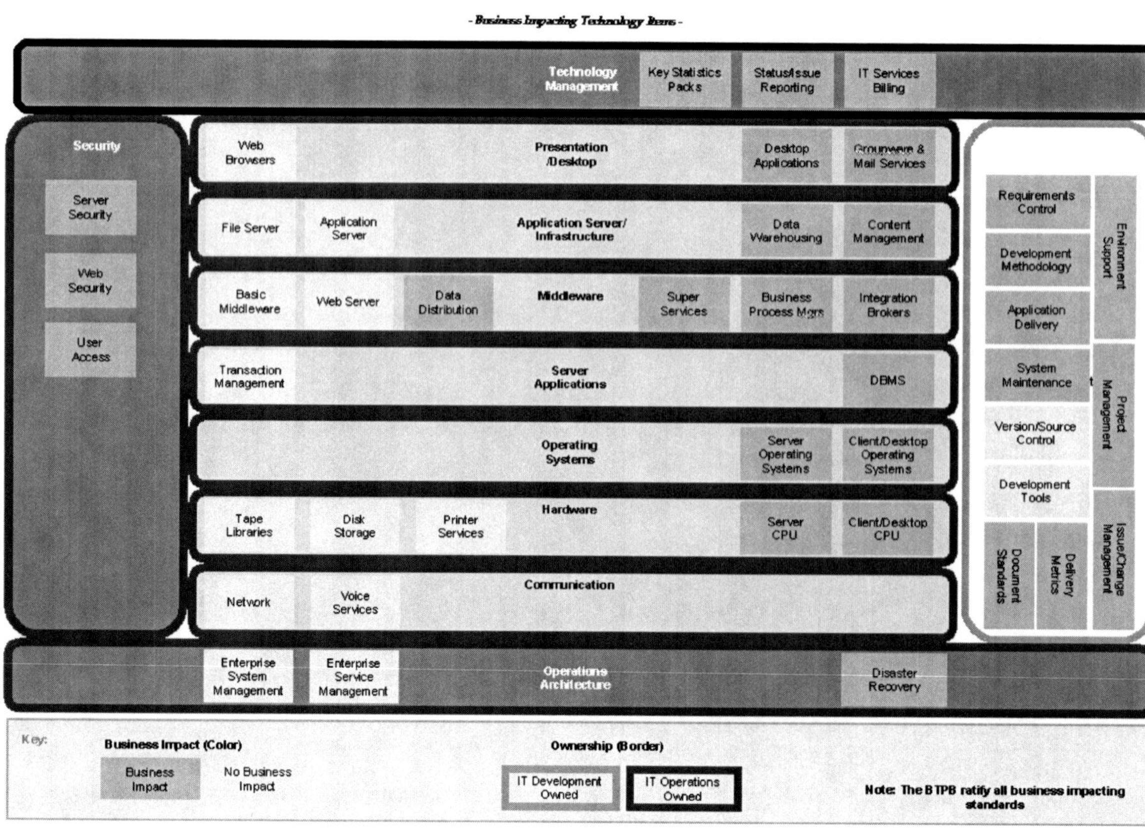

In order to explore how standard selection and control of its usage takes place in this financial services company, we will take a closer look at an initiative to provide the means for corporate IT standards. This initiative, called EITAF, is to support the SBUs to implement IT architectures. It is important to observe that this was not a mandatory process.

EITAF

Alongside the CAT/CART organization a second initiative was launched in mid 1998, the Enterprise Information Technology Architecture Framework (EITAF). It was created in order to improve integration capabilities of applications globally and to reduce the costs and time-to-market of the IT development process. It involved establishing an organization and process in order to develop and implement systems 'under Architecture'. The EITAF Vision was as follows: "*Supporting our business in the world of demanding customers by enhancing our customer relationship capabilities and improving the flexibility and time to market of the delivery processes by introducing CBD and Middleware technologies*"

EITAF consisted of three deliverables:

1) Rules, guidelines and architecture building blocks;
2) A component-based development (CBD) environment (re-usable software modules);
3) Middleware selection - the foundation for better inter-system operability using gateway technology.

Component-based development was defined by EITAF as the development of uniquely identifiable, reusable pieces of software that describe and/or deliver meaningful business functionality via well-defined interfaces to assemble applications and services. The objective of the second deliverable was to produce CBD Methods & Tools. This included a lightweight development environment; a development method / route map (process, guidelines, techniques); and a repository to store and retrieve components and component related information. It also consisted of CBD Training and Support (courses for CBD developers and project support). The third deliverable comprises: 1) functional specifications and architecture document for enterprise-wide deployment for the EITAF Enterprise Service Bus (C-Bus)[3]; 2) a roadmap for further development of the C-Bus and a pilot implementation (Multi Channel Platform proof of concept) based on Windows NT, UNIX, IMS and IBM MQSeries™ 3) integration with the development environment (CBD). C-Bus is an in-house developed gateway technology and basically is an implementation of a Service Oriented Architecture (SOA) that connects applications on any system and any domain.

We will further zoom in on the first deliverable as an example of how standard selection and control took place in this company. An architecture framework is a reference model for information systems, comprising of hardware, software, data, and communications networks. Without such a model, new information systems are built separately resulting in inefficiencies and potential incompatibilities. The main reason that was stated for developing a technical *architecture* framework was *to enable standardization* in IT development and support globally.

In the EITAF model, the process of defining IT architectures and standards commences at the business departments. To come to an application and technical infrastructure architecture, the business processes are described and translated to technical terms before any application or infrastructure development takes place. More specifically, there are 5 domains identified to reach an aligned IT infrastructure, as depicted in Figure 2. It starts at the Business Domain Architecture level that answers questions like: 'What is our reason for existence?', 'What are our main challenges?' and 'Where do we want to be in the future?'. The Business Process Domain Architecture describes how business is to be performed (its processes and related data), who are the stakeholders and what information will be produced. The Application Domain Architecture describes the business services and applications required supporting the business and finally the Technical Domain Architecture describes the implementations of a specific technology.

To ensure alignment between Business and IT, a description of the business processes is made in a Business Process Model. In this model the business processes are defined at a level that is detailed enough to arrive at service descriptions. Subsequently, the application and technical domain architecture definition takes place. It is the responsibility of the business departments to describe the Business Domain and Business Process Domain Architecture. IT is responsible for describing the Application Domain Architecture of a domain and the Technical Domain Architectures.

In order to come to e.g. the technical domain architecture, standards are set for connectivity (network, hardware and operating systems and technical services like security, Messaging and GroupWare, system & service management, etc) and will be proposed as corporate standards. These corporate standards are to be maintained and enforced by the IT organizations of the Business Units. To that end CATs were installed for ongoing development activities (for example, a Middleware CAT) that became part of the existing CAT/CART organization coordinated by the Corporate IT Strategy & Architecture department.

Maintenance and enforcement by the IT organizations of the Business Units of such corporate IT standards turned out to be a major pitfall as 1) these standards were not widely adopted because of a lack

Figure 2. EITAF's domain architecture model

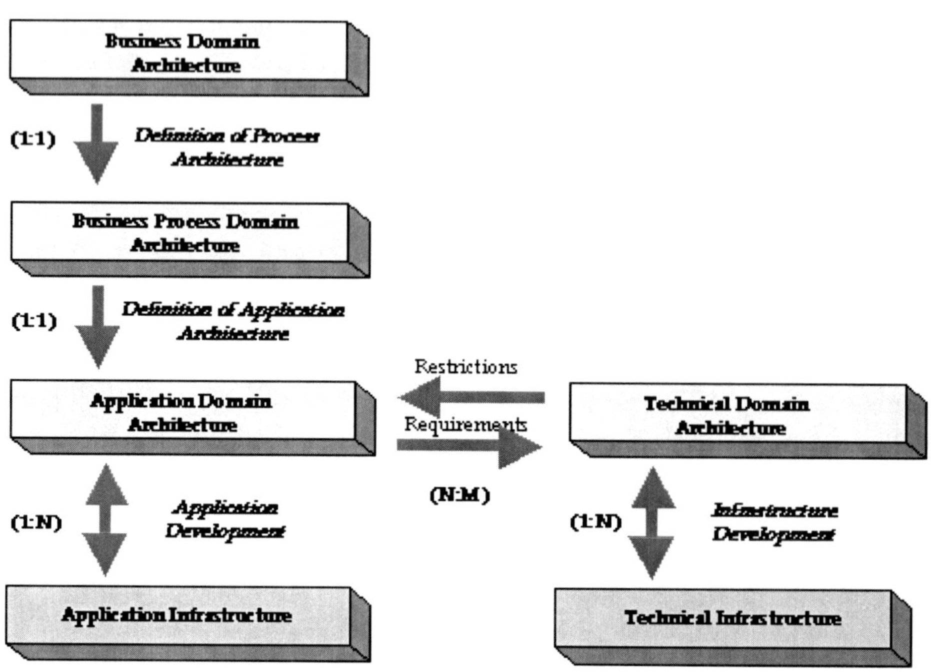

of commitment by the Business Units; 2) the standards were in practice not mandatory as these could be easily deviated or even discarded; 3) specific implementation details were absent for these standards, which resulted in different configurations being used.

Architecture and standards are closely linked, since standards can be regarded as a specific set of guidelines within the architecture framework. In this case, the standards are facilitated by architecture and the EITAF Architecture Method refers wherever applicable to these standards, which were set and managed by the CAT/CART organization. EITAF itself also went through the formal CART and CSPC approval process to become a corporate standard (although it didn't become a mandatory one).

The head of Group IT commented on a number of predicaments related to IT architecture and standardization in this company. In particular this concerned the lack of alignment between Business and IT. It is hard for the business departments to specify functional requirements and their knowledge of IT is only limited. As a consequence the full potential of IT architecture and standards for the Business strategy and models can not be optimally harvested. Secondly, there is still too little standardization at both hardware and system software level resulting in development and maintenance costs that are higher than necessary. The IT standardization initiative at the SBU corresponds to this latter comment.

Lessons Learned

The pilot case provided insight into the basic issues being studied, especially from the selection and control perspective. This information was used in parallel to the literature study satisfying the main objective of this initiative, being to complement existing literature with new empirical observations to build the conceptual model.

Both in the EITAF approach as well as argued by the interviewees, the business model is leading in the selection of standards and these standards have to meet business drivers and requirements. The relationship between architecture and standards was elucidated also. It was observed that there was a strong "not invented here" attitude from the Business Units with respect to corporate IT standards. The general feeling was that corporate IT was not well aligned with the Business Units and that such standards were felt as a control instrument (i.e. power) by corporate IT rather than really beneficial for the SBUs. In other words the buy-in from the Business Units' IT departments to establish corporate IT standards was low. But the Business-IT alignment within Business Units was not good either, even though we have shown an initiative to improve this issue (see Figure 1). It was also found that there was no direct involvement by Business representatives in the CAT/CART organization, but at the high CSPC level only, which did not help in this respect either.

It was observed quite clearly that the SBUs did not usually adopt initiatives at corporate level, like EITAF, since these typically had no mandatory nature. Nor was there a central authority that effectively enforced the usage of these standards. Furthermore, the SBUs were only very slightly involved in the selection phase. The lack of commitment from the IT departments of the SBUs worsened this situation, as these perceived such standards as 'unwanted'.

Moreover, adopted standards by the Business Units typically were not accompanied by implementation specifics to guide projects. In other words, a standardized implementation process of the selected IT products and process standards was not provided. This resulted in dissimilar implementations, hindering for example interoperability and ease of maintenance. Finally, because agreed upon corporate IT standards could not be enforced effectively, SBUs just disregarded such company standards or at least could deviate from these standards quite easily. As a consequence its usage was left to the tender mercies of cooperating IT departments of the Business Units.

Therefore, conclusions from this pilot case regarding the selection of standards are:

- Business model & drivers prerequisites are the primary input for the corporate IT architecture and standards
- Standards should satisfy business requirements
- Standards serve as guidelines within an architecture framework

With regard to the control on the usage of these standards it was learned that the following variables are essential to its success or failure:

- The level of commitment of Business and IT management
- The level of formalization and prescription of related processes and procedures
- The level of enforcing the usage of the standard by the organization

MANAGERIAL IMPLICATIONS

The pilot case showed us the following practical implications for this case company, that could also hold in a more generic setting. Input of all stakeholders, not in the least Business representatives, at an early stage in the development of IT standards is a good practice and will increase likelihood of successful application of company standards. Maintenance and enforcement of mandatory standards is also key to makes sure these are not easily deviated or discarded. A mandatory exception process will also add to this success of the standards. Deviation requests must at least contain: its reason, an assessment of risks, the agreement by senior management, possible alternatives. Specific implementation details for company IT standards will also add to successful application as this prevents different configurations will be created in projects.

INITIAL CONCEPTUAL MODEL

Note: *this section is primarily intended for scholars and researchers in IS. An initial conceptual model is drafted that will be subsequently tested in a number of case studies and further detailed in Chapter 8. Practitioners interested in the final standardization management framework could read Chapter 8 directly instead.*

The goal of a theory is to reduce the complexity of the empirical world and to describe it based on explanations and predictions. Bacharach (1989) characterizes a theory as a system of constructs and variables that are related to each other by propositions and hypotheses respectively. Constructs are not directly observable whereas variables are the operationalized derivatives that can be measured. The constructs and propositions described in this section have been derived from the previous two chapters and the pilot case study. From these lessons and the problem stated in the introduction, this study integrates these constructs into the initial conceptual model, which tries to explain changes in process performance due to the usage of IT standards. This model represents the subject under investigation and will be used to clarify the research problem and the underlying relationships between constructs and variables. The basic unit of analysis in this study is the Business Unit where the standard is used.

It was learned from Chapter 2 that there is extensive literature on standards development, ranging from proprietary products and processes that may become de facto standards via consensus standardization to regulatory standardization. Unfortunately, there are only a few examples in literature on the selection, implementation and usage of standards within a company (specified by Cargill (1989) as internal standardization). One of these examples is the research on IT product standards that has been carried out by Kayworth and Sambamurthy (2000). Rada and Craparo (2001) also contributed to this topic by discussing some control mechanisms when using an IT process standard (see Section on Utilization of IT standards in Organizations). It was discussed earlier that the concept of flexibility is highly dependent on the context in which it is being used. Evans (1991) identified strength, scalability and extensibility as important fundamentals related to flexibility. Duncan (1995) defined flexibility as the degree to which IT resources are sharable and reusable.

From the previous two chapters and the pilot case study, four constructs have been identified that will constitute the initial conceptual model. It was also discussed that there are two major impetuses determining the effects of application of IT standards within a company. Those are 1) the internal standards selection process and 2) the control of these standards in the operation (e.g. level of enforcement). In Chapter 3 the concept of IT value and business performance was discussed, with main result that business performance can be practically assessed one abstraction layer down, namely that of business processes. Business performance, including those of business processes, can be assessed from various vantagepoints (Kaplan and Norton, 1992): financial, client satisfaction, internal and learning & growth. The frameworks of Weill and Broadbent (1998) and Melville et al. (2004), on the impact of IT investments in general on business performance and of the IT Business value respectively, turned out to be useful too. This fourth construct, business process performance, will be expressed in terms of effectiveness and efficiency.

In addition, the pilot case study showed us that success factors for IT standard selection are the relationship with the business model, drivers and requirements, and indicating that the level of Business-IT alignment is an important variable to be considered in the conceptual model. The pilot case study also showed that regarding control on IT standards, three variables were key in the effective usage of standards: 1) level of *commitment* of management 2) the level of facilitation and *prescription of adherence* to the related processes, including ones for implementation and 3) the level of *enforcement* of the standards by the organization.

So, four constructs can be identified. The selection process how to decide on the company IT standard[4], to be used in the company, makes up the first construct. The way the IT standard is being implemented and used in the organization comprises the second construct. A third construct relates to the IT standard's influence on the business process performance. The control on the IT standard constitutes the fourth and final construct. Control of its usage moderates the relationship between the IT standard that is being used and the process performance due to this standard. As a result, the following four constructs have been defined:

- *Process of Standard Selection* relates to the way the company IT standard is chosen.
- *Application of Standard* relates to the way the company IT standard is implemented and used in the company.

- *Process Performance* relates to the efficiency and effectiveness of the process as a result of using the company IT standard, and is expressed in the four Business Balanced Scorecard perspectives.
- *Control of Standard* relates to the control on the application of the IT standard, which includes prescription, enforcement and restriction of using the standard.

These constructs will be discussed in more detail in the next sections. The relationships between the constructs have been derived from the lessons learned above. As a consequence, the following four propositions can be formulated:

- **Proposition 1:** An effective (ineffective) IT standard selection process positively (negatively) influences the application of these standards.
- **Proposition 2:** The application of appropriate IT standards contributes to better process performance and this performance is dependent on the control of its usage.
- **Proposition 3:** A low process performance due to the applied IT standards leads to changes in the way these standards are controlled.
- **Proposition 4:** A low process performance due to the applied IT standards leads to reselection of these standards.

The selection process is considered effective[5] if the operational referents of this construct are considered adequately, which is explained further on. Both constructs and relationships are depicted in the conceptual model of Figure 3. Two organizational learning loops are included with the objective of improving the process performance if this is not at the desired level. One feedback loop drives the control on the standards' usage and another one results in the re-evaluation of the IT standard. This should ensure that standards are adequately enforced, are kept up to date and are responsive to changes in the business environment.

In the next four sections the constructs will be refined and relevant variables that provide an operational referent to the constructs will be determined based on the literature study and pilot case study. The motivation why the Balanced Scorecard has been chosen as a measurement tool will be provided. But reliability and validity of the constructs will be examined first.

Figure 3. Initial conceptual model to determine influence of IT standards on business process performance

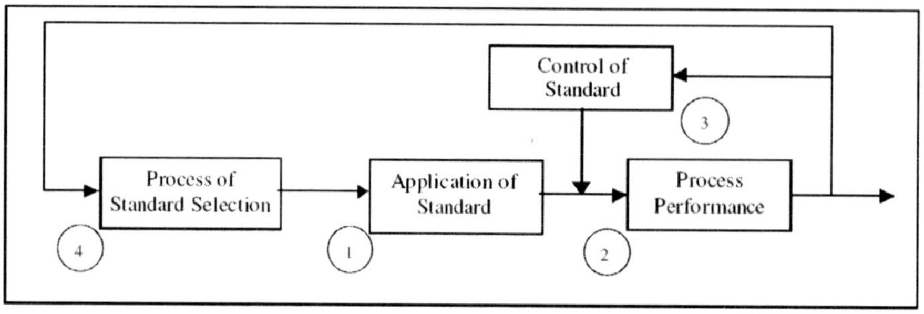

Construct Validity

Are the variables that operationalize the construct valid measures? There is no direct and conclusive empirical way to validate the operational definitions of the variables against the constructs in a theory (Friel, 2003). It is critical, therefore, to understand that a research study is only a direct test of the propositions and not a direct test of the theory. So the extent to which the operational definitions of the variables are valid measures of the constructs in the theory is key. In most cases, this extent is an assumption only and not a fact. There is no direct or conclusive method to test these assumptions. However, there are a number of indirect and inductive approaches that can be used, including 1) Convention; 2) Factor Analysis; 3) Meta-analysis; 4) Measurement Triangulation. In the next sections approach no. 3 is used, i.e. based on literature study and pilot case study operational measures are determined. Then again, the results from this analysis are no guarantee of construct validity, but do serve as a necessary prerequisite in any inductive generalizations about validity (Friel, 2003, p. 38). Moreover, the suggested tactics by (Yin, 1994) to enhance construct validity, were stringently followed as well.

A further discussion on construct validity is related to the so-called formative versus reflective nature of variables and its consequences for validity. This area of research on methodology is mainly based in the fields of sociology/psychology, marketing and strategy (Bollen and Lennox, 1991; Diamantopoulos and Winklhofer, 2001; Bagozzi and Fornell, 1982). MacKenzie (2003, p. 325) provides recommendations for defining constructs. The construct's conceptual theme should be specified in unambiguous terms, in a manner consistent with prior literature (content validity) and in a way that clearly distinguishes one construct from related constructs (discriminant validity). Poor construct conceptualization could result in measure deficiency and contamination of the conceptual domain often leads to measurement model misspecification and raises doubts about the credibility of the hypotheses (p. 324). When developing variables for a construct it is vital to ensure that a) the variables reflect all key aspects of the conceptual domain, b) no contamination occurs by adding variables which are not part of the conceptual domain, c) the variables are properly worded. The relation between these variables and the construct should be a matter of serious attention. Basically, two distinct types of measurement relations have been identified in literature (Bagozzi and Fornell 1982; Bollen and Lennox 1991):

1. *Reflective* indicator measurement models posit that causality flows from the construct to the measures.
2. *Formative* indicator measurement models posit that causality flows from the measures to the construct.

A well-known reflective construct is Perceived Ease of Use (Davis et al., 1989) that consists of six variables such as 'clear and understandable' and 'easy to use'. An increase in the value of the construct is reflected by an increase in the variables that are expected to be correlated. But, performance (e.g. of an organization or process) is a construct that should be modeled formatively if the variables are related to different aspects such as financial, customer and operational excellence perspectives (Rai et al., 2006).

When a construct is not clearly defined, it is hard to determine which of these two fundamentally different types of measurement relations is the most appropriate. This is important as misspecification of the measurement model could undermine both construct validity and reliability. In Jarvis et al. (2003, p. 203) the following causality criteria are listed to determine whether constructs should be modeled as reflective or formative. A construct should be modeled as having formative variables if the following conditions prevail:

a. the indicators are viewed as defining characteristics of the construct,
b. changes in the indicators are expected to cause changes in the construct,
c. changes in the construct are not expected to cause changes in the indicators,
d. the indicators do not necessarily share a common theme,
e. eliminating an indicator may alter the conceptual domain of the construct[6],
f. a change in the value of one of the indicators is not necessarily expected to be associated with a change in all of the other indicators[7], and
g. the indicators are not expected to have the same antecedents and consequences.

On the other hand, a construct should be modeled as having reflective indicators if the opposite is true. These causality criteria are thus most important to decide a priory whether a construct is a formative or a reflective one, as misspecification of the direction of causality can lead to inaccurate conclusions about the relationships between the constructs (Law and Wong, 1999). Jarvis et al. (2003, p. 203) argue that further refinement of the conceptualization of the construct may be needed when there are inconsistencies or difficulties in answering some of the questions. As this is not the case for all constructs in this conceptual model, which will be demonstrated in the next sections, this is a good indication of the validity of the four constructs and their formative variables.

Reflective constructs have clear guidelines for validation (Straub et al. 2004), but the methodological literature provides relative few guidelines in assessing the validity of formative constructs. Construct validity (i.e. convergent, discriminant, content) examines the measurement properties *between* constructs whereas reliability examines the internal consistency *within* the construct (Boudreau et al. 2001). Validation criteria for formative constructs differ from reflective constructs as the measurement error occurs at the construct level rather than at the variable level (Diamantopoulos and Winklhofer 2001).

- Although correlations among variables for formative constructs is not a cause for concern due to the direction of causality, *convergent validity* ("do the measures of the construct belong together?") is likely to be meaningful only for items that contribute heavily to the composition of the formative construct (Loch et al. 2003).
- *Discriminant validity* ("are the measures empirically distinguishable from measures of other constructs?") was guaranteed by ensuring that the constructs did not share variables (Bacharach, 1989).
- *Content validity* ("are all facets of the construct measured?") of the formative constructs has been ascertained by 1) evaluation whether the set of variables map to specific areas in the theory base; 2) expert validations of the case study questionnaire's variables (Boudreau et al. 2001, Diamantopoulos and Winklhofer 2001, Straub et al., 2004). In this model all variables of the constructs have the same relative weights.
- *Reliability* tests are available for quantitative analysis that are typically assessed using Cronbach's alpha. However, reliability is irrelevant for formative constructs as the variables are potentially examining different aspects of a construct (Bollen and Lennox, 1991).

Based on the literature review of Chapters 2 and 3, in the next sections the constructs' variables will be discussed, including the rationale for it being an operational referent. In every instance the causality and validation criteria have been taken into account.

The Construct 'Process of Standard Selection'

The construct 'Process of Standard Selection' deals with standard selection within a company to determine company standards. The formal and informal standardization processes that have been extensively examined by others as discussed in Chapter 2 are explicitly not covered. Standard selection within a company is described in Section 'IT Standardization in Organizations' of that Chapter. With regard to this construct the following was learnt from the literature on both standardization and business performance.

Cargill (1995) argues that there is often a lack of business rationale for standardization and standards in companies whereas the pilot case study showed that the level at which the *business model* was taken into account was important in determining suitable company standards. Jakobs et. al. (1996) mention there can be several *business drivers* for standardization, such as integration or internationalization and according to Cargill (1989, p. 63) company standards should be chosen directed by an understanding of the strategy of the company. Also Duncan (1995), from a flexibility perspective, addresses the importance of considering business objectives when dealing with IT infrastructures. The importance of considering business drivers in the selection phase was also found in the pilot case study (EITAF). Next to that, several authors emphasize the importance of *user/customer involvement* during the process of standard selection (Poppel and Goldstein, 1987; Cargill, 1995; Naemura, 1995; Rutkowski, 1995; Jakobs et. al., 1996; De Vries, 1999; Fomin and Keil, 2000; Spivak and Brenner, 2001).

Rada and Craparo (2001) exemplified the importance of *Business* and *IT involvement*[8] and *alignment* in the standard selection of organizational standards. Furthermore, Monteiro and Hanseth (1999) and Duncan (1995) stress the importance of alignment of IS plans to business objectives. In the pilot case study the importance of Business IT alignment for selection of organizational standards has been discussed as well. Moreover, Kayworth and Sambamurthy (2000) recognized that active collaboration between IT and Business in the selection phase is one of the important factors for company standards to be successful.

Kayworth and Sambamurthy also recognized that *management knowledge* of standards is important for the standard selection process. Moreover, Boynton et al. (1994) found that managerial IT knowledge is a dominant factor in explaining effective IT usage in general. As part of this, the classical distinction of the standard's origin ("de facto, consensus, de jure") is to be taken into account when selecting standards, as commercial interests of vendors and lock-in problems should be considered.

Given this assessment of both literature and pilot case study the variables (i.e. the operational referent for a phenomenon described on a more abstract level (Bacharach, 1989, p.502)) listed in Table 2 seem to make up this construct. The rationale is given why a variable is an observable entity for this construct.

The Construct 'Application of Standard'

The construct 'Application of Standard' deals with any selected company IT standard of the categories defined by David and Greenstein (1990): a reference, minimum quality or interface/compatibility standard. The *reach* of a standard can either be a single department or up to the whole enterprise, whereas

Table 2. Variables of the construct 'Process of Standard Selection'

Variable	Rationale for being an operational referent
Business model consideration	If the business model (e.g. franchise or holding company) is not taken into account during the standard selection process, the company standard that is used in the company's business processes may not meet the requirements related to that model. So the *level of consideration paid to the business model* is considered as an operational measure.
Business driver consideration	As standardization is not an aim in itself, standards should be chosen based on sound business rationale. Failure to do so may lead to misalignment of the business objectives, such as integration or quality improvements. The *level of consideration paid to the business drivers* is considered as an operational measure
Business involvement	Business model or Business driver considerations do not guarantee Business involvement. Lack of Business involvement during the standard selection process may result in ignoring these standards by the Business, as these may not reflect their requirements. So the *extent in which the Business was involved* in the selection process is considered as an operational measure.
IT engineering involvement	If IT engineering is not involved during the standard selection process, this may result in standards that are not adequate, from a technological point of view. Therefore, the *level of IT engineering involvement* is considered as an operational measure.
IT operations involvement	If IT operations is not involved during the standard selection process, this may result in standards that are inadequate, from an IT support point of view. Therefore, the *level of IT operations involvement* is considered as an operational measure.
Level of B-IT alignment	Lack of Business-IT alignment could result into an inefficient and/or ineffective standard selection process and thus of the IT standard. Therefore, the *level of B-IT alignment* is considered as an operational measure.
Management knowledge	The *level of management knowledge on standards* can influence the selection process of standards and is considered as an operational measure

the *range* could be a single communication protocol up to the whole IT infrastructure[9]. Both reach and range have an impact on the application (Hanseth and Braa, 2001; Ross, 2003; Weill and Ross, 2004).

Kayworth and Sambamurthy (2000) showed that, as part of the organizational context, local *IT expertise* of the standards plays an important role in the effective application of standards. Standard *awareness* is yet another factor that plays an important role in the application of standards, which was recognized by Wakid and Radack (1997) and Mähönen (2000). In addition, Rada and Craparo (2001) explained that staff was made aware of the company standards by providing training to employees to address e.g. competency gaps. Finally, Boynton et al. (1994) recognized that the quality of *project management* was a dominant factor in explaining the effectiveness of IT in general and we will analyze whether this holds for IT standards as well.

Given this assessment of both literature and pilot case study the variables listed in Table 3 will be considered in the conceptual model.

The Construct 'Control of Standard'

The construct 'Control of Standard' embodies checks and balances (such as prescription, enforcement, restrictiveness and endorsement) for using the standard.

Cargill (1989) basically distinguishes two extremes of company standard control: from laissez faire to strict *prescription* and *enforcement* and anything in between. Vlaar (2006) discussed formalization in organizational relationships including the enabling to coercive nature of inputs, outputs and processes as a whole. Hanseth and Braa (2001, p.271) showed the negative consequences of ineffective enforcement of standards. In Chapter 2, the key standards management task of enforcing (Weill and Broadbent, 1998,

Table 3. Variables of the construct 'Application of Standard'

Variable	Rationale for being an operational referent
Reach	The *extent to which the standard is used intra-organizationally*, influences its application in a company and is considered as an operational measure as a result.
Range	The *number of used standardized products or processes in the company* influences its application in a company and is, as a result, considered as an operational measure.
IT expertise	The *competence level of the IT department* that applies the standard, affects the effectiveness of the standard and is considered as an operational measure for that reason.
Awareness	The attention paid to the standard affects the effectiveness of the standard, so *the level of cognizance of the standard* is considered as an operational measure.
Project Management	The way in which the standard is implemented in the organization could effect its usage, so *the project management quality* of the standardization project is considered as an operational measure.

p. 266) was identified in a cluster of infrastructure services. Rada and Craparo (2001) showed that management fully supported the enhanced control of standards. They discussed the formalized control and enforcement of software development standards. The pilot case study also confirmed the importance of this aspect. Furthermore, Kayworth and Sambamurthy (2000) showed that three key aspects influence the usage of IT standards: the degree of standard prescription, the level of enforcement and the level of *restrictiveness*. In this same section Weill and Ross (2004) stress the importance of a standards exception process to allow *deviations,* which reinforces the IT infrastructure if these are incorporated as new requirements into the company IT standards.

The level of management commitment or *endorsement* as a key factor that affects IT standardization and standards usage has been since long recognized (Cargill, 1989). Robert et al. (1998) identified this factor during standardization of a software development methodology. Ample evidence of this aspect was also found in the pilot case study, especially the level of commitment by IT departments to comply with company standards. Kayworth and Sambamurthy (2000) showed that the organizational context, especially the participation of stakeholders, plays an important role in the effective application of standards. This has been typified by Corporate IT/Business Unit *collaboration*, which includes information sharing and the rationality of decisions. Such an issue was found in the pilot case study and exemplifies this aspect.

Akkermans and Van der Horst (2002) argued that the *maturity* of an organization is important as to how standards should be used (collaborative or coercive. A same rationale can be found in Ross (2003) related to IT architecture. Weill and Ross (2004) identified the level of Business Unit autonomy (*centralization* / decentralization) as another important aspect of IT control in general, whereas Ross (2003) specifically discusses this for IT standards. Boynton et al. (1994), introduced the 'IT management process effectiveness' as a key factor that affects IT usage. This includes effects on application maintenance. They also recognized that control structures were a moderating factor in explaining the value of IT in general and it is anticipated this holds good for IT standards as well, like *processes and procedures* for adhering to the standards. At least the pilot case study showed that the existence of implementation procedures was an aspect of the successful control on IT standards.

Given this assessment of both literature and pilot case study the variables itemized in Table 4 will be considered in the conceptual model.

Table 4. Variables of the construct 'Control of Standard'

Variable	Rationale for being a operational referent
Prescription	Whether standards are mandatory or recommended only, affects the application of standards. So the *prescription level of the standards* is considered as an operational measure.
Enforcing	Although standards can be formally prescribed, these could be defined by e.g. business departments. So the *level of enforcement to comply with these standards* (i.c. implementation and usage) is considered as an operational measure.
Restrictiveness	Variations within the standard could affect the application of standards, as users could perceive a single choice as being too restrictive. So the *level of restrictiveness of the standard* is considered as an operational measure.
Deviations	The manner in which exceptions to the standards are dealt with, affects the application of the standards. So the *quality level of a standards exception process* is considered as an operational measure.
Endorsement	Management support for standards affects the application of standards, so the *level of endorsement by management for standards* is considered as an operational measure.
Collaboration	The relationship between corporate IT and local IT departments affects the application of the standards, so the *level of collaboration between corporate IT and local IT* is considered as an operational measure.
Maturity	The maturity of the organization could affect the standard's effectiveness, so the *maturity level of the organization that applies the standard* is considered as an operational measure.
Centralization	The *level of centralized control of the standard* affects its application and is, therefore, considered as an operational measure.
Processes	Processes and procedures could play an important role in the effective application of standards, so the *quality level of processes and procedures for implementation and usage of standards* is considered as an operational measure.

The Construct 'Process Performance'

The construct 'Process Performance' is expressed in efficiency and effectiveness/flexibility and relates to business processes. It can be observed from various perspectives, such as financial, customer, internal business and learning & growth, as discussed earlier in Chapter 2. In the following section, the reason for choosing the BSC will be given.

Rationale for Using a Balanced Scorecard

Measuring the impacts of IT standards usage, benefiting business processes, and associated IT investment could be carried out via several approaches. There are the traditional methods such as return on investment (ROI), net present value (NPV) and the internal rate of return (IRR). More sophisticated techniques like information economics and the Balanced Scorecard (BSC) include intangibles next to financial measures. Where ROI, NPV and IRR are not well-suited for contemporary IT services, even the two domains of information economics (business domain and technological domain) fail to fully capture the range of business benefits offered by today's IT services (Martinsons et al., 1999, p72.). It was discussed in Chapter 2 that a well-established method to measure performance, taking into account both tangibles and intangibles, is the Balanced Scorecard.

Attempts have been made to apply the Balanced Scorecard to performance measurement in settings such as electronic commerce (Hasan and Tibbits, 2000), project management (Eickelmann, 2001), ERP Systems (Rosemann & Weise, 1999; Chand et al., 2005) and the alignment between IT and the competitive strategies of a firm (Hu and Huang, 2005). Measuring performance via the Balanced Scorecard approach has also been recognized for evaluating IT and its investments. This was initially proposed by Gold (1992) and Willcocks (1995) and further developed by Van Grembergen & Van Bruggen (1997) and Martinsons et al. (1999). Furthermore, Hatten and Rosenthal (2001, p. 59) argue that there is no need to wait for top management to adopt a BSC or any other performance measurement system. Middle management could intervene with performance measurement enhancements that are useful to their Business Unit.

It is relatively easy to tailor the Balanced Scorecard framework to the specific needs of IT investment evaluation (Milis and Mercken, 2004, p. 94). Therefore, some authors (Van Grembergen & Van Bruggen 1997; Maltz et al., 2003) propose adaptations to the original Business Balanced Scorecard framework since the initial framework focuses on the impact of the Business on the external market, whereas IT for example can be considered as an internal support function. However, others argue (Papalexandris et al., p.223) that the model should be kept unchanged, because of its simplicity and compactness, and more importantly, because other perspectives could be orthogonalized to the original perspectives.

Martinsons et al. (1999) suggest a methodology for creating a Balanced Scorecard for strategic IT management. They propose that "*The BSC concept can also be applied to measure, evaluate and guide activities that take place in specific functional areas of a business. It can even be used to shed greater light on performance at the individual project level.*" (p.75). They conclude "*The cases we studied reinforced a belief that while the specifics of a balanced IS scorecard will differ from company to company, it is beneficial to build upon a standard framework, such as the one presented here, rather than starting from scratch.*" (p.85).

Elsewhere, Van Grembergen & Van Bruggen illustrate how the BSC approach can be applied to the IT function by redefining the original perspectives as user-orientation, corporate contribution, operational excellence and future orientation. An example is given in Table 5. The application of their IT Balanced Scorecard is demonstrated at a Financial services group (Van Grembergen & Saull, 2001). The adapted perspectives of that scorecard contain objectives and measures that are related to perceived IT issues of the case company.

A same line of reasoning is used for IT standards, as these support business processes as well, and IT standards are basically a subset of IT in general. That is why in this research business process performance will be expressed using the BSC approach. A BSC should have set objectives, Key Performance Indicators (KPIs) and related targets (see example, Table 5).

In the case studies described later on, planned and realized values are to be obtained to assess the impact of IT standardization within a company. These values must be compared to the situation before standardization has taken place. The actual contribution will probably depend on the ability of the organization to exploit these benefits.

Four Perspectives of Process Performance.

The lessons learned from the literature review in Chapters 2 and 3 revealed the following as regards process performance:

- For IT usage in general, several impacts on the **financial** side of a company have been identified such as the costs of application development (Weill and Broadbent, 1998; Chapter 3, Figure 2). Again, in this research it is supposed that this will also be true for investment in IT standards and results of further case studies will validate this assumption. De Vries (1999) showed that the use

Table 5. Example of an IT Balanced Scorecard (adapted from Van Grembergen & Saull, 2001)

BUSINESS CONTRIBUTION (Financial Perspective) **Perspective question** How does management view the IT department? **Mission** Contribute to the achievement of the business goals of our clients through effective delivery of value based information services. **Objectives** ■ Strategic Initiative Delivery ■ Synergy Achievement ■ Management of IT Expenses ■ IT Governance ■ Benefit Realization on IT Investments **KPIs** ■ Strategic project success ■ Achievement of integration cost reductions ■ Attainment of expense and recovery targets ■ IT governance gap closures ■ Internal I.T. project success	**USER ORIENTATION (Customer Perspective)** **Perspective question** How do users view the IT department? **Mission** Be the supplier of choice for all information services, either directly or indirectly through supplier partnerships. **Objectives** ■ Delivery Project Performance ■ Service Level Performance ■ Client Satisfaction ■ IT/Business Partnership ■ Portfolio Management **KPIs** ■ Delivery project success ■ Attainment of service level targets (weighted % of services) ■ Client satisfaction survey scores ■ IT/business partnership index ■ Account management effectiveness
OPERATIONAL EXCELLENCE (Internal Perspective) **Perspective question** How effective and efficient are the IT processes? **Mission** Deliver timely and effective information services at targeted service levels and costs. **Objectives** ■ Process Performance ■ Process Maturity ■ Technology Infrastructure Mgmt **KPIs** ■ IT process effectiveness ■ IT process maturity ratings ■ Compliance to technology infrastructure policies ■ Attainment of technology roadmap objectives	**FUTURE ORIENTATION (Learning & Growth Perspective)** **Perspective question** How well is IT positioned to meet future needs? **Mission** Develop the internal capabilities to learn, innovate and exploit future opportunities. **Objectives** ■ Employee Satisfaction ■ Employee Management Effectiveness ■ Enterprise Architecture Evolution ■ Emerging Technologies Research ■ Knowledge Management (future) **KPIs** ■ Employee satisfaction scores ■ Employee turnover ■ Attainment of employee utilization targets ■ % of staff achieving professional development plans ■ Development/update of enterprise architecture documents

of standards contributes to efficiency since one does not have to develop it oneself, so the *cost to develop* is considered an important aspect of the usage of IT standards. Nybo (2002) states that financial institutions that do not use standards, spend a lot of their software development effort on building system interfaces. But also the *cost to support*, for example, the costs per workstation are considered as important aspects of using IT standards. De Vries (1999) argues that procurement costs could decrease due to quantity rebates whereas Akkermans and Van der Horst (2002) showed that standards allow variety reduction to enable economies of scale, resulting in cost efficiency. Kayworth and Sambamurthy (2000) described that higher cost to support could be used as a sanction if one does not want to conform to standard products. In Chapter 3, Figure 2, financial figures related to the impact of IT, were mapped to four hierarchical levels of performance. The cost figures are included in the financial perspective to account for changes in cost and productivity performance (Kaplan and Norton, 1996, p. 56, 306). These figures will be considered as variables in the conceptual model and it should be noted that these are located in the two bottom levels of the hierarchy by Weill and Broadbent's scheme (see Chapter 3, Figure 2).

Table 6. Variables of the construct 'Process Performance', financial perspective

Variable	Rationale for being an operational referent
Cost to develop IT	Due to the application of standards, efficiency increases in IT development are expected, therefore, the *costs to develop new IT services* are considered as an operational measure.
Costs to support IT	Due to the application of standards, efficiency increases in IT support are expected, therefore, the *costs to support the IT infrastructure* are considered as an operational measure.
Economic value-added	Because of costs savings as a result of the application of standards, *Economic Value-added* is expected to increase and is therefore considered as an operational measure.
ROI	Although an approximate measure, *Return On Investment* is considered as a variable of this construct as this a figure frequently available in organizations.

David and Greenstein (1990) argue that standards reduce entry costs and risks for new firms, which may lead to increased price competition as more competitors could enter the market space. De Vries (1999) explains also that positive consequences of product standards for market share have been found. In addition he mentions increased price competition between suppliers. Young (1996) argues that the economic significance of standards is to reduce transaction costs. Furthermore, Hitt and Brynjolfsson (1996) identified increases in productivity due to IT investments. It is anticipated, therefore, that *Economic Value-added* is affected by using IT standards. Another element that is introduced is the Return On Investment *(ROI)* of efforts to reach the company standard (see Chapter 3, Table 2). Although an inaccurate method, this is often used by companies to investigate whether investments will pay off.

'Return On Assets' and 'Revenue Growth' could also be affected. Spivak and Brenner (2001) explain that a company strategically positions its products to expand market share and collects royalties by licensing intellectual property rights (Chapter 2). These indicators are located in the two top levels of the hierarchy scheme by Weill and Broadbent (see Chapter 3, Figure 2). Unfortunately the effects of these investments, including those for IT standardization and standards, are diluted or swamped by many other factors, which makes it very difficult to directly pinpoint the effects of IT standards.

So, for the initial conceptual model, the BSC financial perspective contains the variables as itemized in Table 6.

- Out of five core measures of the Customer Perspective (Kaplan and Norton, 1996, p.68, 306), namely, Market Share, Customer Acquisition, Customer Retention, Customer Satisfaction and Customer Profitability, only Customer Satisfaction is likely to be practically measurable in the context of company IT standard usage. The other measures are too much diluted by other effects next to the use of IT standards. Furthermore satisfaction of staff and internal customers seems to be relevant only given the research scope. When standards are being used, changes in *client satisfaction* could be observed. David (1995) argues that standardization can bring efficiency gains only at the cost of suppressing some sources of consumer/client satisfaction. However, Shafer and Byrd (2000) argue that IT usage in general leads to improved **customer**/client satisfaction. Improvements in client satisfaction due to IT investments were also identified by Hitt and Brynjolfsson (1996). In addition, Kayworth and Sambamurthy (2000) showed that the *perceived complexity* of standards plays an important role in the effectiveness of standards because complicated standards are less likely to be adopted easily. These variables, that operationalize this construct, are listed in Table 7.

Table 7. Variables of the construct 'Process Performance', customer perspective

Variable	Rationale for being an operational referent
Customer satisfaction	The application of standards could impact on the working practices of customers/clients so the *level of customer/client satisfaction with the standard* is considered as an operational measure.
Perceived complexity	Effectiveness of standard is subject to the *perceived complexity of the standard by customers* that use the standard and is considered as an operational measure of this construct.

- A third perspective on business process performance is the **internal** one. For organizations to become more responsive to changes in the market place, Boynton (1993) argues that information systems should deliver management information efficiently and effectively. *On-time service delivery* and minimal *throughput time* of service requests are key to be successful in the market. *Error and rework rates* are supposed to be dropping when a company starts to use IT standards. One of the advantages of using standards found in literature were decreased inefficiencies due to trial and error processes. Robertson (2001) also identified a reduction of manual error when using an IT standard.

Another positive effect identified is the reduction of *time to develop* when using standards (Weill and Broadbent, 1998; De Vries, 1999; Nybo, 2002). Weill and Broadbent consider this as a general effect of IT investments whereas De Vries argues that the use of standards contributes to efficiency; one doesn't have to develop standards oneself and can employ the existing standards immediately. Nybo described that financial institutions spent over 70% of their software development effort on building and maintaining system interfaces in 1999. A same line of reasoning can be taken for *time to support,* which was also listed by Weill and Broadbent (1998). Next, Besen and Saloner (1994) pointed out that lack of standardization in electronic interconnectivity has negative influences on several strategic initiatives to improve services.

Risk is also affected by the usage of standards. David and Greenstein (1990) argue that the usage of standards reduces risks whereas Arnold (1994) elaborates on the risks of using de facto and consensus standards. Akkermans and Van der Horst (2002) argue that a lot of regulatory standards are enforced by law and are created to achieve risk reduction and interoperability.

As discussed earlier, one of the general aims of using standards is to achieve time-savings, hence *Time to market* is expected to decrease. Nybo (2002), for example, noticed that integrating an API is time consuming and requires significant lead-time to test and deploy whereas using a standard interface this can be done far more rapidly. Also from a flexibility point of view, 'time' (speed and response) is an important element (Evans, 1991; Avison et al., 1995; Goldon and Powell, 2000). Weill and Broadbent (1998) also consider 'Time to market' as another important indicator on the impact of IT investments in general. The same is true for product or *Service quality*.

So for the BSC internal perspective the variables in Table 8 will be included in the conceptual model, which are located in all but the top level of Weill and Broadbent's hierarchical scheme (see Chapter 3, Figure 2).

- The fourth perspective on business performance is the **Learning & Growth** one. Weill and Broadbent (1998) suggest infrastructure *availability*[10] as an important indicator on the impact of IT investments in general. It is hypothesized that this will also be true for investment in IT

Table 8. Variables of the construct 'Process Performance', internal perspective

Variable	Rationale for being an operational referent
On-time service delivery	Due to the application of standards, efficiency gains are expected so the *% of on-time service delivery* is expected to increase and is considered as an operational measure.
Throughput time requests	Due to the application of standards, efficiency gains are expected so the *throughput time of service delivery requests* is expected to increase and is considered as an operational measure.
Error and rework rates	Due to the application of standards, more effective and efficient processes are anticipated, so the *error and rework* are considered as an operational measure.
Time to develop	Due to the application of standards, efficiency increases in IT development are expected, therefore, the *time to develop new services/products* is considered as an operational measure.
Time to support	Due to the application of standards, efficiency increases in IT support are expected, therefore the *time to support the IT infrastructure* is considered as an operational measure.
Risk	Due to the application of standards, maintenance is expected to be carried out easier resulting in a lower risk exposure / improved risk profile, so the *level of risk* is considered as an operational measure.
Time to market	Due to the application of standards, efficiency increases in IT development and support are expected, therefore the *time to market to develop new services/products* is considered as an operational measure.
Service Quality	Due to the application of standards, overall IT service quality is expected to increase (e.g. information integrity) so *service* is considered as an operational measure.

standards. The case studies to be carried out later on are to verify this claim. Interoperability is another important effect of using standards that have been recognized by many authors. Bonino and Spring (1991) and Akkermans and Van der Horst (2002) acknowledged that standards facilitate interoperability since they allow effective communication at both the organization and IT level. De Vries (1999) and Wolters (2002) argue that clearly defined and separable interfaces are required to make modules interoperable. The three hierarchies on *compatibility* (interconnection, interchangeability, interoperability) by Stegwee and Rukanova (2003), who addressed this topic in a more general sense (see Chapter 2, Table12), were very useful in this matter.

From a flexibility perspective, several authors address the importance of reusability of standards. Boynton and Victor (1991) and Boynton (1993) argue that information-processing capabilities must be more reusable and modular, to make possible anticipation of frequent, rapid unpredictable change in the competitive environment. Duncan (1995) identified three aspects, compatibility, connectivity/interconnection and *modularity* which play an important role in the effective application of standards and she argues that the degree to which resources are sharable and reusable determines the flexibility of IT infrastructures.

Robustness, *scalability* and *adaptability* are other important aspects of (Evans, 1991) and these may be facilitated by standards. In this same section Goldin and Powell (2000) identified robustness as well. Boynton and Victor (1991) also identified scalability as the capacity to quickly reconfigure in order to produce related products and adaptability as the capacity to adapt to changing and often uncertain product demand. Similarly, Nybo (2002) addressed adaptability, related to proprietary APIs that can quickly be modified to adapt to changing needs.

Staff motivation could be affected by the usage of IT standards. Kayworth and Sambamurthy (2000) stated that aversion against standardization may manifest itself in e.g. job estrangement and feelings of incapacity to be motivated for one's tasks. Kayworth and Sambamurthy (2000) remarked that aversion to standardization might demonstrate itself in feelings of incapacity to *innovative*. In addition, Brunsson and Jacobson (2000) argued that standardization is often seen as an unwelcome, unnecessary and harmful intrusion because it may hinder innovation.

Given this assessment of both literature study (Chapter 2 and 3) and the pilot case study the following variables will be considered in the conceptual model:

Given the discussion on construct validity, the conclusion is that the four constructs of the conceptual model are formative in nature. Since the causality and validation criteria for formative constructs were met, the conclusion is also that the constructs and its variables are sufficiently specified and validated.

FIRST ASSESSMENT AND FURTHER RESEARCH OUTLINE

Assessment of the Pilot Case Study

The added value of the pilot case study is derived from the fact that both constructs and relationships found in this study were confirmed by literature. This is an indication that the initial conceptual model can be used meaningfully in the subsequent case study research. The assessment of the propositions of the initial conceptual model, based on the pilot case study, shows the following.

Table 9. Variables of the construct 'Process Performance', learning & growth perspective

Variable	Rationale for being a operational referent
Availability	Because of the standardized infrastructure a less complex environment is expected to emerge, positively impacting *the availability of the service/product*. Therefore this figure is considered as an operational measure.
Compatibility	Because of the usage of a standardized infrastructure the interconnection, interchangeability, or interoperability of IT components is expected to increase, positively impacting the *level of compatibility of the service/product with other services/products*. Therefore this figure is considered as an operational measure.
Modularity	The *level of modularity of the infrastructure* is chosen as an operational measure because it plays an important role in the effective application of standards and it is supposed to reflect the learning /growth of the organization in relation to the usage of its standardized infrastructure.
Robustness	Because of the standardization, the *level of robustness of the infrastructure* is expected to increase because there are fewer errors and faults expected during changes and interdependencies between infrastructure components are easier to maintain. So this figure is considered as an operational measure for this construct.
Scalability	Because of the standardization, uniform configurations are applied and the *level of scalability of the infrastructure* is expected to increase, so this figure is considered as an operational measure for this construct.
Adaptability	Because of the standardization, changes can be carried out more easily and the *level of adaptability of the infrastructure* is expected to increase, so this figure is considered as an operational measure for this construct.
Staff motivation	Standards could impact on the working practices of staff, so *level of staff motivation in applying the standard* is considered as an operational measure.
Innovativeness	Standards could impact on the way staff operates, so *the level of innovativeness of delivered IT products or services* is considered as an operational measure

- **Proposition 1:** *An effective (ineffective) IT standard selection positively (negatively) influences the application of these standards* - In the pilot case study it was described that selection of standards should be based, among other things, on business requirements. The EITAF architecture methodology can be regarded as an IT process standard. The buy-in and subsequent cooperation from the business side was only marginal. This is exemplified by the fact the standard was not of a mandatory nature. As a consequence most of the (S)BUs did not apply the architecture method nor other deliverables like CDB route-maps and C-BUS, therefore, the effectiveness of the selection is considered low. Proposition 1 tentatively holds.
- **Proposition 2:** *The application of appropriate IT Standards contributes to better business process performance and this performance is dependent on the control of its usage* - The pilot case study was primarily focussed on the standard selection and maintenance processes and not on assessing business process performance following a company standards' usage. We have seen, however, that since the EITAF standard had no mandatory nature (which is one of the control aspects as identified by Kayworth and Sambamurthy (2000)) its usage had a negative impact, so the moderating element in this proposition has been shown to exist and Proposition 2 tentatively holds.
- **Proposition 3:** *A low business process performance due to the applied IT standards leads to changes in the way these standards are controlled* - The pilot case study focussed on the selection and maintenance processes of standards and not on assessing business process performance, although no changes in control at Corporate IT level were observed. Then again, it was also found that individual IT departments could practically ignore the corporate IT standards, as these were not effectively enforced, and some were even setting up control processes for IT standards themselves. Whether this was a result of lower business process performance or motivated by other factors, such as company politics, remains uncertain. Proposition 3 remains undetermined.
- **Proposition 4:** *A low business process performance due to the applied IT standards leads to reselection of these standards* - Again, the pilot case study focussed on the selection and maintenance processes of standards. Nevertheless, as part of the maintenance process a bi-annual review on the usefulness of corporate IT standards was identified in the pilot case study. Furthermore, we have seen that some SBUs selected separate IT standards altogether. One of the reasons was that executives thought these corporate standards were not good enough to ensure superior business performance. But since no business process performance measures were taken to check this claim, Proposition 4 remains undetermined.

Variables

The formative constructs and its variables identified in both literature study and pilot case study are specified in Table 10 (e.g. for rating purposes as part of the case study protocol or design of hypothesis). Table 10 has four columns. The first column lists the four constructs of the conceptual model. The second column shows each variable that has been introduced in the previous sections. For each variable the type of scale[11] is provided: Nominal, Ordinal, Interval or Ratio. In addition, the variables of the construct 'Process Performance' are expressed in terms of the Balanced Scorecard perspectives as identified by Kaplan and Norton (1996) and a specification is given of its location in Weill and Broadbent's hierarchical scheme (Chapter 3, Figure 2). The fourth column provides some examples that relate to the variables. Numeric values of the variables will be determined as much as possible in the semi structured interview sessions during the fieldwork of the case study research.

Subsequent Research Outline

In this chapter a pilot case study was described and the construction of a conceptual model with its propositions and relationships was discussed (i.e. theory development). In the next chapters, case study research into standardization projects, performed at several Business Units of FINCORP, will be described and analyzed (i.e. theory testing). These in-depth case studies have been carried out using this initial conceptual model with the goal to test this theory and possibly amend this conceptual model (i.e. theory refinement). The following three chapters (see Figure 4) will provide details of these in-depth case studies.

The rich analysis of three case studies is described in Chapters 5 to 7 and deals with:

Chapter 5 Client/Server Standardization (Retail Bank Division)
Chapter 6 Software Development Standardization (Retail Bank Division)
Chapter 7 HR Product & Process Standardization (Services Unit)

Table 10. Constructs and variables of the initial conceptual model

Construct	Variable	Scale	Example
Process of Standard Selection	Business model consideration	Ordinal	SBU structure
	Business driver consideration	Ordinal	Increase time to market; cost cutting
	Business involvement	Ordinal	
	IT engineering involvement	Ordinal	
	IT operations involvement	Ordinal	
	B-IT alignment	Ordinal	Business and IT understanding, openness, information exchange on standards
	Management knowledge	Ordinal	Business and IT understanding of standards
Application of Standard	Reach	Ordinal	From a single department to the whole enterprise
	Range	Ordinal	A single standards or a whole set of standards
	IT expertise	Ordinal	Local IT (of Business Unit) knowledge on standards
	Awareness	Ordinal	Consciousness at Business and IT on standards
	IT project management	Ordinal	Quality of project deliverables
Control of Standard	Prescription	Ordinal	Nature of compliance, mandatory / prescribed or just advised / recommended
	Enforcing	Ordinal	Level of obligation to comply with these standards (i.c. implementation and usage)
	Restrictiveness	Ordinal	Vendor choice
	Deviations	Ordinal	Level c.q. quality of standards exception process
	Endorsement	Ordinal	Level of management commitment
	Collaboration	Ordinal	Corporate IS/Business Unit partnership
	Maturity	Ordinal	Organizational maturity level
	Centralization	Ordinal	Level of Business Unit autonomy
	Processes	Ordinal	Implementation process and procedures for IT standards; IT project management

continued on following page

Table 10. continued

Construct	Variable	Scale	Example
Process Performance	*BSC Financial Perspective*		*Note: Numbers refer to the 4 levels inFigure 2, Chapter3*
	Cost to develop IT	Ratio	2 - Project costs to implement IT standard - Transition costs (e.g. Depreciation of old technology; Setting up standardization process/governance; Building into processes i.c. standards); Development; Implementation; Education and Training
	Costs to support IT	Ratio	1 - Costs per work station 2 - System and Service Management: Upgrades (easier); Monitoring standardization within enterprise; Standardization web site; Training (End users; Technical staff); Others (e.g. Single tooling; Licenses; Support contracts).
	Economic value-added	Ratio	4
	ROI	Ratio	4
	BSC Customer Perspective		
	Client satisfaction	Ordinal	3 - Using standardized environment
	Perceived complexity	Ordinal	3 - Ease of usage
	BSC Internal Perspective		
	On-time service delivery	Ratio	1 - Percentage of requests resolved as agreed
	Throughput time requests	Ratio	1 - Resolve time of service requests
	Error and rework rates	Ratio	1 - Maintenance time of environment
	Time to develop	Ratio	2 - New applications
	Time to support	Ratio	2 - Effort to process total number of service requests
	Risk	Ordinal	3 - Lower operational risks
	Time to market	Ratio	3
	Service Quality	Ordinal	3 - data consistency
	BSC Leaning & Growth Perspective		
	Availability	Ratio	1 - Higher IT service availability
	Compatibility	Ordinal	2 - Level of interconnection, interchangeability, interoperability
	Modularity	Ordinal	2- Level of reusability; unsharable
	Robustness	Ordinal	2- Level of fault tolerance; Yielding to pressure
	Scalability	Ordinal	2 - Level of expandability; Capacity for new situation
	Adaptability	Ordinal	2 - Level of portability; Susceptibility of modification
	Staff motivation	Ordinal	3 - Of IT staff and end-users
	Innovativeness	Ordinal	3 - Faster implementation of new products; Number of new services introduced

Figure 4. Subsequent research outline (see also Chapter 1, Figure 3)

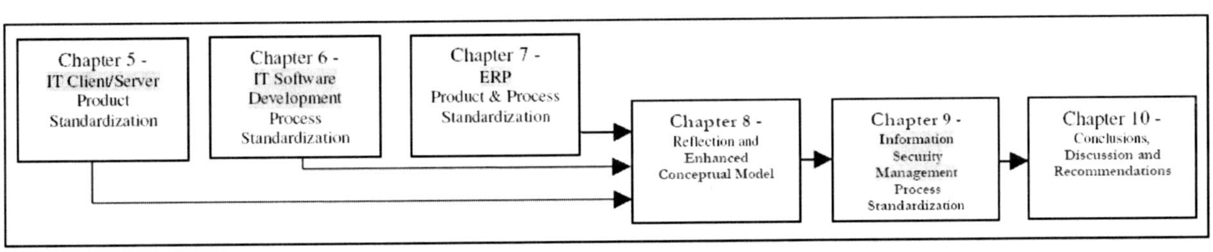

Of course this raises the questions *why three case studies?*, and *why these specific ones?* As the number of case studies is to a certain extent arbitrary, and has nothing to do with the need for enough statistical samples, one could also argue "just two" or "at least five". The primary reason to undertake a number of case studies is to enable replication logic as part of analytic generalization (Yin, 1994)). These specific ones have been chosen because the cases deal with process or product company standardization in the IT domain. The cases differed in a number of ways including: the type of standard; the reach and range of the standard, the level of Business involvement; the level of endorsement of the standard. There were also a number of similarities including: the case studies were carried out at in the same company, the prescription level of the standard, the drivers of standardization.

The case studies results and cross case analysis allows theory refinement in this research area. Accessibility of quality data and staff availability for the interviews also contributed to this specific choice. As far as internal & external validity and reliability is concerned the following holds for all case studies:

- Internal validity is relevant to explanatory or causal studies, not to descriptive or exploratory ones.

As the forthcoming case studies are explanatory in nature, validity was guaranteed by explanation building i.e. by establishing causal relationships (pattern matching and explanation building).

- External validity, to establish the domain into which a study's findings can be generalized, relates to theoretical replication (two disparate cases) and literal replication (two similar cases).

This research will be based on this replication logic by executing multiple-case studies, which will improve the external validity. In Chapters 5 to 7 the initial conceptual model will be tested whereas in Chapter 9 the extended conceptual model, that is based in the insights gained from these three case studies, will be tested also.

- Reliability for all forthcoming case studies is guaranteed by making use of a case study protocol (e.g. the data gathering procedures and tooling) and a case study database.

In addition several semi-structured and unstructured interviews were carried out and the interviewees approved the transcriptions.

The insights gained from these case studies enabled a further detailing of this initial model which is discussed in Chapter 8 "A reflection upon the case studies". A fourth in-depth case study was carried out which is described in Chapter 9 "Information Security Management". This deals with the application of an Information Security Management standard at the Investment Bank Division of the case company. Finally the concluding Chapter 10 "Conclusions" contains the findings and outlines future directions for research.

REFERENCES

Akkermans, H. A., & Van der Horst, H. (2002). Managing IT infrastructure standardisation in the networked manufacturing firm. *International Journal of Production Economics*, *75*(1-2), 213–228. doi:10.1016/S0925-5273(01)00201-8

Arnold, D. (1994). Conformance testing ICT Standards: Costly chore or valuable insurance? *StandardView*, *2*(4), 182–187. doi:10.1145/223282.223283

Avison, D. E., Powell, P. L., Keen, J., Klein, J. H., & Ward, S. (1995). Addressing the need for flexibility in information systems. *J Mgmt Syst*, *7*(2), 43–60.

Bacharach, S. B. (1989). Organizational Theories: Some Criteria for evaluation. *Academy of Management Review*, *14*(4), 496–515. doi:10.2307/258555

Bagozzi, R. P., & Fornell, C. (1982). Theoretical Concepts, Measurement, and Meaning. In Fornell, C. (Ed.), *A Second Generation of Multivariate Analysis* (2nd ed., pp. 24–38). New York: Praeger.

Besen, S. M., & Saloner, G. (1994). Compatibility standards and market for telecommunications services. In Allen, T. J., & Scott Morton, M. S. (Eds.), *Information technology and the corporation of the 1990s: research studies*. New York: Oxford University Press.

Bollen, K. A., & Lennox, R. (1991). Conventional Wisdom on Measurement: A Structural Equation Perspective. *Psychological Bulletin*, *110*, 305–314. doi:10.1037/0033-2909.110.2.305

Bonino, M. J., & Spring, M. B. (1991). Standards as change agents in the information technology market. *Computer Standards & Interfaces*, *12*, 97–107. doi:10.1016/0920-5489(91)90059-9

Boudreau, M.-C., Geffen, D., & Straub, D. W. (2001). Validation in Information Systems Research: A State-of-the-Art Assessment. *Management Information Systems Quarterly*, *25*(1), 1–26. doi:10.2307/3250956

Boynton, A. C. (1993). Achieving dynamic stability through information technology. *California Management Review*, *35*(2), 58–77.

Boynton, A. C., & Victor, B. (1991). Beyond flexibility: building and managing the dynamically stable organization. *California Management Review*, *34*(1), 53–66.

Boynton, A. C., Zmud, R. W., & Jacobs, G. C. (1994). The influence of IT management practice on IT use in large organizations. *Management Information Systems Quarterly*, *18*(3), 299–318. doi:10.2307/249620

Brunsson, N., & Jacobson, B. (2000). *A World of standards*. New York: Oxford University Press Inc.

Cargill, C. F. (1989). *Information Technology Standardization: Theory, Process, and Organizations*. Bedford, MA: Digital Press.

Cargill, C. F. (1995). A five-segment model of standardization. In Kahin, B., & Abbate, J. (Eds.), *Standards Policy for Information Infrastructure*. Cambridge, MA: MIT Press.

Chand, D., Hachey, G., Hunton, J., Owhoso, V., & Vasudevan, S. (2005). A balanced scorecard based framework for assessing the strategic impacts of ERP systems. *Computers in Industry*, *56*, 558–572. doi:10.1016/j.compind.2005.02.011

David, P. A. (1995). Standardization policies for network technologies: the flux between freedom and order revisited. In Hawkins, R., Mansell, R., & Skea, J. (Eds.), *Standards, Innovation and Competitiveness. The politics and economics of standards in Natural and Technical Environments*. Aldershot, UK: Edward Elgar Publishing Limited.

David, P. A., & Greenstein, S. (1990). The Economics of compatibility standards: An introduction to recent research. *Economics of Innovation and New Technology, 1*, 3–41. doi:10.1080/10438599000000002

Davis, F. D. (1989). Perceived usefulness, perceived ease of use, and user acceptance of information technology. *Management Information Systems Quarterly, 13*, 319–340. doi:10.2307/249008

de Vries, H. J. (1999). *Standardization: A Business Approach to the Role of National Standardization Organizations*. Boston, MA: Kluwer Academic Publishers.

Diamantopoulos, A., & Winklhofer, H. M. (2001). Index construction with formative indicators: An alternative to scale development. *JMR, Journal of Marketing Research, 38*(2), 269–277. doi:10.1509/jmkr.38.2.269.18845

Duncan, N. B. (1995). Capturing flexibility of Information Technology Infrastructure: A study of Resource Characteristics and their Measure. *Journal of Management Information Systems, 12*(2), 37–57.

Eickelmann, N. (2001). Integrating the Balanced Scorecard and Software Measurement Frameworks. In van Grembergen, W. (Ed.), *Information Technology Evaluation Methods and Management* (pp. 240–252). Hershey, PA: Idea Group Publishing.

Evans, J. S. (1991). Strategic flexibility for high technology maneuvers: a conceptual framework. *Journal of Management Studies, 28*(1), 69–89. doi:10.1111/j.1467-6486.1991.tb00271.x

Fomin, V., & Keil, T. (2000). Standardization: Bridging the gap between economic and social theory, International Conference on Information systems (ICIS). In *Proceedings of the 21st International Conference on Information Systems, Brisbane* (pp. 206-217).

Friel, C. M. (2003). *From Theory to Hypothesis- Variables and Hypothesis Testing*. Lecture Handouts, College of Criminal Justice, Sam Houston State University.

Gold, C. (1992). *Total quality management in information services - IS measures: a balancing act*. Research Note Ernst & Young Center for Information Technology and Strategy, Boston, MA.

Golden, W., & Powell, P. (2000). Towards a definition of flexibility: in search of the Holy Grail? *Omega, 28*, 373–384. doi:10.1016/S0305-0483(99)00057-2

Hanseth, O., & Braa, K. (2001). Hunting for the treasure at the end of the Rainbow: Standardizing Corporate IT Infrastructure. *Computer Supported Cooperative Work, 10*, 261–292. doi:10.1023/A:1012637309336

Hasan, H., & Tibbits, H. (2000). Strategic Management of Electronic Commerce: An Adaptation of the Balanced Scorecard. *Internet Research, 10*(5), 439–450. doi:10.1108/10662240010349453

Hatten, K.J., Rosenthal, S.R. (2001). Why-and How- to systematize performance measurement, *Journal of Organizational Excellence*, Autumn, 2001, 59-73.

Hitt, L. M., & Brynjolfsson, E. (1996). Productivity, Business Profitability, and Consumer Surplus: Three Different Measures of Information Technology Value. *Management Information Systems Quarterly, 20*(2). doi:10.2307/249475

Hu, Q., & Huang, C. D. (2005). Aligning IT with Firm Business Strategies Using the Balance Scorecard System. In *Proceedings of the 38th Hawaii International Conference on System Sciences.*

Jakobs, K., Procter, R., & Williams, R. (1996). Users and Standardization - Worlds Apart? The Example of Electronic Mail. *StandardView, 4*(4), 183–191. doi:10.1145/243492.243495

Jarvis, C. B., MacKenzie, S. B., & Podsakoff, P. M. (2003). A critical review of construct indicators and measurement model misspecification in marketing and consumer research. *The Journal of Consumer Research, 30*(2), 199–218. doi:10.1086/376806

Kaplan, R. S., & Norton, D. P. (1992). The Balanced Scorecard - Measures that Drive Performance. *Harvard Business Review, 70*(1), 71–79.

Kaplan, R. S., & Norton, D. P. (1996). *The Balanced Scorecard: Translating Strategy into Action.* Boston, MA: Harvard Business School Press.

Kayworth, T., & Sambamurthy, V. (2000). Facilitating localized exploitation and enterprise-wide integration in the use of IT infrastructures: The role of PC/LAN infrastructure standard. *The Data Base for Advances in Information Systems, 31*(4), 54–81.

Keen, P. G. W. (1991). *Shaping the Future: Business Design through Information Technology.* Boston, MA: Harvard Business School Press.

Law, K. S., & Wong, C. S. (1999). Multidimensional Constructs in Structural Equation Analysis: An Illustration Using the Job Perception and Job Satisfaction Constructs. *Journal of Management, 25*(2), 143–160. doi:10.1016/S0149-2063(99)80007-5

Loch, K., Straub, D., & Kamel, S. (2003). Diffusing the Internet in the Arab World: The Role of Social Norms and Technological Culturation. *IEEE Transactions on Engineering Management, 50*(1), 45–63. doi:10.1109/TEM.2002.808257

MacKenzie, S. B. (2003). The dangers of poor construct conceptualization. *Academy of Marketing Science Journal, 31*, 323–326. doi:10.1177/0092070303031003011

Mähönen, P. (2000). The Standardization Process in IT - Too Slow or Too Fast? In Jakobs, K. (Ed.), *Information Technology Standards and Standardization: A Global Perspective* (pp. 35–47). Hershey, PA: Idea Group Publishing.

Maltz, A. C., Shenhar, A. J., & Reilly, R. R. (2003). Beyond the balanced scorecard: refining the search for organizational success measures. *Long Range Planning, 36*, 197–204. doi:10.1016/S0024-6301(02)00165-6

Martinsons, M., Davison, R., & Tse, D. (1999). The balanced scorecard: a foundation for strategic management of information systems. *Decision Support Systems, 25*(1), 71–88. doi:10.1016/S0167-9236(98)00086-4

Melville, N., Kraemer, K., & Gurbaxani, V. (2004). Information Technology and Organizational Performance: Integrative Model Of IT Business Value. *Management Information Systems Quarterly, 28*(2), 283–332.

Milis, K., & Mercken, R. (2004). The use of the balanced scorecard for the evaluation of Information and Communication Technology projects. *International Journal of Project Management, 22*, 87–97. doi:10.1016/S0263-7863(03)00060-7

Monteiro, E., & Hanseth, O. (1999). Developing corporate infrastructure: implications for international standardization? In K. Jakobs & R. Williams (Eds.), *1st IEEE Conference on Standardization and Innovation in Information Technology, Aachen, Germany, Sept. 15- 17*. IEEE Press.

Naemura, K. (1995). User involvement in the life cycles of information technology (IT) and telecommunication standards. In Hawkins, R., Mansell, R., & Skea, J. (Eds.), *Standards, Innovation and Competitiveness. The politics and economics of standards in Natural and Technical Environments*. Aldershot, UK: Edward Elgar Publishing Limited.

Nybo, A. (2002). *A fixed-income protocol: too late or too early?* TowerGroup, Needham MA, USA, research paper 030:03S.

Papalexandris, A., Ioannou, G., Prastacos, G., & Soderquist, K. E. (2005). An Integrated Methodology for Putting the Balanced Scorecard into Action. *European Management Journal, 23*(2), 214–227. doi:10.1016/j.emj.2005.02.004

Poppel, H., & Goldstein, B. (1987). *Information Technology: The Trillion-Dollar Opportunity* (p. 6). New York: McGraw-Hill.

Rada, R., & Craparo, J. S. (2001). Standardizing Management of Software Engineering Projects, *Knowledge, Technology, &. Policy, 14*(2), 67–77.

Rai, A., Patnayakuni, R., & Patnayakuni, N. (2006). Firm Performance Impacts of Digitally-Enabled Supply Chain Integration capabilities. *Management Information Systems Quarterly, 30*(2), 225–246.

Robert, T. L. Jr, Gibson, M. L., Fields, K. T., & Rainer, K. Jr. (1998). Factors that impact implementing a system development methodology. *IEEE Transactions on Software Engineering, 24*(8), 640–649. doi:10.1109/32.707699

Robertson, E. (2001). *OFX and IFX: The Standards Challenge*. TowerGroup, Needham MA, USA, research paper 028:61N.

Rosemann, M., & Wiese, J. (1999). Measuring the performance of ERP software—a balanced scorecard approach. In *Proceedings of the 10th Australasian Conference on Information Systems, Wellington* (pp. 773–784).

Ross, J. W. (2003). Strategic IT architecture competency. *MIS Quarterly Executive, 2*(1), 31–43.

Rutkowski, A. M. (1995). Today's Cooperative Standards Environment and the Internet Standards-Making Model. In Kahn, B., & Abbate, J. (Eds.), *Standards Policy for Information Infrastructure*. Cambridge, MA: MIT Press.

Shafer, S. M., & Byrd, T. A. (2000). A framework for measuring the efficiency of organizational investments in information technology using data envelopment analysis. *Omega*, *28*, 125–141. doi:10.1016/S0305-0483(99)00039-0

Spivak, S. M., & Brenner, F. C. (2001). *Standardization Essentials. Principles and Practice*. New York: Marcel Dekker Inc.

Stegwee, R. A., & Rukanova, B. D. (2003). Standard Making: A Critical Research Frontier for Information Systems. *MISQ Special Issue Workshop Standard Making: A Critical Research Frontier for Information Systems. Pre-Conference Workshop, International Conference on Information Systems, December 12-14, 2003, Seattle, Washington* (pp. 161-170).

Straub, D., Boudreau, M.-C., & Geffen, D. (2004). Validation Guidelines of IS Positivist Research. *Communications of the AIS*, *13*(24), 380–427.

van Grembergen, W., & Saull, R. (2001). Aligning Business and Information Technology through the Balanced Scorecard at a Major Canadian Financial Group: its Status Measured with an IT BSC Maturity Model. In *Proceedings of the 34th Hawaii International Conference on System Sciences*.

van Grembergen, W., & van Bruggen, R. (1997). Measuring and improving corporate information technology through the balanced scorecard technique. In *Proceedings of the Fourth European Conference on the Evaluation of Information technology, Delft, October 1997* (pp. 163-171).

Vlaar, P. W. L. (2006). *Making Sense of Formalization in Interorganizational Relationships: Beyond Coordination and Control*. Doctoral Dissertation, ERIM Ph.D. Series Research in Management 75, Erasmus University Rotterdam, The Netherlands.

Wakid, S., & Radack, S. (1997). Measurement Based Standards for future Information Technology Systems. *StandardView*, *5*(1), 36–40. doi:10.1145/253452.253479

Weill, P., & Broadbent, M. (1998). *Leveraging the new Infrastructure. How Market Leaders Capitalize on Information Technology*. Boston, MA: Harvard Business School Press.

Weill, P., & Ross, J. (2004). *IT Governance - How Top Performers Manage IT Decision Rights for Superior Results*. Boston, MA: Harvard Business School Press.

Willcocks, L. (1995). *Information management. The evaluation of information systems investments*. London: Chapman & Hall.

Wolters, M. J. J. (2002). *The Business of Modularity and the Modularity of Business*. Doctoral Dissertation Erasmus University Rotterdam, ERIM Ph.D. Series in Management 11, The Netherlands TRAIL Research School.

Yin, R. K. (1994). *Case Study research, Design and Methods* (2nd ed.). Thousand Oaks, CA: Sage Publications Inc.

Young, H. P. (1996). The Economics of Convention. *The Journal of Economic Perspectives*, *10*(2), 105–122.

ENDNOTES

1. One of the interviewees, however, elaborates that in practice this did not work out as anticipated by the corporate standardization organization.
2. This criterion may reinforce lock-in.
3. The functionality of C-Bus includes several middleware type services like messages exchange, file transfer, publish & subscribe and brokers and APIs for applications and services (C, C++, COBOL, JAVA). Transport should be middleware independent but is initially based on IBM-MQ series. In the future this would include others like TIB, EJB and CORBA.
4. ranges from IT infrastructure (products). to data entities and processes.
5. Proposition 1 is not self-evident. An example of application of standards that resulted in complete disaster was the Mars Explorer mission of NASA in 1999. In the application phase it turned out that metric and imperial measurement standards were mixed up, in spite of earlier effective selection of measurement systems by the respective teams. See e.g. Standards and Crashing on Mars: http://weblog.ipcentral.info/archives/2006/01/standards_and_c.html (Retrieved on 2007-07-25)
6. Dropping an indicator would be similar to dropping a part of the construct (Bollen and Lennox, 1991) and should not be done once an indicator is verified as part of a construct.
7. Due to the direction of causality with formative models, high correlation between the indicators is not expected, neither required, nor a cause for concern.
8. This will be subdivided into IT engineering and IT operations given the organizational structure of the case company.
9. The concepts of 'Reach and Range', introduced by Keen (1991) originally describe the business scope of a companies IT infrastructure. Reach refers to the locations the infrastructure is capable of connecting, whereas Range refers to functionality in terms of business activities that can be seamlessly shared across each level of Range.
10. Availability is considered in the fourth perspective because usage of standards could improve IS availability and this is considered as learning & growth by the organization in question (Kaplan and Norton, 1996, p.44).
11. Nominal: no ordering, e.g. arbitrary labels; Ordinal: ordered, no constant scale as differences between values expresses an order, not a difference, e.g. a Likert scale of 1..5 reflecting your degree of satisfaction; Interval: ordered, constant scale, but no natural zero, e.g., dates; Ratio: ordered, constant scale, natural zero, e.g. length or age.

Section 4
Three In-Depth Case Studies

As part of in depth case study research, in this section multiple case studies will be carried out, with the intention to gain experience with the initial conceptual model and to make generalization possible, as part of the theory testing phase.

The first case study is about product standardization of both back-end and front-end of a desktop environment. We will check what the main objectives were and how the case company accomplished the intended business benefits. The second case study is about process standardization within a software development department. We will investigate how this process standard was chosen and implemented and what its effects were on business performance. The third in-depth case study relates to an IS product standardization, the ERP HR modules of PeopleSoft, which include the accompanying HR processes. This initiative included company-wide standardization of data (both syntax and semantics) which is known to be very difficult to accomplish.

Chapter 5
Client/Server Standardization "Uniform Case"

INTRODUCTION

It is often said that the use of standards in IT saves money. An example is given by Nash (2001) which shows that annual end-user support at a company using a standardized IT environment costs $5400 per workstation, compared with $7400 at a company that uses a mix of technologies. As part of in depth case study research, this type of observations will be further substantiated. Multiple case studies will be carried out, enabling both literal and theoretical replications. The first one is about product standardization of both back-end and front-end of a desktop environment.

As described in Chapter 2, Ross (2003) argued that in the 'standardized technology architecture stage', with lead-times that range from 2 to 6 years, IT resources are put in a shared infrastructure allowing cost savings by e.g. significant reduction in the number of vendor packages that offer similar functionalities. This also increases IT maintainability, reliability and security.

CASE DESCRIPTION

At the head office of FINCORP the IT environment consisted of a plethora of different hardware and software products. Managing this environment was difficult; it involved high support costs and long

DOI: 10.4018/978-1-61520-759-6.ch005

resolution times. Because of the lack of standardization, upgrades were difficult to implement. Therefore, a two-year IT standardization project was carried out affecting 10,000 end-users of one of the company's Business Units. The scope of the project, which included *de facto* standards of hardware and software at both the front and back ends of the Business Unit, ranged from desktop productivity tools to applications for complex financial transactions.

The main objectives of the standardization project were to reduce the total cost of ownership or TCO[2] with 18% (calculated against industry benchmarks) and to facilitate change flexibility. Cost reductions were needed especially in the fields of procurement and support, and they were expected to result in a decrease of the environment's complexity by reducing the variety at both the hardware and software levels. More specifically this entailed:

- Reduction of development costs;
- Reduction of support costs;
- Reduction of purchase and license costs;
- Easier SLA management;
- Increased efficiency of end-users.

With respect to flexibility the most important requirements were to make possible free seating, allowing staff to easily relocate from one workspace to another, and the seamless rollout of changes. Because of the standardized IT platform, migration to new technologies should become easier as well. In this section we will describe the project's implementation as well as its results in terms of efficiency and effectiveness of the company's IT delivery and support processes.

This case deals mainly with de facto Client/Server (C/S) standards that have both a wide reach and range. The reach of these standards is the complete Business Unit and some small sections of other departments that require applications in this environment. The range is all applications that are used within this Business Unit (from desktop productivity tools to applications for complex financial transactions).

Implementation and Usage

The IT products specified in the new set of IT standards were selected by the Business Unit involved and the company's IT engineering department, working in close cooperation. The Business Unit not only set the project's cost saving targets but also defined the future standard's functional requirements, which rendered the project business-oriented rather than technology-focused. A three-tier approach was followed to arrive at the new set of standards: hardware standardization, system software standardization, and application software standardization.

Hardware Standardization

In order to decrease complexity and facilitate the possibility of free seating (with the aim to ease staff accommodation) an environment was chosen that is known as server-based computing, terminal server remote desktop or as server-based thin client. This set-up minimized the dependencies between the system's hardware components and consisted of three main elements:

- thin clients (PCs set up with a minimum of local applications);

- web servers and terminal servers hosting the applications;
- back-end servers hosting the user data.

Thin clients are in essence the successors of devices that are known as 'dumb' terminals except for the fact that it supports graphics instead of a character based interface. Long before these thin clients, workstations connected to a mini computer were designed to be networked with a file and print server. When multi-tasking PC software appeared, the same concept was adopted at a lower cost.

The new environment consisted of 10,000 thin client workstations, 1,000 laptops, 1,000 terminal servers, a couple of web servers and 300 back-end servers. User and group data were stored on the terminal servers and replicated daily to the central storage facility. Laptops in this free seating environment were an interesting part from a cost point of view, as these numbers should be reduced significantly because of the virtual desktop concept within all the head office buildings (see later in this section).

System Software Standardization

The original desktop environment was hard to manage because it consisted of a large collection of locally installed applications on fat client desktops. Implementing changes could take as long as three to four months. Therefore, whenever technically possible, the new system software was not installed on desktops. End-users used browsers to access applications from their PCs. The browser-based applications were run on the web servers in a multi-application hosting environment on an S/390™ mainframe. To this end a product called WebSphere® was used; Java Virtual Machines was used to facilitate PC independence.

Applications without browser-based equivalent were installed on terminal servers running on Wintel, also using Websphere. No multi-application hosting was allowed on terminal servers to minimize the interdependencies between these logical nodes. The Web-servers took care of the applications that were truly web based and the web-browsers on the standard PC used Java Virtual Machines to provide PC independence. User and group data were stored on the local terminal servers and replicated daily to central storage.

Application Software Standardization

When work began on standardizing the IT environment, the Business Unit was asked what kind of functionalities it required (not which applications they wanted). The answer was a 300-page requirements document that would have involved staggering amounts of money. Of course, this was not the way forward so the IT department was asked how this could be rationalized. Theirs was the suggestion to script applications for browser-based access where technically possible and financially feasible, and to introduce terminal servers for applications that could not be ported. Only some legacy applications and office productivity tools like word processors and spreadsheets were installed locally on the PCs themselves, mostly for performance reasons. After inventorizing, the number of applications needed was reduced from more than six thousand to 265 – over twenty-two[1] times less!

This rationalization and standardization process was not easy. It required much effort, and it took time to convince all stakeholders of the added value. Cost reduction was always the most important argument. Interestingly, the biggest savings were achieved by the reduction of license fees: formerly several hundreds of licenses were paid for (some for very few or even no users at all), simply because no-one could keep track of all the software installed on thousands of locally run PCs. Therefore, the guiding principle in this project phase was that only one type of software was allowed - preferably the latest version - unless this would significantly degrade business functionality. The balance between functionality and support & license costs was the main criterion for listing applications as standard software. Such lists were drawn up for each department, subject to approval by their business managers. The following departments were in scope:

- Corporate Clients
- Corporate Sales
- Marketing
- Products
- Management and Secretaries' Offices
- Change Management
- HRM
- Finance
- Securities Operations
- Operations International Payments & Services
- Operation Risk Control & Services
- IT-Development
- IT-Services

All user data and available hardware were identified. The user data were copied to the new environment. Departments were standardization efforts were relatively easy were Secretaries' Offices and Change Management. Several subprojects were distinguished as listed in the following table:

Single sign on technology was used as much as possible to facility user authentication. New applications were as much as possible Web-browser based and existing ones were adapted, when technically possible. This should provide the opportunity to migrate from the WINTEL platform and would be

Table 1. Subprojects of C/S standardization

Subproject	Activity
Development	Migration of the remaining applications to the terminal server environment
	Setting up data storage via ESM
	Creating tools for testing and distribution
	Amending contingency plan, backup and recovery procedures
Implementation	Execution per Business Unit and department
	Within each building/domain dedicated terminal servers were installed
Support	Creating new services and SLA's
	Setting up governance structure
Organizational change	Migration and/or integration of IT departments
	Involvement of Workers Councils
Business assistance	Conscientious communication and supply of information
	Learning how to use the new environment

Table 2. The final set of IT Product from an end-user perspective

IT product	Example	Remarks
Desktops		Multi language MS Windows and Office 2000; Http browser; Adobe Acrobat reader; Winzip; Lotus Notes; Norton Anti Virus
Flatscreens	17" LCD	
Printers		Network printer, minimal staff: #10
Laptop		Non personalized, fully interchangeable
Work at home facilities	RAS	Via Internet/SSL and replaces most Laptops
Palmtops		
Scanners		
DVD / CD-ROM drives		
RSI-prevent tools	Special mouse	
Smartcard readers		Standard integrated with keyboard
Specials		Braille for poorly sighted

an excellent way to progress and yet provide continuity. The final set of IT products from an end-user perspective as part of the standardized IT environment, is presented in Table 2.

Several potential risks were identified in the implementation phase that could have caused the project to fail. These included organizational and HR risks, because the IT support organization had to be dismantled and its staff relocated to set up a new, centralized IT support department. Financial risks were taken because the estimates of operational revenues and expenditures were just that: estimates. And then there were some specific project risks that could have endangered its deliverables. The most important of these are listed in Table 3, with a reference to the constructs of the conceptual model (Chapter 4). This table includes countermeasures taken to prevent these risks from materializing.

Minimizing the total number of applications was a laborious and time-consuming effort and resistance was to be expected. Expected drawbacks from an end-user perspective were: 1) loss of some functionality; 2) effort of getting used to new applications. The reduction of the number of applications, which

Table 3. Project risks related to constructs of conceptual model

Risk	Possible Impact	Countermeasure	Construct
The Business Unit's management shows no commitment to the project.	Business Units do not commit to the new set of IT standards. The costs reductions and flexibility required are not achieved.	Maintain close contact between the Business Unit's managers and the company's general management, who must be actively involved.	Control of Standard
The reduction of the number of applications is not achieved.	Potential benefits of scale aren't fully exploited. More licenses and terminal servers are needed. Support remains costly and complex.	Continuously watch and enforce the maximum number of applications.	Process of Standard Selection
Organizational change is carried out too arduously.	IT staff morale deteriorates, which is reflected in lower service quality.	Pay special attention to staff involvement and open and honest communication.	Control of Standard

was a key element of the project, generally resulted in an uncooperative attitude of staff involved. Guidance of staff and the correct attitude of senior Business Unit's management were essential to realize the objectives of the standardization project. These two drawbacks were countered and solved by offering adequate software alternatives and education respectively.

In addition, because of the new IT infrastructure the support organization had to be restructured. Existing support staff morale was negatively affected by the necessary organizational changes. A new support organization was created with significantly less staff than before. In the new and centralized support organization special attention had to be paid to the security administration for which additional staff was recruited. The existing IT units were guided in the organizational change process and the business departments in the usage of the new environment.

A concession has been made on the amount of applications that still remained in service in the course of the project. In theory the final list of 265 applications could have been even smaller. However, internal company politics caused that some allegedly vital applications used by a few departments (Marketing; IT Development) remained on the list. It was decided that these applications were not put on terminal servers but remained installed locally on a few workstations. These applications are not supported by the newly created IT support organization. Another compromise was the total amount of laptops that were not reduced to a theoretical minimum. Practical circumstances, in this case the status of having such a device, resulted in a larger number of laptops that had to be supported than was anticipated when the project started. Finally it was decided by the project management to keep the roll out of laptops out of the scope of the project. Roll out was postponed until a new work at home facility via Internet became available, called 'RAS'. From that moment on it was easier to restrict the amount of laptops. Both these situations resulted in slightly smaller cost savings than could have been achieved theoretically.

Control

There are several ways in which new standards can be enforced once they have been implemented: the regulatory style, the laissez faire, or a combination of these two. Our FINCORP Business Unit adopted the first style, as was expressed in their maxim 'each and every desktop must have the same configuration'. Therefore, the way in which the set of standards was formalized and prescribed was very strict, as were the restrictions applied to any deviations. The standardized C/S environment was the exclusive ownership of the Business Unit and was supported by its IT department, which was also responsible for any changes and modifications to this standard.

In principle, end-users could choose from standard applications and hardware only. Basically, changes to the set of standards were relatively easy to make because of the C/S environment's modular structure. But anyone requesting functionality modifications would first have to try to realize these within the set of IT standard's possibilities. If that didn't work, those responsible would only be convinced to make structural changes on the basis of sound business rationale, which involved indicators such as added value, the number of users affected, the possibility of charging someone for it, and the total costs involved. Planning and controlling the standardized IT environment was the task of a number of key players with clear accountabilities (Table 4).

When a deviation request was granted, there were two options: either the requested product was adopted into the set of IT standards (the preferred option) or an exception was granted, but then on a temporal basis only. This policy was supported by four rules:

Table 4. Staff responsible for managing the standardized IT environment

Function	Accountability
IT architect	Preserves infrastructure consistency and evaluates the overall impact of deviation requests.
IT product manager	Responsible for managing costs, charging the business, the reduction of expenses, and increasing cost transparency. Calculates the financial impact of deviation requests. Accountable for all assets, budget-responsible for infrastructure depreciations and of all support contracts.
IT product coordinator	Translates functional and technical requirements into IT products and assesses deviation requests from a technical point of view.
IT support coordinator	Plans and controls the IT operations and reviews change requests from an IT operations viewpoint.

- There must be as little dependence as possible between developments at the application and operating system levels. These levels should be uncoupled.
- The computing platform must be upgraded without large investments to update in-house developed applications.
- Only COTS* products were allowed, to prevent legacy applications from being kept operational, which would cause security and stability problems and high support and license costs.
- To ease maintenance and increase security, no business-specific applications were allowed on workstations; these should be completely de-personalized.

To support this environment two key players are active: a product coordinator and a product manager. The product coordinator is responsible for translating technical interpretation into products. Functional requirements are translated into technical implementation (e.g. the "Flash" application with separate proxy for bank shops). Key activities of the product manager are managing costs, reduction of expenses, increasing costs transparency. The product manager is contact owner of all (support) contracts and responsible for all assets, and depreciations in the infra domain. The dedicated technical review team that took care of projects and its associated standards for this C/S environment was in line with the observation of Rada and Craparo (2001) described in Chapter 2.

Results

Planned

The initial investments of the project, with duration of 19 month, were estimated at € 30,355,000. Half of it were investments on terminal servers, new support tools and replacing old PCs. The other half was roughly spent on personnel costs (99 FTE). Some unexpected costs occurred when software code had to be rewritten or bought in order to migrate to the new standard environment.

The benefits were estimated at € 22,971,000 per year. This resulted in a payback period of 1.3 year, disregarding interests and index. These numbers are derived from the business case that used an internally performed independent benchmark by Gartner®[3]. Expected benefits were related to the general ones as summarized earlier:

- Shorter time to market - introduction of new applications will be faster;

- Costs savings - fewer development tools and less staff needed; less local support and fewer installations; easier support and governance; reduced license costs;
- Faster and cheaper relocation of staff - workstations needn't be moved anymore, it allows flexibility in workplaces;
- Higher availability - less downtime, proven standard COTS products and computing environment;
- Fewer conversion problems - less software versions are used.

Actual

The factual costs and benefits were as follows. Project expenses involved € 32M which is an excess of 5% compared to the planned ones. Benefits were calculated by comparing the former non-standardized C/S environment and its standardized successor. The direct costs (on 1/1/2003) of the former environment were € 4600 per desktop per year (and those were very nearly the costs that were calculated separately by the Garner TCO exercise). These costs are used as a reference for comparing the direct costs of the new standardized C/S environment that were set at € 2392 per desktop per year. The data in Table 5 show the costs being charged per 1/1/2004 to the departments and are based on data of the finance department. Depreciations are done immediately and the useful life is set at 4 years.

At the start of 2004, there were still workstations in use of the old environment and these desktop costs have increased from € 4600 to € 5235 per year. The increase is explained by dividing fewer desktops through support costs of the old back-end that remained more or less the same. This old environment was phased out within a year.

With these data it is easy to compare and calculate the savings. Calculating on the basis of 10,000 desktops, a four-year life span and using the values € 4600 and € 2392, the actual pay back period turned out to be 1.45 year[4], which was quite near the original planned one. In addition, the return on investment rate[5] was 176% and the internal rate of return[6] 58%.

CASE ANALYSIS

In this explanatory case study the initial conceptual model (Chapter 4, Figure 3) is used to assess the business process performance due to the application of the C/S standards. Each construct will be ana-

Table 5. Direct costs per 1/1/2004 in Euro per desktop per year

	Before standardization	**After standardization**	**Cost reduction**	**1/1/03**
Expenses (licenses)	1212	322	*73%*	**1400**
Other Direct Costs	318	245	*23%*	**450**
Depreciations	911	801	*12%*	**1550**
Support Costs (staff)	792	216	*73%*	**1200**
Internet Browsing	574	40	*93%*	
Network	793	768	*3%*	
Total	€ 4600	€ 2392	***48%***	**€ 4600**

lyzed using the results from the semi-structured interviews and the relevant documents obtained from the field research.

The four constructs ' Process of Standard Selection', 'Application of Standard', 'Process Performance', 'Control of Standard' and its derived variables are prominently present in this case, although mainly qualitatively. In Chapter 4 these constructs were discussed based on the literature review. In the next section the results of this case study are presented which will be related to these constructs. *Italics* refer to variables of the conceptual model, as described in Chapter 4, Table 10.

Constructs

Process of Standard Selection

The Business Unit took the initiative for the standardization project. It had two main reasons to do so: cutting costs and increasing flexibility. These two goals were to be accomplished by rationalizing the IT applications used by the Business Unit and by simplifying their maintenance, objectives that in turn were to be achieved through standardizing the IT infrastructure. Cutting costs was accomplished by, among other things, allowing one type of software only. The balance between the new applications' functionality and their support and license costs was an important factor for its success. As a result of using the modular structure, limiting integration at both the client and the server ends, the new IT environment was given maximum flexibility.

The hardware company C/S standard specified the following products[7]: HP desktop, HP server, IBM notebook and Philips® displays. Overall software tactics for the C/S standard were "be a Microsoft follower", which identifies the standard as an established, de facto product standard. As both hardware and software were all well established products one could typify this company as a late adopter of these de facto product standards. The Corporate Architecture Team (CAT) representing all Business Units, set these standards. Key factors for selection were functionally and costs. The CAT set requirements on e.g. CPU-speed, amount of memory, speed and capacity of hard disk drives and type of warranty. Then the corporate purchase department selected the most profitable offer in a tender process. An important parameter for this department was the availability of a product line for at least one year, therefore, there has been chosen for type A-brands only. For this C/S standard only 4 configuration types were distinguished among which the ARBO workspace with Braille printer of € 12000 was the most expensive version.

Although the business departments set the requirements, the *Business model* did not play a dominant role in the standardization process[8]. This was in contrast to the *Business drivers*, which were to realize costs savings and to enable organizational flexibility, while a decrease in end-user functionality was not allowed. Therefore, the conclusion is that this standardization process was more managerially than technically focussed. *IT engineering* and the *Business* departments were both heavily *involved* in setting the IT standards whereas *IT operations involvement* was small. On the whole the *alignment* between business departments and the IT department was considered as close. For example, IT staff had to teach practices at the business departments and middlemen were assigned for each department. Concerning the *knowledge* on standards: IT Management had strong knowledge whereas business Management only had marginal knowledge.

Application of Standard

Referring to variables that are an aspect of the application of a product/process standard (*reach, range*; see Chapter 4, Table 10), the description in the previous section shows us that this C/S standard is an established de facto product standard. It is being used in a single Business Unit (approximately 27.000 FTE) of a globally operating financial services company (approximately 100.000 FTE).

To succeed, the project was carried out in a joint effort of the Business Unit and its IT department and *awareness* of the effects and the resulting IT standards was considered as high. Because the project involved many people, processes and technological changes, five sub-projects were installed, each was covering distinct aspects (Table 6). A total of 51 FTEs were involved, including the program manager and the project office.

The project was organized as shown in Figure 1 the five sub-projects reported to a program manager who was supported by the project office. The program manager in turn reported to a steering group whose members came from both the business departments and the IT department. This steering group was accountable for managing the sub-projects' costs and progress; approving project changes; monitoring implementation quality; deciding on organizational changes; and controlling the type and number of applications. The importance of adequate *project management* in this IT standardization project concurs with the finding for IT in general by Boynton et al. (1994).

Support of the computing environment was carried out based on incidents and daily reports. *IT expertise* was high and could be described as both reactive and proactive. To increase stability and ease of support, applications were not be grouped on large servers. This is because the IT department proved that the costs of integration and support are higher than the additional costs of separate servers dedicated to one type of functionality. For the new desktop environment, applications were scripted for browser based access whenever technically possible. On Wintel servers, end-users could pick additional applications that are made available via the normal web browser on the standard workstation.

Control of Standard

As we have seen, the Business Unit's objectives were to accomplish a reduction in costs and to increase flexibility. The IT department, with an organizational *maturity* that can be considered as high, was fully committed to these goals, and they realized that cost cutting alone would not be good enough. Business departments, after all, were in some cases willing to pay substantially more rather than less for non-standard elements. The deviation process, therefore, had to be very strict to ensure that only genuine requests would be made. Any such requests were then assessed by an IT policy group taking

Table 6. Sub-projects of the server-based computing project

Sub-project	Objective	FTEs
Development	Preparing the applications for terminal servers; scripting, conversion and testing	29
Deployment	Rolling out the new infrastructure per department	8
Service levels	Setting up service level agreements with the Business Unit	7
Organizational change	Managing the IT department's organizational change caused by the project	3
Business support	Counseling and liaising with the business departments	2

Figure 1. Project organization

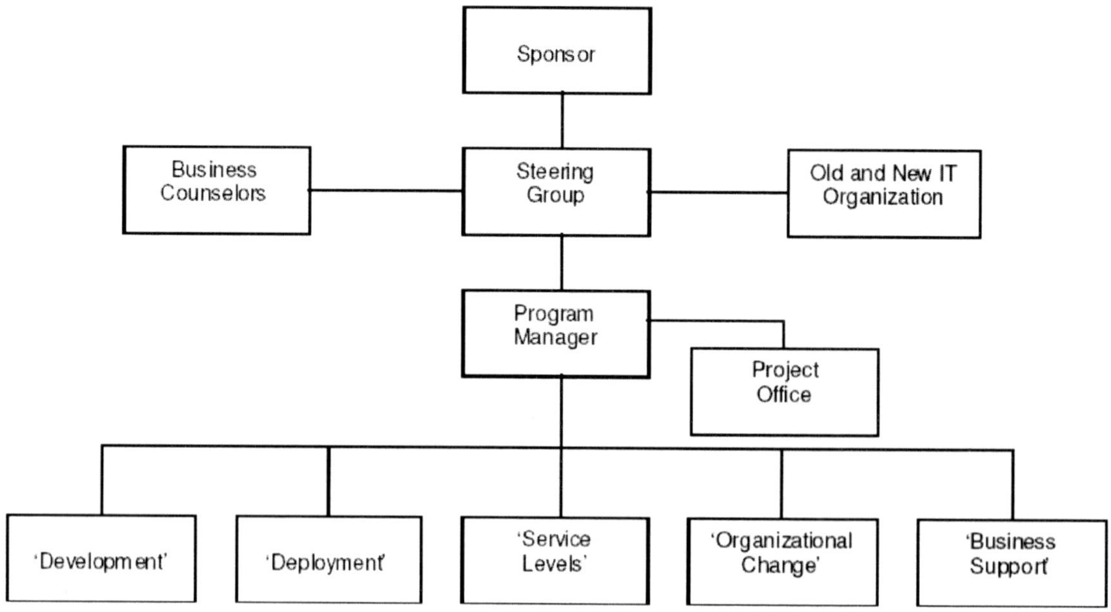

both business and technological considerations into account. Only serious arguments stood a chance of convincing this group to allow *deviations*, and these would then have to be reported to IT management on a monthly basis. Through this policy, the organization learned that a strict IT standards deviation process proved to be worthwhile, which is in line with Weill and Ross' (2004) observations. Firstly, because it provided input to adapt the set to changing business needs, but also as only genuine requests would enter the process.

The adage for this set of C/S standards was "each and every desktop has the same configuration". The *restrictiveness* in deviations from, and *prescription* level of these standards was considered strict. The whole process was also heavily *enforced*. In principle, one could choose from standard applications and hardware only. In general implementation requests were modified in such a way that they would still conform to the standard even when it negatively impacted user-friendliness. For example, if a "Java applet" only ran with a specific JVM version that deviated from the desktop standard it was put on a separate terminal server and was charged separately. In case this was not possible "to keep tigers and sheep in one cage", then the deviation from the standard was rejected in almost all instances. Notwithstanding, sound business rationale might result in structural standard amendment, but alternatives on requested functionality had to be considered first within the standard. Main considerations were the possibility of charging, added value, costs (direct and indirect) and amount of users involved. Choices to amend were considered by the IT department: first by a product coordinator, secondly by an IT architect. Additions to the standards could be carried out rather easily because of the modular structure of this set of C/S standards. The bottom line was that there were no deviations since approved changes were institutionalized, by adding them to the existing set of standard IT products. This positively impacted the acceptance and usage of this set of C/S standards. Exceptions to the deviation process were workplaces with special tools for the blind or hearing impaired. For those configurations the automatic installation of updates was not possible because the special software enhancements could be easily broken. As a result these type of configurations were expensive and were charged separately.

Enforcing the set of standards was a task executed *centrally* by IT at Business Unit level; the company's corporate IT unit was not involved, so *collaboration* was nonexistent. Senior business Management was fully aware and supported these standards as long as the objectives were accomplished (i.e. cost cutting and organizational flexibility). The attitude of business Management towards standards was one of skeptic pragmatism. The *endorsement* was dependent on the type of business department. For one selling mortgages, the IT costs were just a marginal part of the total costs, whereas for a support center the IT costs were the most significant part of the total expenses. IT management was really committed to these standards.

The scope of this case study on C/S standardization was limited to one Business Unit only although the technology could have been used throughout the enterprise. Before this C/S standardization, a project was launched called "Corporate Desktop Standard" but this failed to deliver. The main reasons were problems with how to implement IT delivery and support, driven by internal company politics. This concerned questions on centralization of support and activities like installation of patches and updates. Basically, the issues were "who decides what and when?" and "who does what?". The autonomy of the Business Units prevailed over the synergies of using a corporate wide C/S infrastructure. Another difficulty was multi-language support, which was not facilitated properly at that time. There were also some country-specific legal aspects, but those could have been overcome as well. On the other hand, hardware standardization at corporate level is almost accomplished within this company. Corporate procurement was in charge of this initiative.

Earlier on, a similar discussion took place within this very Business Unit between the local branches (that used the 16 bit Windows for Workgroups de facto standard) and head office (that used the 32 bit Windows NT 4.0 de facto standard). These two IT standards existed within a single Business Unit, because the departments were said to be too distinct to make a single IT desktop standard possible. A different organizational setup was one of the main reasons as control and charging differed between head office and branches. The costs and charging of the new platform have now been well defined which includes desktop, network and servers. These turned out to be significantly lower than before, even lower than commercial third parties. Consequently, it was very difficult for the head office to reject this new desktop standard. Besides, the C/S standard had already been implemented successfully at the branch offices of the Business Unit.

In line with the observations published by Rada and Craparo (2001), a technical review team carried out the verification of the specified IT product standards in projects. Strict conformity to the related service and project management *processes* were key elements in the successful usage of the set of IT standards. The team also reviewed any upgrades, replacements or patching needed. Standards are being reviewed once every 2 years in the CATs. The full review process often resulted in a new product that was incorporated in the set of IT standards, reflecting developments in both the technological and business environment.

Process Performance

In this case study the advantages of economies of scale are well demonstrated, as specified in literature. Increased efficiency and effectiveness, including flexibility, were demonstrated. To assess the new set of IT standards not only the project's financial results were evaluated but also several intangible aspects of IT service delivery and support were evaluated as well. The four perspectives identified in the Balanced Scorecard (BSC) will be discussed: financial, customer, internal-business-process, and learning & growth.

Financial Perspective

Many costs were eliminated by introducing the standardized IT environment. This included the following *costs to support*: a) reduction in the number of applications that were supported and licensed (with a factor of 22 using the functional equivalent principle); b) reduction of IT support staff; c) no more local installations and easier support of applications; d) no more hardware movements when staff relocated (that took approx. 25% of total former desktop costs). In short, the new environment costs half as much as the previous one (see Table 5). In general, the service levels of the standardized workstations were lower than before, so support costs per workstation were lower as well. Support was considered as less critical since all workstations had the same configuration. Because of the free seating concept[9] staff could easily use a nearby workstation. A department called 'distributed systems' was responsible for application support on both terminal servers and workstations. This department also coordinated hardware problems that were fixed by a third party, which was also responsible for the logistics. In essence this is a swap service. When hardware broke down after the guarantee period it is just replaced with a new one. More and more, the workstation evolved into a commodity with the only remaining other costs those for the network. Because of these developments the number of support staff dropped with approximately 130 FTE (from 383 FTE). In addition, logistical costs for computer equipment were no longer charged when staff had to move from one location to another. License management also became far better than in the old environment when application instances were often kept on the desktop computer systems or copied erroneously to the new location when staff moved or changed jobs. This behavior could easily double the number of licenses or kept licenses for that program occupied.

But not only support costs decreased, the *costs to develop* decreased as well since one had to develop for a standardized platform only and thus less specific expertise was necessary. Although dissimilar C/S environments existed in the several Business Units, these could be implemented on the same type of hardware standard. The resulting economies of scale enabled the company to negotiate significant global purchase discounts from their suppliers. After four years, its economical end of life, the system was replaced by the latest hardware (company) standard.

Another reason for the previous expensive desktop environment was that costs were roughly divided among all participants, because no standard configuration existed. For example, costs of high-end workstations with expensive video cards and additional memory and basic workstations were charged the same. In the new standardized environment staff used their web browsers to pick up any additional applications needed on their thin client e.g. AutoCAD® at 11,057 € /year or SAP at 1,609,165 € /year. The extent to which they used such applications determined those workstations' variable costs. Authorization to do so was obtained through an application also used for license management, giving the Business Unit maximum transparency and cost control. To minimize costs of application licenses and the (server) infrastructure even further, regular investigations were made on how many instances of an application was actually being used. This is done to tailor and keep the costs to a minimum. In this way the Business Unit is able to adapt its installed base when required.

Whether or not the investment in the standardized IT environment is practical from an economic point of view, Figure 2 shows the cash flow for four years. The initiative results in a positive cash flow of +56M € in the fourth year. The bottom line is that the new IT environment cost only about half as much as the old. The direct costs of the old and new IT environments, as calculated on 1 January 2003 and 2004 fell from € 4600 per desktop per year to € 2392 (Table 5).

In conclusion: significant cost reductions have been achieved at both development and support level. This contributed indirectly to the *economic value-added* of the company. The *ROI* was calculated at 176%. In addition, payback and internal rate on return could be determined from the obtained field study data, which were 1.45 year and 57.59% respectively. Unfortunately due to the fact that the effects of IT standards are diluted by many other factors, it is practically impossible to quantify other important financial indicators such as sales from service, profit growth, turnover, market share and revenue per employee. The best that can be said about these indicators is that the positive contribution of the C/S standard to the business performance only seems to be quite marginal.

Customer Perspective

The customers in this case were the Business Unit's staff and it took them some time to become acquainted with the new IT environment. Initially, their attitude was not positive: 'We will lose all flexibility...' But this changed and End-user/*client satisfaction* with the new environment could be described as acceptable. Most of the Business Unit's staff were more satisfied with IT delivery and support than before. More than half considered the change an improvement, 30% were indifferent and only some 10% were less satisfied than before – and those, interestingly enough, were predominantly IT engineering staff.

IT staff had some complaints on functionality and security restrictions that resulted in, for example, 20 local Websphere installs on the desktop. These were permitted temporally only (designated as separate workstation type). One could even find examples of offering a dedicated server to a single user for heavy-duty applications instead of upgrading or purchasing a high-end workstation. Such a workstation is physically bound to one location with e.g. logistical costs in case of relocations. It turned out to be the most efficient type of exploitation in such instances. But more importantly to staff than the standardization of their desktop was the higher speed of the new PC they got...

Figure 2. Cash flow following investment in the standardized IT environment

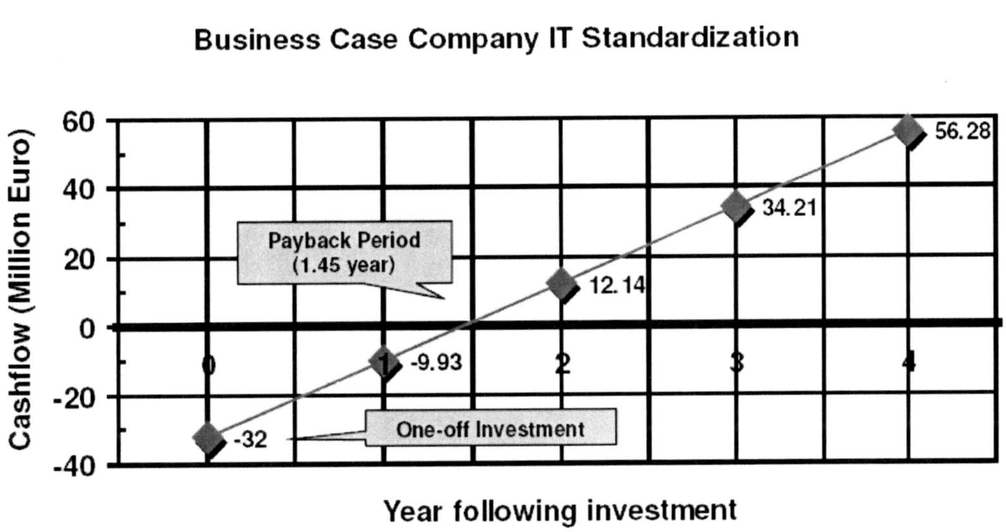

So generally speaking end-users were happy, as with just a few clicks they were now able to select from a set of over 250 applications, that could be made available within 15 minutes (see Figure 3). They could use more applications more easily and the *perceived complexity* of the set of standards was low. Incidents could be reported and requests for new hardware and software made through a web-interface. The free seating concept allowed staff to move to other locations whenever necessary, and use another workstation with exactly the same features. The fact that all workstations were the same also made them less dependent on delivery and support. For the company as a whole this meant decreased costs; for its staff it meant less hassle and therefore an improved working environment.

Internal Perspective

With the introduction of the C/S environment, significant improvements were achieved with respect to *on-time service delivery*, from decreased *throughput time* of service *requests* to the implementation of a standardized IT environment for a whole department (*time to market*). New projects showed lead times that were up to 75% shorter than before. New applications could be made operational within a few weeks; deploying the standardized environment typically took no more than a month.

So service performance increased from both the development and the support point of view, including *time to develop* and *time to support* which both deceased because of the reduced complexity of the new environment. In addition, a higher security level (*risk* profile) was achieved through automated anti-virus updates and the uniform patching of operating system and applications. Smart cards were used for application log-on procedures, so that a single sign-on was enough. Only with respect to *error and rework rates* no significant improvements were achieved: the former organization had already been responsive. Overall the *service quality* improved.

Leaning & Growth Perspective

In this case, the Business Unit decided to use the de facto standard software products of Microsoft. Potential lock-in effects could occur if one becomes bound to a single supplier of hardware or software.

Figure 3. Start Page with terminal server applications

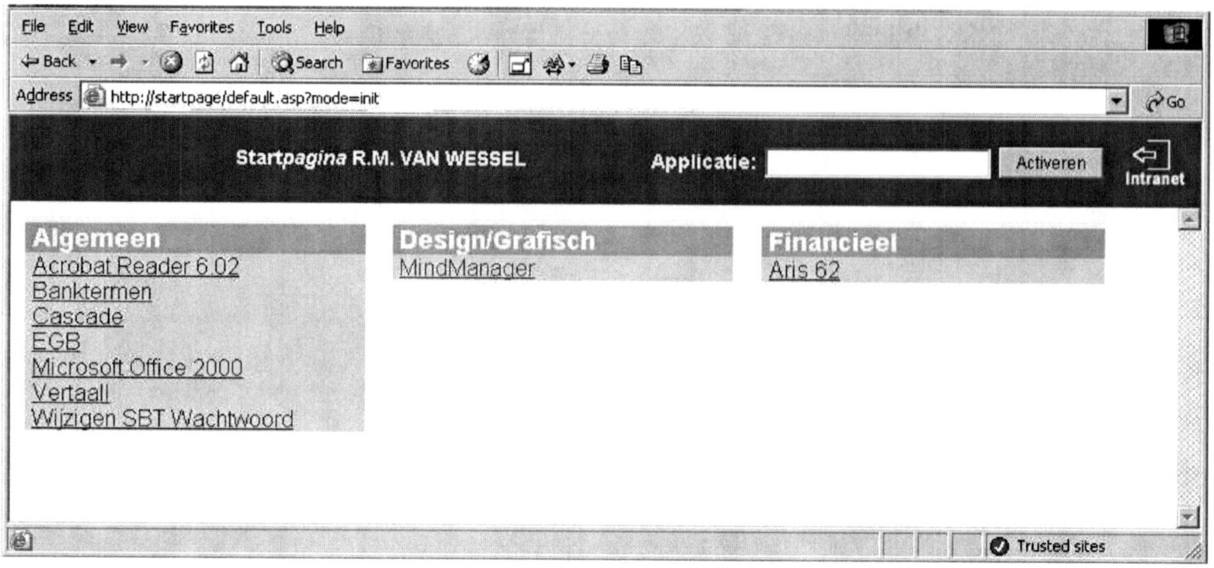

Generally speaking, this presented no problems, although *adaptability* and *compatibility* became more difficult when applications were integrated that deviated from the Microsoft standard. But these lock-in effects were considered far less important than the benefits to be achieved. Hardware seemed to present almost no such risks at all; and even for system software these were considered less important since the modular set-up of the environment would allow changing front-end or back-end software relatively easily.

Regarding *innovativeness*, this thin client concept was the first in this financial services company and probably also in the financial services industry in general. It turned out to be both flexible and *robust* because of the way the thin client/server based computing technology is being used (a highly granular environment with dedicated terminal servers per application). Desktop downtime became negligible since almost all instability had been application-related, not hardware-related, hence the new IT environment proved to be highly *available*. It is therefore considered to be an innovative concept. Moreover, no lowering of *staff motivation* was observed or as one of the interviewees said "*motivation of staff is more affected by reorganizations than by tooling*".

The standardized IT environment facilitated increased technical, organizational and financial flexibility. Technical flexibility was achieved in terms of *adaptability, scalability* and *robustness* because of the server based computing principle. ATMs used by customers of FINCORP, for example, could be included in this environment as essentially just another peripheral. Furthermore, the IT environment allowed running several versions of an application (Lotus Notes 5 and 6, for instance) simultaneously on a single desktop, since they were installed on separate terminal servers. Another example are so called 'Internet pillars' in the consumer bank offices that are being equipped with thin client configurations (browser and terminal server client, ROM bootable without hard disk). A department (International Payments) using a special, dedicated LAN environment exemplified organizational flexibility. The IT environment now allowed the department's staff to work anywhere, irrespective of their physical location. This meant its business functionality could be spread over several locations. And last, Financial flexibility was achieved because application and hardware use were paid on the basis of the actual number of subscriptions: workstations were charged according to how much they accessed the web and terminal servers. So when a department reduced or increased its staff, the bill changed automatically. Of course, for the IT organization this kind of flexibility presented some financial uncertainty, but the users' flexibility was considered necessary to accomplish a more effective exploitation environment.

The set of C/S standards was refined further to make it possible for other Business Units with complex set-ups to adapt this application and storage centric solution. The internal politics of the enterprise, however, was not ready yet for this to happen corporate wide. In spite of this, the reusability of this standardized environment was far better compared to the previous one, mainly because of its modular architecture. There was *modularity* at both ends: 1) at the client side was the standardized computing platform with applications and peripherals 2) at the server site modularity could be found in the form of servers per applications, limiting integration as far as possible. An example of the reusability of this standardized environment was the preparation for usage with ATMs that in essence were just another peripheral. The terminal servers and web servers could be seen as modular back-end components of this C/S environment that were connected with a standardized interface at the front-end (the terminal emulator and browser respectively). Therefore it could be stated that technical flexibility was achieved by not integrating thus flexibility through modularity. Or in other words: through integration comes inflexibility.

A final look may be taken at the project's results from the perspective offered by Evans' flexibility framework Evans (1991). This framework consists of: a) the capability to yield to pressure by offering an increased robustness; b) the capability to accommodate new situations (scalability); and c) the capability to be modified or adapted according to the needs of the organization (adaptability). As described above, the new IT environment scored well on all three aspects.

Propositions

In Chapter 4 four propositions were formulated. Using the analysis results from the previous sections it is argued whether these propositions are supported by this case or not.

Discussion Proposition 1

- An effective (ineffective) IT standard selection positively (negatively) influences the application of these standards.

The chosen standards were based upon prudent standard selection as described in the analysis section. Furthermore, flexibility requirements were an integral part of the standard selection process. We have seen hat the alignment between Business and IT during the selection process was close. Given these results it is concluded that proposition 1 is **supported by this case**.

Discussion Proposition 2

- The application of appropriate IT standards contributes to better process performance and this performance is dependent on the control of its usage.

Positive results on efficiency and effectiveness (including flexibility) were clearly identified in this case study and include: 1) cost reductions; 2) increased flexibility; 3) increased security. The data obtained on business performance were considered from four perspectives: financial, customer, internal business and learning & growth. Positive effects on the *financial* side of using IT Standards resulted in significant cost reductions. Cost savings in development have been accomplished and support costs were roughly halved. Most other effects on variables of the conceptual model could not be determined because the effects of IT standards are diluted by many other factors. From the *customer* perspective positive influences were identified, since for more than half of the end-user community (60%) satisfaction increased, 30% were indifferent and only 10% were less satisfied with the new desktop environment. At the *internal business* side service performance (such as throughput time and time to market) showed great improvements and flexibility has been achieved at organizational, financial and technical level. From an *innovation* point of view positive results also have been identified, like the value add of the exception processes to IT standards. The performance due to these standards is also based on strict control as described earlier in this Chapter. Management is committed to these standards and standards are strictly enforced. Flexibility requirements are an integral part of the selection process. Given these facts proposition 1 is **supported by this case**. This result is also in line with the results found by Kayworth and Sambamurthy (2000).

Discussion Proposition 3

- A low process performance due to the applied IT standards leads to changes in the way these standards are controlled.

This proposition basically says that IT standard control is amended when triggered by undesired 1) financial, 2) customer, 3) internal or 4) learning & growth outcomes. These kinds of activities were observed and discussed earlier, such as changing the standards' deviation process to counter rising costs (financial perceptive). It is concluded that proposition 3 is **supported by this case** as well.

Discussion Proposition 4

- A low process performance due to the applied IT standards leads to reselection of these standards.

This proposition basically says that IT standard selection is more useful when triggered by results from one or more of the four business process performance perspectives. For example a change of a standard application is required because end-users complain of its stability (customer perspective) or the time to market is too slow (internal perspective) make this necessary. We have seen, for example, that one of the reasons to choose the new C/S standards was the lack of scalability/adaptability and high operating costs (both related to the business performance) of the former environment. Furthermore, it was already discussed that these C/S standards are reviewed at regular intervals and updated periodically. Therefore it is concluded that proposition 4 is **supported by this case**.

The final results are listed in Table 7.

CONCLUSIONS

Case Conclusions

This C/S standardization project finished in January 2004 and positive results were clearly found. A cross-reference with the five summarized anticipated improvements in business performance resulting from usage of IT in general (Shafer and Byrd, 2000) shows us:

Table 7. Evaluation of the propositions

No	Proposition	Supported by this case
1	An effective (ineffective) IT standard selection positively (negatively) influences the application of these standards.	Yes
2	The application of appropriate IT standards contributes to better process performance and this performance is dependent on the control of its usage.	Yes
3	A low process performance due to the applied IT standards leads to changes in the way these standards are controlled.	Yes
4	A low process performance due to the applied IT standards leads to reselection of these standards.	Yes

Table 8. Improvements resulting from the standardized IT environment

Area	Result
Improved quality	• Easy and fast introduction of new applications. • Straightforwardness and fewer errors.
Reduced costs	• Time and costs to develop (no tailoring and no unnecessary integration) and support (reduction of 50%) decreased significantly.
Increased flexibility	• The standardized server based computing concept facilitates organizational, financial and technical flexibility more easily.
Improved customer satisfaction	• For more than half of the end-user community (60%) the satisfaction of using this standardized environment increased. One of the effects that exemplifies this is the throughput time of requests which decreased significantly.
Overall improvements in operations	• The new environment is more stable because only proven products are applied. Perception of availability is a lot higher because of the modular architecture of the standardized server based computing environment. Terminal servers are very robust, the IT architecture has interdependencies and there is an increased level of security. • 80% of the server based applications are running faster compared to running on a desktop.

Lessons Learned

When carrying out this case study, the initial conceptual model was used. It was shown for three constructs ' Process of Standard Selection', 'Application of Standard' and Control of Standard' that the related variables were present in the case material. Most of these are of a qualitative nature only.

For the fourth construct 'Process Performance' the four BSC perspectives, as proposed by Kaplan and Norton (1996), were assessed and corresponding variables from Chapter4, Table10 were linked to an augmented four-tier scheme (see Chapter3, Figure 2). Using this scheme it was shown that for the first three levels the values of the variables of the conceptual model could be determined. Variables at the fourth and highest level, related to the Financial business performance could not be properly assessed. This is because there are numerous other factors apart from the influence of the usage of IT standards that affect the business performance as well. Summing up, therefore, only the first three levels in this scheme can be considered in order to determine the influence of IT standards on process performance.

MANAGERIAL IMPLICATIONS

Two key objectives drove this standardization initiative: to cut costs and to increase flexibility for change.

Essential element in cutting costs was to allow one type of hardware and (application) software only. The adage for this set of C/S standards was "each and every desktop has the same configuration". Key factors for selection were functionally and costs. The balance between functionality and support/license costs was the main criterion for putting hardware and software on the list of company IT product standards. Furthermore, as a result of using the modular structure, limiting integration at both the client and the server ends, the new IT infrastructure was given maximal flexibility.

Another essential ingredient in meeting these two objectives was related how the deviation process of standards was managed. The restrictiveness in deviations from, and prescription level of those standards was strict. Enforcing the set of standards was a task executed centrally by IT at Business Unit level. The deviation process ensured that only genuine requests would be made. In case of with sound Business rationale only, deviations were allowed temporally. But in most cases those products were institutionalized, by adding them to the existing set of company IT product standards.

In the following two chapters more case studies on IT product and process standardization will be carried out in order to perform a cross case analysis.

REFERENCES

Boynton, A. C., Zmud, R. W., & Jacobs, G. C. (1994). The influence of IT management practice on IT use in large organizations. *Management Information Systems Quarterly*, *18*(3), 299–318. doi:10.2307/249620

Evans, J. S. (1991). Strategic flexibility for high technology maneuvers: a conceptual framework. *Journal of Management Studies*, *28*(1), 69–89. doi:10.1111/j.1467-6486.1991.tb00271.x

Kaplan, R. S., & Norton, D. P. (1996). *The Balanced Scorecard: Translating Strategy into Action*. Boston, MA: Harvard Business School Press.

Kayworth, T., & Sambamurthy, V. (2000). Facilitating localized exploitation and enterprise-wide integration in the use of IT infrastructures: The role of PC/LAN infrastructure standard. *The Data Base for Advances in Information Systems*, *31*(4), 54–81.

Nash, K.S. (2001, March 8). Study: Use of standards in ICT saves money. *Computerworld.*

Rada, R., & Craparo, J. S. (2001). Standardizing Management of Software Engineering Projects, *Knowledge, Technology, &. Policy*, *14*(2), 67–77.

Ross, J. W. (2003). Strategic IT architecture competency. *MIS Quarterly Executive*, *2*(1), 31–43.

Shafer, S. M., & Byrd, T. A. (2000). A framework for measuring the efficiency of organizational investments in information technology using data envelopment analysis. *Omega*, *28*, 125–141. doi:10.1016/S0305-0483(99)00039-0

Weill, P., & Ross, J. (2004). *IT Governance - How Top Performers Manage IT Decision Rights for Superior Results*. Boston, MA: Harvard Business School Press.

ENDNOTES

1. Calculated on the basis of the functional equivalent principle.
2. Total cost of ownership, a Gardner™ indicator on efficiency of IT
3. In the Gartner report an TCO was calculated of direct costs of € 4,580 per workspace.
4. Pay back = $32 \times 10^6 / \{(4600-2392) \times 10^4\} = 1.45$ year
5. ROI = $\{(4600-2392) \times 10^4 \times 4 - 32 \times 10^6\} / 32 \times 10^6 = 176\%$
6. $$32 \times 10^2 = \sum_{j=1}^{4} \frac{(4600 - 2392) \times 10^4}{(1+i)^j} \Rightarrow i = 0.5759$$

7 The preferred supplier status continues for three years after which the standard selection process reinitiates. Typically this consists of three steps: 1) a RFP phase focussing on technical and ergonomics requirements; 2) price negotiation by means of reversed auction; 3) acceptance test with two products resulting in the choice of the preferred one.

8 The C/S standard was designed for the branches' organization first and was subsequently adopted by the head office, which demonstrated its flexible architecture.

9 Although free seating technically works as anticipated, the concept does not seem to work as well as expected because it also required a change of attitude of staff involved. Staff have selected 'their' specific flexible workspace in spite of the fact that all workstations were configured exactly the same.

Chapter 6
Software Development Standardization "CMM/DSDM Case"

INTRODUCTION

Pijl et al. (1997) point out that strict adherence to software quality standards could be counterproductive if tailoring for specific types of systems is not possible. They also argue that current quality standards are focussed on standardization processes and procedures, whereas innovative projects require creativity. However, as has been pointed out in Chapter 2, standardization can be beneficial to creativity when one does not have to focus on basic quality issues. On the other hand standardization could impede creativity when it limits the number of possible solutions. Therefore one should not focus on standardization of processes alone. As Mintzberg (1984) argues there are other coordination mechanisms such as standardization of skills, outputs and communication.

The second case study is about process standardization within a software development department. We will investigate how this process standard was chosen and implemented and what its effects were on business performance.

DOI: 10.4018/978-1-61520-759-6.ch006

CASE DESCRIPTION

Introduction

In shortening timeframes and with lower costs, flexible information systems have to be developed and supported. This has consequences for the application development processes. By employing a standardized development methodology, an BPR program was launched that intended to accomplish fundamental changes in the way Business and IT created new software products.

This BPR program, called INSPIRATION[1], was launched in August 2000 following two benchmark studies carried out by Gartner® and Compass® at the end of 1999 that showed that there was 'room for improvement' within the Software Development functions of FINCORP. The function in question was the IT Development organization, part of the Dutch retail division, that consisted at that time of 2000 staff (including software developers, project managers, application supporters, line managers).

A number of external benchmark studies in 1999 and 2000 showed that, compared to other companies, development costs of software were much higher. A second issue was the discrepancy between requirements defined by the business departments and the final product. In other words the alignment between the business departments and its software development organization could improve as well[2]. The overall picture was:

- Concerns about IT productivity and increasing costs
- Insufficient project / budget control, limited steering options, projects delivered late
- Barriers between business departments and IT development and IT support departments
- Lack of a structured development process as several methods were used
- Inefficient allocation of employees to projects by IT project management
- Application-technology old and complex
- Hardly any reliable measurements

As a consequence, the central issue throughout the Inspiration program has been the quality of the software developed for the Business Unit that in its turn influences the quality of services the bank can offer its customers. Furthermore, the Inspiration target was to achieve a 20% improvement in productivity (Harmsen and Kleijnen, 2003). The total costs of the whole program, which ran four years in succession, added up to 5-7% of the yearly budget available for this Business Unit. A payback period of the program was calculated of 24 to 30 months.

In the past another initiative to standardize the software development process was introduced called "OA" but this utterly failed because of lack of support from both management and staff. Before the merger of FINCORP, the 'Method/1' (Andersen, 1988) waterfall approach was used in Company 1 and another method called "SOMA" was used in Company 2. Although 'Method/1' was the would be company standard it was not widely accepted and with the failure of OA, each contracting party that developed software for FINCORP tried to introduce its own process and tools.

For this reason, when Inspiration was launched, staff in general was very skeptic indeed. A key difference in the implementation strategy of Inspiration compared to previous initiatives was that it refrained from "*Theoretical guides like Method/1 or exercises with no links to reality such as 'OA'*" as said by of the interviewees. At the start of 2001 no standard development methodology was used, whereas at the end of 2003 the standardized software development process was implemented. This makes comparisons possible between projects either using a standardized methodology or not. The organizational structure at the start of the Inspiration program is depicted in Figure 1.

Key objectives of the Inspiration program (related to the status in 2000) were to:

- Improve the quality of delivered products and to make both project schedule and costs more predictable (by the introduction of metrics and measurement systems through quantifying performance and analysis of processes)
- Reduce costs by continuous software development productivity growth. The overall productivity of the application development and maintenance functions is to be increased by at least 20% and accelerate (rapid) application development up to 50%[3] in particular.
- Respond more rapidly and effectively to change (shorter time to market)
- Improve the co-operation between business and IT departments in projects and increase user acceptance and satisfaction
- Add value to organization and employee. Increase professionalism and maturity of all staff, increasing job satisfaction and job attraction to (new) staff.

With a number of sub-projects, the project Inspiration lasted for four years towards the above goals. It started with four sub-projects: a) Dynamic System Development Method (DSDM), b) Benchmark Short Term (BMST); c) Benchmark Recommendations Long Term (BREL); d) Balanced Scorecard (Dashboard). Later on, the following projects were added to the Inspiration scope: e) Professionalize Project Management (PPM); f) The Capability Maturity Model (CMM); g) Professional Attitude (PA). The project was strongly advised by the external consultant firms: Cap Gemini Ernst & Young® (DSDM), MphasiS® (CMM), Coach & Commitment™ (PA).

A short description of these projects follows, and later on in this chapter we will focus on DSDM and CMM only. The rationale is that these two are de facto/industry standards whereas the others are not within the research scope of standardization of IT processes or products. On the other hand some attention will be paid to the PA initiative as this is closely linked to CMM and DSDM and can be seen to a certain extent as standardization of skills and communication.

Figure 1. The IT Development organization

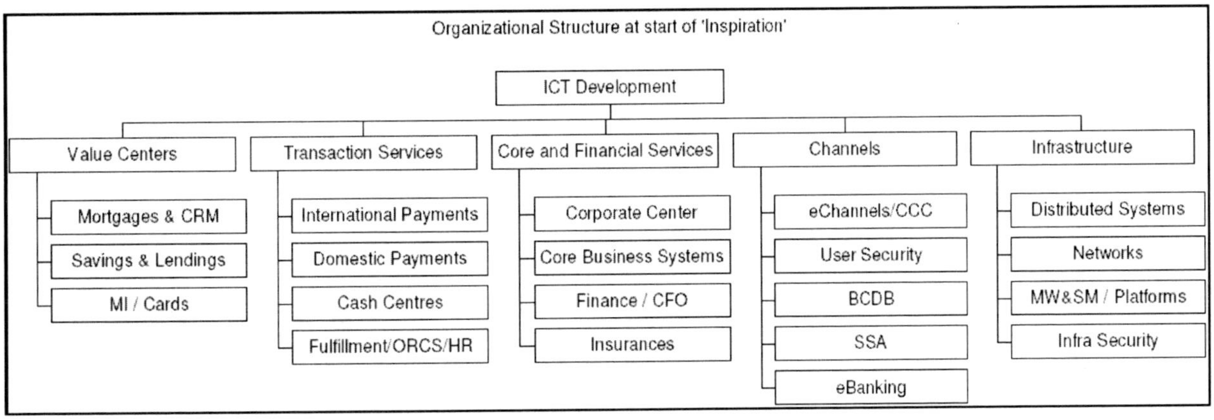

- DSDM facilitates the introduction of a standardized software development process. DSDM describes the *how* in this respect, with as key elements a user-focused solution and time boxing of deliverables and this method helps to satisfy requirements of CMM level 2. DSDM should improve software development and maintenance, productivity and delivery time (time to market). DSDM was initiated per product column[4] that was headed by a Senior Solution Integrator.
- BMST was aborted shortly after start-up because of budget constraints. Only a system called 'Dashboard' has been completed and is still being used. This enables measurement and analysis of the performance of definitions of key processes. The measurement system is based on the Balanced Scorecard (Kaplan and Norton, 1992) and contains project productivity data. These data are expressed in terms of 'function points per FTE' (or 'EURO per PF')
- BREL was an organizational project that resulted in organizational entities called Full Expertise Teams (FET), that embodied staff from both application development and support organizations to improve internal alignment. The rationale was to make the necessary modifications to the organization to make DSDM successful.
- PPM was to improve Business and IT (both development and support) alignment that includes project management capabilities, processes (e.g. knowledge management), organization and staff. PPM was to focus on professionalizing all project management staff but PPM was also canceled shortly after start-up because of budget constraints.
- The CMM process framework describes *what* one should do, not how one should do it. CMM was the framework used as reference to assess the maturity of the application development and support processes. CMM was intended to improve the maturity of the software development processes in terms of an evolutionary path from ad-doc and chaotic to controlled and disciplined. CMM started within three domains (Insurances, BCDB and Networks) and was launched parallel to the DSDM implementation. CMM was initiated per domain, that was headed by a Solution Integrator / Portfolio manager.
- In order to address the organizational side of software development, apart from process and tooling, a project called Professional Attitude (PA) was added to DSDM and CMM in 2002. The aim of the PA initiative was to place greater emphasis on personal behavior to achieve a cultural shift from reservedness to openness and honesty.

The Dashboard sub-project was lifted out of the project scope to become part of the IT organization in general. As mentioned above, DSDM and CMM started as separate pilot projects and were launched in different departments, basically because of distinct implementation strategies and corresponding timelines. As time went by, however, this turned to be an ineffective implementation scenario. Therefore it was decided to join both efforts to come to an Integrated Quality System called IQS[5] in mid 2002. CMM procedures were rewritten in such a way that it incorporated the DSDM requirements hence implementation became more efficient and effective.

IQS was to ensure that projects were carried out in a structured manner and were to result in IT products of better quality and tailored to the business departments needs. According to the Inspiration program manager the integration of the DSDM software development standard and the CMM quality management system standard has been an unique and distinctive achievement (Zwart, 2003). IQS has been incorporated into the processes of the organization, although it was considered by some as being 'heavy', especially for relatively small projects. Tailoring for such projects was not implemented consistently.

In July 2004 the project ended and structures were put into place to ensure that IQS and PA became firmly embedded in the organization and were to be developed further. For IT staff, roles were clearly defined and rules of play communicated. Experiences with new projects showed where improvements were still to be made. Professional Attitude was incorporated into line management and features of it in the Personal Performance Plans.

Professional Attitude

One of the crucial lessons that has been learned during the implementation of the Inspiration program is that one could not change a process without giving careful thought to behavior as well. So for CMM and DSDM to take root in the organization, a complementary action learning project Professional Attitude (PA) was launched to improve commitment, competence, trust and quality. It intended to be the guideline to develop both the professionalism of the individual and that of the organization as a whole. The anticipated end result was a professional organization that was both enjoyable to work in and that offered ample opportunities for personal development. Key patterns of behavior to be increased were:

- Customer orientation - put oneself in the customer's position
- Result focus - show initiative and think of solutions not problems
- Commitment to standards - unconditional usage of standards and creativity in deliverables
- Cooperation - fall back on each other and work as a team
- Receiving and giving feedback - be open and responsive
- Coaching - managers do not direct but are tutors instead

Each member of staff had to follow a two-day course and was appointed a change agent. Project management staff acted as coaches and discussed face to face how to improve the behavior of project members. In addition staff members, with a quality focus, were appointed in order to ensure both CMM and DSDM became embedded in the organization. Furthermore HR resource managers acted as change coaches for this program as part of their job to develop people. IT staff, however, being by nature rather opinionated, often saw these coaches as DSDM/CMM police.

In short, CMM and DSDM were the tools and PA was the human side dealing with how to use these tools. DSDM was generally perceived as agreeable to work with, predominantly because of the workshops integrally linked to this software development method. For CMM, on the other hand, the perception was rather like "*one had to fill in just the corresponding template*". The effects of CMM or DSDM were measured individually but the effects of Inspiration were assessed as a whole (results can be found in Table 6). As the DSDM project leader explained: "*If you put them together into a single program, you should measure it as one*".

DSDM Implementation and Usage

Implementation of the system development method Dynamic Systems Development Method (DSDM™), (Stapleton, 2002) is one of the key elements of the Inspiration program. This process standard for rapid application development was chosen for the following reasons:

- At that time DSDM was an emerging de facto standard for rapid application development[6] offering expertise and training for staff by several external companies that specialized in this method.
- DSDM should offer guarantees regarding quality of project members. Internal staff can become certified (which enhances them professionally) but also offers assurances on the competencies of contractors.
- DSDM is supplier independent therefore the risk of vendor lock-in is relatively small. In addition, the organization was able to participate in further DSDM developments and could influence future developments of the standard.
- DSDM facilitated the aspiration to reach uniformity in application development and offered the flexibility for departments to tailor it according to their needs, for example, support of legacy applications at the same time.

DSDM is an established software development standard in the Netherlands and the United Kingdom. It has a large customers group, including FINCORP.

Core principle of DSDM is the extent (60% must have, 40% should/nice to have) to which new software functionality will be delivered to ensure both budget delivery (fixed resources) and timely delivery (fixed timelines). In this way the notorious project performance triangle (Lock, 2003) is mitigated, i.e. the typical trade-off made by project managers between functionality and time or functionality and budget (Figure 2).

DSDM Components

DSDM consists of several components that can be divided into three, partly overlapping, groups (Klei, 2002):

These components will be described shortly; details can be found on the DSDM consortium website[7]. The DSDM development process consists of five *phases* that result in several *products*, as listed in Table 2. The first three phases contain a risk log.

DSDM distinguishes several *roles* that do not necessarily relate to individuals on a one-to-one basis. One person may cover two or more roles or that same role could be allocated to a number of individuals, which often depends on the size of the project. The following 10 project roles are defined in DSDM:

Figure 2. The DSDM software development method facilitates variable functionality delivery

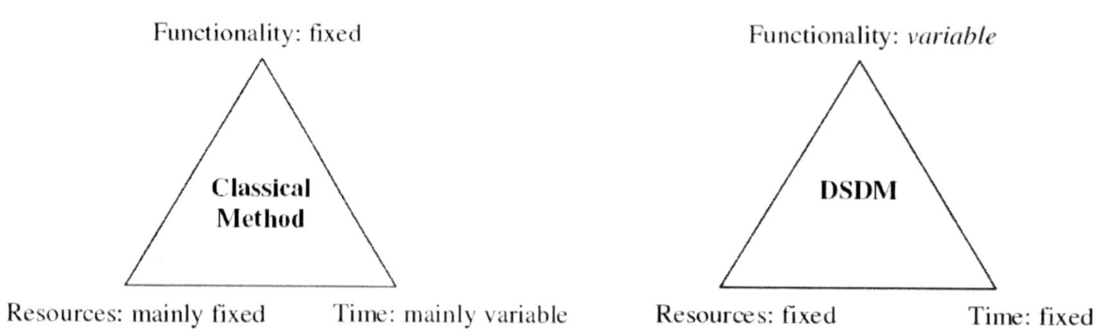

Table 1. Key components within DSDM

Group	Component
Framework	Phases, Products, Roles
Philosophy	Roles, Principles, Time boxing
Technique	Time boxing, Prioritization, Workshops, Prototyping

Table 2. DSDM phases and products

Phase	Description	Products
Feasibility Study	Assessing whether DSDM is the right approach, both technically and economically	Feasibility report and prototype Outline Plan
Business Study	Determining business requirements and technical constraints	Business area definition Prioritized requirements list System architecture definition Development plan
Functional Model Iteration	Refining the business based aspects of the information system	Functional model, prototypes and review records Non-functional requirements list Implementation and timebox plans Development Risk analysis log
Design and Build Iteration	Building the information system	Design prototype and review records Tested system and test records
Implementation	Handing over the system from development to the operational environment.	User documentation Delivered system Trained user population Project review document

Executive Sponsor; Visionary; Ambassador User; Advisor User; Project Manager; Technical Co-ordinator; Team Leader; Developer; Tester; Scribe. In addition there are the facilitator and specialist roles. A typical DSDM project organization is depicted in Figure 3.

DSDM is based on the following nine *principles*:

1. Active user participation - all the way through the development process, the end user is involved in order to guarantee that final product requirements are met.
2. DSDM teams are empowered to make decisions - the end users in the development team are skilled and able to make decisions
3. Periodic feedback of results - the focus is on frequent delivery of products; think in terms of product delivery in stead of carrying out activities.
4. Fitness for business purpose is the key acceptance criterion of deliverables - this makes sure that priorities are set correctly
5. Iterative and incremental development leads to correct business solutions - a basic assumption is that software can not be built instantaneously without errors.
6. All changes during development can be reversed - alterations in environment and ideas are possible
7. Requirements are baselined at a high level - this makes it possible to empower DSDM teams

Figure 3. The DSDM project organization (Adapted from DSDM Consortium Ltd.)

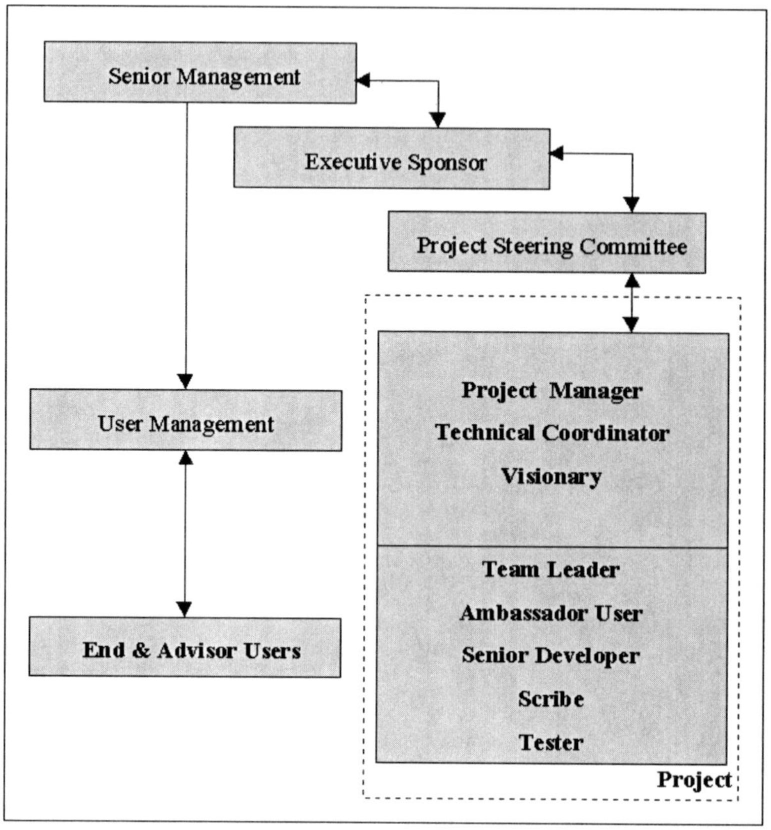

8. Tests are an integral part of the development phase - there is no distinct test phase
9. All stakeholders have a cooperative and collaborative mindset - barriers should fade between all parties involved.

Finally, several techniques are used such as *Time boxing*, *Workshops*, and *Prototyping*. *Prioritization* is carried out according to "MoSCoW": Must have, Should have, Could have and Want to have.

Claimed DSDM Benefits and Preconditions

The DSDM consortium claims this method to have benefits such as:

- End users are more likely to claim ownership of the application;
- The risk of building 'wrong' applications is reduced;
- Time to market decreases compared to other methods;
- Implementation is easier and deadlines are more easily met;
- Business and IT cooperation increases naturally.

Although DSDM can be used for any software development project, it is claimed that there are certain characteristics, which make DSDM the method of choice to develop an information system when:

- The system has a clear and interactive user interface;
- There is a distinctly defined user group;
- Complex sections can be split up into smaller functional sections;
- The project is constrained with hard deadlines;
- The requirements are not fully crystallized and/or are subject to change and can be reprioritized.

The DSDM consortium warns that this method is less appropriate for the following uses:

- Process control and real time applications;
- Requirements which have to be fully specified before any work can begin;
- Safety critical applications, since tests in DSDM are not as robust as they should be for such applications;
- Delivering re-usable components.

Finally the DSDM consortium states the following *critical success factors*:

1. Acceptance of the DSDM philosophy before commencement of work;
2. The decision making powers of the end-users and developers in the development team are respected;
3. There is commitment of senior user management to provide significant end-user involvement;
4. One sticks to incremental delivery;
5. Easy access by developers to end-users is guaranteed;
6. The size, stability and skills of the team;
7. A supportive commercial relationship;
8. The development technology is adequate.

DSDM Implementation

The DSDM method has been implemented gradually per product column (see Figure 1) in the course of one year. The implementation schedule was as follows:

1. Formation of a steering committee
2. Creating and executing a communication plan
3. Assigning key staff to follow DSDM courses
4. Identification and execution of pilot projects
5. Evaluation of these pilot projects
6. Full implementation

At first a few projects were piloted followed by a full rollout per Channel. Experience from the 12 pilots (3 pilot projects in 4 Channels each) led by DSDM experts, was documented by a Knowledge Center and used, before domain wide implementation took place. A dedicated intranet site containing papers on software development and project management was launched as well. The DSDM usage at the pilot projects was optional at first and interest of staff was small. That is why the method became compulsory and gradually all staff got acquainted with DSDM, making it more and more easy to carry out projects with minimal supervision. During the implementation period there were 14 DSDM coaches working in 20 domains.

DSDM has links with existing disciplines such as project management, architecture, testing and service level management. DSDM can be part of any project management method, whereas DSDM route maps are linked to architectural processes. Also included are documents like Business Area Definition and System Architecture Definition, which are discussed in the DSDM Feasibility and Business Study phases. Regular testing is an integral part of the software development cycle of DSDM and the existing test method was incorporated. In the Business Study the agreements described in the 'DSDM route maps' were reflected in the final SLA. These route maps are practical aids to develop information systems that consist of method (approach, support, and directives), tools (templates, checklists) and deliverables (environments, manuals). These were put together by the IT project manager and the IT architect. For this financial services company there were several *route maps* at hand even before DSDM was introduced: 1) COOL:Gen™; 2) JAVA; 3) Web Domino®; 4) Package Solution; 5) Data warehousing; and 6) COBOL. DSDM supplemented the route maps with its specific requirements, and from then were called DSDM route maps.

There is a clear relationship between DSDM and CMM as DSDM is a concrete implementation of CMM as regards the software development process and DSDM supports an organization to operate at CMM level 2[8]. At the end of 2001 it was decided to merge the implementation of the hitherto two distinct projects DSDM and CMM. The problems of continuing with two separate projects were larger than the risk of combining the two. One of the reasons was because domains were reorganized and some staff were already educated in CMM but not in DSDM and vice versa. Especially for the sequence CMM after DSDM, one encountered resistance as staff had just learned the DSDM way and were then told to carry out activities more strictly as prescribed by CMM. Another advantage of the merger was that CMM made sure the DSDM software development processes took root in the organization.

Both the DSDM project and its follow-up, the Integrated Quality System (IQS) had active commitment of IT management although this could have been more in the start-up phase of the DSDM project. The implementation of DSDM was not via a 'big bang' but via a gradual introduction into the several domains. One of the main reasons was to compare notes from the pilot studies. Project staff learned from each other's faults, which in turn improved stakeholders' collaboration. There were around 10% early adopters (that typically get less interested in due course), 80% staff indifferent towards DSDM and 10% adversaries to it. One of the interviewees argued that "*Especially these last 10% are an interesting section since, once convinced of the benefits of these standards, they can be great allies*".

In November 2004 DSDM had been in full swing for one year and was being used as intended. Productivity measurements were carried out also as part of the Dashboard initiative. The IQS had been fine-tuned by, for example, streamlining requirements and checklists and deleting redundant sections. In addition, tailoring was introduced to accommodate smaller projects.

Main contributors to the successful implementation of DSDM in this organization were supposedly:

1. Management shows some patience when implementing the process and knows that results will not be instant.

2. The product is flexible in the sense that it is possible to adapt it to the organization.
3. Skillful communication, including that of the DSDM coaches.
4. The direct involvement of both Business and IT support during all phases of the project

A number of key differences, related to DSDM roles and empowerment, were observed in comparison to the default DSDM implementation. First of all, end user participation in projects was almost non-existent in spite of its prominent casting in the DSDM principles and processes (see the DSDM 9 principles earlier). Requirements were fed by head-office delegates from the project sponsor in most cases and not by end users of the branches. The default DSDM roles were also changed, to align them with existing roles in the organization. Secondly, the advocated empowerment of DSDM teams was not fully realized, as these teams were not quite autonomous in practice. Issues and key decisions were still dealt with by higher management. In what way these choices have negatively influenced the overall end result remains uncertain.

In the next section, we will discuss the implementation and use of the CMM quality management system standard in the control of quality of the information systems development process.

CMM Implementation and Usage

A growing number of companies use standards as guidance for their quality management systems and some go one step further to have their quality systems certified. Two well-known quality standards in the areas of software development are ISO 9000-3 and the software Capability Maturity Model. ISO 9000-3 (ISO, 1991) was specifically designed for systems development and was popular in Europe and Japan. However, we will not go into further details since this standard is not within the scope of this case study.

CMM Levels

The software Capability Maturity Model (CMM) has been developed by the Software Engineering Institute[9] (SEI) of the Carnegie Mellon University (Paulk et. al, 1991, 1993) and is a tool to assess and gradually improve the maturity of software development organizations. The aim of SEI was to improve the quality of software products by focussing on the way these products were made.

It is based on the work of Nolan & Gibson (1974) and Humphey (1989) who described a staged model on the allocation of IT in organizations. CMM is basically a quality system related to processes of software development and support and has become a de facto standard in the USA. CMM is descriptive and not prescriptive since it describes "what" practices are recognized as critical to success for software development efforts and not "how" the activities are to be performed. Inspired by the work of SEI a multitude of other maturity models were presented, such as the IT Service CMM and Test Process MM.

Five levels of maturity are defined in CMM ranging from initial to optimized (see Table 3). Each level has certain Key Process Areas (KPA's) which in turn consists of goals and key practices. By measuring the degree of implementation of these key practices, the maturity level of the system development organization is determined. Measurement of each key practice is ascertained as being I) Insufficient, P) Partly sufficient or S) Sufficient whereas a KPA can be either Sufficient or Insufficient.

Claimed CMM Benefits and Preconditions

Each CMM quality level can be seen as a well-defined stage on the way to a fully mature organization. CMM focuses on all relevant aspects: project management, the technique of application development and the organization of software development and support. The whole idea behind CMM is that the higher the maturity degree the better the software systems delivered in terms of quality, costs, timelines and client satisfaction. Industry results have shown that the implementation of CMM within various organizations results in significant productive improvements, ranging from 10 to 50%.

The core principles behind CMM are:

- CMM is characterized by a gradual approach to each higher quality level. All KPAs should be met before transition to the next level.
- CMM is a specification and not a prescription - The KPAs describe the 'WHAT' and not the 'HOW'.[10]
- Changes in behavior are institutionalized - the evolvement to the next CMM level only succeeds when changes in behavior have become second nature.
- Process improvements support business objectives - enhancements in the software development processes should be aligned with the business purposes.

Table 3. The software Capability Maturity Model

CMM Level	Description	Key Process Area (KPA)
Initial	Unstable environment • Ad hoc, occasionally even chaotic • Project success not guaranteed and depends on individual effort	None
Repeatable	Stabilized environment • Costs controlled • Product oriented reactive management system	Project management • Requirements management • Software project planning • Software project tracking and oversight • Software subcontract management • Software quality assurance • Software configuration management
Defined	Develop common processes • Process standardized and documented • Tailored standards for each project	Engineering management • Organization process focus • Organization process definition • Training program • Integrated software management • Software product engineering *) • Inter group coordination • Peer reviews *)
Managed	Control variation • Process understood, measured and controlled	Quantitative management • Quantitative process management • Software quality management
Optimized	Continuously improve • Focus on process improvement	Change management • Defect prevention • Technology change management • Process change management

*) These Level 3 processes were implemented in the organization where this case study took place

The main advantages of working with the CMM model are[11]:

- Increased confidence and satisfaction at the Business side for the software deliverables. These will closely match the Business requirements.
- Software will be built at lower costs since it is designed more efficiently and with fewer errors.
- Projects will finish at the planned end date and at the specified costs.
- Processes and procedures have been standardized so roles and deliverables are unambiguously defined and templates, checklists, etc are available ready-made.
- There will be a structural attention to continuous process improvement.
- One can give free reign to one's creativity in designing software and need not bother about what process or procedures needs to be followed.

CMM Implementation

The organization chose to further professionalize its software development and support functions. Inspiration started with the goal of a 10% increase in productivity after the first year of the project in a domain and a 20% improvement in productivity within two years. Whereas DSDM offers the framework on the *how*, CMM describes the *what*.

One of the main goals was to achieve productivity improvements through CMM process design. The CMM framework has been used as reference to assess the maturity of the application development processes. Areas of attention are: requirements management; project planning; project tracking and -overview; subcontract management; quality assurance, and configuration management. DSDM assists to reach a 2 to 3 CMM maturity level as a properly documented and standardized software development process is aimed at. The CMM implementation at this financial services company was characterized as:

- Co-operation and participation. Staff in the domains were in the "driver's seat" and were in control of the implementation process. Both external (MphasiS) and internal consultants coached the staff.
- The primary focus of the implementation phase was to achieve business objectives. However, the Business was not involved as an integral part of the project team. To counter objections from the business departments on the way forward, they only became more involved after two years.
- The IT support organization also participated in the implementation to augment the support for CMM.
- Processes were designed bottom-up and the re-use of best practices was encouraged.
- Pilots started in three domains (Insurance, Business Contact Database (BCDB) and Networks). Lessons learned (e.g. same gaps found in the domains and same process enhancements required) in these pilots were incorporated into other domains[12].

The CMM implementation embodied four phases, as listed in Table 4, and took well over a year per domain. The 8:8:16:26 weeks was the default time frame used during the implementation phase. Originally, these phases were separate but after experiences in the pilot project the first two and the last two phases were combined.

During phase 1, a gap analyses was carried out to determine the difference between existing and desired level. The desired level was set at CMM level 2+ which meant that all KPA's of level 2 had to

Table 4. CMM implementation schedule for a Domain - 58 weeks

Phase	Description	Duration
1	Analysis and Gap report	8 weeks
2	Define and document CMM processes	8 weeks
3	Implementation of processes	16 weeks
4	Institutionalization of process	26 weeks

be met and two KPA's of level 3 (software product engineering & peer reviews). In addition an initial productivity assessment was carried out. These baseline metrics were necessary to demonstrate the required 20% productivity increase to determine the positive effects of the CMM implementation later on. The initial data were gathered from interviews and workshops with staff members. Finally the gap report was created that contained a list of necessary improvements. The nature of these activities changed from identifying gaps into creating awareness because the CMM coaches became more and more familiar with the existing gaps in the organization.

In the second phase the Process Improvement Team described the required process enhancements in close conjunction with domain experts. As much as possible one used existing processes to gain buy-in of staff. This activity also matured and the team changed into a Process Acceptance Team with domain experts simply agreeing with the required process enhancements. This phase was combined with phase 1 after a few pilots, resulting in 6 weeks in total instead of 16 weeks.

Based on the gap report, the domain experts prioritized the process enhancements. In addition internal audit findings and user feedback were used. Supervised by CMM coaches existing projects were selected and amended.

In the final phase the newly furnished software development processes were adopted as standard working practice. The main facilitation vehicle was the "Professional Attitude" project that apart from CMM institutionalization also incorporated DSDM working practices. Finally the preparation for the CMM assessment commenced that was carried out by a CMM certified external consultant.

Control

The BU' IT Management was committed to ensure the Integrated Quality System (IQS[5]) became fully embedded as the software development quality standard of BU-NL. In spite of software development off-shoring initiatives, the IQS remained of great importance. One of the aims of IQS (as part of the KPA subcontract management) was to be 'in control' of the software development activities of third parties. To that end the Software Engineering Process Group (SEPG) was established during the Inspiration program. This highest organizational body dealing with software development in the Business Unit was accountable for:

- Initiating and implementing a software development process for the entire Business Unit;
- Planning, tracking and co-ordination of process improvements and assessments;
- Defining and planning software process performance indicators and targets[13];
- Reviewing process training requirements.

It was made up of the following members (see Figure 4):

- Infrastructure Delivery Managers (IDM);
- Portfolio Managers (PFM);
- The head of Project Office IT (PO ICT);
- The Central Quality Officer (CQO);
- Route map owners (Full Expertise Teams, FET)
- Project management representatives of the business departments

IT Management budgeted 7 FTEs for 2004 and built a Quality Management organization. A number of QA roles were created: Process Improvement Managers (PIM), Project Quality Assurance Leaders (PQALs) and Configuration & Change Managers (CCM). In addition, a Central Quality Officer (CQO) was appointed at the end of the Inspiration program who had overall responsibility of IQS' usage, quality and support. The CQO owned the software development and maintenance policy and had two main tasks:

1. **to oversee the supervision of IQS' maintenance and usage in the various domains carried out by the PIMs.** Already during the Inspiration program, in order to properly monitor the quality of projects (i.e. process compliance) and its delivered software, PIMs were appointed that were responsible for a number of domains and reported to the project manager of CMM (later CQO), and the PFM, IDM. A quality assurance tool was used that contained Project Performance Indicators (PPI) to assess IQS compliance. When necessary the PIM created Process Improvement Plans (PIP) to make sure the software delivery process in a domain met ISQ requirements. The PIM had several PQALs in each domain that supported a specific project, typically 4 hours a week, in how to use the IQS and fill in PPI's. In addition assessments were carried out that

Figure 4. Organization at IT Development Department to control the process standard (IQS) at end of Inspiration program[14]

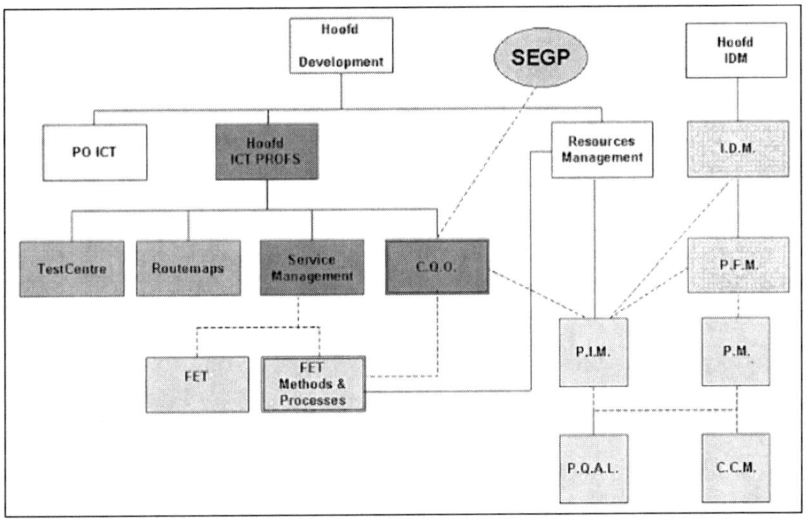

determined the quality of quality assurance itself. These were sent to the CQO as well. Although the PQALs were the ears and eyes for IQS implementation in projects, the quality of the project deliverables remained the project manager's responsibility.

2. **to manage the support of the route maps carried out by the FETs.** After the Inspiration program, day to day IQS support was carried out by a so-called Full Expertise Team (FET Methods and Processes) which had the following tasks:
   - To maintain, improve and disseminate knowledge on DSDM, CMM and the project management process.
   - To support and maintain all relevant IQS processes and content, like requirement identification and its related acceptance criteria.
   - To develop and provide IQS training sessions for stakeholders.
   - To facilitate the introduction of IQS into other (trans-domain) IT processes.

Changes to the DSDM route maps were allowed subject to approval of the PIM and CQO. These were approved when compliance to CMM was not at risk. One of the interviewees argued that initially control on IQS compliance was too tight: "*Before Inspiration it was far too loose but now the balance has tipped over to the other side*". For example, CMM allows tailoring so not all templates need to be filled in as long as it is documented why these are not used. Nor need all DSDM roles or principles be met (e.g. the 20% MoSCoW 'should haves'). "*First enforce the standards and accomplish discipline, then make requirements looser and allow tuning and tailoring. It is not about IQS but about accomplishing a good software product. But of course retain the good elements!*", he said. A few months after implementation, project staff was indeed allowed to deviate if certain aspects of IQS were not adding value, like some prescribed DSDM roles that did not make sense in small projects as part of tailoring.

The CQO role was fully embedded in the IT organization and monitoring and management of compliance of Business projects was still to be included. The expansion of scope was anticipated as follows: 1) IT projects and processes at IT; 2) IT projects at business; 3) Business projects at business; 4) Business processes at business. It was expected that the latter would only be added in the future. Then, the role of CQO should be moved from IT to Business according to one of the interviewees.

Results

Results DSDM & CMM

The implementation of DSDM was completed in October 2003 and that of CMM in June 2004. The goals of the Inspiration program were to: 1) Improve quality; 2) Increase productivity and reduce costs; 3) Respond more rapidly to change; 4) Improve co-operation between Business and IT; 5) Increase job satisfaction and attractiveness to staff. It was found that some of these goals were accomplished, whereas effects of others were less conclusive.

1. Quality improvements specifically attributed to DSDM or CMM could not be found as DSDM and CMM implementations were combined. Although results of key DSDM objectives like 'fitness for business purpose' and indicators related to the manageability of software were not available the amount of rework decreased. Quality improvements can be predominantly attributed to CMM, with 8 domains certified at level 2 and two at level 3 (January 2004). One of the DSDM coaches argued

that IQS resulted in a higher level of software quality because of: a) CMM requires configuration management including version control; b) CMM requires change management that ensures better control on all assets; c) The integral test process of DSDM ensures that most errors are revealed. Errors are unveiled related to for example requirements and the system architecture solution. As a consequence a drop of up to 80% of change requests related to errors was noted.

2. Productivity and costs savings were reached (and a saving of EUR 23 million for 2004 was expected). This contribution came from both DSDM and CMM. Based on the measurement data in Dashboard (function points per FTE) a cost reduction has been observed of between 10 and 20% compared to projects that did not use CMM and DSDM. The workshops enhanced communication between the stakeholders whereas prioritization urged the business departments to reflect on the financial consequences of requested software functionality. Adequate requirements management contributed to these savings too. As far as the reduction of the total development time is concerned, no convincing improvements were found, partly because DSDM was used for mainframe applications. The development in such an environment in combination with DSDM is not an optimal combination, since prototyping is more difficult than in a C/S environment.
3. Responding more rapidly to change was mainly contributed by DSDM although, CMM demanded one followed a change request process that formally documented such requests. In two-weekly workshops the results were presented to the end-user project members. Implementations that did not fully meet the requirements or changes in functionality could be satisfied easily. Responsiveness and flexibility improved significantly making a rollback of only 2 weeks possible, instead of a couple of months. In spite of this the overall time to market did not improve significantly.
4. As regards appreciation at the business side for the Inspiration initiatives, CMM played a less visible role, whereas DSDM contributions were obvious to Business and IT staff. For example, higher user satisfaction was achieved because participants felt they were taken seriously during workshops as part of DSDM. Although prototyping during workshops was considered as valuable, the co-operation between Business and IT did not improve significantly because the latter was not fully involved during the first two years of the Inspiration program. The CMM/DSDM combination, therefore, was perceived as a dictate from IT, which negatively impacted acceptance.
5. In general there was enthusiastic and close cooperation between the project members. A high level of user involvement due to DSDM workshops and prototyping was accomplished. Almost all IT staff followed DSDM courses and some of those even became DSDM practitioners. A perceived disadvantage of DSDM was that it had no ready-made templates nor predefined workflow, therefore, it became an "Inspiration" project deliverable. A list of other disadvantages and advantages based on a workshop with Business and IT staff is listed in Table 5. With CMM being less visible to staff, the appreciation for CMM was less on the whole than that of DSDM. Effects on creativity of staff using IQS were not available. Inspiration program management anticipated that this would increase, as staff should not worry about the process but should focus on the content and solutions. However, measurements were not carried out and there was no initial measurement anyway.

Regarding the effects of these IT process standards the following was found. There has been a significant increase in the productivity (FP/hr) although the initial phases took longer (e.g. Business study, see Figure 5). This is because of the requirements are discussed far better during the workshop sessions which also resulted in an 80% drop of follow-up changes after the project was finished. The throughput

Figure 5. Typical planned and realized budget allocation of software development projects with DSDM

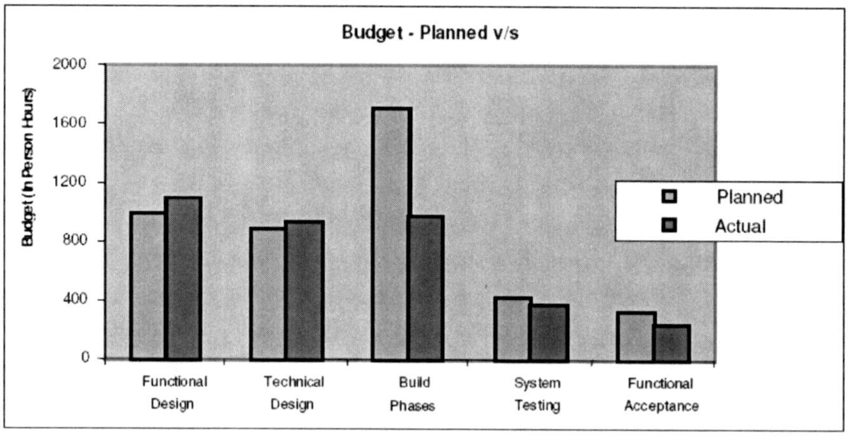

time of requests did not change. The increase in service performance can certainly be ascribed to the DSDM/CMM standards being utilized as will be discussed in later on in this Chapter

Also as a result of the workshops, staff motivation of all project members increased because the participant felt their comments and suggestions were better addressed. This was also true for risks that were integrally taken care of since these are part of the DSDM framework. Potential risks did not result in disclaimers but were actively being mitigated. Another spin-off of the workshop methods was an increase in innovative thinking. As staff on a project team came from both Business and IT disciplines, this made them reflect on existing business processes and thereby come to inventive solutions more easily. According to the interviewees the time to support the developed applications, client satisfaction, and time to market of new applications were positively influenced.

At the end of this field study (December 2004) an outsourcing initiative was announced using third party software development vendors in India. It was questionable whether it was still advantageous to DSDM as this method works fine in a single culture with limited geographical scope. This method was not well known and popular in India's software development industry. But even more importantly, some essential DSDM ingredients, like two-weekly prototyping workshops, are less appropriate in an off-shore setting. It was to be expected, therefore, that the waterfall method for software development would be introduced once again. The most likely scenario is that IQS will be updated to reflect the new conditions. For example, only parts of DSDM are kept, such as workshops in the Business Study and Functional Model Iteration (see Table 2).

And last but not least, unfortunately there was more control on decision making by line management than necessary, at least from a DSDM perspective. In other words the development teams did not feel they were as empowered as they should be, which was one of the reasons time to market did not drop. The other reason was already identified in Table 5: a longer Business Study phase.

Table 5. Perceived advantages and disadvantages of using DSDM

Perceived advantages	Perceived disadvantages
Requirements are set better and unambiguously	Requirements phase takes longer
Requires one to make choices in functionality	Projects are too heavy and bureaucratic
More control over functionality	By default no templates nor workflow are available
More attention is paid to quality	Too much documentation
Improved cooperation Business and IT	Learning curve is slow
More and rapid insight into costs	Existing roles and links to DSDM roles confusing.
	Too much focus on process and project administration and too less on deliverables
	Empowerment of teams in practice too little; frequent escalations still required.

Results Professional Attitude

Initially the plan was to implement a new quality system (i.e. CMM/DSDM). However, Professional Attitude (PA) was a prerequisite to make sure the DSDM and CMM standards were adopted successfully in the organization because of the necessary attitude/cultural change. This became apparent to the Inspiration program management after two years. Soon afterwards, the organization went through a consciousness-raising process with mixed success. The following successes have been achieved:

- Professionalism was on the daily agenda of almost all staff and people act accordingly;
- A large majority of the project teams assessed the PA project as good / very good;
- Internal coaches were generally well appreciated (rated 3.5 out of a 5 point scale);
- The project attracted the attention of other divisions and even from outside the bank.

There were certain aspects, however, that did not work out as intended. The main issues were:

- An off-shoring initiative drew attention away from PA for both staff and managers to a considerable degree;
- PA behavior agreements were included in the work agreement process but were not always met because of lack of commitment;
- Some contractors failed to adopt PA.

PA was incorporated into line management and features in the HR Personal Performance Plans. The implementation of PA was completed in June 2004. Unfortunately, only few measurements were carried out on staff acceptance and satisfaction of this project.

At the end of the case study fieldwork the following challenges still existed:

1. Staff had to show more discipline regarding time registration of project activities (in AIMS) to allow further assessment of productivity improvements.

2. Function Point analysis for all projects larger than 0.5 FTE had to be improved, also to assess further improvements.
3. More projects, including non software development ones, had to follow IQS

One of the interviewees pointed out that besides the Inspiration program other factors influenced the organization as well, like the fact that senior management indicated that they would be more actively involved in quality and quantity and that they expected this from all the staff accordingly. Furthermore to make these things visible a lot of effort was made in creating the Balanced Scorecard. These all resulted into the before mentioned productivity improvements.

Overall Results

Data from a time registration tool and productivity graphs were used to determine changes in performance. A study on the plausibility of these graphs showed that these were considered as acceptable (Schalken, 2004). The graphs showed the progressive average of the software project productivity (some150 projects) expressed in Euro/Function Point. This company used function points, as defined by NESMA (1997), that measures the functionality of software based on information flows (retrieval, storage, etc) and data files. Job point counters, most of them NESMA-certified, determined the function points. Schalken (2004) showed a decreasing trend, from 2646 Euro/FP in July 2002 to 1769 Euro/FP in September 2003. Another set of project related data, in the period from January 2001 to January 2003, revealed that costs expressed in Euro/FP decreased from 2250 to 1400 which resulted in an overall drop in costs of 20%. The Project Office published these figures every month in the Dashboard.

In Table 6, a comparison was made between projects that were carried out in four domains, with and without using the CMM/DSDM methodology. From these data it can be concluded that an increase up

Table 6. Measured productivity increases at some domains[15]

Domain	Domain Baseline	Productivity increase - (CMM/DSDM projects)	Productivity increase - (non CMM/DSDM projects)	Comparison - (CMM/DSDM v.s. non CMM/DSDM projects)	Platform/Technologies (Route Maps)
Core Business Systems (CBS)	2853 €/FP	+27%	+7%	*+20%*	Mainframe, COBOL
Customer Contact Center (CCC)	2697 €/FP	+20%	+6%	*+14%*	COBOL, Java, J2EE, JSP, Servelets, App Servers (Weblogic 5.1/6.1 and Tomcat) ASP, ASP.Net, DB2, IMS/DB-DC, JCL
eChannels	3806 €/FP	N/A	+6%	N/A	COBOL, Java, J2EE, JSP, Servelets, App Servers (Weblogic 5.1/6.1 and Tomcat) ASP, ASP.Net, DB2, IMS/DB-DC, JCL
Savings & Lendings	3225 €/FP	+22%	N/A	N/A	COBOL, Java, J2EE, JSP, Servelets, App Servers (Weblogic 5.1/6.1 and Tomcat) ASP, ASP.Net, DB2, IMS/DB-DC, JCL

to 20% was achieved by making use of the standardized software development methodology. Another observation was that other effects next to this standardization effort have resulted in an increase of 7% for these domains.

This productivity increase of 20% due to the application of the CMM/DSDM process standards was confirmed by Schalken et al. (2006), who used a number of statistical techniques and regression models to exclude potential impacts of project size and/or a domain (department).

Referring to the key objectives of the Inspiration program, the following overall results have been achieved.

Quality of deliverables increased and the number of error related changes decreased. There is also more insight into the costs and planning of the projects.

Productivity increased up to 20%. The 50% speed up of RAD was not accomplished, largely because tailoring (as part of CMM level 3) was not properly implemented. Nevertheless, first results in the DSDM phases were accomplished earlier.

An overall increase in time to market was not found.

Business-IT alignment improved mainly because of workshops and other user participation. However, the key stakeholder, Business Management, was not involved in the Inspiration program in the beginning, which had a severely negative impact on this key objective.

Attitude changed positively until the off shoring initiative was announced.

CASE ANALYSIS

The four constructs ' Process of Standard Selection', 'Application of Standard', 'Control of Standard' and 'Process Performance' and its derived variables will be discussed again, based on the results found in the previous section. After that the 4 propositions will be revisited.

Constructs

Process of Standard Selection

The choice of the standards for the Inspiration program relied heavily on the *business drivers*, which were: 1) to improve the quality of delivered products and to make both project schedule and costs more predictable; 2) to reduce the costs by continuous software development productivity growth; 3) to be able to respond more rapidly and effectively to change; 4) to improve co-operation between Business and IT in projects and increase user acceptance and satisfaction; 5) to add value to organization and employee. Little to no consideration was given to existing or emerging *business models* neither at the IT department or the whole Business Unit. *Involvement* from the Business side and Business IT *alignment* was low. The latter failed as of day one since the business departments were not involved in the program. No proper stakeholder analysis was carried out and only after two years the business departments became more involved. Involvement from IT engineering was high and that of IT operations medium to low. The DSDM and CMM process standards were selected in two separate ways:

- DSDM has been chosen for the following reasons: DSDM 1) was an emerging de facto standard; 2) should offer guarantees regarding quality of project members; 3) is supplier independent thereby minimizing the risk of lock-in; 4) facilitates the aim to reach uniformity in application development and offers at the same time the flexibility for departments to tailor it according to their needs

- CMM has been chosen for the following reasons: CMM 1) can be used as guidance for a quality system for software development and support on the way to a fully matured organization; 2) was already a de facto standard in the USA.

IT *Management knowledge* on standards was medium, whereas that of the corresponding business Management was low. With regard to the origin of the standards, both are a result of consortium collaboration whereas the first one is a regional standard (Europe only) and the second is a globally established de facto one.

Summarizing, the key business drivers in the standard selection were quality, costs, productivity, timelines and client & staff satisfaction.

Application of Standard

The description in the previous section showed a unique combination of two process standards had been implemented: DSDM and CMM. Apart from benefiting from synergies during implementation, DSDM can be used as enabler for CMM level 2. From the case description in the previous section one can conclude that the quality of the *Project management* was high. These process standards were used in a software development department, as part of an IT organization (approx. 2.000 FTE) of single Business Unit (approx. 27.000 FTE) of a globally operating financial services company (approx. 100.000 FTE). This characterizes the standards' *reach* and *range*. The *Local IT expertise* and *Awareness* at IT were both considered as high. Awareness at the Business side was low.

Unfortunately, both in the selection phase as well as in the application phase these standards were treated separately at first because it was thought that DSDM implementation could be carried out far more quickly than CMM. This caused inefficiencies and inconsistencies and later on both tracks were merged to overcome inefficiencies and inconsistencies.

Because of the off-shoring initiative it is doubtful whether DSDM will be used to its full extent in the future, since key attributes of DSDM are rapid Prototyping and intensive user involvement in all stages which will be more difficult to accommodate. CMM on the other hand is a well established quality management system standard for software development which is especially practiced in India, the 'would be' locating for software engineering in the near future for this financial services company. Therefore it is expected that CMM will remain to be used in this company and only the initial phases of DSDM (e.g. workshops with end users).

Control of Standard

During the Inspiration program, as part of CMM requirements, a number of QA roles were introduced in a QM organization with PIMs and PQALs to ensure IQS compliance. A department FET Methods and Processes was to maintain and improve the IQS processes and content (including the route maps) and to disseminate knowledge on DSDM/CMM to the stakeholders. Another initiative was the Software Engineering Process Group (SEPG), as part of CMM requirements. The SEPG was to plan, track and co-ordinate the software process performance and process improvements. Secondly they were to review the organization's software process database and training requirements. Furthermore, the quality improvements listed at the Internal perspective could be attributed to improved configuration/asset management, change control and risk management. These activities and the route maps can be considered as examples related to the variable *processes* and procedures of this construct.

The IT management team, including those of the software development departments, was committed (*endorsement*) to make IQS the quality standard of IT BU-NL, to ensure its performance and objectives. To that end they appointed a Central Quality Officer (CQO) that oversaw the use and maintenance of the software development and maintenance process standards (i.e. a *centralized* setup). The organizational *maturity* of the IT development can be considered as high but *collaboration* with corporate IT was low. The latter was not involved in the program.

In general the existing quality standard was considered to be too *restrictive* as regards compliance to the process standards. Therefore one was allowed to *deviate* if certain aspects of IQS did not add value, with approval of the PIM and ratified by the CQO. A version for small projects was developed also next to the possibility of tailoring. The idea was to first *enforce* the standards and accomplish discipline, then allow tuning and tailoring. To meet requests from the IQS customers, at the end of the Inspiration program the usability of IQS was improved (making it lean and mean) and all non-essential ingredients were eliminated. Overall IQS can be typified as fully mandatory (i.e. high level of *prescription*).

Process Performance

Key results were listed earlier: 1) Productivity improvements are determined expressed in €/FP from 2650 to 1500 in a three year timeframe; 2) Client satisfaction improved mainly because of workshops as part of DSDM. But on the whole this was poor as the business departments were not involved in the standardization program at the start of the project; 3) Quality of the developed software increased and number of error related changes decreased, because of improved configuration, change and test management as part of the IQS. Related to the BSC this maps to financial, customer and internal perspectives respectively. This will be discussed in the following four sub-sections.

Financial Perspective

As discussed earlier, other influences on productivity improvements next to the DSDM/CMM implementation were recognized. These included the announcement by management that performance data were measured and subsequently visualized in a BSC. From Table 6 it was found that next to the DSDM/CMM standardization effort an increase in productivity was found of 7%. Based on these measurement data a productivity increase was found of between 10 to 20% compared to projects that did not use CMM/DSDM. This was achieved by e.g. making use of the DSDM principles of facilitated workshops and prioritization according to "MoSCoW" and the CMM focus on project, configuration and quality management. A saving of EUR 23 million for 2004 was anticipated because of the usage of the process standards, but the actual *costs to develop* nor the *costs to support* the software were not precisely calculated by the organization.

Nevertheless, significant productivity and costs reductions resulted from the CMM/DSDM standard. In Figure 6 data from 290 software development projects are plotted with project start dates ranging from Jan 2001 (the official start of Inspiration) till July 2004. The data originate from the IT project office and includes per project, the costs per function point (€ /FP). Inspection of the data resulted in clean up and

Figure 6. Average project costs during Inspiration program

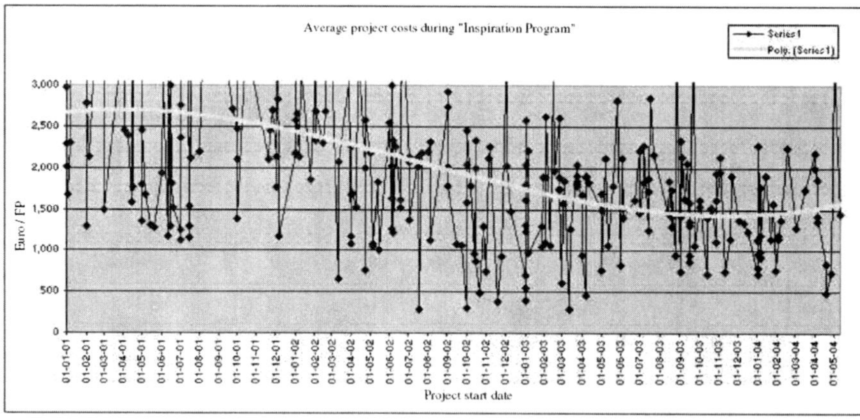

removal of 2 outliers. A third order polynomial trend line was calculated that shows an overall decrease from € /FP 2650 (January 2001) to € /FP 1450 (November 2003)[16].

A dissection of the data into smaller and larger projects (at 130 Function Points) or filtered on Project Manager (domain) showed a similar trend line as in Figure 6. Other financial figures, like Sales from Service and Revenue growth (Chapter 3, Figure 2) were not measured by the organization and could not be determined either with the data available.

Customer Perspective

A high level of user involvement was achieved because end-users felt that they were taken more seriously in the whole DSDM software development process. When implementations did not meet requirements or changes in functionality were necessary, every 2 weeks there was the opportunity to do so. Due to these workshops and prototyping an increase in *user satisfaction* was achieved but the relation between IT and Business did not improve significantly because of the lack of alignment during the implementation of the program. This negatively impacted on DSDM user participation in the projects. In general, with CMM being less visible to staff it was appreciated less (*attractiveness*) than DSDM. The *perceived complexity* of DSDM and CMM was medium.

Internal Perspective

Overall the service performance improved. *Quality* improvements were mainly attributed to CMM because of 1) configuration management 2) change management 3) *errors* within projects dropped and were revealed more easily. Potential *risks* were actively being mitigated as well.

Requirements were discussed much better during the DSDM workshops and in conformance to the CMM KPA requirements management that demands a mandatory review of the requirements resulted in a 80% drop of follow-up changes after the project. Quantitative data on the *Time to support* of developed applications were not available although interviewees argued this dropped slightly because of the usage of a single methodology. In spite of being one of the prime objectives, the *Time to market* for new applications only increased marginally. Nor were significant improvements found in this case found for *on time service delivery, throughput time of* service *requests* and *Time to develop.*

Leaning & Growth Perspective

Because of the workshops, *staff motivation* of all project members increased, as they felt more involved in the projects. In general, software development staff was positive towards the DSDM/CMM standard, however, for project members that were already working according to best practices, the maturing to the next CMM level(s) went too slowly. Another contribution of DSDM was the ability to respond more rapidly to change (*adaptability*) during the project. Although staff from both Business and IT disciplines from a project team tended to think over current business processes and could potentially come up with more inventive solutions, no increase in *innovativeness* was observed. With respect to *compatibility* of the developed software, no hard measurement data were recorded, although some improvements were made as all projects used the same kind of development routemaps. No changes were found concerning *robustness, scalability* and *availability* of the software. There were discussions on a 'reusability office' but no additional funding was available to make the software *modularized*. To do so, cost had to be funded by the running projects and this did not result into reusable software apart from some interfaces.

Propositions

In Chapter 4 four propositions were formulated. Using the analysis results from the 'Case Analysis' section it is discussed whether these propositions are supported by this case or not.

Discussion Proposition 1

- An effective (ineffective) IT standard selection positively (negatively) influences the application of these standards.

During the selection phase CMM and DSDM were selected to be used as intra-organizational IT process standards, but in the selection phase they were not treated as a single (combined) standard. As a consequence the standards were implemented separately in the first phase of the project. Furthermore, although the rationale for selecting the DSDM/CMM process standards was fully based on a set of business requirements, the business departments were not involved in the selection phase. This had direct negative consequences for the usage of these standards, such as lack of management buy in and lack of business participation. Consequently, this process is considered as ineffective. Based on the 'Case Analysis' section, therefore, one can conclude that the standard selection negatively influenced its usage (e.g. lower business participation and cooperation during the projects and CMM and DSDM teams that did not really work as a single entity) and proposition 1 is supported; in this case ineffective IT Standard selection negatively influences the application of IT Standards.

Discussion Proposition 2

- The application of appropriate IT standards contributes to better process performance and this performance is dependent on the control of its usage.

We have seen a significant drop in the costs (expressed in € /FP) of software development and an increase in productivity of up to 20% due to the introduction of a standardized software development process. Other process performance aspects from the customer, internal and learning & growth perspectives also showed improvements as well. Control was typified as formal and strict, including the deviation process, which all contributed to the successful application of this standard. Therefore it is concluded that this case supports proposition 2.

Discussion Proposition 3

- A low process performance due to the applied IT standards leads to changes in the way these standards are controlled.

We have seen that for small projects the DSDM/CMM quality management system allows tailoring, to comfort client satisfaction. Improvements to the IQS were also made based on input from the software development project teams and dedicated QA staff (PIMs and PQALs). Furthermore, changes in the way of implementing the standards were found. At first DSDM and CMM were implemented separately, but to mitigate inconsistencies, to improve staff acceptance and to overcome inefficiencies (higher costs) it was decided by IT management to combine these two projects with positive results. It is therefore concluded that this case supports proposition 3.

Discussion Proposition 4

- A low process performance due to the applied IT standards leads to reselection of these standards.

The DSDM/CMM standards were gradually introduced as of 2001 and were implemented fully per June 2004, so it was too early to discuss whether a low business performance would lead to reselection. Up to the end of the field research, IT Management tried to influence the performance by changing the control (in both the implementation and use) of these standards. Therefore the outcome of this proposition for this case is inconclusive.

The final results are listed in the Table 7.

Table 7. Evaluation of the propositions

No	Proposition	Supported by this case
1	Effective (ineffective) IT Standard selection positively (negatively) influences the application of IT Standards.	Yes
2	The application of IT Standards leads to improved business process performance and this performance is dependent on the control of its usage.	Yes
3	A low business process performance leads to changes in the way IT Standards are controlled.	Yes
4	A low business process performance leads to reselection of IT Standards	N/A

Table 8. Improvements resulting from the standardized software development process

Area	Result
Improved quality	Requirements were much better discussed during workshops (DSDM) and of mandatory reviews (CMM) resulted in an 80% drop of follow-up changes after completion of the projects.
Reduced costs	Development costs reduced significantly because of an increase in productivity of 10 to 20% compared to projects that did not employ the process standards for software development.
Increased flexibility	Responsiveness and flexibility were significantly improved because of the prototyping and workshops and a rollback is only 2 weeks max.
Improved customer satisfaction	The business departments were more satisfied with the end result although the time during the initial phases of the software development project took more of their time than before. Business IT alignment did not reach the intended level because of insufficient Business involvement.
Overall improvements in operations	This was not identified in this case study. For example, improvements in application availability (in operational phase) or throughput time of requests did not change (as requirements phase took longer).

CONCLUSIONS

Conclusions from this case study are as follows. The Inspiration program started in January 2001 and ended in June 2004. In these three and a half years the effects of this process standardization initiative have been identified in the analysis section and are summarized in Table 8. Of the 5 key objectives of the Inspiration program: 1) quality up, 2) costs down, 3) decrease time to market, 4) improve Business-IT alignment and 5) increase professionalism, only the time to market one was not met.

A cross-reference with the five anticipated improvements in business performance resulting from usage of IT in general (Shafer and Byrd, 2000) shows us:

MANAGERIAL IMPLICATIONS

During the implementation of the Inspiration program it became apparent one could not change the way staff used processes without giving careful attention to behavior as well. Furthermore, for small projects, IQS was considered as too heavy and this should have been recognized earlier on in the implementation process. Although there was the possibility of tailoring for small projects this was not carried out effectively throughout all domains.

A key governance issue, concerning Business participation in the project, was addressed late in the implementation process. The business departments became more involved after two years, which partially relieved the negative sentiment of Inspiration being "something of IT". Another governance issue was found regarding empowerment of development teams. They didn't feel as empowered as they should have been from a DSDM perspective as the balance of decision making resided more with line management than with these teams. So key is to involve all stakeholders early on in the selection and implementation process and to hold on to essential ingredients of the standard.

Finally, measurements, quality checking and tracking of project data were vital to drawing conclusions and making the correct decisions by the project team on how to apply these process standards. Basically the costs per function point were available but a lot of other data were insufficiently measured, such as employee satisfaction. To sell your company standardization initiative and to further improve your business performance one should make sure that all BSC perspectives are included in your performance measurements.

REFERENCES

Andersen, A. (1988). *Method/1 User Manual*. Arthur Andersen & Co.

Davenport, T. H. (2005). The coming commoditization of processes. *Harvard Business Review*, (June): 100–108.

De Zwart, C. (2003). Bank naar Hoger niveau. *Computable*, *14*, 16–19.

Harmsen, F., & Kleijnen, J. (2003). Invoering van DSDM, Informatie, Maart 2003 (in Dutch).

Humphrey, W. S. (1989). *Managing the Software Process*. Addison Wesley.

ISO 9003 (1991). *Quality management and quality assurance standards, part 3*. Guideline for the application of ISO 9001 to the Development, Supply and Maintenance of Software, International Organization for Standardization, Geneva, Switzerland.

Kaplan, R. S., & Norton, D. P. (1992). The Balanced Scorecard - Measures that Drive Performance. *Harvard Business Review*, *70*(1), 71–79.

Klei, O.P. (2002). DSDM voor legacy Omgevingen, Grotere betrokkenheid, tastbase resultaten. *Software Release Magazine*, *7*(11) (in Dutch).

Lock, D. (2003). *Project Management*. London: Gower.

Mintzberg, H. (1984). *Structures in Fives: Designing Effective Organizations*. Englewood Cliffs, NJ: Prentice-Hall.

NESMA. (1997). Definitions and counting guidelines for the application of function point analysis: A practical manual (2.0 Edition). Amsterdam, The Netherlands.

Nolan, R.L., & Gibson, C. (1974). Managing the four stages of EDP growth. *Harvard Business Review*, Jan.-Feb., 76 -88.

Paulk, M. C., Curtis, B., & Chrissis, M. B. (1991, August). *Capability Maturity Model for Software* (Tech. Rep CMU/SEI-91-TR24). Software Engineering Institute.

Paulk, M.C., Curtis, B., Chrissis M.B., Weber, C.V. (1993). Capability Maturity Model for Software, Version 1.1, Software Engineering Institute, CMU/SEI-93-TR24, August 1993.

Pijl, G. J., Swinkles, G. J. P., & Verrijdt, J. G. (1997). ISO 9000 versus CMM: Standardization and certification of IS development. *Information & Management*, *32*, 267–274. doi:10.1016/S0378-7206(97)00019-0

Schalken, J. (2004). *Inspiration Info - Productivity in more detail*. Internal publication FINCORP, 17, January 2004.

Schalken, J., Brinkkemper, S., & van Vliet, H. (2006). *Using Linear Regression Models to Analyse the Effect of Software Process Improvement* (p. 15). Amsterdam, The Netherlands: Publication of Vrije Universiteit, Department of Computer Science.

Shafer, S. M., & Byrd, T. A. (2000). A framework for measuring the efficiency of organizational investments in information technology using data envelopment analysis. *Omega, 28*, 125–141. doi:10.1016/S0305-0483(99)00039-0

Stapleton, J. (2002). *Framework for Business Centered Development: DSDM Manual version 4.1*. Kent, United Kingdom: DSDM Consortium, Ltd.

ENDNOTES

1 "INitiative for Software Process Improvement and Re-engineering of FINCORP's Terminology, Implementation and OrganizatioN" in order to create a professional and inspiring working environment.

2 One of the interviewees said that at first the business management was not really interested "*Hoe zo moet ik meedoen, het is jouw feestje. Wat heb ik met je productiviteit te maken...*" (In English: Why should I bother to cooperate? It is your baby and I have nothing to do with your productivity issues.)

3 The 50% increase has never been accomplished. Moreover the only measurements that were carried out were Function Point Analysis, so it was impossible to assess this objective.

4 A column (e.g. Channels) contained several domains (for example CCC, Customer Contact Center). There were 5 columns in total, see Figure 1.

5 The IQS integrated the following. IQS = DSDM + CMM + FINCORP specifics. DSDM has certain life cycles and proposes products. CMM sets certain requirements per product. FINCORP specifics were the project management part (different roles than in DSDM to comfort company politics), the route maps (incl. architecture) and elements of PA. During the field research DSDM 4.1 was used.

6 It did not reach a dominant position globally as DSDM was successfully challenged by the Rational Unified Process, RUP (Computable 10 Sept. 2004). Towards the end of 2004, DSDM was popular in the UK and the Nordic countries but certainly not in the US and India.

7 http://www.dsdm.org

8 DSDM by itself is not enough to comply with CMM level 2 (e.g. it does not satisfy the requirements review criteria of CMM).

9 www.sei.cmu.edu

10 Davenport (2005) mentions this as the primary reason for its success: "*Finally, a key reason for the popularity of the CMM is the flexibility of its use and application within organizations. It provides a framework for improvement but doesn't specify how an organization should improve*".

11 ref: FINCORP leaflet "Inspiration en het Capability Maturity Model"

12 CMM implementation in a domain resulted in a DQS (Domain Quality System). As best practices in a domain were more or less the same, DQS migrated to a SQS (Standard Quality System). Next, SQS in combination with DSDM resulted in IQS (i.e. DSDM integrated in the CMM framework).

13 Examples included: Euro/Function Point (with target 2004: Euro 1600), Hours/Function Point, Euro/Hour (tariff programmer), IT efficiency ratio: IT costs/ volume of business.

14 ref: The last Inspiration newsletter, Edition 19, June 30, 2004.

15 Source: Presentation "IT Domains Productivity Trend - Presentation to MT, June 2003"

16 Since November 2003 the productivity indicator seemed to be rising again which might have been caused by external influences, like the announcement of outsourcing and off-shoring of the complete software development organization.

Chapter 7
HR IS Standardization "CHRISP Case"

INTRODUCTION

To gain further experience with the conceptual model, as part of the theory testing phase, a third in-depth case study was carried out at FINCORP. The IS product standardization in this study relates to ERP HR modules of PeopleSoft®[1], which include the accompanying HR processes. These modules were selected as company IT standard.

As discussed in Chapter 3, measuring the real costs and benefits of IT investments is a notoriously complex problem (Brynjolfsson and Hitt, 1998). Asif and Schuff (2005) acknowledge that this becomes even more complicated when considering ERP technologies that impact on a variety of processes across the value chain. Chand et al. (2005, p.560) also acknowledge the problem of assessing the benefits of ERP systems is less well studied and understood, and illustrate the applicability of the Balanced Scorecard (BSC) to ERP systems. They list various reasons that motivate organizations to implement ERP systems, which can be split into financial and non-financial benefits (Table 1). Anticipated benefits related to company IT standardization can be clearly identified.

Furthermore, they integrate the four Kaplan and Nortons' Balanced Scorecard perspectives with Zuboff's *automate, informate and transformate* goals of information systems (Zuboff, 1985) in an at-

DOI: 10.4018/978-1-61520-759-6.ch007

Table 1. Reasons for ERP adoption (Chand et al., 2005)

	Business reasons for ERP adoption	Technical reasons for ERP adoption
Financial benefits	Accommodate business growth Reduce business operating and administrative expenses Reduce inventory carrying costs and stock outs	Replace hard to maintain interfaces Reduce software maintenance burden through outsourcing Eliminate redundant data entry Decrease computer operating costs
Non-Financial benefits	Acquire multi-language capability Acquire multi-currency IT support Improve inefficient business processes Eliminate delays and errors in filling customers' orders for merged businesses Provide integrated IT support Standardize procedures across different locations Present a single face to customer Acquire worldwide "available to promise" capability Streamline financial consolidations Improve company wide decision support	Reduce data errors Integrate applications cross-functionally Ease technology capacity constraints Improve IT architecture Consolidate multiple different systems of the same type

tempt to measure the contributions and impacts of ERP systems at operational, tactical and strategic levels. However, in this case study we will use the original perspectives to make comparison with the other case studies possible.

Enterprise Resource Planning

Enterprise Resource Planning (ERP) is basically a special instance of company standardization, although this field of research has not had much attention in the core IS standardization community. ERP systems are promoted as systems that improve organizational efficiency through both enhanced information capture and organizational redesign around defined best practices (Newell et al., 2003). ERP systems are highly standardized, requiring data standards across the enterprise and entail a great deal of process standardization as well (Gattiker and Goodhue, 2004). To date two vendors (SAP® and Oracle®) dominate the ERP market.

In academic literature there is mixed evidence on the success of implementing ERP systems, ranging from true success stories to dramatic failures. A myriad set of factors influence the outcome. Some even ague that results could be influenced by a mismatch between national and organizational culture by the stakeholders' values and beliefs (Krumbholz & Maiden, 2001).

On the whole, academics do not appear to be highly interested in ERP, apart from reasons for implementation or on challenges of the implementation project itself (Akkermans et al., 2003) and only very limited research has been carried out on the effects of ERP usage on business performance. Examples describing positive and negative effects include Ross & Vitale (2000), Gattiker & Goodhue (2004) and Staehr et al. (2004).

One of the founding fathers of the process approach of business improvement summarizes the following motivations for using ERP programs (Davenport, 1998):

- business process integration and its positive effects on manufacturing productivity and customer responsiveness;

- the provision of consistent data from a single source;
- cost reductions by staff reductions and decommission of legacy systems.

Davenport relates ERP failures to 1) the inherent technical complexity and 2) a mismatch between business requirements and technical specifications. The core problem, however, does not seem to be technical but people related, such as lack of support by senior management and inability to change work practices. Success factors reported by Ross & Vitale (2000) include:

1. Development of a clear business case, clarify performance objectives and establish appropriate metrics;
2. Assignment of your best people, 100% of the time, to the project and provide adequate resourcing in the post-implementation stage;
3. Demonstration of senior management commitment by communicating goals, program scope and the established a long-term vision;
4. Adequately addressing resistance to change;
5. Facilitate management reporting requirements.

Most of the literature focuses on the implementation of ERP and more specifically on the implementation in the manufacturing sector. Botta-Genoulaz & Millet (2005) are among the few that provide insight into the approach of implementing ERP packages in the service sector. They summarize the main reasons for ERP implementations in service companies that include: 1) to solve technical anomalies; 2) to reduce administrative workloads; 3) to replace unreliable management systems or dispersed legacy systems; 4) to make real-time data processing possible. They carried out case study research in the service sector and point out that on the whole financial service companies are hesitant about extending their ERP systems apart from some functional areas. Only a few modules are used focusing on financial, human resources and customer relationship. Motivations for introducing ERP systems and problems encountered during implementation are on the whole similar to general IS literature. Partial implementations of ERP modules in service companies are a salient detail. They suggest that the difference in importance of material flows and labor in manufacturing and service companies respectively could explain the dissimilarities of ERP configurations in service companies. Finally, for four out of six case studies, no ROI was performed.

CASE DESCRIPTION

Introduction

In November 1997, HR Managers from all (S)BUs of FINCORP decided to launch a project called 'Common Human Resources Information System Program' (CHRISP) consisting of an integrated HR management system and a global HR data warehouse. The intended goals of the global HR information infrastructure were:

1. provision of quality services that enable the enterprise to improve its HR function;
2. cost savings through empowerment of employees (self service) and therefore reduction of HR headcount and reduced HR IS costs;

Table 2. Current and future states of HR service delivery at project commencement

Current HR state	Planned HR state
Disparate HR departments and services	Single HR organization, process and tool
Several points of contacts per service	One point of contact for all services
System focused	HR-user and staff focused
One password per HR application	Single sign on for all HR applications
Requested information difficult to obtain	Easy information access
Branding differs per website	All web-sites have the same look and feel
Training required for each new service	Only a Minimal amount of training necessary

3) to comply globally with requirements of data privacy and protection regulations, rules of accounting and related HR corporate policies.

The main driver was the lack of consistency of HR information available in existing HR information systems and the impossibility of consistent analysis and reporting. The HR administration was based on dispersed spreadsheet-like tools and often no historic data were available. Frequently, questions from the head office could not be answered adequately or addressed in the optimum timeframe due to the fact that information had to be processed manually. Table 2 lists the difference between current and intended states as per 1998.

The root cause of the problematic HR service delivery was largely related to the decentralized organizational structure. The case company consisted of three strategic business units that were able to dismiss centrally issued requirements by the head office. In our discussion on standards control we will elaborate on this topic.

Implementation and Usage

In 1998 the steering group of the project selected the PeopleSoft Human Resources Management System ERP package and Business Objects as reporting tool. Selection of PeopleSoft (version 8.1 or higher) was based on its Best-in-Class rating. More specifically, PeopleSoft:

- had been rated Best-in-Class by all leading HRMS industry analysts;
- had been chosen by 75 of the top Fortune 100 and chosen by all 10 of Fortune Global 10;
- was number 1 HRMS vendor, worldwide over 50 million employees were listed in PeopleSoft HR packages.

Anyhow, the required functionality offered by PeopleSoft was the main reason for its selection. PeopleSoft started in the HR Business, whereas other vendors like SAP started in finance and added HR functionality later on. Because of this background, to date it is still the de facto standard for HR solutions. The fact that a large company as this financial services company chose PeopleSoft with accompanying free publicity resulted in interesting purchase and license savings as well.

In the case study it was determined how the implementation of PeopleSoft was carried out, whether it was possible to deviate from or customize the chosen standard and how this is reflected in the standard's usage. Implementation started in April 1999 as a conference room pilot of 10 days in which HR representatives from all over the world participated in workshops to determine process scope and functionality. Initially, there were no standard HR processes, reports, data definitions, etc. A basic set was defined and a successful pilot implementation in three countries proved the concept worked. In September 1999 the business case was approved by the Management Committee. On the basis of that implementation scenario a standard implementation toolkit, consisting of the PeopleSoft Basic HR Administration (back office HR processes, forms, and templates) was created and rolled out in other countries. The basic HR processes in scope were: 1) New and re-hire; 2) Leave, Suspension and Termination; 3) Job related changes (e.g. Transfer, Promotion and Demotion); 4) Fixed and variable compensation details (e.g. performance rating); 5) Compensation related changes; 6) Employee deductions and dependant details (e.g. change in Marital Status, Address changes); 7) Head Office expatriates.

Almost all HR processes were to be standardized, at a high level. For example, the recruitment process is basically the same for all countries. As a consequence, identical processes and Graphical User Interface could be used. These HR-processes were based on best practices of the case company, other enterprises and, of course, the knowledge integrated in the ERP package. But small differences remained at a more detailed level. An example of this is graduate recruitment, since school systems differ per country. HR data syntax and semantics of the data warehouse were standardized as far as feasible. One of the interviewees explained that these standards were based on corporate or country-specific standards. A 100% standardization globally could not be achieved because of country-specific's, for example legal and tax related requirements. Hence there were basically two distinct sections in CHRISP: a global part and a country-specific part. Table 3 lists some examples of country specific requirements.

Implementation was as much as possible plain-vanilla PeopleSoft, unless local constraints dictated otherwise, to minimize support costs and increase adaptability and portability. There are examples of companies that opted to fully customize ERP packages, that resulted in massive costs and an environment difficult to manage (e.g. Gattiker and Goodhue, 2004). As regards the different languages used throughout the enterprise there was the tradeoff between user acceptance and costs of implementation and support. This holds good for both the user interface and data storage. The language strategy was to provide a system that could support both local and global needs. For each specific country, therefore, implementation of both the English and local language was carried out as far as possible.

The blueprint of CHRISP defined the HR IS standard (PeopleSoft/Business Objects with menus, data entities, etc) which delineated how HR processes could fit in. Later on the implementation strategy changed as part of the Human Resources Transformation Programme (HRTP, see further on in this Chapter) that started with standardized HR processes (holiday allowance, promotion, etc) and only then aligned PeopleSoft/Business Objects with these processes. Before HRTP, the approach was to implement the basic functionality (PeopleSoft Admin workforce) in a country that was followed with a gap analysis. The basic premise was to implement plain PeopleSoft software and only to deviate when

Table 3. Country specific storage requirements prohibit a 100% standardized implementation

Country	Obligatory	Forbidden	Specifics
USA	Racial Origin	Date of birth	Tax facilities
Netherlands		Racial Origin	Occupational health and safety regulations
Germany	Military Service		Data protection act

local, fiscal or legal requirements dictated it (e.g., keep résumés for 5 years). In practice, timelines for implementation of other modules were set at the discretion of the country. When the gap analysis showed that some functionality was not available in the existing service offerings, the project tried to identify requirements from other countries to arrive at a new global HR process. As part of the gap analysis a local data conversion plan was made according to the following guidelines:

- Only data belonging to in scope business processes were captured in PeopleSoft.
- Historical data would not be loaded for small sites. Medium-size sites could load historical data, however, the amount of history to be loaded had to be agreed on by project management. Large sites were allowed to load historical data in the new information system.
- For any new data / functionalities that were agreed to be part of the local country implementation, the project assessed the effort required to amend the CHRISP-tools for automated transfer. The additional data had to be transferred manually if existing conversion tools could not be amended easily.
- On completion of the data upload, the local country users would be required to complete user acceptance of the conversion system. This was a formal sign-off by the project management before its release into the Production environment.

An example of a new HR process, following a gap analysis, was the global recruitment process and tooling that originated from a request by the US branch. This same concept was institutionalized with HRTP with the exception that in HRTP one started with the HR-processes and not with the PeopleSoft information system. A so-called process stream in HRTP was exclusively dedicated to HR-processes that delineated the required functionality. Then CHRISP was advised whether this functionality could be implemented in PeopleSoft. Not surprisingly, when CHRISP was included in HRTP it became the IS part of this transformation project.

PeopleSoft was implemented in phases. Initially, the Basic HR Administration was implemented such as Starters, Leavers, Suspension and Termination. HR policies were translated into best practice core processes that were presented to BU representatives for validation and approval. Later on, other processes/functionalities were added such as e-recruitment, employee self services, staff performance modules and helpdesk. Each new functionality constituted its own project. These additions were carried out at the BUs' request and were designed by the project in close conjunction with corporate HR. Any change to page, table (entity, attribute), logic or menu was considered as a customization. For small sized locations customizations could be requested only if it was legally required to make a modification, whereas for medium size implementations customizations could be requested only if changes would fit into existing modules. The project team assessed and decided whether and how to implement these changes. The functional scope, therefore, differed per country since implementation of the full PeopleSoft HR-suite was not strictly mandatory. In the Netherlands, for example, only the Back Office functionality was implemented.

Global implementation partner was a large consultancy firm who had between 60-70% staff of the 140 FTE allocated to CHRISP (consultancy costs were around €20M per year). Total projects costs were EURO 50M per year. After transition, the permanent organization would constitute around 30-40 FTE worldwide.

In May 2005, 60% of staff were serviced from PeopleSoft whereas the data warehouse (DWH) contained almost 100% of all staff. This DWH was used to support the local HR processes and to provide global strategic HR metrics. Three types of common Business Objects® reports were provided: 1) operational reports that assist countries in performing an efficient HR service (e.g., recent joiners and future leavers); 2) management information reports that allow tactical and strategic analysis of the organization (e.g. quarterly headcount per month or gender); 3) exception reports that allow countries to focus on quality assurance (e.g. report of all employees without a local ID).

The configuration of the technical infrastructure was as follows:

- One centralized system implementation, fully redundant in architecture;
- PeopleSoft ERP HR suite version 8.1 or higher in a 4-Tier architecture;
- Oracle version 8 or higher as RDBMS and Business Objects as reporting engine;
- HP-UX Operating System for HRMS, CRM and Portal.

PeopleSoft HRMS incorporated a four-tier architecture comprised of a Database Server, an Application Server, a Web Server and a user's web browser (see Figure 1). The Database Server, Application Server and Web-Server were stored at a secure location and communication between servers was considered secure (Secure Socket Layer, SSL Protocol). All communication between the PeopleSoft system and the end-user was carried out between the Web-Server and the Internet Browser on the end-user's machine, so a user would never contact the Application Server or the Oracle Database directly. When a user viewed a PeopleSoft page in a browser, it did not exist as a static page but was created dynamically on the web-server. Contingency arrangements were made to address long term loss of processing, in line with business requirements. The computer systems were fully mirrored and located in two separate computer centers.

Control

The CHRISP initiative that originated from Corporate HR started in 1999 and was heavily affected by the SBU formation a year later. As the newly formed SBUs were increasingly encouraged to settle own Profit & Loss', the rationale to implement an ERP/HR tool like PeopleSoft (and thus to change its HR-processes) became more difficult. In addition, there was a great deal of resistance because it was perceived as a dictate from head office and because of the large changes that are inherently related to implementations of ERP packages. Synergies were endangered since participating countries in the (S)BUs reduced implementation scope or even stopped it entirely. In January 2005, CHRISP became part of an organizational change program called Human Resources Transformation Program (HRTP) that resulted in an accelerated implementation rate of the intended PeopleSoft functionality. HRTP was structured into Group Shared Services (GSS) HR, which included the previously dispersed HR departments of the SBUs. CHRISP used to be run as a corporate project that did not have the mandate to enforce changes in the (S)BUs. HRTP was in essence the continuation and extension of CHRISP but now with a direct mandate from the managing board. Before its move to GSS HR, the project could not direct from the SBUs and/or countries to harmonize their HR artifacts (processes, data syntax and semantics, tooling, etc). This resulted in just 50-60% harmonization of all intended HR processes.

The implementation of the PeopleSoft HR IS standard accelerated because of two key changes. Firstly, because of the difference between CHRISP and HRTP which was twofold: 1) a system versus process focus regarding the related standards; 2) the implementation of the HR IS standard changed from a recommended to a mandatory nature as a result of increased management commitment to standardization

Figure 1. The 4-Tier Architecture of the PeopleSoft implementation

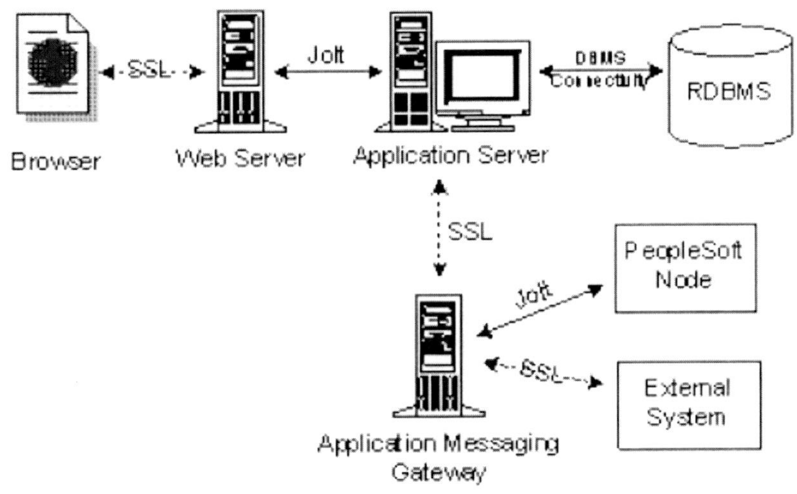

by GSS HR. Secondly, the arrangement of a number of operational units around the globe (HR shared service centers) that provided HR services based on PeopleSoft implementation. The HR shared service center concept required a global HR information system infrastructure. Countries could no longer refrain from migrating to PeopleSoft since the new HR services were based on PeopleSoft whilst HR support was delivered from these centers only.

With HRTP, no deviations were allowed from using PeopleSoft, requirements were hard and harmonization of processes and data became as much as 80%. This included general staff data, a recruitment system, performance management of staff, the payroll interface and career development. All HR departments worldwide had to comply with these standards unless there were country-specific fiscal or legal restraints. As an example, the HR learning & growth modules would be implemented unconditionally which could not have been accomplished by CHRISP alone. With HRTP, considerable commitment to CHRISP existed at various levels:

- Sponsorship by the Management Board;
- HR directors and HR professionals across all (S)BUs;
- Increasing business demands for strategic HR input.

In spite of this commitment, neither the product nor the implementation process has been incorporated in the set of corporate standards. The corporate standardization organization was not involved in the standard selection process of the HR IS standard whereas implementation standards are not part of the standardization methodology of this enterprise. At corporate level there was an initiative to standardize HR data semantics (such as hours per FTE, retirement age, working hours per week) as much as possible but which failed because of internal politics. Basically, there was a governance issue regarding HR data, where roles and responsibilities were not adequately assigned.

In conclusion, with the amended HRTP approach along with full endorsement at the highest management levels and strict enforcement, standardization of HR processes and related tooling progressed better than before with CHRISP.

Results

In this section the four perspectives of the BSC framework will be analyzed.

Financial perspective - CHRISP was in essence a 'soft' project and a prerequisite set of tools to turn HR into an efficient and effective organization. To that end, HR processes (pragmatics) and related end data (semantics and syntax) were standardized as much as possible and costs were of secondary importance. Although project costs, investments, depreciations and ongoing maintenance calculations were taken into account, it was hard to determine the financial benefits for the business case. The reason was that most countries could not provide the required figures of existing HR costs. This by itself was a very strong argument to introduce a global HR information system. Nevertheless, an indication of financial benefits was provided by the HR ratio (i.e. the number of HR staff to the number of total staff). The original figures differed per region from 1:50 to 1:150 and the general aim was to increase this ratio to 1:200. Referring to one of the key objectives of CHRISP, through the implementation of, among others, PeopleSoft employee self-service modules (e.g. address changes), a significant reduction in the number of HR staff was anticipated (up to one third of the total HR community).

As regards the CHRISP data warehouse (DWH), the interviewed team lead indicated that cost savings were very difficult to quantify, as the perceived benefits were typically 'soft'. For example, since all staff data are stored in the DWH one could easily query whether men and women in comparable roles were rewarded the same way (the answer was "yes"). Moreover, it turned out that career opportunities for women seemed to be even better, as the average age of women in senior management positions and the amount of time they worked for the bank was lower than those for men. Without the DWH, in order to gather these data, over a hundred questionnaires would have had to be sent, completed and analyzed. Obviously, this would have cost lots more in terms of time and money.

Customer perspective - In general, staff was satisfied (based on feedback the project got from Luxembourg, Germany and France) and the PeopleSoft GUIs were perceived as user-friendly. For end-user satisfaction the key success factor was that the system allowed easy changes (e.g. in home address and marital status). A few anomalies had to be taken into consideration. One of the interviewees mentioned an example of a number of HR staff in France who had never used Personal Computer systems before so that switching to PeopleSoft proved to be a major change.

Customers of the data warehouse were very pleased as well, since they could use a service that was not available earlier. Information was presented using Business Objects user-customizable reports. Certain requests could not be met since some information was not available. Examples included cross-country comparisons of cashiers or bond traders as no global role description nor rewarding system existed as yet.

Internal/business process perspective – Because of the standardized IS, the quality of the HR data in the DWH improved significantly. For example, headcount/FTE figures which used to differ 15% from numbers of the annual report (these numbers were obtained via an alternate route) decreased to less than 3%. Other examples included gender (initially too few women were reported) and date of birth (at first many were set to the default value of 1 Jan. 1900). Since 2001 the number of PeopleSoft implementations increased and covered 60% of 100.000 FTE FINCORP staff at the end of the fieldwork (November

Figure 2. Data ownership and effects on data quality

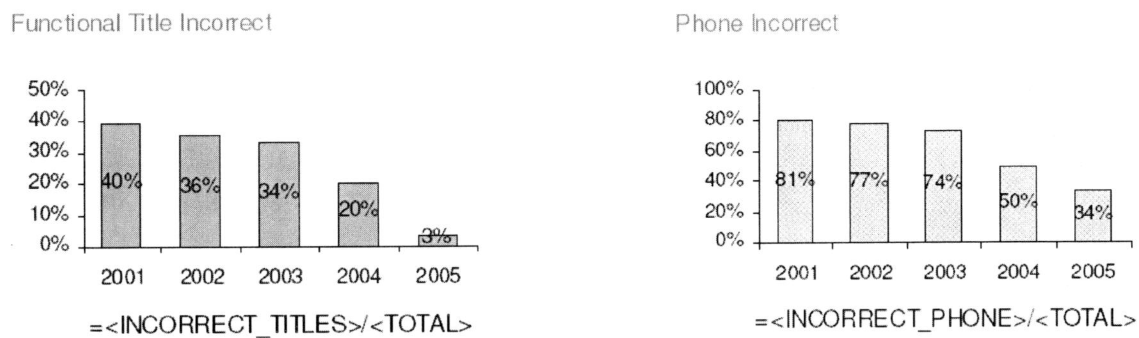

2005). Furthermore, in Figure 2 the progress in data quality of the title of staff and their phone numbers is depicted. "Functional Title" is part of basic HR administration and as the correct contents matters from a HR perspective, a steady progress of correctly assigned functional titles is observed. It is notable that HR owns this data element, as for the second one "Phone" ownership was unassigned yet. As a consequence, one third of phone numbers are still blank[2].

The quality of the data even became so good, that one could spot potential errors by looking at the average age of staff for departments that had recently been entered in the DWH. When, for example, dates of birth were entered as 1967 in stead of 1976 the mean age was above average. There were lots of other benefits (such as checks on the number of software licenses related to staff housed per building; starters' and leavers' data to update user access entries of information systems; staff turnover per department/country/business unit) that resulted from the DWH as data were readily available. For countries that already had an adequate local HR information system, the benefits were not that great. Nevertheless, introduction was still advantageous at corporate level since this allowed transparency and enhanced interoperability and flexibility. Moreover, with the existence of standardized data elements and structure it was possible to instantly report such figures with an increasing level of accuracy. Before introduction of the DWH it took an enormous effort to produce this management information. Such reporting, part of the introduction of the PeopleSoft product and process HR IS Standard, improved strategic decision-making. The quality of the PeopleSoft implementation as a whole also improved. One of the interviewees elaborated that "*during the course of the project the total number of support staff doubled, the number of supported end-users increased by more than a factor of two, whereas the number of incidents concerning the PeopleSoft application per support staff remained the same.*"

Learning & Growth perspective - Considering this final perspective, HR staff activities, job satisfaction and IS availability have been evaluated. HR staff satisfaction differed per country since each country had its own implementation. Differences in implementation were observed as regards: 1) HR staff participation, 2) implemented functionality, 3) added value of the new system compared to the legacy HR system. The responses of HR staff from the different countries varied, partly depending on the way PeopleSoft was implemented. If hardly any HR IS was available, improved satisfaction could be easily met. For countries that already had a local HR IS infrastructure, HR staff had mixed feelings. In small countries, for example, browsing through a large number of PeopleSoft pages for new hires was considered a burden. Another remarkable example was found in the Netherlands, where feedback was

Table 4. Anticipated changes in activities for HR staff

	Before introduction PeopleSoft	After introduction PeopleSoft
Strategic	10%	20%
Tactical	20%	50%
Operational	60%	30%

not positive since only the back-office part of PeopleSoft was implemented. This occurred because the full scope of the HR ERP suite was not mandatory and thus one could not speak of a standardized way of implementing the suite. As a consequence, a lot of manual work, which in the PeopleSoft self service philosophy would be performed by employees, had to be done twice because no automated link existed between front and back-office applications. Obviously, this had to be fixed by the introduction of the Front Office tools later on. In the North America branch, though, the PeopleSoft suite was implemented fully (both Front and Back Office functionality) and responses have been very positive indeed. For all other countries, reactions are in between these two extremes.

Another important success factor was the level of HR staff participation during the project. Satisfaction was high when participation was large and vice versa. Satisfaction also depended on the amount of functionality that had been requested and which % was actually implemented. At the individual level, there was a negative feeling since HR staff perceived PeopleSoft as the primary reason they lost part of their autonomy. In addition the standard software affected their employability, which of course, is typical for any BPR/ERP implementation. Because of the efficiency gains through employee self-service, the core of the daily activities of HR staff shifted from operational to tactical tasks, as listed in Table 4.

As far as the IS availability is concerned, this was considered to be sufficient and corresponding to the importance of this system. The system had a fully redundant high available system architecture. No differences were reported between hardware or software failures, which were low anyway. Although there were no quantitative data available from the old environment the new system was a significant improvement compared to the disparate and dispersed legacy HR-systems.

CASE ANALYSIS

Constructs

Process of Standard Selection

The HR IS standard was selected based on its Best-in-Class rating by the following stakeholders: senior SBU HR representatives, project management and corporate HR. The *management knowledge* of such standards was moderate to high. The *business drives* to come to the standard were clear and a key reason to start the standardization initiative (quality up; costs down; comply with local and international regulations). The HR *business model* also played a principal role in the selection phase, as the HR IS standard was to be used in a centralized organizational set-up. Because this standard concerned an ERP/HR information system the selection process not only ended at the tool and its embedded HR processes.

Agreement also had to be reached on data syntax and semantics which proved to be difficult because a number of idiosyncrasies, for example in country-specific legal and tax regulations.

But even more improperly, as roles and responsibilities between stakeholders were not effectively assigned, they did not succeed in standardizing (or even defining) all relevant HR data elements (entities). As a consequence, the data standardization process was limited to a relatively small set of entities. In the DWH (part of the IS Standard) only a few corporate and country-specific standardized semantics were accomplished. A same line of reasoning holds for the HR processes in the initial phase of the project. Some HR processes were excluded since no enterprise-wide agreement could be reached. This was especially the case for HR processes linked to PeopleSoft Front Office functionality. Altogether, the selection process, especially that of the data entities, was not considered as effective. Both *Business* and (corporate) *IT* were heavily *involved* but the level of *Business IT alignment* was considered as low to medium only. Involvement of local IT was low.

Application of Standard

The selected HR IS standard and its embedded processes have been implemented and used throughout the enterprise, across all HR organizations which typifies its *reach* and *range*. It was found that a limiting factor in full standardization was caused by country-specific legislation. Local IT *expertise* on HR IS standards was in general low, which was to be expected as they were not involved in the selection process and standard *awareness* by the Business and IT were high and low respectively. Overall the *project management* quality was considered as low (overrun in time and lack of project deliverables).

The most important development during the implementation of the HR IS was the change in focus from a system (CHRISP) to a process (HRTP) one. The process focus turned out to be the preferable one, since this forced the stakeholders to unequivocally follow the standardized process flow that was subsequently implemented as part of the information system. Doing it the other way round showed that this did not necessarily result in the standardized HR-processes that was aimed at. This resulted in a big change in the project structure as the original CHIRSP project became embedded in the HRTP project.

For countries with only small offices, like Uzbekistan, it was only after the introduction of Shared Services Centers that it became cost efficient to introduce PeopleSoft. Before GSS there were only roll-outs of PeopleSoft at country level for countries with more than approximately 50 staff. The first HR Shared Serve Center was launched at the US branch in April 2004. These service centers included a call center, data entry and helpdesk and functional specialists as well. In addition support for the CRM product of PeopleSoft was delivered. For the whole enterprise, 4 Hubs (Chicago, Sao Paulo, Amsterdam and Mumbai) would be implemented.

Control of Standard

The HR IS standard was implemented, in principle, as plain-vanilla PeopleSoft as much as possible to minimize project and ongoing maintenance costs. Only in the case of country-specific requirements *deviations* were allowed. The project team could override customization requests if these were too costly or if they negatively affected the manageability of the system. However, as implementation of the full scope of the HR IS functionality was not mandatory (concerns variable *prescription*), some countries carried out a partial implementation (e.g. backoffice functionality) only. In most locations, the local HR business was heavily involved during the implementation and was authorized to make key decisions.

For example, new functionality within the standard was added at local HR's request to increase buy-in for this project and enhance cooperation with the project team (too less *restrictiveness*). In addition, it turned out that the HR business in some business units did not fully support the standard (lack of *endorsement*). There were several evasive maneuvers to prevent full implementation of the HR IS in a country. Since the local HR business had a decisive say in the implementation timeframes, this allowed for slippage or even cancellation of parts of the implementation. As a result there was no standardized way of implementing the HR IS (concerns variable *processes*) which negatively influenced the overall applicability. The *maturity* of the HR organization can be considered as low and *collaboration* between corporate IT and local IT was low.

It was discussed why the formulation of syntactical and semantical HR data standards shattered. This was a combination of 1) lack of mandate and decision rights, and 2) the nature of the advises (recommended instead of mandatory - prescription). Lack of ownership of some HR data elements remained an issue. A similar issue arose during the course of the implementation of the HR IS standard. Process performance did not improve at the pace initially anticipated. Furthermore, implementation time took too long as the project had been running for 6 consecutive years and the end was not in sight. Moreover, the project scope remained too narrow since only 60% of staff used (parts of) the HR IS standard with just 50-60% of the HR processes in scope standardized. Because of that, organizational embedding and control were rigorously changed in early 2005 with the move of CHRISP from Corporate HR to a newly formed HR services mandated by the Managing Board (concerns variable *centralization*). This resulted in positive effects to the application of the IS standard:

- Project scope became fully mandatory, which allowed no ad-hoc deviations and resulted in a project scope that could be effectively enforced and that approached the one originally intended.
- Senior management endorsed the implementation and use of the HR IS standard, which resulted in *enforcement* of the standard adoption and in an 80% standardization of HR processes and data.
- Implementation scenario changed from a system focus into one with a process focus, which required the stakeholders to adopt the standardized HR processes that were subsequently implemented as part of the HR information system.
- Establishment of the HR shared services concept changed roles and responsibilities regarding HR IS support, which resulted in the impossibility of countries to circumvent this service and its related standards.

Process Performance

The four perspectives on business process performance showed a number of changes as a result of the usage of this company HR IS standard.

Financial Perspective

At the end of the field study (December 2005) the project had not yet been completed, so that actual figures on cost savings were not available. No precise calculations were made, in terms of *ROI* etc, as it was impossible to get some key cost figures from the local HR departments. Soft financial benefits were identified, such as prompt and high quality management reporting in stead of costly manual processing. Implementation costs were at least 20M Euro a year, with the project already running for 6 consecutive years. The *costs to develop* this new environment were anticipated to be lower as changes can be carried out far more easily because of the standardized HR IS. Structural cost savings, the *costs to support,* were to be achieved as a result of reductions in HR staff, using the HR ratio moving up from 1:50 to 1:200, with this HR IS standard as an important precondition. Reduction of HR staff through employee self service, however, did not take into account the new indirect costs resulting of staff now performing administrative activities themselves.

Customer Perspective

The *perceived complexity* of the HR IS standard was high for small countries, which considered it as overkill and medium for other countries. Regarding the different languages used throughout the enterprise the tradeoff had to be made between user acceptance on the one hand and costs of implementation and support on the other hand. By and large, the HR IS standard has been perceived as satisfactory by the end-users, with ease of usage as a key success factor. Customers of the DWH were very *satisfied* because of the new functionality offered, enabled by standardization. As to the satisfaction of HR staff, feelings were mixed (see Leaning & Growth perspective).

Internal Perspective

The quality of HR related data improved significantly which resulted in, for example, enhanced correctness, completeness and timeliness of management information. In addition, during the ongoing global rollout, the relative number of incidents related to the usage of the HR IS standard decreased (*error and rework rates*). Because of a number of problems during implementation the *service quality* differed country by country but overall it improved, especially the management information. Risks related to HR activities were anticipated to be lower as the HR IS implementation was dedicated specifically to adhering to both global and country specific requirements. Qualitative values of other variables of the conceptual model related to this construct *(on-time service delivery, throughput time requests, time to market* and *time to develop* and *support*) could not be determined. Either these were not measured by the case organization or because the project was not yet finished, although the general comment from the interviewees was that these would change for the better.

Leaning & Growth Perspective

Responses and satisfaction/*motivation* of HR staff varied depending on the level of HR staff project participation and the amount of requested HR IS functionality that was implemented. Secondly, there was negative sentiment of HR staff at times due to perceived lost of autonomy and potential negative impact on employability. As far as *innovativeness* is concerned the daily workload of HR staff is to change from an operational to a tactical focus.

Because now a single standard is being used, it is expected that *compatibility, adaptability* and *scalability* become easier, so changes can be implemented faster. End result of all the efforts is a more stable (*availability, robustness*) and integrated HR IS environment (so not *modular*). The availability of the system already proved itself.

A striking contrast with the C/S case study was that one of the conclusions was to integrate as little as possible. The key difference in this HR IS case study is that one deals with a process oriented environment with just a single application whereas the C/S case study dealt with a multitude of (hardware and software) products.

Propositions

In Chapter 4 four propositions were formulated. Using the analysis results from the earlier sections it is discussed whether these propositions are supported by this case study or not.

Discussion Proposition 1

- An effective (ineffective) IT standard selection positively (negatively) influences the application of these standards.

During the selection process several key stakeholders agreed on the chosen HR IS standard, based on functionality, costs and market dominance. These stakeholders were senior HR business representatives, project management and corporate HR and played a crucial role in the selection process. Accountabilities with respect to standardization of HR processes and data elements were not assigned effectively because no enterprise-wide agreement could be reached. Although the chosen HR IS standard has been implemented and has been used throughout the enterprise the selection process can not be considered as effective because:

- Some local HR business did not support this standard and could obstruct implementation of both timelines and project scope (e.g. HR front office processes).
- Standardization of HR data syntax and semantics remained at a bare minimum.
- There was no input from end users in the selection process.

In conclusion, the standard selection process of both HR processes and data were ineffective and negatively influenced the implementation and usage of the IT standards (no standardized implementation, the scope differed per country; some data elements had no ownership). It is concluded, therefore, that proposition 1 is supported by this case.

Discussion Proposition 2

The application of appropriate IT standards contributes to better process performance and this performance is dependent on the control of its usage.

A number of changes in business process performance related to the four BSC perspectives were presented as a result of the usage of this HR IS standard, which was by and large positive. The full HR IS functionality, however, was not of mandatory nature during the CHRISP phase which negatively influenced its usage. Local HR business was allowed to make key decisions (for instance on functionality, scope, implementation timeframes) which increased collaboration with the project staff but had negative effects on the overall performance. In the HRTP phase, which basically was a change in controlling the implementation and usage of the standard, a positive shift in process performance was found. In conclusion, proposition 2 is supported by this case. This proposition also supports the results found by (Kayworth and Sambamurthy (2000).

Discussion Proposition 3

A low process performance due to the applied IT standards leads to changes in the way these standards are controlled.

During the course of the implementation and usage of the HR IS standard, business process performance was not improving at the pace initially anticipated. Time to implement took much longer than expected (the project was running for 6 consecutive years) and the scope remained too narrow (with only 60% of the community using the HR IS standard, and with only 50-60% standardization of the HR processes in scope). Not enough HR data elements were standardized globally either. It was discussed that in early 2005 the control of the HR IS standard changed because of the issues listed above:

- scope and standards became fully mandatory;
- senior management became fully committed and endorsed implementation and use;
- implementation changed from system focus to process focus;
- introduction of HR shared service centers (i.e. centralization).

So, it is concluded that proposition 3 is supported by this case.

Discussion Proposition 4

A low process performance due to the applied IT standards leads to reselection of these standards.

In this case study it was found that a lower than required process business performance changed the way the IS standard was controlled, such as the change of implementation from a system focus to process focus. Although the project was running for 6 consecutive years, and required process performance was not met (in terms of lowering HR costs, customer satisfaction, process scope & data quality) this did not result in reselection of the IT standard. As discussed above, a lot of changes were made including the switch to another third party implementation partner, however, reselection of the HR IS standard was not taken into consideration at all. It is concluded that proposition 4 is not supported by this case.

The final results are listed in the Table 5.

Table 5. Evaluation of the propositions

No	Proposition	Supported by this case
1	An effective (ineffective) IT standard selection positively (negatively) influences the application of these standards.	Yes
2	The application of appropriate IT standards contributes to better process performance and this performance is dependent on the control of its usage.	Yes
3	A low process performance due to the applied IT standards leads to changes in the way these standards are controlled.	Yes
4	A low process performance due to the applied IT standards leads to reselection of these standards.	No

CONCLUSIONS

The four constructs of the conceptual model, based on the literature study and pilot case study, were clearly present and several variables have been identified to possibly control business process performance.

A cross-reference with the five anticipated improvement areas resulting from IS usage in general (Shafer and Byrd, 2000), Tale 6 lists the results of the usage of this company HR IS standard.

Apart from the observed negative effects in customer satisfaction, other drawbacks related to introduction of global HR information system are: 1) At country level and specifically for countries that already had proper HR processes and tooling, the advantages of a global HR information system were only marginal; 2) It required a tremendous amount of time and effort to align all stakeholders to come to a standardized environment. Resistance to change and even counterproductive behavior was experienced by both project and corporate HR.

Finally other influences, besides the application of the HR IS standard, might account for the observed changes in process performance as well. Contributing factors could be organizational change, active involvement of senior management and the fact that there is change anyway, which was also found in the DSDM/CMM case study. As part of our conceptual model, however, these are almost all related to the introduction of the HR IS standard and its accompanying standardized HR processes.

MANAGERIAL IMPLICATIONS

The IS standard has been *selected* based on functionality, costs and market dominance. The main drivers to introduce the HR IS standard were cost savings and the lack of quality HR services. A default *implementation* has been chosen as much as possible in order to minimize support costs and increase adaptability and portability. Apart from the phased approach to alleviate the considerable changes required for successful implementation, the HR IS implementation has been piggybacked on an even larger organizational change program to take advantage of that momentum. Another important observation was that the implementation sequence "technology, process" or "process, technology" impacts the end-result. In other words, to agree on processes first, then on the supporting technology pays off. Furthermore, the fact that only a single module of an ERP Suite has been implemented confirms the

Table 6. Improvements resulting from the standardized IS environment

Area	Result
Improved quality	Positive: Consistent and timely management reporting; improved HR data correctness and completeness.
Reduced costs	Positive: Reduction in HR staff; decommissioning of legacy HR systems.
Increased flexibility	Positive: Global changes (business processes and IT) can be effected easily.
Improved customer satisfaction	Positive: In general, end users are satisfied. Negative: Local HR business felt that they lost a significant part of their autonomy and it negatively impacted on their employability.
Overall improvements in operations	Positive: Better maintainable technical environment and thus more stable; creation of global information infrastructure that satisfied local and fiscal requirements. Negative: For countries that already had adequate HR processes and tooling, the advantages were only marginal. For small countries the IS was even considered to be over the top.

findings of Botta-Genoulaz & Millet (2005). They showed that by and large financial service companies are hesitant about extending their ERP systems outside some functional areas.

Furthermore, there was a governance issue regarding HR processes and data (semantics) as no enterprise-wide agreement could be reached. Accountabilities with respect to standardization of HR processes and data elements were not adequately assigned. These were by and largely resolved by making clear the 1) mandate and decision rights of all stakeholders, 2) accountabilities and ownership of HR data 3) roles and responsibilities of both project and HR organization, 4) nature of the advises being mandatory instead of recommended.

Three variables related to IS standard *control* identified in the pilot case study: senior management commitment; facilitation of and adherence to implementation processes; enforcement of the selected product and process standards were all found to be important success factors in this case study as well. The managing board has mandated the standard adherence. Furthermore, the decentralized organizational structure of the case organization, which is closely related to the IS standards control (i.e. *governance*), has been identified as a key determinant that influences business process performance. Moreover, the effects of company politics related to implementation and usage of the IS Standard, played an important role and these have been mitigated by means of strict mandates from top management and a change in the organizational structure.

REFERENCES

Akkermans, H. A., & Van der Horst, H. (2002). Managing IT infrastructure standardisation in the networked manufacturing firm. *International Journal of Production Economics*, *75*(1-2), 213–228. doi:10.1016/S0925-5273(01)00201-8

Asif, A., & Schuff, D. (2005). A process-based framework for assessing IT value. In *Proceedings of the Eleventh Americas Conference on Information Systems, Omaha, NE, USA, August 11th-14th 2005*.

Botta-Genoulaz, V., & Millet, P.-A. (2005). An investigation into the use of ERP systems in the service Sector. *International Journal of Production Economics*, *99*(1), 202–221. doi:10.1016/j.ijpe.2004.12.015

Brynjolfsson, E., & Hitt, L. M. (1998). Beyond the productivity paradox. *Communications of the ACM*, *41*(8), 49–55. doi:10.1145/280324.280332

Chand, D., Hachey, G., Hunton, J., Owhoso, V., & Vasudevan, S. (2005). A balanced scorecard based framework for assessing the strategic impacts of ERP systems. *Computers in Industry*, *56*, 558–572. doi:10.1016/j.compind.2005.02.011

Davenport, T. H. (1993). *Process Innovation: reengineering work through Information Technology*. Boston: Harvard Business School Press.

Gattiker, T., & Goodhue, D. (2004). Understanding the local-level costs and benefits of ERP through organizational information processing theory. *Information & Management*, *41*, 431–443. doi:10.1016/S0378-7206(03)00082-X

Kayworth, T., & Sambamurthy, V. (2000). Facilitating localized exploitation and enterprise-wide integration in the use of IT infrastructures: The role of PC/LAN infrastructure standard. *The Data Base for Advances in Information Systems*, *31*(4), 54–81.

Krumbholz, M., & Maiden, N. (2001). The implementation of enterprise resource planning packages in different organisational and national cultures. *Information Systems*, *26*, 185–204. doi:10.1016/S0306-4379(01)00016-3

Newell, S., Huang, J. C., Galliers, R. D., & Pan, S. L. (2003). Implementing enterprise resource planning and knowledge management systems in tandem: fostering efficiency and innovation complementarity. *Information and Organization*, *13*, 25–52. doi:10.1016/S1471-7727(02)00007-6

Ross, J. W., & Vitale, M. (2000). The ERP revolution: surviving versus thriving. *Information Systems Frontiers*, *2*, 233–241. doi:10.1023/A:1026500224101

Staehr, L., Shanks, G., & Seddon, P. (2004). Understanding the Business Consequences of ERP Systems. In Adam, F., & Sammon, D. (Eds.), *The Enterprise Resource Planning Decade: Lessons Learned and Issues for the Future* (pp. 72–91). Idea Publishing Group.

Zuboff, S. (1985). Automate/informate: The two faces of intelligent technology. *Organizational Dynamics*, *14*(2), 5–18. doi:10.1016/0090-2616(85)90033-6

ENDNOTES

[1] In January 2005, Oracle Corporation acquired PeopleSoft. Its products continue to be used under the product line "PeopleSoft Enterprise"

[2] In 2004 and 2005 some branches saw the added value of the DWH and started to use HR phonebook, instead of building their own local system. This explains the increase in correct phone numbers. It is an example that shows how IS standardization can improve customer satisfaction and enhance data quality and reduce costs.

Section 5
A Reflection Upon the Case Studies:
Towards a Corporate IT Standardization Management Framework

In this chapter a cross case analysis will be carried out using replication logic tactic (Yin, 1994, p.46). The case studies will be compared and the initial conceptual model, including its propositions, will be reassessed. The insight gained will be discussed resulting in an enhanced conceptual model. This enhanced model will be tested in a fourth and final case study to increase validity of the case study research.

Chapter 8
A Reflection Upon the Case Studies

Before the Corporate IT Standardization Management Framework is presented, first a summary and cross case analysis of the previous three case studies is given provided.

SUMMARY OF THE CASES

Case Study I (De Facto Product Standards)

Selection: At the head office a Client/Server (C/S) standardization project was carried out within a 2-year timeframe, affecting 10.000 end users of a business unit. Main objectives of the standardization project, which included hardware and software of both front and back end, were 1) to reduce costs of development and support of both hardware and software; 2) to facilitate change flexibility. One of the core components of this program was application software rationalization, which ranged from desktop productivity tools to applications for complex financial transactions. Guiding principle in the application rationalization phase was that only one type of software was allowed, preferably the latest version, unless business functionality was impaired considerably. The balance between functionality and support/

DOI: 10.4018/978-1-61520-759-6.ch008

license costs was the main criterion for putting an application on the list of standard software. The total number of client and server applications was downsized rigorously by approximately a factor 22 (from 6000 to 265). This list of software products and C/S hardware constituted the set of IT standards.

Application & Control: Heavy load applications that used to run on (midrange) desktops were migrated to high-end servers. This server based computing concept allowed running such applications on low-end desktops, which resulted e.g. in low overall hardware purchase and maintenance costs. In line with the observations by Rada and Craparo (2001), a technical review team carried out the verification of the specified IT product standards in projects. Strict conformity to the related service and project management processes were key elements in the successful usage of the set of IT standards. The team also reviewed any upgrades, replacements or patching needed. Standards were reviewed every 2 years and the review process often resulted in a new product that was incorporated in the set of IT standards, reflecting developments in both the technological and business environment.

Case Study II (Informal Process Standards)

Selection: This standardization initiative was launched at the main Software Development department with the aim of bringing about fundamental changes in the way Business and IT developed software products. The goals of the program were to: 1) Improve quality; 2) Increase productivity and reduce costs; 3) Respond more rapidly to change; 4) Improve co-operation between Business and IT; 5) Increase job satisfaction and attractiveness to staff. The company standards consisted of a combination of the Capability Maturity Model (CMM) (Paulk, 1991) and the Dynamic System Development Method (DSDM™). DSDM was used to assist to reach CMM level 2.

Application & Control: In the implementation phase, control of the separate CMM and DSDM projects was merged to increase staff acceptance and to deal with inefficiencies (higher costs). These process standards were implemented accompanied by an organizational change process, which proved to be important for the overall success. The control on these process standards was considered as strict but one was allowed to deviate if certain aspects of the standard did not add value, as long as it was approved by the QA organization. A version for small projects was developed as well as the possibility of tailoring. The idea was first to enforce the standards and exert discipline, then allow tuning and tailoring. A weakness in the implementation was the lack of alignment between Business and IT that negatively impacted on the whole program.

Case Study III (Propriety ERP Product)

Selection: An ERP HR suite that included core HR processes, was selected by the HR Business as company standard, based on its Best-in-Class rating by the HR profession. This initiative included standardization of data (both syntax and semantics) which is known to be complicated (Boh and Yellin, 2007). The main driver was lack of consistency of HR information in existing HR information systems and the impossibility of proper analysis and reporting. The HR administration was based on dispersed spreadsheet-like tools often lacking historical data. The goals of the global HR IS were: 1) cost savings through empowerment of employees (self service) and consequently a reduction of HR headcount and reduced HR IS costs; 2) provision of quality services that enable the enterprise to improve its HR function; 3) comply globally with legal and fiscal requirements. The standardization process, especially that of the data semantics, turned out to be ineffective as roles and responsibilities between corporate and local HR units were not effectively assigned. This included 1) lack of mandate and decision rights from the corporate core, 2) the nature of advise (recommended instead of mandatory) 3) lack of ownership of HR data elements. As a consequence, the data standardization process was limited to a relatively small set of entities.

Application & Control: HR departments in some business units did not fully support the standard. To get buy in from local HR, therefore, no standard way of implementing the HR IS was enforced. The possibility to implement optional features of the standard did not help to make this project an immediate success either. As the implementation took too long and the scope of the deliverables remained too narrow a rigorous change in the way of implementing the standard was made which resulted in positive effects on the application of the company IT standard:

- Project scope became fully mandatory, which allowed no ad-hoc deviations and resulted in a project scope that could be effectively enforced.
- Senior management endorsed the implementation and use of the HR company IT standard, which resulted in enforcement of the standard adoption and in an 80% standardization of HR processes and data.
- Implementation scenario changed from a system focus into one with a process focus, which required the stakeholders to adopt the standardized HR processes.

Establishment of the HR shared services concept changed roles and responsibilities regarding HR IS support, which resulted in the impossibility of countries to circumvent this service and its related standards.

CROSS CASE ANALYSIS

In this section the three case studies will be analyzed from an overall perspective. This means that similarities and/or differences will be investigated and possible explanations will be provided. First, an overview of the propositions will be given which will be analyzed from a cross case context. Then the constructs and related variables of the initial conceptual model will be investigated from a cross case context as well and overarching themes will be discussed. In addition, cross-case process performance change inspections will be carried out using the Balanced Scorecard framework.

Propositions

Table 1 lists the evaluation of the propositions for three case studies.

This shows that for all case studies the first proposition holds. This means that the selection process of standards, which will be used in companies, must be carried out conscientiously if these standards are to be implemented and used effectively. Which variables influenced the selection of the standard will be described shortly.

Following proposition two, cross case analysis also shows that the application of IT Standards has lead, overall, to improved process performance. The proposition also holds well as far as the control on the usage of standard is concerned. Details of this performance and specific control elements will be discussed as part of the analysis of the individual variables (see later on in this Chapter).

Table 1. Evaluation of the propositions, based on the three case studies

No	Proposition	Supported by Case Study I	Supported by Case Study II	Supported by Case Study III
1	An effective (ineffective) IT standard selection process positively (negatively) influences the application of these standards.	Yes	Yes	Yes
2	The application of appropriate IT standards contributes to better process performance and this performance is dependent on the control of its usage.	Yes	Yes	Yes
3	A low process performance due to the applied IT standards leads to changes in the way these standards are controlled.	Yes	Yes	Yes
4	A low process performance due to the applied IT standards leads to reselection of these standards.	Yes	N/A	No

With reference to the third proposition, it was found for all case studies that control on the standards' usage changed when triggered by one or more undesired process performance outcomes as regards 1) financial, 2) customer, 3) internal or 4) learning & growth perspectives. In the first case study, for instance, the standards' deviation process was changed to counter rising costs. We have seen in the second case study that the DSDM/CMM quality system was tailored because customers complained about the massive volume of the process standard for small projects. In the implementation phase, control of the separate CMM and DSDM projects was merged to increase staff acceptance and deal with inefficiencies (higher costs). In the third case study, for example, triggers related to problems in compatibility (different scope of implementations – related to the variable range) resulted in changes in control of the standard implementation.

Only one of the case study results sustains the fourth proposition. In the C/S case study, changes to the standard were made based on approved deviation requests made by customers. We have seen that amendments to the standard were made as part of the deviation process to ensure the set of products reflects up to date business requirements. In the second case study a reselection was not considered (yet) as improvements could still be made within the existing two process standards, for example by changing control on its implementation and usage. But the life span of the IT standards also plays an important role in this respect. A key difference was found related to the lifecycle of IT product and IT process standards. The first ones typically last 1-3 years, whereas the others have a longer life span of between 3-5 years. In the third case study, reselection of the standard was not considered, even after the project had been running for more than 6 years, but changes in control countered the lack of required process performance.

So one can conclude that reselection of standards is not necessarily based on process performance outcomes but could be triggered by other effects, and timeframes differ between product and process standards because of the distinct lifecycles of these types of standards.

Later on in this section we will propose, as part of an enhanced conceptual model (i.e. the corporate standardization management framework), that reselection of the standards is not triggered directly by process performance but will be linked to the company standards' management and governance.

Valuation of Constructs and Variables

In this section the constructs with their respective variables are analyzed across the cases and overarching themes will be discussed. Table 5, which has six columns, will be used in this cross case analysis. Similar to Table 10 in Chapter 4, the first two columns show the constructs and its respective variables. For each construct and variable a quantitative value has been calculated which values are presented in the third to fifth column for cases I to III respectively. In the rightmost column of Table 5 a discussion is provided per variable across the three cases.

The calculated values are based on a five-point Likert scale (which ranges from 1 to 5 of the case study questionnaire that was used during the field research. The value is a weighted[1] number based on the ratings from a) some of the interviewees individually (denoted as 'n') and b) the remaining case study materials, which includes the interviewees that did not provide a rating for a variable (denoted as 'm'). In Table 2 the values of 'm' and 'n' are listed that were used in the calculation. Subsequently the average value of the individual variables was calculated which equals the value of the construct.

Next to this value, a valuation (Table 3) of the variables and the constructs will be carried out to provide a check of the qualitative assessments of the propositions provided in Table 1. Any value between 1 up to 3 was considered to be Low achievement whereas values from 3 up to and including 5 were considered to be High achievement.

The main findings from the cross case analysis (Table 5) are summarized as follows:

- The level of consideration paid to the business model was low in those cases where initiatives originated from IT.
- Business drivers were the principal reason to start the company IT standardization initiative.
- Requirements from IT operations from the company standards were for all cases marginal at best.
- The chosen company IT standards are well-established products and processes available in the market place, based on a risk mitigation strategy.

Table 2. Interviewee related data

	Case Study I (C/S standard)	Case Study II (DSDM/CMM)	Case Study III (ERP HR)
Number of Interviews	8	8	7
Number of interviewees (m)	6	6	6
Number of interviewees that provided valuation (n)	3	3	2

Table 3. Definition of "Low" and "High" valuation

Value of variable	Valuation of variable
[1, 3>	Low
[3, 5]	High

- For all cases there was mis-alignment between Corporate IT and Local IT as the selected company IT standards were not developed in a mutual effort.
- Adequate project management played an important role in mitigating risks during the implementation phase.
- For all three cases, during implementation and usage, formal centralized control of the prescribed standards was carried out which contributed to the effectiveness of the company IT standards. This included high levels of prescription, enforcing, restrictiveness and a strict deviation process.
- High levels of management endorsement for the standards contributed to its effective implementation and usage. The same is true for on ownership of the standard that must be clear for the company standard to be effective.
- Also other process and procedures played an important role in the effective implementation of the standard. Without implementation specifics the danger exists of creating incompatible versions of the company standard.
- From a BSC performance perspective an overall improvement was found as specified in Table 6. A further discussion on these performance changes is provided in Table 8.

Furthermore, from Table 5 the following conclusions can be drawn:

- The quantitative values of the constructs, including the related variables, correspond to the qualitative values described in the in-depth case studies of the preceding chapters.
- Valuation of the construct in relation to its variables corresponds to almost all variables. In other words, variables with a "High" valuation correspond to a "High" valuation of its construct. For those that have a valuation opposite to its construct, this does not necessarily mean there is a validity issue regarding this variable. It could also be the case that the value of the construct would have been even higher if the variable had been of the same valuation. This is in conformity with the nature of formative constructs (see Chapter 4 - *Construct Validity*).
- Some variables could not be determined or turned out to be typical control variables, whereas a few others emerged from the case studies as relevant operational referents of the constructs[2]. Details can be found in Table 4.

Control variables in a conceptual model are to account for contextual differences (Baron & Kenny, 1986, p.1179; Zhu et al., 2006, p.525) and are in particular useful in large numerical data sets (e.g. surveys). The use of such variables helps to control for the differences in, for example, the reach and range of the organizational IT standard that might affect its application in the company.

Table 4. Changes in variables due to the three case studies

Construct	Control variable	New variable	Discarded variable
Selection	Origin	-	-
Application	Reach, Range	-	-
Control	-	Level of agreed ownership	-
Process Performance	-	Payback Period; IRR (financial perspective). Attractiveness of standard: (customer perspective)	Economic value-added

Table 5. Cross-case analysis at the end of the each field research - rating of variables

Construct	Variable	Case Study I (C/S standard)	Case Study II (DSDM/CMM)	Case Study III (ERP HR)	X-Case Analysis
Process of Standard Selection		**High (3.5)**	**Low (2.5)**	**Low (2.9)**	
	Level of consideration paid to the business model	*Low (2.8)*, although a C/S standard more or less presupposes a centralized control	*Low (1.3)*	*High (4.0)*, this was an important criterion (i.e. staff self service model; centralization of management and setting up four operational Hubs)	Consideration paid to the (expected) business model was inadequate in 2 of 3 cases (Low) and these initiatives both originated for IT (IT Monarchy). The standardization initiative rated High originated from Corporate HR.
	Level of consideration paid to the business drivers	*High (4.8)*, cost reduction was the main driver and to facilitate flexibility of change	*High (4.2)*, relied heavily on business drivers: quality improvement, cost reduction, shorter timelines and higher client and staff satisfaction	*High (4.0)*, quality improvement, cost reduction, and ensuring compliance with legal requirements were important drivers	Business drivers (quality, costs, time to market, customer satisfaction, compliance and functionality) were the primary rationale to start with standardization in this company and the level of consideration was high in all cases. Overall the tendency was towards the operational excellence value proposition (lower costs, shorted time to market) complemented with customer intimacy aspects (client/staff satisfaction).
	Extent of Business involvement	*High (3.7)*	*Low (1.4)*	*High (3.2)*	A striking similarity between the cases was that in the selection process IT engineering and the business department cooperated whereas input from IT operations (primary stakeholder in the use phase of the standard) was far less.
	Extent of IT engineering involvement	*High (4.7)*	*High (4.8)*, as they were Initiator	*Low (2.0)*, only involvement from corporate IT	
	Extent of IT operations involvement	*Low (2.0)*	*Low (2.2)*	*Low (1.0)*	
	Level of B-IT alignment	*High (3.7)*	*Low (1.6)*	*Low (2.4)*	The level of understanding between Business and IT was not high quality in 2 of 3 cases. There is no apparent causality with the level of business model consideration.
	Level of management knowledge on standards – Business	*Low (2.7)*	*Low (1.8)*	*High (3.0)*	The level of knowledge of standards, including its potential and effects, was considered for IT management, whereas that of the Business was only medium
	Level of management knowledge on standards – IT	*High (3.8)*	*High (3.0)*	*High (3.2)*	
	Origin[*)]	Chosen for de facto (lagger) and A-marks	Chosen for well established standards	Chosen for Best-in-class rating	The company has a clear stance on choosing standards that are well established, based on a risk mitigation strategy, as these standards will be supported by large companies during the standards' lifetime. No valuation (control variable).

[*)] These variables will be considered as control variables and were not included in the valuation (rating) of the construct. Although these are not aspects (operational referents) of the constructs in question, the variables can still be used to account for contextual differences.

continued on following page

Table 5. continued

Construct	Variable		Case Study I (C/S standard)	Case Study II (DSDM/CMM)	Case Study III (ERP HR)	X-Case Analysis
Application of Standard			**High (4.3)**	**High (3.6)**	**Low (2.4)**	
	Reach*)		Single BU	Single BU	Whole Enterprise	The cases involved both BU and enterprise wide scope so the range of the standards swept from single organizational to intra organizational. No valuation (control variable).
	Range*)		Full Client/Server infrastructure	Full software development lifecycle	Full HR	The range of the standards was pushed as far as these standards allowed. This means that the full range of client server products, the complete software development lifecycle and all HR services were covered by the respective standards. No valuation (control variable).
	Level of local IT expertise		*High (5.0)*	*High (4.0)*	*Low (2.0)*	Local expertise of the standards was high for the two cases that originated from the BU whereas this was low in the case where the standards selection originated from the corporate department. For all cases there was an alignment gap between corporate IT and Local IT.
	Level of awareness	Business	*High (3.4)*	*Low (2.2)*	*High (3.2)*	The awareness of the selected standards was considered as adequate for all cases.
		IT	*High (4.6)*	*High (4.0)*	*Low (2.2)*	
	Project management quality		*High (4.0)*	*High (4.0)*	*Low (2.0)*	Project management was considered as adequate in 2 out of 3 cases. It played an important role in mitigating risks.
Control of Standard			**High (3.8)**	**High (3.4)**	**High (3.4)**	
	Prescription (prescription level of the standards*)*		*High (3.9)*, standards are fully mandatory	*High (3.9)*, standards are fully mandatory	*High (4.8)*, standards are fully mandatory (HRTP)	For all three cases there was formal control of the prescribed standards (during implementation and usage) and this was considered as 'High'.
	Enforcing (level of enforcement to comply)		*High (4.5)*, standards were enforced strictly	*High (4.0)*, standards were enforced strictly	*High (4.8)*, standards were enforced strictly (HRTP)	The level of enforcement to comply with the prescribed standards (during implementation and usage) was considered as 'High' for all three cases.
	Level of restrictiveness		*High (3.5)*, one had very limited choice within the selected set of products	*High (3.6)*, one had no choice other then using the CMM/DSDM combination	*High (3.8)*, one had very limited choice	The possibility to select flavors within the standard was only very limited.
	Deviations (quality level standards exception process)		*High (5.0)*, adequate process; deviations were allowed in case of good business rationale	*High (4.0)*, adequate process; deviating from the standard was allowed in case of e.g. small projects	*High (4.0)*, only few deviations were allowed (HRTP)	For all three cases, deviations from the prescribed standards were allowed only in case of sound business rationale.

*) These variables will be considered as control variables and were not included in the valuation (rating) of the construct. Although these are not aspects (operational referents) of the constructs in question, the variables can still be used to account for contextual differences.

continued on following page

Table 5. continued

Construct	Variable		Case Study I (C/S standard)	Case Study II (DSDM/CMM)	Case Study III (ERP HR)	X-Case Analysis
Control of Standard	Level of endorsement by management for standards	Business	*High (4.0)*	*Low (2.0)*	*High (4.0)*	Commitment to the standards was considered adequate. This included both selection and usage. But in the implementation phase endorsement by management was also important to make sure the projects delivered what was agreed on.
		IT	*High (4.0)*	*High (4.0)*	*Low (2.0)*	
	Collaboration (level of collaboration between corporate IT and local IT)		*Low (1.0)*, no collaboration between central and local IT	*Low (1.0)*, no collaboration between central and local IT	*Low (2.0)*, difficult collaboration between central and local IT as the latter could not deal with lot of implementation requests	Collaboration between corporate IT and local IT departments, with respect to selection, implementation and usage, was poor.
	Maturity (maturity level of the organization that applies the standard)		*High (4.0)*, organizational maturity was high	*High (4.0)*, organizational maturity was high	*Low (2.0)*, organizational maturity was low	The maturity of the organization that selected and applied the standards played a important role in allowing to setup process and organizational structures to control the standards (e.g. the QA organization in the software development case)
	Centralization (level of centralized control on the standard)		*High (5.0)*, regulation from centralized unit (BU specific)	*High (4.0)*, regulation from centralized unit (BU specific)	*High (4.0)*, regulation from centralized unit (from corporate to services, both centralized)	Control of the applied standards was in all three cases carried out from a central unit.
	Processes (quality level of processes and procedures for implementation and usage of standards)		*High (4.0)*, adequate service and project management processes	*High (4.0)*, e.g. the development routemaps	*High (3.0)*, only as of HRTP, a standardized way of implementation was available	Process and procedures played an important role in the effective implementation of the standard. If no implementation specifics were available this could easily lead to incompatible versions of the standard. During selection and usage, such as selection criteria and service management processes respectively, this was an important aspect on the control of the standards.
	<New variables orginating from case study>		Exclusive ownership of the product standards by the Business Unit (high)	Clear ownership by the IT department of the process standards (high)	Ownership was clear for HR processes - by local HR (high) Level of (agreed) ownership for data entities was far less (medium)	The *level of agreed ownership* of the standard and/or entities within the standard is included as a new variable going forward as this is a measure that can be operationalized as part of the control on the standard. The importance became evident in the HR ERP case as lack of ownership of data entities resulted in lack of data quality.

*) These variables will be considered as control variables and were not included in the valuation (rating) of the construct. Although these are not aspects (operational referents) of the constructs in question, the variables can still be used to account for contextual differences.

continued on following page

Table 5. continued

Construct	Variable	Case Study I (C/S standard)	Case Study II (DSDM/CMM)	Case Study III (ERP HR)	X-Case Analysis
Process Performance		**High (4.4)**	**High (3.5)**	**High (3.8)**	
	BSC Financial Perspective	**High (4.9)**	**High (3.9)**	**High (4.5)**	
	Cost to develop	*High (4.8)*, decreased	*High (4.8)*, decreased	*High (4.8)*, anticipated lower	These variables concern the cost to develop and support the product or process standards in the its respective IT (Client/Server; Software development; HR). A "High" rating implies lower costs (i.e. improved performance). One of the primary business drivers for starting the standardization projects, to lower costs, was accomplished or was at least anticipated. Lower costs during the development phase were accomplished because the diversified landscape of products and methods was heavily rationalized so implementation was carried more efficiently and effectively.
	Costs to support	*High (5.0)*, decreased	*High (3.0)*, anticipated lower	*High (4.8)*, anticipated lower (HR ratio up)	The same is true for the costs to support, mainly due to: 1) fewer staff required to support specific expertise (both products and processes) 2) rationalization of the process and product landscape so, again, changes could be carried out more efficiently and effectively.
	Economic Value-added	Couldn't be determined	Couldn't be determined	Couldn't be determined	As the EVA due to the IT standards could not be determined in all three cases, effects of using the standards are diluted by many other factors, this variable will be dropped going forward.
	ROI	*High (4.9)*, 176%	*High (4.0)*, exact value could not be calculated	*High (4.0)*, exact value could not be calculated	Although ROI is considered as an inaccurate measure, it has been calculated as part of a standardization project proposal. For 2 out of 3 case studies there were insufficient data to calculate this figure anyway.
	<New variables orginating from case study>	<Payback Period>: 1.45 year <IRR>: 49%	<Payback>: 2 to 3 year, depending on scope	Couldn't be determined	Based on available case study data, *payback period* and/or the *internal investment rate* have been calculated as well. These are considered as more accurate than ROI as the time value of money is taken into consideration. All in all, the financial parts of the business cases were not drawn up in detail.
	BSC Customer Perspective	**High (4.0)**	**High (3.4)**	**High (3.0)**	
	Client satisfaction (level of customer/ client satisfaction with the standard)	*High (4.0)*, Improved	*High (3.8)*, Improved	*High (4.0)*, Improved	For product and process standards, analysis in Chapters 5 to 7 showed that, customer (i.e. internal clients) satisfaction increased on the whole.

*) These variables will be considered as control variables and were not included in the valuation (rating) of the construct. Although these are not aspects (operational referents) of the constructs in question, the variables can still be used to account for contextual differences.

continued on following page

Table 5. continued

Construct	Variable	Case Study I (C/S standard)	Case Study II (DSDM/CMM)	Case Study III (ERP HR)	X-Case Analysis
Process Performance	Perceived complexity	*High (4.0)*, C/S standard complexity was perceived as low	*High (3.0)*, DSDM Perceived complexity high CMM Perceived complexity medium	*Low (2.0)*, high for small countries, low for others	Customer perception of the complexity of the used standards differed case by case. Note: a perceived high complexity results in 'Low' ranking; low complexity results in 'High' ranking.
	<New variables orginating from case study>	Attractiveness high	Attractiveness DSDM high Attractiveness CMM medium	Attractiveness medium	The *level of attractiveness* (i.e. fitness for use) is included as a new business process performance variable going forward as this is a measure that can be operationalized as part of the customer perspective.
	BSC Internal Perspective	**High (4.4)**	**High (3.6)**	**High (3.8)**	
	On-time service delivery (% of on-time service delivery thanks to the standardized infrastructure)	*High (4.2)*, improved	*High (3.4)*, improved slightly	*High (3.0)*, didn't change	Analysis of these three case studies didn't show convincing overall increase in value of this variable, which is surprising, as efficiency is one of the key rationales for standardization. For the DSDM/CMM case study one of the reasons is that the requirements phase took longer. And for the ERP case study, for example, sub-optimal solutions (such as limited standardization of semantics) were implemented.
	Throughput time requests (throughput time of service delivery requests due to the standardized infrastructure)	*High (5.0)*, decreased	*High (3.1)*, Decreased slightly	*High (3.2)*, decreased slightly	In line with the observation at 'On-time service delivery' for this variable no convincing overall x-case improvements were found either. This variable is part of the operational IS phase.
	Error and rework rates (because of the standardized infrastructure)	*High (3.4)*, decreased slightly	*High (4.2)*, decreased	*High (4.0)*, anticipated lower	This variable shows an x-case improvement that was anticipated as it relates to one of the objectives of these standardization initiatives, namely an increase in quality (see also variable 'Service Quality'). Note: "High" means lower error and rework rates (i.e. increased process performance).
	Time to develop (time to develop new services/products from the standardized infrastructure	*High (4.6)*, decreased	*High (3.4)*, Decreased as a single methodology was used	*High (3.3)*, anticipated lower	Overall, in the phase during IS development, a decrease was found which can be explained because of the rationalization of products and processes (easier migrations, fewer exceptional). Note: "High" means shorter time to develop.

*) These variables will be considered as control variables and were not included in the valuation (rating) of the construct. Although these are not aspects (operational referents) of the constructs in question, the variables can still be used to account for contextual differences.

continued on following page

Table 5. continued

Construct	Variable	Case Study I (C/S standard)	Case Study II (DSDM/CMM)	Case Study III (ERP HR)	X-Case Analysis
Process Performance	Time to support (time to support the standardized IT infrastructure)	*High (4.6)*, decreased	*High (3.3)*, decreased slightly	*High (3.0)*, anticipated lower	For this variable, which relates to the operational IS phase, no grand x-case improvements were found either. Note: "High" means shorter time to support.
	Risk (level of risk resulting from using the standardized environment)	*High (4.2)*, improved security	*High (4.0)*, improved, fewer errors in newly developed software	*High (3.8)*, improved security and compliance	A clear x-case decrease of risk was found for these three cases mainly because of the easier development and maintenance and as a single product/process was applied. Note: "High" means low remaining risk.
	Time to market (time to market to develop new services/products from the standardized infrastructure)	*High (4.8)*, only indirect effects	*High (3.4)*, Improved slightly	*High (4.0)*, only indirect effects	This variable does not seem generic enough, as it only made sense in Case II to determine it. In the other Cases only indirect effects were anticipated.
	Service Quality (service quality as a result of using the standardized infrastructure)	*High (5.0)*, improved	*High (4.0)*, improved	*High (4.0)*, Improved overall, especially the MI	For all three cases the quality of the service (in terms of data consistency, etc) improved overall.
	BSC Learning & Growth Perspective	**High (4.1)**	**High (3.1)**	**High (3.9)**	
	Level of availability	*High (5.0)*, increased because of high level of granularity	*High (3.0)*, Didn't change	*High (4.2)*, improved	For two out of three cases the IT availability increased because changes and maintenance are easier when using a single product. No improvements were found as regards the availability of the developed software.
	Level of compatibility	*High (3.6)*, more interoperable	*High (3.8)*, Improved because of standardized software development route maps	*High (5.0)*, anticipated higher	Compatibility increased because of the application of single process/product standards.
	Level of modularity	*High (4.2)*, increased because of highly modular set-up	*Low (1.7)*, modularity was not aimed at, nor is this DSDM aligned.	*High (3.2)*, anticipated higher because of ERM system that contains modules	A more modular set-up of the environment in the C/S product standards and ERP cases were found because the standards facilitated such a set-up. In the software case this was not facilitated in the standards, nor was this true for the developed software, although this could have been accomplished but management chose not to do so.

*) These variables will be considered as control variables and were not included in the valuation (rating) of the construct. Although these are not aspects (operational referents) of the constructs in question, the variables can still be used to account for contextual differences.

continued on following page

Table 5. continued

Construct	Variable	Case Study I (C/S standard)	Case Study II (DSDM/CMM)	Case Study III (ERP HR)	X-Case Analysis
Process Performance	Level of robustness	*High (5.0)*, increased because of high level of granularity	*High (3.0)*, didn't change	*High (4.0)*, anticipated higher	An important result from the analysis of the three case studies is that flexibility did not decrease after introduction of the process/product standard. In fact robustness, scalability and adaptability did increase or were anticipated to increase.
	Level of scalability	*High (4.8)*, increased as there were almost no restrictions in this respect	*High (3.0)*, didn't change	*High (4.2)*, anticipated higher	
	Level of adaptability	*High (3.8)*, increased, easy to make changes because of modular structure within standard set	*High (4.0)*, improved only during development	*High (4.8)*, anticipated higher, because of single standard that makes changes easier	
	Level of staff motivation	*High (3.0)*, didn't change	*High (3.9)*, increased	*Low (2.4)*, various, from High to Low	Staff motivation working with the standard, x-case, varied because of a number of reasons. Overarching theme was the way these standards affected their daily work practices. If these influences were positive then motivations increased, and vice versa.
	Level of innovativeness	*High (3.8)*, new C/S infrastructure considered as innovative set-up, because it was a leading technology that was successfully implemented.	*High (3.3)*, increased because of more focus on content than on process. The successful combination of DSDM/CMM is uncommon too.	*High (3.2)*, HR activities from operational to tactical, so considered moderately innovative.	For all three case studies a positive effect was found as a result of the introduction of the product or process standards

*) These variables will be considered as control variables and were not included in the valuation (rating) of the construct. Although these are not aspects (operational referents) of the constructs in question, the variables can still be used to account for contextual differences.

Altogether the variables that originated from literature study and pilot case study can be used successfully to describe the constructs.

Recheck of Propositions

For all case studies the initial values (denoted as "Before") and the values at the end of the each field research (denoted as "After") have been determined (Table 6). These values will be used to have another look at the propositions. In other words, a recheck of the qualitative assessments of the propositions will be carried out based on the valuations of Table 5.

An assessment of Table 6 suggests that ineffective selection (Cases II & III) and application (Case III) can be compensated with effective control of standards as process performance turned out to be "High" in all three Cases at the end of the field research.

Table 6. Valuations of constructs before the standardization initiatives (Cases I & II) or change in control of standard (Case III) and after the field research

		Process of Standard Selection		*Application of Standard*		*Control of Standard*		Process Performance	
Case Study I	Before	Low	1.8	Low	2.0	Low	1.6	Low	1.9
(C/S standard)	After	High	3.5	High	4.3	High	3.8	High	4.4
Case Study II	Before	Low	1.5	Low	1.8	Low	1.7	Low	1.7
(DSDM/CMM)	After	Low	2.5	High	3.6	High	3.4	High	3.5
Case Study III	Before	Low	2.9	Low	2.2	Low	2.3	Low	2.8
(ERP HR)	After	Low	2.9	Low	2.4	High	3.4	High	3.8

Proposition 1: An effective (ineffective) IT standard selection process positively (negatively) influences the application of these standards.

- Case 1: this case clearly supports this proposition as both the selection and application are valued as 'Low' before and 'High' after the standardization initiative.
- For Case 2: at a glance these results are not supporting this proposition. Selection was rated 'Low' because the business departments were not heavily involved in this process nor were current or emerging business models taken into consideration. One could argue, however, when selection would have been valued as 'High', application would have been rated higher than 3.6 (i.e. application was indeed negatively influenced by selection), so in this sense the proposition is supported by these case results as well.
- Case 3: clearly supports this proposition, both before and after the change in control of this standard.

This shows that for all case studies the first proposition holds good, which means that selection of organizational standards must be carried out conscientiously if these standards are to be implemented and used effectively.

Proposition 2: The application of appropriate IT standards contributes to better process performance and this performance is dependent on the control of its usage.

- Case 1: this case supports the proposition that a successful 'High' application of the standard (both during implementation and usage) resulted in 'High' process performance. Contributing to this 'High' process performance was 'High' Control.
- Case 2: the reasoning for case 1 holds well for this case as well.
- Case 3: this case also supports the proposition. Before the change in control, it was 2.2 'Low' and the Process Performance was 2.8 'Low'. At the end of the field research the Control became 3.4 'High' resulting in 3.8 'High' process performance.

From case studies 2 and 3 it can be concluded that ineffective selection and/or application can be compensated for with effective control of standards. Following proposition 2, cross case analysis also shows that the application of IT Standards has lead to improved process performance overall. The proposition also holds good as far as the control on the usage of standard is concerned.

Proposition 3: A low process performance due to the applied IT standards leads to changes in the way these standards are controlled.

- Case 1: proposition is supported as control (regarding deviations) changed, to positively affect 'Low' process performance (financial perspective), resulting in the 3.8 'High' valuation. So the low process performance resulted in stricter control.
- Case 2: proposition is supported as control during implementation changed, to positively affect process performance (financial & customer perspective), resulting in the 3.4 'High' valuation. So the low process performance led to stricter control.
- Case 3: proposition is supported because at the end of the field research the control became 3.4 'High' as well resulting in 3.8 'High' process performance. Again, a low process performance led to stricter control.

With reference to the third proposition, it was found for all case studies that control on the standards' usage changed when triggered by one or more undesired process performance outcomes regarding 1) financial, 2) customer, 3) internal or 4) learning & growth perspectives. In the first case, for instance, the standards' deviation process was changed to counter rising costs. In the second case the DSDM/CMM quality system was tailored because customers complained about the top heaviness of the process standards for small projects. In the third case, for example, triggers related to problems in compatibility (different scope of implementations) resulted in changes in control of the standard implementation.

Proposition 4: A low process performance due to the applied IT standards leads to reselection of these standards.

For case studies 1 and 2 a 'Low' business process performance (1.9 and 1.7) was the trigger to initiate a standardization program in the first place, so this can not be linked to 'reselection of IT Standards'. As far as results after the standardization initiative are concerned, the following can be said:

- Case 1: proposition is supported only from a theoretical perspective as reselection was possible as part of regular reviews.
- Case 2: no evidence was found; no other standards were reselected. Changes in process performance were dealt with by changing the control of the standard.
- Case 3: not supported (no new standard selected, control changed instead).

Just one of the case results sustains the fourth proposition. In the C/S case, changes to the standard were made based on approved deviation requests made by customers. We have seen that amendments to the standard were made as part of the deviation process to ensure the set of products reflects up to date business requirements. In the second case a reselection was not considered (yet) as improvements could still be made within the existing two process standards by, for example, changing control on its implementation and usage. But the life span of the IT standards plays an important role in this respect too. A key difference was found related to the lifecycle of IT product and IT process standards. The first ones are typically 1-3 years, whereas the others have a longer life span of between 3-5 years. In the third case, reselection of the standard was not considered, even after the project running over 6 years, but changes in control countered the lack of required process performance.

Therefore, low process performance outcomes do not necessarily lead to reselection of standards and timeframes differ between product and process standards because of the distinct lifecycles of these types of standards. Proposition 4 is therefore rejected.

Table 7 lists the evaluation of the propositions for three case studies, based on this recheck.

The recheck of the propositions, using the quantitative values and its related valuations, has resulted in the same assessment of the causal relationships as the qualitative assessments listed in Table 1 that were carried out earlier in Chapters 5 to 7. This increases confidence with respect to internal and construct validity (Yin, 1994).

Overall Performance

Table 8 lists changes in process performance from the four Balanced Scorecard perspectives as a result of using of the IS product or process standards in the business units. These can be qualified as positive overall.

The lessons from this overall process performance view, based on these case studies, result in "in-flight conclusions" that can be linked to the conceptual model:

1. Quality and flexibility increase whereas costs decrease when using appropriate IT standards (internal and financial perspectives).
2. Customer satisfaction increases when using IT standards, but this is dependent on the level of business participation (customer perspective).
3. IT process and/or product standards should be integrated as little as possible (learning & growth perspective).
4. Overall improvement in operations due to application of standards but constrained by country specific regulations (internal perspective).

Towards the Corporate Standardization Management Framework

The initial conceptual model turned out to be useful in describing and explaining the results of the preceding three case studies. So far the construct control of the conceptual model has been applied in terms of "operational use and practical applicability of company IT standards". To explain effects on process performance due to selection and application of standards even better the conceptual model will be extended by incorporating governance elements related to company IS standards.

Rationale for this decision is that case studies showed not only 'control' elements (such as awareness, endorsement, enforcing, prescription, restrictiveness and reusability) which had an effect on the

Table 7. Evaluation of the propositions, based on the three case studies

Proposition No.	Supported by Case I	Supported by Case II	Supported by Case III	Overall
1	Yes	Yes	Yes	Sustain
2	Yes	Yes	Yes	Sustain
3	Yes	Yes	Yes	Sustain
4	Yes	No	No	Reject

Table 8 Changes in process performance, due to usage of IS standards, as found in the three case studies

Perspective	Case Study I (C/S standard)	Case Study II (DSDM/CMM)	Case Study III (ERP HR)	Overall Assessment
Financial	*Positive*: Reduction of time and costs to develop (no tailoring or unnecessary integration); support costs decreased from € 4600 to € 2392 per desktop per year. *Negative*: -	*Positive*: Development costs reduced from 2650 to 1450 €/ FunctionPoints and productivity increased up to 20%. *Negative*: -	*Positive*: Reduction in HR staff; decommissioning of legacy HR systems; cost reductions by automation of management reporting. *Negative*: Project costs higher that originally anticipated.	Overall drop in development and support costs.
Customer	*Positive*: For more than half of the end-user community the satisfaction with the standardized environment increased. *Negative*: Minority perceived set of standard products as too restrictive.	*Positive*: The business is more satisfied with the end result. *Negative*: initial phases of project (a.o. requirements gathering) take more time than before.	*Positive*: End users are satisfied in general. *Negative*: end users have higher workload because of employee self-service.	Customer satisfaction increases when using appropriate IT standards, but this is dependent on the level of business participation.
Internal	*Positive*: higher availability because of modular architecture; increased level of security; 80% of server-based applications running faster compared to running on a desktop. *Negative*: -	*Positive*: quality improvements because of configuration and change management and formal review of requirements and deliverables. *Negative*: throughput time of requests did not change.	*Positive*: consistent and timely HR management reporting; improved HR data correctness and completeness; better maintainable technical environment and thus more stable; created global information infrastructure that satisfied local and fiscal requirements. *Negative*: Relatively small amount of semantical standardization accomplished.	Overall quality improvement (fewer errors, increased stability and maintainability; improved security and data consistency).
Learning & Growth	*Positive*: Increase in scalability and adaptability; easy and fast introduction of new applications; straightforwardness and fewer errors; strict IT standards deviation process proved to be worthwhile. *Negative*: Large number of IT staff was made redundant because of new environment.	*Positive*: Responsiveness and flexibility improved significantly because of prototyping and workshops. *Negative*: B-IT alignment was inadequate because the business departments were involved at a late stage in the implementation of the project only; IT department was not able to exploit the full potential of the standards (e.g. software development teams were not empowered adequately by management).	*Positive*: global changes (business processes and IT) can be effectuated easily. *Negative*: Local HR business felt they lost a significant part of their autonomy and it negatively impacted their employability; countries that already had adequate HR processes and tooling, advantages were only marginal. For small countries IS was even considered as over the top.	Overall increase of flexibility. Standardization resulted in staff redundancies.

application of the standard, but also elements that were strictly speaking *issues related to decision rights and its accountability*, see sections:

Chapter 5

- Ownership and decisions to modify the standard resided at the Business, not IT;
- The initiative for the standardization project was taken by the business unit;
- This steering group was accountable for managing the sub-projects' costs and progress;
- Failure of Corporate Desktop Standard because of issues in decision rights and responsibilities.

Chapter 6

- End users in the development team should be skilled and empowered to make decisions;
- ... end user participation in projects was almost non-existent, in spite of its prominent casting in the DSDM principles and processes;
- QA roles have been introduced in an QM organization in each domain, the CQO has overall responsibility of the IQS;
- A key governance issue, concerning Business participation in the project, was addressed late in the implementation process. The Business only became more involved after two years...

Chapter 7

- As roles and responsibilities between stakeholders were not effectively assigned, they did not succeed in standardizing...
- The local HR business was heavily involved during the implementation and was authorized to make key decisions.
- Because of that, organizational embedding and control were rigorously changed in early 2005 with the move of CHRISP from Corporate HR to a newly formed HR services mandated by the Managing Board;
- Accountabilities with respect to standardization of HR processes and data elements were not assigned effectively because no enterprise-wide agreement could be reached.
- Furthermore, the decentralized organizational structure of the case organization, which is closely related to the IS standards control (i.e. governance), has been identified as a key determinant that influences business process performance. Moreover, ...strict mandates from top management and a change in the organizational structure.

In addition, the construct 'control' will be generalized to the construct 'management' because the case studies showed ample evidence of the importance of the elements of planning, organizing, and directing on the effects of the standard selection, implementation and usage as well. Moreover the construct management will not only be modeled as moderator for the application of standards only but also for selection and implementation of standards. This model enhancement is in correspondence with the observation of Schwab (1980, p. 11) of construct validation being an interactive process involving changes through time in both construct and measure.

Before detailing the standardization management framework we will first discuss the concepts IT governance, including the centralization / decentralization topic, and management as these are expected to play an important role in this model and the remainder of this research.

IT GOVERNANCE

In the past, information technology was dealt with mainly from a technological perspective with little attention and consideration paid to business requirements. Responsibilities for governing and managing the IT environment were, therefore, limited to IT managers. In the last decade this situation changed drastically as enterprise stakeholders became more concerned about risk, because of changes in the IT environment (e.g. outsourcing) and legislative, legal and regulatory pressures. IT governance is a structure that could address these challenges. Critical success factor in IT governance is adequate attention of management. In fact, as Weill and Ross (2005) point out, 'senior management awareness of IT governance is the single best indicator of its effectiveness.' One could argue that this is also the case of IT standards governance. We will investigate this later on.

In order to understand the governance of IT standards we first have a look at some definitions of IT Governance. COBIT (2000) defines IT Governance as: "*A structure of relationships and processes to direct and control the enterprise in order to achieve the enterprise's goals by adding value while balancing risk versus return over IT and its processes.*" ITGI (2003) expresses it as: "*Leadership, organizational structures and processes that ensure that the organization's IT sustains and extends the organization's strategies and objectives.* Remark: It is the responsibility of the board of directors and executive management and an integral part of enterprise governance."

IT Governance is, according to the IT Governance Institute (ITGI), concerned with delivering value and mitigating risks. ITGI (2003) describes five main focal areas for IT governance, driven by stakeholder value, as depicted in Figure 1. This picture also holds well for information security governance ITGI (2001, p. 16). Attention should be paid to:

1. *Strategic Alignment* – focuses on aligning IT with the business and collaborative solutions;
2. *Value Delivery* – concentrates on minimizing expenses and proving the value of IT with focus on knowledge and IT infrastructure;
3. *Risk Management* – addresses safeguarding of IT assets and business continuity;
4. *Resource management* – optimizes IT capabilities and ensures competence of IT staff;
5. *Performance Measurement* – concentrates on success of business and IT leadership in carrying out the strategy.

Weill and Ross (2004) have a different view and argue that IT governance is to address three key questions: 1) *What* decisions must be made to ensure effective management and use of IT; 2) *Who* should make these decisions; 3) *How* will these decisions be made and monitored (Weill & Ross, 2004, p.10)?

Figure 1. Focus Areas of IT governance (Adapted from ITGI, 2003, p. 20)

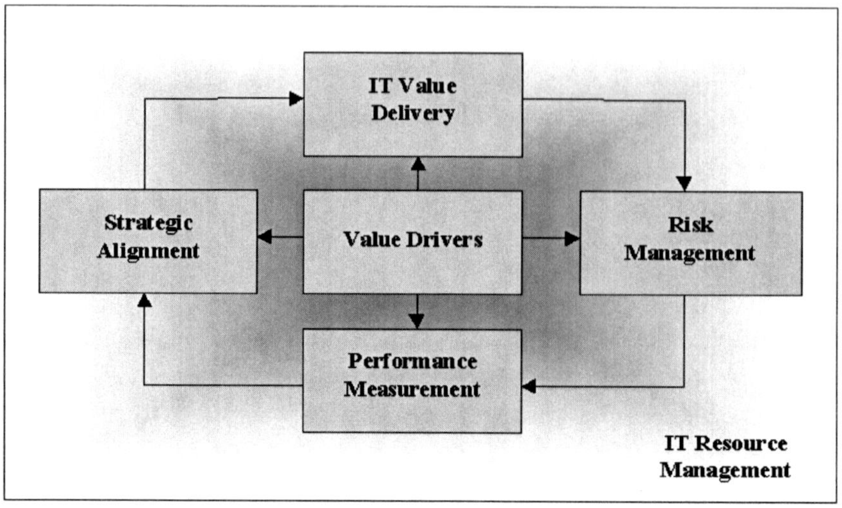

With regard to '*What*' they identified five major interrelated decision areas in IT governance (p. 10):

- *IT principles* – Clarifying the business role of IT.
- *IT architecture* – Defining integration and standardization requirements
- *IT infrastructure* – Determining shared and enabling services
- *Business application needs* – Specifying the business needs for purchased or internally developed IT applications
- *IT investment and prioritization* – Choosing which initiatives to fund and how much to spend

In relation to IT standards used in a company the following issues can be identified (see Table 9).

In designing IT governance, a key activity is to determine *'Who'* should make the decisions and who should be held accountable for these decision areas. This allocation of decision rights is highly dependent on the organizational context, which has been classified by Weill and Ross into six archetypal approaches: 1) Business monarchy, 2) IT monarchy, 3) Feudal (BUs individually), 4) Federal (corporate core/centre and a BU, with or without IT), 5) IT duopoly, and 6) Anarchy. These describe combinations of people who have either decision rights or input to IT decisions. Per decision area the approach may differ.

The 'How' question depends strongly on the firm's strategic objectives (e.g. leading on profit or leading on revenue growth). Firms that lead on profit had more centralized governance to facilitate cost control, standardization and reduce duplication by for example providing shared services. Firms that lead on revenue growth typically had more decentralized IT governance. The business predominantly sets IT principles in an attempt to balance the goals of the business units and firm wide goals. Typically the IT principles focus on growth and empower the Business Units to focus on functionality and speed, leaving little room for standardization.

Table 9. IT standards governance: related decision areas in IT governance (Adapted from Weill & Ross, 2005)

Decision Area	**Description**	**IT Standard Issue**
IT principles	High-level decisions about the strategic role of IT in the business	What are desirable IT Standards?
IT architecture	Integrated set of technical choices to guide the organization in satisfying business needs	Which technical capabilities should be standardized enterprisewide to support IT efficiencies and facilitate process standardization and integration? What activities must be standardized enterprisewide to support data integration?
IT infrastructure	Centrally coordinated, shared IT services that provide the foundation for the enterprise's IT capability	Which infrastructure services should be implemented enterprisewide?
Business application needs	Business requirements for purchased or internally developed IT applications	How can business needs be addressed within architectural standards? When does a business need justify an exception to a standard?
Prioritization and investment decisions	Determine how much and where to invest in IT	What is the relative importance of enterprisewide versus business unit investments? Do actual investment practices reflect their relative importance?

Apart from these *decision-making structures* two other governance mechanisms can be identified which are *alignment processes* (e.g. tracking the business value from IT investments) and *formal communications* (e.g. justifications of exceptions to a company standard). As each organization has its own strategy, structure and value proposition, an optimal model of IT governance is organization dependent.

Ribbers et al. (2002) address procedural and social mechanisms of IT governance and show that environmental contingencies, especially dynamism & turbulence in organizations, are important moderating variables. Contingency variables include corporate governance, management style and IT maturity which influence effective decision-making and thus IT governance processes and their outcome.

De Haes and Van Grembergen (2005) argue that IT governance can be implemented as a mix of processes, structures and relational mechanisms. Examples are respectively: 1) COBIT and ITIL, Balanced Score Cards, Service Level Agreements; 2) organizational structures, roles, responsibilities and accountabilities that locate decision-making responsibilities and 3) Business and IT participation and collaboration, partnership rewards and incentives. Likewise, IT Standard Governance is defined by Van Wessel et al. (2005) as: the procedures (processes), organizational embedding (structures) and techniques (relational mechanisms) for implementation and usage of standards within a company.

It should be noted, however, that definitions of IT governance are broad and diverse, indicating a lack of clarity of this concept (Webb et al., 2006, p.6). In their analysis of 12 definitions on IT governance, five recurring elements illustrate the broad reach of IT governance. These elements are:

1. Strategic Alignment
2. Delivery of business value through IT
3. Performance Management
4. Risk Management
5. Control and Accountability

These elements provide the basis for their proposed "definitive" definition of IT governance:" *IT Governance is the strategic alignment of IT with the business such that maximum business value is achieved through the development and maintenance of effective IT control and accountability, performance management and risk management." (p.7)*

As IT standards are a subset of the IT domain (Weill and Broadbent, 1998; West, 2003; Weill and Ross, 2004) these standards should be governed as well. That is why in this research we will adopt the definition of IT governance by Weill and Ross (2004, p.8) as this is considered by the author a lean and mean definition, that clearly excludes management related activities: "*Specifying the decision rights and accountability framework to encourage desirable behavior in use of IT*" and arrange it for the company Information Technology standards:

Box 1.

Governance of company IT standards
Specifying the decision rights and accountability framework to encourage desirable behavior in the selection, implementation and use of IT Standards within an organization.

As indicated earlier on, little empirical research has been conducted to verify claimed benefits (such as easing co-ordination problems and increasing efficiency) and drawbacks (such as local solutions that may not be optimal) of using IT standards. The same holds well for governance of IT standards. One of the few examples available carried out recently, is related to a survey research on the use of Enterprise Architecture (EA) IT standards (Boh and Yellin, 2007). They investigated to what extent the use of EA standards facilitate organizations to improve the *sharing and integration* of IT resources across the enterprise and how different *governance mechanisms* affect the use of EA standards. They considered the following four governance mechanisms:

1. Define key architecture roles;
2. Institutionalize mechanisms to involve key stakeholders;
3. Institutionalize monitoring processes for EA standards;
4. Centralize IT decision making.

The outcome of using EA standards concerning sharing and integration was not considered from a business process point of view but from an IT architecture one. They examined the extent to which use of EA standards affected the following outcomes: 1) heterogeneity of IT infrastructure components across business units, 2) replication of IT services across business units, 3) business application integration across the enterprise, and 4) enterprise data integration. Their empirical results showed that the use of EA standards was significant in helping organizations to effectively manage these types of IT resources.

They also found that each type of governance mechanism had a different impact on the type of EA standard used (i.e. IT standards for infrastructure, application integration and data integration). Standards of the first type, which include desktops, are claimed to have only indirect effects on users of business units. Its use is predominantly associated with centralization of IT infrastructure management and institutionalization of monitoring and control processes of standards setting and conformance. Using standards of the second type is more complex and requires more business involvement. It needs coordination across business units through clearly defined architecture roles and to have architects to set and implement a feasible set of EA standards. Finally, managing EA standards for enterprise data appears to be the most difficult problem, as it is hard for stakeholders in enterprise data standardization to come to an agreement. Only centralization of IT decision making had a significant impact.

Centralization vs. Decentralization

The choice between centralization or decentralization is a governance decision in particularly. King (1983) discusses that control (delegation) is the key determining issue in IT centralization / decentralization decisions. Delegation is the transfer of decision rights from high levels in the organization to the lower levels.

Zannetos (1965) argues, however, that the level of de-centralization is no measure for level of delegation. A same line of thought comes from Nielen who defines decentralization as "*the allocation of an identical aspect to one or more units*" (Nielen, 1969, p.34). Zannetos argues that hierarchical structures do not necessarily prejudice the nature or form of centralization and decentralization. This has been depicted in Table 10 and Figure 2.

Table 10. Delegation and centralization / de-centralization

	Centralization	De-centralization
No delegation	All units have to comply with directives from high levels in the organization **(1,1)** – The traditional view on Centralization.	All units decide for themselves **(2,1)**.
Delegation	All units have to comply with directives from a central department delegated by high levels in the organization **(1,2)** - This type of centralization is discussed by (Zannetos, 1965).	Units are authorized to make important independent decisions, delegated by high levels in the organization **(2,2)**.

Figure 2. Centralization and delegation in an organization (numbers refer to Table 10)

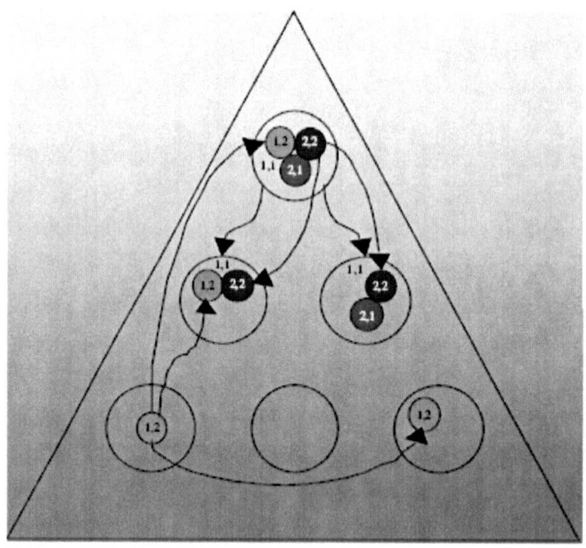

According to Zannetos, centralization has the following advantages compared to de-centralization: 1) prevents sub-optimization and double work; 2) allows economies of scale; 3) allows specialization and 4) reduces coordination costs and time. With regard to de-centralization he distinguishes the following advantages: 1) responsiveness - no loss of flexibility; 2) robustness; 3) innovativeness 4) no necessity to compromise.

Evaristo et al. (2005) discuss there have been several shifts in the decentralization/centralization trend with inflection points at the end of eighties and late nineties (see Table 11). The current trend is still one of recentralization, which was indeed found in the three case studies, although confined to the Business Unit level only.

They argue that the degree of IT hardware centralization depends on the size of the organization, its structure and dependency on real-time information, and its value chain.

Nielen (1969, p. 78) argued that standardization and centralization show the same sort of characteristics, such as a single department that decides on procedures to be used. *Standardization requires centralization to some extent* (Nielen, 1993, p. 141) because centralization facilitates standardization (e.g. each unit has the same type of Desktop) whereas *de-centralization in general impedes it* (e.g. each unit decides on its own type of Desktop).

Table 11. Trends in corporate IT decentralization/centralization (Evaristo et al., 2005)

Why Centralize	Why Decentralize
Early 1960s - technology did not allow for alternative architectures	
	Mid 1970s - Improve responsiveness and flexibility Early 1980 - Introduction micro computer
End 1980s (1987) - data integration; economies of scale	
	Early 1990 (1992) - perceived service quality; OS limitations towards Web solutions
Late 1990s - reliability and security; geographically independent instantaneous data access.	

IT MANAGEMENT

As the concept of management is broad there are a plethora of definitions, however, keywords such as controlling, directing and organizing are commonly used. ISO 9000 (2000) defines it from a quality management perspective as: "*Coordinated activities to direct and control an organization*[3]". Looijen (1989, p.43) characterizes management[4] from an IT perspective as: "*All activities performed to provide and maintain ICT resources for electronic data processing and the provision of information*". Karimi et al. (2000, p.212) define IT management as planning, controlling, organizing and integrating activities within a firm. According to Karimi et al., planning relates to aligning IS plans from a top-down with the firms' business objectives and to disseminate IT within the firm. Controlling should be based on benefits, priorities and technical standards, to meet organizational goals. They argue that organizing is about responding to the changing needs of users and leveraging the IT investments more effectively whereas integration should aim at firm-wide identification and exploitation of IT opportunities rather then automation on an application-by-application basis.

Following the same rationale that IT standards are a subset of the IT domain, IT standards are to be managed as well. Based on Boynton and Zmud (1987) that define IT Management as "*the decision-making efforts associated with planning, organizing, controlling, and directing of IT*" our definition of management of company IT standards, therefore, becomes:

In short, 'Governance' is WHO makes the decisions whereas 'Management' is WHAT decisions are made (Weill and Ross, 2004, p. 220).

IT governance defines the conditions (centralized and/or decentralized) under which decisions are made, related to management and operations of IT (see Table 12).

Box 2.

Management of company IT standards
The decision-making efforts associated with planning, organizing, controlling, and directing the selection, implementation and use of IT standards within an organization.

Table 12. Four possible IT governance arrangements

IT Operations	Decentralized		
	Centralized		
		Centralized	Decentralized
		IT Management	

EXTENDED CONCEPTUAL MODEL

The original conceptual model (Chapter 4) consisted of four constructs and their relationships. These constructs were: I) Process of Standard Selection, II) Application of Standard, III) Control of Standard and IV) Process Performance. Lessons learned from three in-depth case studies on process and product standards (Chapters 5 to 7) which were also published in three conference papers (Van Wessel et al., 2005, 2006, 2007) and the previous discussion resulted in:

1. The breakup of the construct 'Application of Standard' into: a) *IT Standard*, b) *Implementation of Standard* and *c) Use of Standard.*
2. The breakup of the construct 'Control of Standard' into: a) *Governance of Standard* and b) *Management of Standard.*

The enhanced model with its constructs and relationships, represented as arrows between the constructs, is depicted in Figure 3. The *Exogenous Factors* relate to the Competitive and Macro environment of the company (see Chapter 3, Figure 3) which are outside the scope of this research. The dotted line

Figure 3. Corporate standardization management framework to determine the influence of company IT standards on process performance

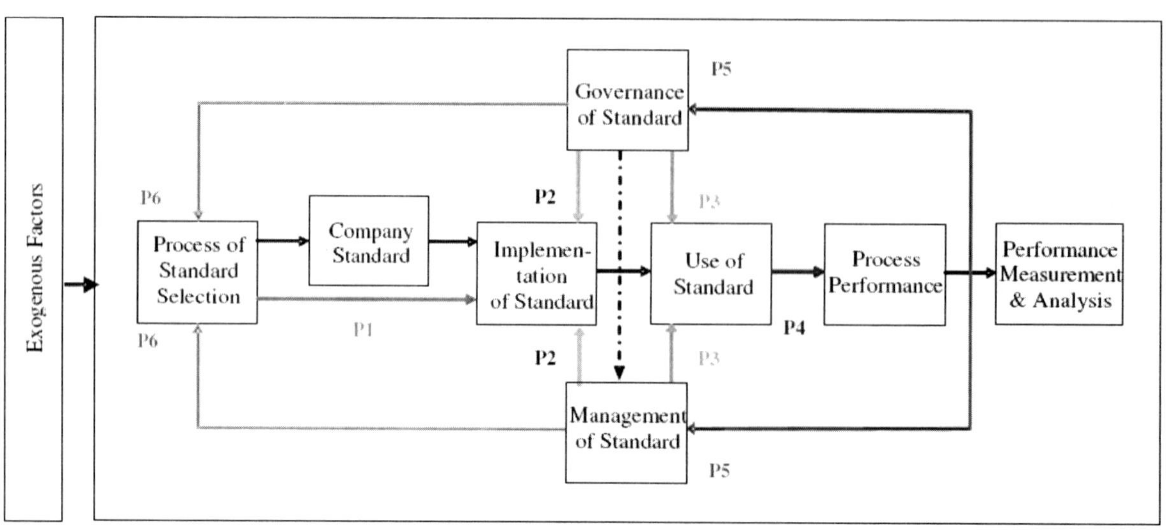

from *Governance of Standard* to *Management of Standard* indicates that governance of company IT standards is pre-conditional to its management.

The main goal is to influence process performance by means of governance and management of selection, implementation and usage of IT standards, in order to achieve the realization of intended business benefits from company IT standardization. As discussed, process performance was assessed from the four Balanced Scorecard (BSC) perspectives. Consideration was given to other IT decision-making methodologies and frameworks like Critical Success Factors, Information Economics and SWOT analysis. However, because of its perceived practicality and to align this study with the three earlier case studies a BSC was considered the most appropriate. The following constructs are of importance:

1. *Process of Standard Selection*: the way the company IT standard is chosen.
2. *Company Standard*: the specification of the IT product or process to be repeatedly and consistently used in the company.
3. *Implementation of Standard*: the way the company IT standard is put into operation.
4. *Use of Standard*: the way the company IT standard is operated.
5. *Process Performance*: the efficiency and effectiveness of the process as a result of using the company IT standard.
6. *Performance Measurement & Analysis*: the way in which efficiency and effectiveness of the company IT standard's use is assessed.
7. *Governance of Standard:* specifying the decision rights and accountability framework to encourage desirable behavior in the selection, implementation and use of the company IT in the organization.
8. *Management of Standard:* the decision-making efforts associated with planning, organizing, controlling, and directing the selection, implementation and use of the company IT in the organization.

Furthermore, the following propositions (P1 to P6) can be formulated based on this model, listed in Table 13:

The Corporate IT Standardization Management Framework consists of the Governance and Management constructs that pertain to propositions 2, 3, 6. Propositions 1, 4, 5 relate to selection, implementation, use and process performance, complementing the remainder of the framework.

Table 13. Propositions related to extended conceptual model

P1 An effective (ineffective) IT standard selection process, positively (negatively) influences the implementation of these standards.
P2 Effective (ineffective) governance and/or management of appropriate IT standards, positively (negatively) influences the implementation of these standards.
P3 Effective (ineffective) governance and/or management of appropriate IT standards, positively (negatively) influences the use of these standards.
P4 Effective (ineffective) use of appropriate IT standards, positively (negatively) influences process performance.
P5 A high (low) process performance due to the applied IT standards, does not lead (leads) to changes in the way these standards are governed and/*or* managed.
P6 Effective (ineffective) governance and/or management of appropriate IT standards, positively (negatively) influences the IT standard selection process.

With reference to the propositions of the initial conceptual model, former Proposition 1 has been revised in P1, from 'application' to 'implementation' to reflect the split of construct 'Application of Standard' as described above. Former Proposition 2 was converted into P4 and P3 and former Proposition 3 is now expanded in P5. Former Proposition 4 was discarded. As a result of the model enhancement one of the research sub-questions (Chapter 1) will be reformulated from "How to control the usage of IT standards?" to "How to govern and manage IT standards?"

A similar model, containing implementation, usage and performance constructs, has been proposed by Naveh and Marcus (2005) who investigated the effects of implementing ISO 9000 on business and operating performance and found experimental evidence of a comparable proposition P4. They did, however, not focus on management and governance of IS standards and how these may influence the process performance.

Extended Conceptual Model Applied to the Three Case Studies

In this section the extended conceptual model will be checked using the results from the three preceding case studies as described in Chapters 5, 6 and 7.

Case Study I

The <u>selection process</u> of the set of IT products, that constitutes the IT standard, was rated as 3.5, 'High' (Table 6), and considered as <u>effective.</u> The selection process positively contributed to the implementation of the IT standard as Business requirements were satisfied and involvement and alignment of Business and IT were high. This resulted in full agreement between Business and IT on the way forward. So proposition P1 is supported by this case.

<u>Governance</u> and <u>management</u> of the standards in this case study is considered as <u>effective</u> as well. Ownership and decision rights of the standard resided at the Business, which allowed them to make key decisions on IT products to satisfy business requirements. As far as management of the standard was concerned, this was executed by IT with strict planning, organizing, controlling, and directing (e.g. deviations) of the standards. The effective governance & management positively contributed to the implementation of the IT standard, application rationalization was carried out successfully and the project completed with only small overrun in budget and time, so proposition P2 is supported by this case.

The effective governance and management also positively influenced the use of the standard. The decision to start the standardization initiative resided at the Business whereas management of the standard, through strict control, was the responsibility of IT. There were only few deviations required and these were incorporated in the set of products that made up the standard. The case also demonstrated that the standard was flexible in use and the majority of customers were satisfied. Therefore, proposition P3 is supported by this case.

The case study showed that the <u>use</u> of the IT standard was <u>effective</u> (cost reductions up to 50%, satisfied customers, increased security and few deviations, increased flexibility). This is reflected in a processperformance rated as 4.4, 'High' (Table 6) due to the applied IT standards. So proposition P4 is supported by this case.

It was shown that management of the IT standard was amended, triggered by undesired 1) financial, 2) customer, 3) internal or 4) learning & growth process performance outcomes. These kinds of activities were observed and discussed such as changing the standards' deviation process to counter rising costs and satisfying customer needs (i.e. financial and customer perspectives). Therefore it is concluded that proposition P5 is supported by this case.

Effective governance & management positively influenced the selection process of the IT standard, again because of decision rights at the Business side and strict planning and organizing regarding the standard at IT. So proposition P6 is supported by this case.

Case Study II

This case demonstrated an ineffective selection process that was rated as 2.5, 'Low' (Table 6). Although business requirements were met, involvement of and alignment between Business and IT were low. This negatively impacted on the implementation of the standards because the Business was not really interested in this initiative. Therefore it is concluded that proposition P1 is supported by this case.

Governance and management of the standard during the implementation phase are typified as ineffective. The Business was not involved in the selection phase and did not endorse it during implementation. In addition IT did not consider the new software development standard as a single (combined) standard. These were two key contributing factors that negatively impacted on the implementation. As a consequence, the standards were implemented separately in the first phases of the project, with CMM and DSDM teams not working as a single entity. Also the business participation and cooperation during the project was found to be inadequate. It is concluded that proposition P2 hold for this case as well.

When the standard was used, the ineffective governance did not change which resulted in a lack of Business commitment and participation. Management of the standard, on the other hand, was effective with formal and strict control on its usage and a deviation process that adequately took account of business rationale. This contributed to the successful usage of this standard (an increase in productivity of up to 20%). Given this result, proposition P3 holds well for this case.

The usage of this standard can be typified as effective as there was a significant drop in costs (expressed in €/FP) of software development due to the introduction of a standardized software development process. Other process performance aspects from the customer, internal and learning & growth perspectives also showed improvements on the whole. This is reflected in the 3.5 'High' process performance rating (Table 6). Given this result proposition P4 is supported by this case study.

At first DSDM and CMM were implemented separately, but to overcome inefficiencies (higher costs), to improve staff acceptance and to mitigate inconsistencies (financial, customer and internal process performance perspectives respectively) a change in the way the standards were managed was made. IT management decided to combine these two projects into a single implementation stream with positive results. Hence, it is concluded that proposition P5 is supported by this case.

Governance and management were typified as not being effective and this negatively influenced the IT standards selection process. A key issue was that there was a lack of Business involvement in the selection phase and this negatively affected the subsequent phases. Proposition P6 holds good.

Case Study III

In this case study the selection process, rated as 2.9, 'Low' (Table 6), was ineffective. There was low Business IT alignment, a lot of business requirements remained unaddressed and the scope of HR processes and data to be standardized was small. These aspects seriously influenced the implementation in a negative way. Local HR in the Business units did not support the selected standard or were even obstructing implementation. Consequently only a small set of processes and data entities kept in scope and standardization of data syntax and semantics remained an issue. It is concluded that proposition P1 is supported by this case.

In this case study two distinct ways of governance and management of the standard were described. During CHRISP, governance and management were ineffective. The cooperation of HR in the BUs with the project and Corporate HR was inadequate. The stakeholders did not succeed in standardizing (or even defining) all relevant HR data elements (entities). Allocation of decision rights between Corporate HR and HR from the BUs was not clear whereas controlling and directing by the project of the set of HR processes to be implemented was ambiguous. Business Units were able to reduce implementation scope or introduce other functionalities, only useful for their specific domain. As a result reach and range of standardized HR processes and data remained too small to be effective. During HRTP, governance and management of the standard became effective: the nature of the standard changed from recommended into a mandatory use, which was fully endorsed by top management. Secondly, centralized HR service centers were installed that provided HR services based on the PeopleSoft HR implementation. As a result of this change, the standard attained an enterprise wide reach and range. Given the above, it is concluded that propositions P2 and P3 hold good for both settings (i.e. CHRISP and HRTP) as well.

In the CHRISP case the usage of this standard can be typified as ineffective. The scope of the standard remained too narrow with only 60% of staff using (parts of) the HR IS standard and with just 50-60% of the HR processes in scope standardized. The CHRISP phase showed a 2.9 'Low' process performance rating (Table 6). In the HRTP case the usage of this standard can be typified as effective. All basic HR processes were standardized as far as possible (constrained by country specific legislation) and user satisfaction increased. The HRTP phase demonstrated a 3.5 'High' process performance rating. It is concluded that these case study results support proposition P4 as well.

During the CHRISP phase, several process performance variables in all four BSC views (such as Cost to develop, Client satisfaction, Time to develop, Compatibility) were rated low and process performance did not improve at the pace initially anticipated. As a consequence, governance and management of the standard changed rigorously. This included centralization of support with the introduction of HR shared service centers; the scope of standards became fully mandatory; full endorsement at the highest management levels; strict enforcement of the standards; implementation changed from system focussed to process focussed. As a result of the standardization of HR processes and related tooling, the process performance improved significantly from 2.8 'Low' to 3.8 'High'. Hence, it is concluded that proposition P5 is supported by this case.

Governance and management in the HRTP phase of the case were typified as ineffective. A key issue was the lack of alignment between Corporate HR and the project on the one hand and HR of the Business Units on the other hand. Although the HR ERP Information System (PeopleSoft) was agreed on, the lack of proper allocation of decision rights and ownership of HR data and processes negatively influenced the standard selection process on data and processes. In the HRTP phase, there was effective governance and management of the standard that resulted, among others, in a much broader range of data elements that were standardized. Proposition P6 holds well.

Results

The results of the above assessment are listed in Table 14.

In the case studies evidence was found that this model works well in describing changes in performance by virtue of the constructs Governance and Management of Standards. In other words, with these new constructs it can describe and even explain the case study outcomes better.

In the next chapter this enhanced model will be used in a fourth and final case to test the model and to possibly extend the theory to a wider set of circumstances (i.e. by making use of replication logic (Yin, 1994)). This case study deals with yet another type of IT standards: a process standard for Information Security management, known as ISO/IEC 17799, that is used in one of the Strategic Business Units.

MANAGERIAL IMPLICATIONS

In everyday practice governance is often confused with management. Basically, governance concerns the "WHO" whereas management concerns the "WHAT". Governance provides oversight of decisions and accountability where stakeholder involvement is essential. Management is about execution of the related activities once the decisions are made.

Weill and Ross (2004) make a clear distinction between governance and management related activities. Based on their definition, governance of company IT standards is the activity of specifying decision rights and an accountability framework to encourage desirable behavior regarding company IT standards and monitoring the outcome of these (strategic) decisions. Next to this, management of company IT standards relates to the decision-making efforts associated with planning, organizing, controlling, and directing the selection, implementation and use of company standards within an organization.

Table 14. Propositions of enhanced model using earlier case study results

Proposition Number	Supported by Case Study I	Supported by Case Study II	Supported by Case Study III
P1	**Yes** (Effective selection)	**Yes** (Ineffective selection)	**Yes** (Ineffective selection - CHRISP)
P2	**Yes** (Effective governance and management)	**Yes** (Ineffective governance and management)	**Yes** (Ineffective governance and management - CHRISP; Effective governance and management - HRTP)
P3	**Yes** (Effective governance and management)	**Yes** (Ineffective governance, effective management)	**Yes** (Ineffective governance and management - CHRISP; Effective governance and management - HRTP)
P4	**Yes** (Effective usage)	**Yes** (Effective usage)	**Yes** (Ineffective usage - CHRISP; Effective usage - HRTP)
P5	**Yes**	**Yes**	**Yes**
P6	**Yes** (Effective governance and management)	**Yes** (Ineffective governance and management)	**Yes** (Ineffective governance and management - CHRISP; Effective governance and management - HRTP)

Although good management processes can reduce the need for governance, governance of company IT standards is pre-conditional to its management. It is essential to keep this distinction in mind and not to mix it up, as clear accountability of company standards is pre-conditional to its effective management.

REFERENCES

Baron, R. M., & Kenny, D. A. (1986). The Moderator-Mediator Variable Distinction in Social Psychological Research: Conceptual, Strategic, and Statistical Considerations. *Journal of Personality and Social Psychology, 51*(6), 1173–1182. doi:10.1037/0022-3514.51.6.1173

Boh, W. F., & Yellin, D. (2007). Using Enterprise Architecture Standards in Managing Information Technology. *Journal of Management Information Systems, 23*(3), 163–207. doi:10.2753/MIS0742-1222230307

Boynton, A. C., & Zmud, R. W. (1987). Information Technology Planning in the 1990s. *Management Information Systems Quarterly, 18*(1), 59–71. doi:10.2307/248826

COBIT. (2000). *Cobit Executive Summary*. IL, USA: Information Systems Audit and Control Foundation.

Davis, F. D. (1989). Perceived usefulness, perceived ease of use, and user acceptance of information technology. *Management Information Systems Quarterly, 13*, 319–340. doi:10.2307/249008

de Haes, S., & van Grembergen, W. (2005). IT Governance Structures, Processes and Relational Mechanisms. In *Proceedings of the 38th Hawaii International Conference on System Sciences*.

Evaristo, J. R., Desouza, K. C., & Hollister, K. (2005). Centralization Momentum: The Pendulum Swings Back Again. *Communications of the ACM, 48*(2), 67–71.

ISO 9000 (2000). *Quality management systems - Fundamentals and vocabulary*. International Organization for Standardization and International Electrotechnical Commission, Geneva, Switzerland.

ITGI. (2001). *Information Security Governance: Guidance for Boards of Directors and Executive Management*. IL, USA: IT Governance Institute - Information Systems Audit and Control Foundation.

ITGI. (2003). *Board briefing on IT Governance* (2nd ed.). IL, USA: IT Governance Institute.

Karimi, J., Bhattacherjee, A., Gupta, Y. P., & Somers, T. (2000). The Effects of MIS Steering Committees on Information Technology Management Sophistication. *Journal of Management Information Systems, 17*(2), 207–230.

King, J. (1983). Centralized vs. Decentralized computing: organizational considerations and management options. *ACM Computing Surveys, 15*(4), 319–349. doi:10.1145/289.290

Looijen, M. (1989). *Management en organisatie van automatiseringsmiddelen*. Deventer: Kluwer Bedrijfswetenschappen. (in Dutch)

Looijen, M. (1995). *Beheer van Informatiesystemen*. Deventer: Kluwer Bedrijfswetenschappen. (in Dutch)

Naveh, E., & Marcus, A. (2005). Achieving competitive advantage through implementing a replicable management standard: Installing and using ISO 9000. *Journal of Operations Management*, *24*(1), 1–26. doi:10.1016/j.jom.2005.01.004

Nielen, G.C. (1993). *Van Informatie tot Informatiebeleid*. Samson Bedrijfsinformatie, Alphen aan den Rijn (in Dutch).

Nielen, G.C.J.F. (1969). *Informatiesystemen en het besturen van ondernemingen*. Samson, Alphen aan den Rijn (in Dutch).

Paulk, M. C., Curtis, B., & Chrissis, M. B. (1991, August). *Capability Maturity Model for Software* (Tech. Rep. CMU/SEI-91-TR24). Software Engineering Institute.

Rada, R., & Craparo, J. S. (2001). Standardizing Management of Software Engineering Projects. *Knowledge, Technology, & . Policy*, *14*(2), 67–77.

Ribbers, P. M. A., Peterson, R. R., & Parker, M. M. (2002). Designing Information Technology Governance Processes: Diagnosing Contemporary Practices and Competing Theories. In *Proceedings of the 35th Hawaii International Conference on System Sciences.*

Schwab, D. P. (1980). Construct validity in organizational behavior. In L. L. Cummings & B. Staw (Eds.), Research in Organization Behavior, 2, 3-43. Greenwich, CT: JAI Press.

van Wessel, R., Ribbers, P., & de Vries, H. (2005). On the effects of IS company standards on business process performance. In *Proceedings of the 4th International Conference on Standardization and Innovation in Information Technology*, Geneva.

van Wessel, R., Ribbers, P., & De Vries, H. (2006). Effects of IS Standardization on Business Process Performance: A case in HR IS Company Standardization. In *Proceedings of the 39th Hawaii International Conference on System Sciences*.

van Wessel, R., Ribbers, P., & de Vries, H. (2007). Towards a Comprehensive Model to master Company IT Standards. In *Proceedings of the 5th International Conference on Standardization and Innovation in Information Technology, Calgary*.

Webb, P., Pollard, C., & Ridley, G. (2006). Attempting to Define IT Governance: Wisdom or Folly? In *Proceedings of the 39th Hawaii International Conference on System Sciences*.

Weill, P., & Broadbent, M. (1998). *Leveraging the new Infrastructure. How Market Leaders Capitalize on Information Technology*. Boston, MA: Harvard Business School Press.

Weill, P., & Ross, J. (2004). *IT Governance - How Top Performers Manage IT Decision Rights for Superior Results*. Boston, MA: Harvard Business School Press.

Weill, P., & Ross, J. (2004). *IT Governance - How Top Performers Manage IT Decision Rights for Superior Results*. Boston, MA: Harvard Business School Press.

Weill, P., & Ross, J. (2005). A Matrixed Approach to Designing IT Governance. *MIT . Sloan Management Review*, *46*(2), 26–34.

West, J. (2003). The role of standards in the creation and uses of information systems, MISQ Special Issue Workshop Standard Making: A Critical Research Frontier for Information Systems. *Pre-Conference Workshop, International Conference on Information Systems, December 12-14, 2003, Seattle, Washington* (pp. 314-326).

Yin, R. K. (1994). *Case Study research, Design and Methods* (2nd ed.). Thousand Oaks, CA: Sage Publications Inc.

Zannetos, Z. S. (1965). On the theory of divisional structures: Some aspects of centralization and decentralization of control and decision making. *Management Science, 12*(4), Series B, Managerial, B49-B68.

Zhu, K., Kraemer, K. L., Gurbaxani, V., & Xu, S. X. (2006). Migration to Open-Standard Interorganizational Systems: Network Effects, Switching Costs and Path Dependency. *Management Information Systems Quarterly, 30*(Special Issue), 563–581.

ENDNOTES

1 $$value\ of\ variable = \left(\sum_{i=1}^{n} (value\ interviewee\#i) + (m-n).(value\ based\ on\ other\ case\ study\ materials) \right) / m$$

Example calculation for Case Study I (n=3; m=6) of variable "Business involvement" with value (3.7) and valuation (High) = = (Value interviewee#1 + Value interviewee#2 + Value interviewee#3 + 3 x Value based on other case study materials) / 6 = (2 + 4 + 4 + 3 x 4) / 6 = 3.7

2 One of the variables that was identified from the case study data was *Attractiveness* of the company IT standard as part of the BSC customer perspective on process performance. In retrospect, the Technology Acceptance Model (TAM) (Davis, 1989) could have been used, instead of the current variables, to operationalize the customer perspective. TAM can be used to determine user acceptance of information technology and consists of two (reflective) constructs: Perceived Usefulness and Perceived Ease of Use. 'Perceived Usefulness' is defined by the degree to which a person believes that using a particular system would enhance his or her job performance (p. 320) and is measured by six variables. 'Perceived Ease of Use' is defined as the degree to which a person believes that using a particular system would be effortless (p. 320) and is also measured by six reflective indicators: 1 Easy to Learn; 2 Controllable; 3 Clear & Understandable; 4 Flexible; 5 Easy to Become Skillful; 6 Easy to Use.

A check has been carried out using TAM, whether significant differences would occur in the valuation of the BSC customer perspective on process performance. This proved not to be the case: e.g. Case Study II with TAM resulted in a High (3.7) compared to High (3.4) using the method from the case study protocol.

3 An organization is a group of people and facilities with an arrangement of responsibilities, authorities and relationships (ISO, 2000).

4 Looijen (1995) defines 'Information Systems Management' as: '*The management, control and maintenance of the information system components and related data processing and information system processes in accordance with user requirements and preconditions and the characteristics*

of the information system components: hardware, software, databases, procedures and people. As such, information systems management offers services in the most effective and efficient way and influences the goals of the organization in a positive way.'

Section 6
A Fourth and Final Case Study to Test the Corporate IT Standardization Management Framework

In this section the enhanced conceptual model, our corporate IT standardization management framework will be tested. The framework now includes the constructs "Governance of Standard" and "Management of Standard" and will be used to determine the effects of IS company standards on business process performance. In the three case studies so far, business processes were respectively those of IT Delivery & Support, Application Software Development and HR Back Office processes. In this study we will focus on the process of Technology Risk Management (TRM) and subsequently link it to the general process of IT Delivery & Support, complementing the general theme of this research.

Chapter 9
Information Security Management Standardization "ISO/IEC 17799 Case"

INTRODUCTION

In this Section an outline will be given on the discipline of Information Security and some of its related standards. Special attention will be paid to the ISO/IEC 17799 process standard as this information security management standard formed the basis of this case study.

Information Security

The objective of Information Security is (ITGI, 2001, p 9): "protecting the interests of those relying on information, and the systems and communications that deliver the information, from harm resulting from failures of *availability*, *confidentiality* and *integrity*." In Table 1 these concepts are clarified.

ISACF (2001) adds to these objectives that business transactions as well as information exchanges between enterprise locations or with partners can be trusted (*authentication*[1] and *non-repudiation*[2]). Furthermore, they list six major activities involved in information security management:

1. *Policy Development:* using the security objective and core principles as a framework around which to develop the security policy;

DOI: 10.4018/978-1-61520-759-6.ch009

Table 1. Objectives of information security (ISO/IEC 17799, 2000, p. VII)

Concept	Description
Confidentiality	Ensuring that information is accessible only to those authorized to have access to it.
Integrity	Safeguarding the accuracy, completeness and timeliness of information and processing methods
Availability	Ensuring that authorized users have access to information and associated assets when required

2. *Roles and Responsibilities:* ensuring that individual roles, responsibilities and authority are clearly communicated and understood by all;
3. *Design:* developing a security and control framework that consists of standards, measures, practices and procedures;
4. *Implementation:* implementing the solution on a timely basis, then maintaining it;
5. *Monitoring:* establishing monitoring measures to detect and ensure correction of security breaches, such that all actual and suspected breaches are promptly identified, investigated and acted upon, and to ensure ongoing compliance with policy, standards and minimum acceptable security practices;
6. *Awareness, Training and Education:* creating awareness of the need to protect information, providing training in the skills needed to operate information systems securely, and offering education in security measures and practices.

In the next section a number of well recognized and accepted Information Security standards are listed and one specific standard will be discussed in more detail. Then the relationship between information security standards and IT governance in general will be addressed, followed by the management and the value of these standards.

Information Security Standards

Roughly speaking, Information Security Standards can be divided into national, international and industry standards. Although there is a wealth of security guidelines, checklists, best practices and controls—that vary considerably in scope, style and purpose—there is no consensus on a single information security management standard. Only a few are well respected and are applied worldwide by the information security profession. Among the most common and generally accepted are ISO/IEC 17799 and COBIT (ISACA, 2005).

Another categorization can be made as regards the purpose of the standard. ISF (2001, p. 12) recognizes three types:

1. *Technical security framework standards:* often originate from open international communities of network designers, vendors, academics and researchers; some of the major bodies include the Internet Engineering Task Force (IETF)[3] and World Wide Web Consortium (W3C)[4];
2. *Technical evaluation standards:* can be used to help evaluate both the inherent security of hardware, software and its security functionality;
3. *Information security management standards:* aimed at the management of information security, not the security of hardware or software.

Table 2. Examples of information security standards (based on ISF, 2001 and ISACA, 2005)

Standard	Category	Owner	Description
BSI — IT Baseline Protection Manual	National - Germany	Bundesamt für Sicherheit in der Informationstechnik	Recommended standard security measures for typical IT systems
BS 7799 Part 2:2002 — Information Security Management Systems; Specification With Guidance for Use	National - UK	British Standards Institution	A specification for an information security management system. Intended to provide foundation for 3rd party audit. Was replaced by ISO 27001 in October 2005 and now aligned with other management standards, such as ISO 9001 and ISO 14001
NIST 800.12 — An Introduction to Computer Security	National - USA	US Department of Commerce, National Institute of Standards and Technology	Describes common requirements for managing and implementing a computer security program and some guidance on the types of controls that are required.
ISO/IEC 13335-1:2004 Information technology – Security techniques – Management of information and communications technology security	International	International Organization for Standardization and the International Electrotechnical Commission	Technical guidance divided into five sections which provide guidance on aspects of information security management. Part 1: Concepts and models for information and communications technology security management.
ISO/IEC 15408:1999 Information technology – Security techniques – Evaluation Criteria for IT security	International	International Organization for Standardization and the International Electrotechnical Commission	Based on the Common Criteria for Information Technology Security Evaluation 2.0 (CC) and is used as a reference to evaluate and certify the security of IT products and systems.
ISO/IEC 17799:2005 Information Technology—Code of Practice for Information Security Management	International	International Organization for Standardization and the International Electrotechnical Commission	A collection of information security best practices based on BS 7799 Part 1.
COBIT — Control Objectives for Information and related Technology	Industry	Information Systems Audit and Control Foundation	A collection of documents that can be classified as generally accepted framework and standards for IT governance, security, control and assurance.
Standard of Good Practice: The Standard for Information Security	Industry	The Information Security Forum	A collection of information security principles and practices.
OCTAVE — Operationally Critical Threat, Asset, and Vulnerability Evaluation	Industry	The Software Engineering Institute (SEI, home of CERT)	A set of principles, attributes and outputs for risk assessment

The standards listed in Table 2 are of the third category, except for ISO/IEC 15408 and OCTAVE which are technical evaluation standards.

There are only a very limited number of empirical studies on information security (Kotulic and Clark, 2004; Spears and Cole, 2006). An analysis of research articles on information security related subjects in top ranked IS journals, during a two-year period (2003-2004), revealed a lack of research in this area, particularly at the organizational level. Moreover, of these articles only 17% pertained to standards (Sinclaire, 2005).

Siponen and Stucke (2006) discuss that existing Information Security Management (ISM) standards focus on ensuring that certain information security processes and related activities exist but leave the content of those processes unaddressed. They argue that future standards should pay attention to how the information security activities are to be carried out, and how objectives of those standards are to be achieved in organizations. At the information security policy level, a similar observation was made by Höne and Eloff (2002) as existing information security management standards describe a range of processes and controls to successfully implement a policy, rather than advising what that policy should look like[5].

Since the case company, prior to this case study, selected the ISO/IEC 17799 standard as their baseline Information Security standard we will provide a short description of this standard. Main rationale for using this standard was that it has a very good reputation and is widely accepted by the information security profession. Furthermore it is considered as a tool for implementation regulatory requirements, like the US Sarbanes Oxley Act[6] and the European Central Banks Basel II[7] directives.

ISO/IEC 17799: An Information Security Management Standard

The International Organization for Standardization and the International Electrotechnical Commission published a standard titled ISO/IEC 17799:2000 "*Information Technology - Code of Practice for Information Security Management*"[8] which was first released in December 2000[9]. It is based on the British Standard BS 7799 - Part 1:1999, with statements written as 'should'. The standard consists of 94 pages and offers internationally recognized security practices that enable an organization to meet audit, regulatory and legal requirements. Furthermore it can be used as part of the basis for certification to BS 7799 - Part 2:2002[10] (with statements written as 'shall'). The standard is very well accepted worldwide and working group ISO/IEC JTC1/SC27 WG1 is responsible for its maintenance. At the end of 2005, a technically revised version has been published (ISO/IEC 17799, 2005)[11].

The standard has been written as a set of guidelines that can be tailored to the specific risks and needs of an organization. By implementing a set of controls, consisting of policies, practices, procedures, organizational structures and software functions, the preservation of information related to confidentiality, integrity and availability is to be achieved. It is important to understand that performance criteria and targets are not included in this ISO standard and it is up to the organization to set them for their specific needs (ISO/IEC 17799, 2005, p. XI).

The 2000 version of this standard is structured into 10 sections that contain 36 objectives and 127 controls: 1) Security Policy; 2) Organizational Security, 3) Asset Classification and Control; 4) Personnel Security; 5) Physical and Environmental Security; 6) Communications and Operations Management; 7) Access Control; 8) Systems Development and Maintenance; 9) Business Continuity Management and 10) Compliance. In the 2005 release some sections have been rearranged and renamed and an additional section has been added: 11) Information Security Incident Management. The standard is now structured into 11 sections that contain 39 objectives and 133 controls. More details can be found in Table 10.

CASE DESCRIPTION

Introduction

The fundamental goal pursued in this book is to determine, describe and possibly control the effects of selection, implementation and usage of IS standards on business processes in order to achieve the intended business benefits. In this section the enhanced conceptual model, that includes the constructs "Governance of Standard" and "Management of Standard" as described in Chapter 8, will be used to determine the effects of IS company standards on business process performance.

In the three case studies so far, business processes were respectively those of IT Delivery & Support, Application Software Development and HR Back Office processes. In this study we will focus on the process of Technology Risk Management (TRM)[12] and subsequently link it to the general process of IT Delivery & Support, complementing the general theme of this research.

There was full access to all relevant measurement data. Key measurement data were analyzed in order to assess the changes in the risk profile as part of a number of initiatives (see next section). This data were analyzed by a number of information security staff (including the author) that were responsible for creating graphs and discussion of results. These were subsequently published as monthly dashboards.

Implementation

In this section the implementation of ISO/IEC 17799, that formed the basis of a case study carried out at the Information Security department of a Strategic Business Unit of our case company, will be described. This company had outsourced almost all of its IT services to third-party vendors and among the few IT services that remained in-house was the information security function. ISO/IEC 17799 was selected earlier as the instrument to be used in the enterprise across all business units to mitigate information risks.

As the information risk profile of that company was not considered to be on an acceptable level, given the number of information risk related issues existing in the IT infrastructure, senior IT management committed to address this situation, and a number of initiatives were launched in the third quarter of 2004 to improve and maintain an acceptable risk profile going forward. The total investments (€10.9M) were approximately 1% of the total yearly IT budget. The case study concerned an information security standardization program that included initiatives such as Technology Risk Accreditation Process (TRAP) and Security Officer Standard Operating Model (SOM) that was rolled out in the organization. These initiatives were basically implementations of (parts of) the guidelines of ISO/IEC 17799 "Code of practice for information security management" and its objectives & deliverables are listed in Table3.

This comprehensive approach was chosen to improve the information risk profile of the business unit considerably. System access had to be managed better, both proactively (Role Based Access Control, Two Factor Authentication, Single Sign On, Emergency Password Process) as well as retroactively (HLAM, Security Officer Standard Operating Model). Furthermore, by means of Project & Operational risk assessments and dedicated Vulnerability Management, the security of the IT infrastructure was to be improved. The approach included a security awareness campaign and it was measured through the monthly reporting cycle. The regular monthly reporting provided the baseline measurement just before the launch of these initiatives. Measurements from the BSC perspectives would be used, as far as available in the case company, to determine business process performance as a result of the application of the ISO/IEC 17799 standard. It should be appreciated that the measurements discussed in this Chapter were not designed as part of a Balanced Scorecard. The available measurement data show that these map to the internal perspective of the Technology Risk Management (TRM) BSC. Initiative 7 is assessed by means of Key Control Indicators that were defined earlier by the case company.

Initiatives 8 to 12 were not implemented successfully; these have been omitted in the further analyses as no (valid) measurement data were available. Explanations of failure to implement were a combination of the following: too complex or wide project scope; lack of properly defined requirements; no clear deliverables or a change in deliverables (e.g. from actual implementation to only an advice on how to implement); lack of project management in general; lack of alignment and cooperation between the departments (i.e. initiatives 3, 10 and 11).

Table 3. Risk profile improvement initiatives

Initiative[13]	Objectives and Deliverables	Implemented
1. Vulnerability Management	• Internal Network Vulnerability Scanning - detection and classification of computer vulnerabilities • External Network Vulnerability Scanning – prevention from the network being exploited to gain unauthorized access to the IT environment • Patch Management - react, in a adequate and timely way, to requests to deal with any critical vulnerability • LCIRT - visibility and control of security incidents that occur locally	Yes
2. Risk Assessments • Operational systems • Projects	• Measure the adequacy of controls for all critical or sensitive applications and amend when required. • For all projects, risks are to be measured and appropriate controls established from the outset	Yes
3. Security Incidents *)	Adequate capturing, reporting and tracking of erroneous and repeating events in the production environment.	Only partially
4. Audit Point Resolution	The implementation of an Audit Issue Control function designed to address audit issues in a timely manner and to enable the IT function to pragmatically resolve potential issues prior to them being the subject of an audit report.	Yes
5. Security Awareness	As awareness is a major building block in the implementation of effective risk management, ensure that all employees are made aware of and are reminded of key policy and best practice.	Only partially
6. Policy Deviation Process	The implementation of an effective IT deviations process to address the current situation in respect of scattered and uncoordinated deviation requests globally.	Yes
7. Security Officer Standard Operating Model	Effectively manage global operational technology risk and govern local security management operational activities and associated risks.	Yes
8. SSO/2FA	SSO: A unified authentication system for disparate, internal systems to provide the required infrastructure to reduce the number of credentials a user needs to remember. 2FA:To provide a high level of confidence in the identity of a user, thus managing the risk of providing electronic access to critical or confidential data. Projects did not deliver in 2005.	No
9. Encryption	Identify the scope of data that requires encryption and implement an adequate standardized solution where appropriate. Project did not deliver in 2005.	No
10. Access Control *)	To improve user account requests, system access reporting and role based access control. The implementation of: 1) a global account request tool (GART), 2) a system reporting to enable user and profile review, and 3) a role based access control (RBAC) determined on pre-defined job roles. Projects stalled in 2005.	No
11. High Level Account Monitoring *)	Identification and reporting on activities associated with High Level / privileged accounts and security controls of Information Systems. Project did not deliver as expected as it got very little attention by Management.	No
12. Infrastructure Remediation	A globally agreed, standardized approach will ensure the security of new infrastructure is adequate before it is deployed. Project did not start, as scope and deliverables could not be agreed upon.	No

Table 4 lists the initiatives that were launched, which have been mapped to the 39 ISO/IEC 17799:2005 control objectives (see Chapter 3).

Usage and Results

To determine the effects (like trend breaches) of the implemented initiatives (Table 3), measurement data that related to the situation just prior to the implementation of these initiatives were, where available,

Table 4. Risk profile improvement initiatives mapped to ISO/IEC 17799 standard

ISO/IEC 17799:2005 Section	Control objective covered by
1. **Security Policy** • Information Security Policy	• To a degree by Security Officer Standard Operating Model – *Policy exception process, Local Security Policies & Standards*
2. **Organizing Information Security** • Internal organization • External parties	• Security Officer Standard Operating Model – *Allocation of information security responsibilities ; Specialist information security advice*
3. **Asset Management** • Accountability for assets • Information classification	• Security Officer Standard Operating Model - *Inventory of system owners, signatories, CIA ratings*
4. **Human Resource Security** • Prior to employment • During employment • Termination or change of employment	• Security awareness program • Security Officer Standard Operating Model - *Security Awareness*
5. **Physical and Environmental Security** • Secure areas • Equipment security	• Security Officer Standard Operating Model - *second line support only - first line via facility management and physical security guards*
6. **Communications and Operations Management** • Operational procedures and responsibilities • Third party service delivery management • System planning and acceptance • Protection against malicious and mobile code • Backup • Network security management • Media handling • Exchange of information • Electronic commerce service • Monitoring	• Risk Assessment of 200 operational applications • Vulnerability Management - Internal and external scanning of computer networks • Tactical High Level Account Monitoring (HLAM) • Security Officer Standard Operating Model - *Vulnerability scanning, anti virus mgt, hot fixes; Support Risk Assessments process; Change Control (CAB); Penetration testing; Audit resolution*
7. **Access Control** • Business requirement for access control • User access management • User responsibilities • Network access control • Operating system access control • Applications and information access control • Mobile computing and networking	• Role Based Access Control (RBAC), Global Access Request Tool (GART) • Two Factor Authentication (2FA) solutions • Simplified Sign On (SSO) solution • Emergency Passwords process • Security Officer Standard Operating Model - *Emergency passwords; System monitoring (Security administration review, Emergency Passwords, Remote Access, Starters & Leavers, Critical High Level Account)*
8. **Information Systems Acquisition, Development and Maintenance** • Security requirements in information system • Correct processing in applications • Cryptographic controls • Security of system files • Security in development and support services • Technical vulnerability management	• Risk Assessments of new applications • Cryptographic enhancement program (CDRAP) • Security Officer Standard Operating Model - *Support Risk Assessments process*
9. **Information Security Incident Management** • Reporting information security events and weaknesses • Management of information security incidents and improvements	• Global and Local Computer Incident Response Teams • Security Officer Standard Operating Model - *Security Incident Management; Investigations; Security Awareness*
10. **Business continuity management** • Information security aspects of business continuity management	• No new initiatives; status unchanged
15. **Compliance** • Compliance with legal requirements • Compliance with security policy and standards • Information systems audit considerations	• Reporting – TRM Dashboard • Security Officer Standard Operating Model - *System Reviews, Legal & Regulatory Compliance*

Figure 1. Hosts and critical vulnerabilities

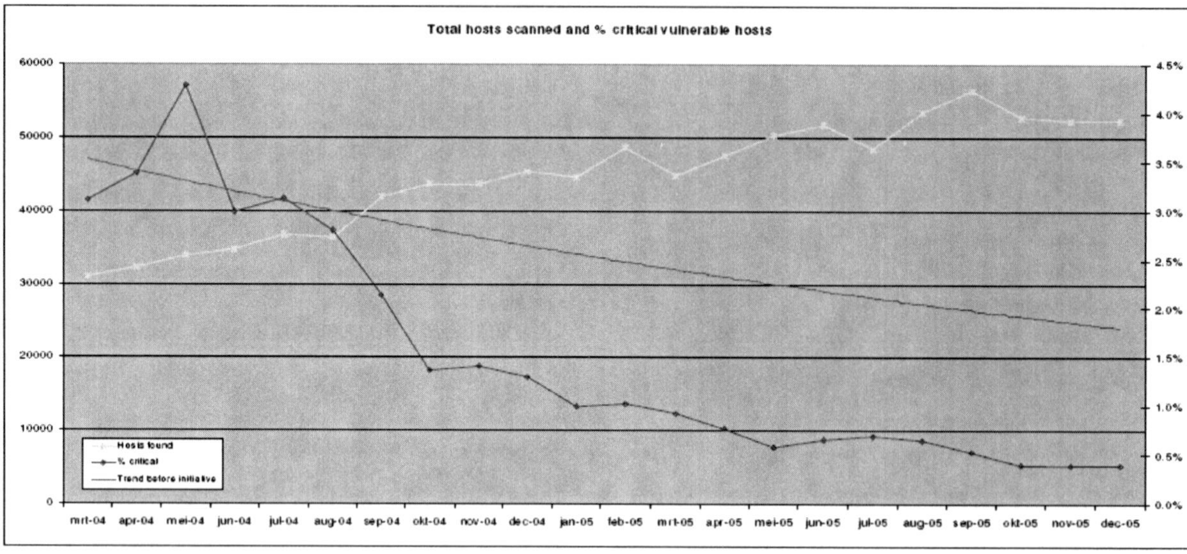

gathered. In addition, data from 'Risk Self-Assessments', 'Other Risk Approval Process', 'Regulatory Compliance' and a Financial Losses database were included to determine possible indirect effects of these initiatives.

Direct Effects of the Usage of the Standard Vulnerability Management

The Vulnerability Management initiative is related to ISO/IEC 17799 Section 10 "Communications and operations management" - *Vulnerability Management*. The objective of vulnerability management is to mitigate the risk related to risk exposures, like inadequate patching levels and out-of-date virus definition files on servers in the computer network.

One of the outcomes of the implementation of the Standard Operating Model (SOM), was increased focus on vulnerability management. As depicted in Figure 1, in December 2004 the total number of hosts found was 45345, whereas in December 2005 this figure rose to 52275. In this same timeframe, the percentage of critical vulnerabilities was considerably reduced from 1.3% to 0.4%. This shows both positive and significant improvements in the vulnerability risk profile. It was determined that the prime contributing factor to the reduction of critical vulnerabilities was the identification of un-patched hosts. These were introduced in the operational environment as a result of failure to follow defined processes. As a consequence, an initiative was established to address this issue, and the breach in trend is clearly visible around August 2004. The activities in this area also contributed to better asset registration.

A further detail of analysis can be added to determine quantification of costs per critical vulnerability. This is part of the recommendations in this Chapter.

Risk Assessments

The Risk Assessment initiative is related to two sections in ISO/IEC 17799 because it covers both operational systems and projects: 1) Section 10 "Communications and operations management" - *Technology*

Figure 2. Project risk assessments

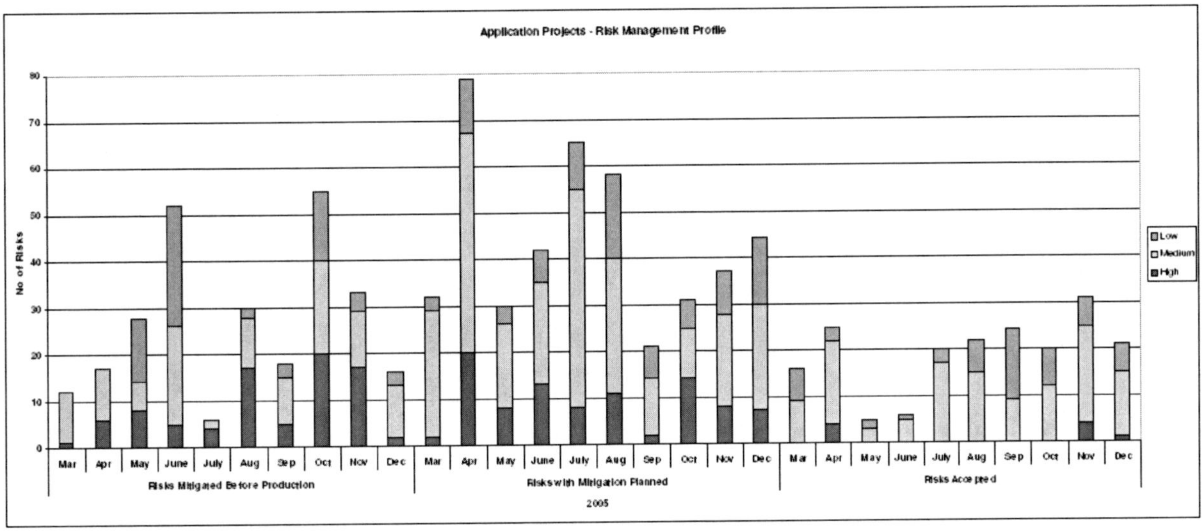

Risk Accreditation Process, and 2) Section 12 "Systems development & maintenance" - *Technology Risk Accreditation Process*.

Figures related to ISO/IEC 17799 Section 12 are presented in Figure 2. Data before March 2005 were not available. In the three subsections (Risks Mitigated Before Production, Risks with Mitigation Planned, Risks Accepted), it shows for the year 2005 per month: 1) the number of risks mitigated before production; 2) the number of risks with mitigation planned and 3) the number of risks accepted. Although no trend is visible in these 3 categories of data, the figure shows effectiveness of the risk project assessments in screening for risks. This is because it shows the appropriate mitigation during the course of development and implementation of project initiated change. This is also reflected by the fact that almost all 'High' risks (Figure 2) have been mitigated either before the IT systems went into production or mitigation of these risks had been planned. As a result of this initiative, the IT infrastructure became more and more secure since only few risks were introduced in the production environment.

Security Incidents

The Security Incident initiative is related to ISO/IEC 17799 Sections 8 and 11, "Human Resource Security" and "Information Security Incident Management" respectively. The available data in this category constitute the number of reported security incidents.

The reduction of Internal Threats[14], over which the organization had more direct control, benefited from the closer management and awareness by the maturing Security Officer Standard Operating Model and the reinforcement of the structure and processes of both Global and Local Computer Incident Response Teams. As far as the External Threats[15] were concerned, the volume of these incidents also reduced across the year, with the single serious exception of a Worm attack in July 2005 (Figure 3), that was handled with minimal impact on the organization.

The Security Incident initiative started in September 2004 and, therefore no preceding data were available for comparison. The increase till April 2005 in the reported number is not necessarily an indication that such incidents were going up. The fact that the numbers increased can also be an indication

Figure 3. Number of reported security incidents

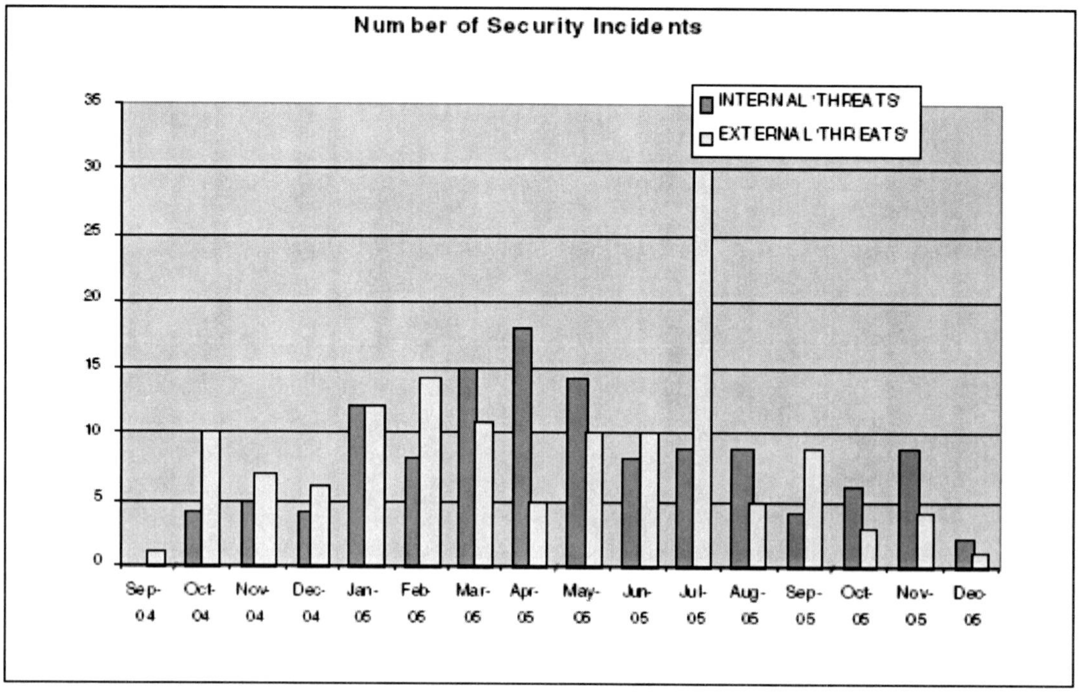

that individuals were reporting more incidents that they previously ignored. Overall a decline in incident numbers is shown which does suggest that there has been a measure of success in incident prevention.

Audit Point Resolution

The internal audit department reports technical and policy deficiencies in information systems as Audit Points to senior management that have to be resolved as a matter of urgency. Reporting of audit points is related to ISO/IEC 17799 Sections 10 and 15 of the ISO/IEC 17799 standard. The number of audit points should reflect a holistic view on the level of information security risks and the level of compliance to corporate policies and standards of the IT infrastructure. The number used, is the number of open (i.e. outstanding) audit points that added up to 650 at the moment of initial measurement (September 2004).

Figure 4 details the status of open audit points throughout the months. The trend line shows the direction in which the number of open audit points was increasing. As from April 2005, however, the graph showed a gradual decrease in the total number of open audit points as a result of the concerted effort of several audit issue resolution taskforces, including the ones that are part of the Security Officer Standard Operating Model. In addition, the implementation of a structured audit issue management process and the establishment of an Area Audit Managers role had a positive impact on the closure of the outstanding issues. The proactive management of potential issues arising from future Audit activity started to develop as well.

Figure 4. Open Audit Points

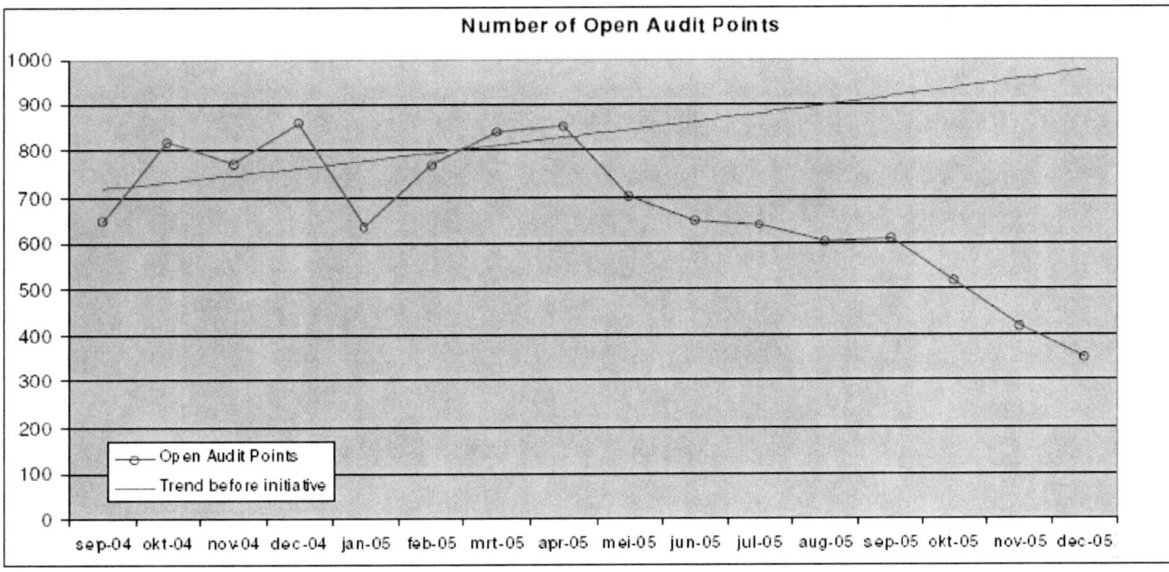

Security Awareness

The Security Awareness initiative is related to ISO/IEC 17799 Section 8. In the assessment period, the awareness of staff in respect of information risk was focused on both the IT community and Business departments of the Strategic Business Unit. As the level of individual awareness was an unknown quantity, no changes in process performance could be determined. A baseline on information security knowledge was established (Figure 5) with the rationale that improving knowledge on information security would improve the awareness. This figure shows the percentage of correctly answered questions by the IT community. The questions on information security were divided into four categories: Information, Computer, Office, and Yourself. For all categories combined the percentage of correctly completed answers (36 in total) was 80%. Additional to the awareness testing, an awareness film was produced and e-learning modules were developed based upon describing information security processes to the Business user community. Another important element in increasing security awareness at the Business community, were electronic wallpapers that were published on the desktops every month. Indirectly, the increase in awareness at the business departments may well be reflected by the increase in incident reporting that was observed in the period the measurements were gathered (see section on Security Incidents).

Policy Deviations

Managing deviations is related to ISO/IEC 17799 Section 5, Policy Exceptions. The policy deviation process had been operational since April 2005, so no data prior to that date were available for comparison. The prime objective of the process was to ensure effective and efficient management of IT related deviations in a consistent manner, without introducing an unacceptable level of risk. Whilst a gradual increase in the number of requested deviations can be observed in Figure 6, with an average number of 100 deviation requests per month, it should be appreciated that this does not necessarily mean an

Figure 5. Baseline information security awareness

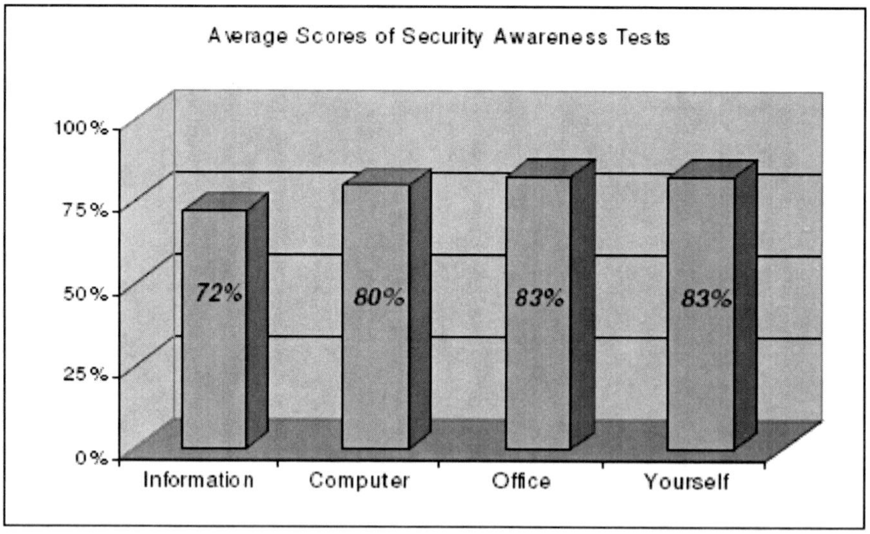

Figure 6. Number of requests related to information security policy exceptions

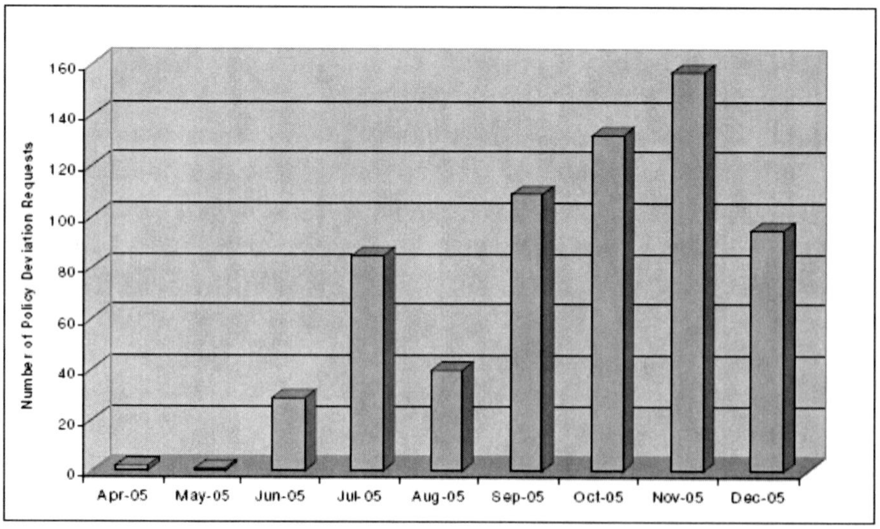

increase in the risk profile. It is more likely that it reflected an increased risk focused attitude of staff, enabling better risk management.

This kind of information enabled not only the identification of those locations that required extra attention, but also those policies and standards that, in a practical business environment, were difficult or impossible to implement. As such it reinforced the best practice that development of policies and standards for any Business should be undertaken with the direct involvement of all elements of the business departments to make these policies and standards as Business aligned as possible. Examples were data encryption policies and standards that had to be amended to make them work in practice. Initially these were created with very little discussion and involvement of the business departments on its impact while in the dynamic financial environment some element of risk is acceptable. So some relaxation of encryption requirements was allowed and implemented.

Security Officer Standard Operating Model

Data of Key Control Indicators (KCIs) are related to ISO/IEC 17799 Sections 5 to 13. Although one should be aware that rating the key controls themselves was carried out rather subjectively, as there were no hard criteria to set the status (red to green), comparison between the current KCIs against those reported at the start of the year showed that, in general, improvement had been achieved.

Primary issues raised by audits include:

- No local person responsible for security management
- Lack of segregation of duties between sec admin and review tasks
- No independent system monitoring being undertaken
- No formal security incident procedures defined
- Lack of asset classification for all local systems
- No local independent reviews being undertaken on key systems/processes
- No comprehensive security awareness being delivered

The continued implementation of the Security Officer Standard Operating Model (SOM) has been a key factor in the progress of global improvement as regards the KCIs, including the issues listed above which is also reflected in Figure 7. A period of uncertainty and doubt was replaced by stabilized risk assessment, recognition of issues, and effective action to address the identified gaps. The SOM provided a risk management delivery mechanism to deliver that with a measure of consistency across the organization.

Indirect Effects of Using the Standard

Risk Self Assessments (RSA)

Data of RSAs are indirectly related to ISO/IEC 17799 Section 8. As the assessments in this area are partly covered by initiatives listed in Table 4, it provided an opportunity to cross reference as 'RSA' remained unchanged. These RSAs were carried out at IT departments worldwide. Assessments showed no change in process performance of the Information Security function from the RSA perspective. At the very least this meant that the perceived level of risk, reported by the participants of these self assessments, did not change.

Other Risk Approval Process (ORAP)

Data of ORAPs are relates to ISO/IEC 17799 Section 12. However the data was neither sufficient in quantity nor quality to make any useful comparative analysis possible.

Financial Losses

The reporting on financial losses due to security incidents is not related to any ISO/IEC 17799 section, although it would fit nicely into the financial perspective of the Balanced Scorecard, if the translation is

Figure 7. Key Control Indicators[16]

Nr.	Key Controls	Q4 2004 EMEA	Q4 2004 ASPAC	Q4 2004 Americas	Q3 2005 EMEA	Q3 2005 ASPAC	Q3 2005 Americas
Security Organisation							
1	Information security function	GREEN	GREEN	AMBER	GREEN	GREEN	GREEN
2	Incident Response-process	GREEN	GREEN	GREEN	GREEN	GREEN	GREEN
Control over Information Systems							
3	Availability of system inventory	LIGHT GREEN	LIGHT GREEN	LIGHT GREEN	LIGHT GREEN	LIGHT GREEN	LIGHT GREEN
4	Assignment of system owner	AMBER	AMBER	LIGHT GREEN	LIGHT GREEN	LIGHT GREEN	LIGHT GREEN
5	Assignment of CIA-label	YELLOW	AMBER	GREEN	LIGHT GREEN	LIGHT GREEN	LIGHT GREEN
6	Risk (re-)assessment and -acceptance	RED	RED	RED	AMBER	AMBER	AMBER
7	Management of risk mitigating follow-up actions	YELLOW	YELLOW	AMBER	LIGHT GREEN	LIGHT GREEN	LIGHT GREEN
Personnel Security							
8	Dual control/segregation of functions	LIGHT GREEN	AMBER	GREEN	AMBER	AMBER	LIGHT GREEN
9	Awareness of staff	LIGHT GREEN	AMBER	YELLOW	GREEN	GREEN	GREEN
Physical and environmental security							
10	Critical processing and storage facilities	LIGHT GREEN	LIGHT GREEN	GREEN	GREEN	LIGHT GREEN	GREEN
11	Clean desk	LIGHT GREEN	AMBER	GREEN	GREEN	AMBER	GREEN
Installation, maintenance and use of computers (incl. PDA's etc.)							
12	SW/HW-maintenance	LIGHT GREEN	AMBER	GREEN	GREEN	LIGHT GREEN	GREEN
13	Disposal of storage media	YELLOW	LIGHT GREEN	AMBER	YELLOW	GREEN	LIGHT GREEN
14	Vulnerability Management-process	n/a	n/a	n/a	GREEN	GREEN	GREEN
15	Malicious code protection	n/a	n/a	n/a	GREEN	GREEN	GREEN
System access							
16	2FA for access to critical system functions	RED	RED	AMBER	RED	RED	RED
17	2FA for access via external connections	LIGHT GREEN	LIGHT GREEN	GREEN	GREEN	LIGHT GREEN	LIGHT GREEN
18	Maintenance of system access rights	AMBER	AMBER	AMBER	LIGHT GREEN	AMBER	AMBER
19	Role based access control	n/a	n/a	n/a	RED	RED	RED
20	Review of access rights	YELLOW	LIGHT GREEN	LIGHT GREEN	AMBER	GREEN	AMBER
21	Control over special privileges	YELLOW	LIGHT GREEN	YELLOW	YELLOW	GREEN	YELLOW
22	External connections	n/a	n/a	n/a	LIGHT GREEN	GREEN	LIGHT GREEN
Workstation security							
23	Encryption of hard-disks	YELLOW	YELLOW	RED	YELLOW	LIGHT GREEN	YELLOW
Systems development and maintenance							
24	Segregation of duties	LIGHT GREEN	AMBER	AMBER	AMBER	AMBER	AMBER
25	Isolation of environments	YELLOW	AMBER	AMBER	LIGHT GREEN	AMBER	AMBER
26	Testing and acceptance of security measures	n/a	n/a	n/a	LIGHT GREEN	GREEN	AMBER
27	Use of test-data	YELLOW	AMBER	AMBER	LIGHT GREEN	LIGHT GREEN	AMBER
Use of cryptography							
28	Storage and transport of secret data	YELLOW	YELLOW	LIGHT GREEN	YELLOW	YELLOW	AMBER
29	Data transported over external networks	YELLOW	YELLOW	AMBER	YELLOW	YELLOW	LIGHT GREEN
	White boxes denote controls introduced 2005 and not assessed in 2004	n/a					

made between incident type and associated costs. It basically represents the outcome of security incidents and other operational anomalies.

From Figure 8 it becomes clear that most of the reported incidents are caused by configuration failures and software bugs. However, as data were available from September to December 2005 only, trend analysis was not possible. Cross-referencing with ISO/IEC 17799 section 12 "Information Systems Development and Maintenance", causal factors could be process failures in this area. Enhanced incident reporting and subsequent financial loss calculations had to be improved to increase its usefulness. As a large proportion of the data recorded in the systems did not relate directly to information risk, this conclusion is only tentative.

Figure 8. Incidents that caused financial losses

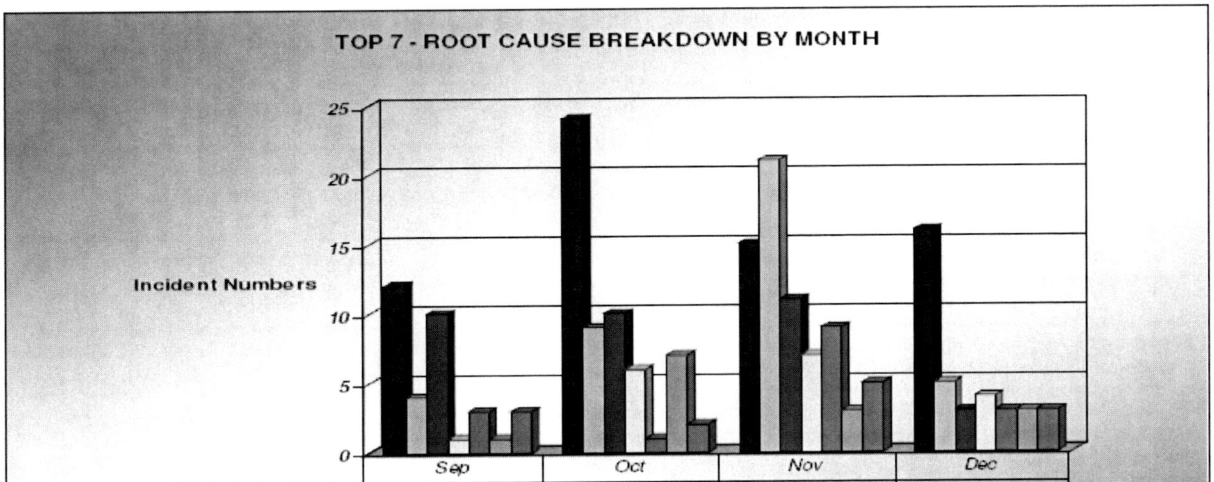

	Sep	Oct	Nov	Dec
Configuration	12	24	15	16
Code Defect	4	9	21	5
Data	10	10	11	3
Process - Bank	1	6	7	4
Human Error	3	1	9	3
Third Party Failure	1	7	3	3
Processing	3	2	5	3

Regulatory Compliance

Data on the level of regulatory and policy compliance (ROC/AIM) are related to ISO/IEC 17799 Section 5 as well. As this area was not directly covered by initiatives listed in Table 4, it also provided an opportunity to cross reference with the other initiatives as 'ROC/AIM Compliance' remained unchanged. Qualitative assessments for 'ROC/AIM Compliance' showed a significant improvement in process performance of the information security function as the number of reported policy compliance exceptions increased from 53 to 102. This showed the intensified compliance checking and awareness and was not a result of a laxity in technology risk management.

CASE ANALYSIS

In this section the constructs of the enhanced conceptual model will be discussed and the propositions of this model will be assessed following the case description of the previous section.

Constructs

Process of Standard Selection

The selection process of the standard itself was not part of the analysis, as ISO/IEC 17799 was previously chosen to be used as company standard. Main rationale for this choice was the broad acceptance in the

Table 5. Success factors for effective implementation and usage of ISO/IEC 17799:2005 (Italics by author)

Success Factor	Case Assessment	Valuation[17]
a) information security policy, objectives and activities should reflect *business objectives*	Objectives and requirements of the initiatives were only loosely aligned with those of the Business.	Average
b) implement, maintain, monitor and improve information security that *is consistent with the organizational culture*	The organizational culture could be described as entrepreneurial, which explains the rather informal way the initiatives were established and executed.	Good
c) visible *support and commitment* from all levels of management	Endorsement for the initiatives came mostly from IT and not from the Business as the alignment between these parties was only average at best.	Average
d) good *understanding* of information security requirements, risk assessment and risk management	In the IT department there was good understanding of these initiatives, but on the Business side this was poor to average.	Average
e) effective *marketing* of information security to all managers, employees and other parties to achieve awareness	Selling of the information security function was done via electronic mailings and regular postings on the intranet site and was typified as average and for some of the initiatives this was even poor.	Average
f) distribution of *guidance* on information security policy and standards to all managers, employees and other parties	Guidance on policy and standards was carried out by means of an intranet side and occasional leaflets	Average
g) provision to *fund* information security management activities	There were ample financial means to carry out the information security management initiatives	Good
h) provide appropriate *awareness, training and education*	Training and education of Business and IT staff comprised of electronic wallpapers with key messages based upon Information Security best practises. Additional to these wallpapers an awareness film was produced for the business community.	Average
i) establish an effective *information security incident management process*	The initiative related to this success factor was only partially implemented because of alignment and ownership issues within the IT departments. As a consequence no consistent end to end information security incident management process was implemented.	Poor
j) implement a *measurement system* that is used to evaluate performance in information security management and feedback suggestions for improvement. Note that information security measurements are outside of the scope of this standard	The measurement system was based only on the BSC internal perspective. Other aspects of performance, including financial and customer perspectives were lacking.	Poor

information security profession because of its perceived usefulness. In fact ISO/IEC 17799 is considered as *the* standard for Information Security Management in Europe (ISF, 2001 and ISACA, 2005).

As far as the selection of the initiatives were concerned (Table 3), it was observed these originated solely from within IT without direct Business input and involvement. These initiatives are subsets of ISO/IEC 17799.

Implementation and Use of Standard

The ISO/IEC 17799 Information Security Management lists 10 *success factors* for its effective implementation and usage (ISO/IEC 17799, 2005, p. Xi) and Table 5 provides a valuation for this case.

Of these 10 success factors, 2 were rated as good, 5 average and 3 poor. These factors were moderated with governance and/or management, in conformance with the enhanced conceptual model. Success factor "a", relates to the standards policy, objectives and activities that should reflect the business

Table 6. Details on the ISO/IEC 17799 related activities

ISO/IEC 17799 related activity	Part of TRM initiatives	Change in process performance
Vulnerability Management	Yes	Positive (direct measurements)
Risk Assessments	Yes	Positive (direct measurements)
Security Incidents	Yes	Positive (direct measurements)
Audit Points	Yes	Positive (direct measurements)
Security Awareness	Yes	Positive (indirect measurements)
Policy Deviations	Yes	Positive (direct measurements)
Security Officer Standard Operating Model	Yes	Positive (direct measurements)
Risk Self Assessments (RSA)	No	No effect (indirect measurements)
Other Risk Approval Process (ORAP)	No	Undetermined
Financial Losses	No	Undetermined
Regulatory Compliance	No	Positive (indirect measurements)

objectives, which is typically a concern of governance. Adequate alignment between Business and IT as to accountability and decision rights is required to meet this success factor. Some success factors "b, c, and i" involve both governance and management concerns. These success factors can be satisfied only with adequate alignment between Business and IT on how to implement and use these factors. Management aspects, like organizing and controlling the related activities, are also required to meet these success factors. The remaining success factors "d, e, f, g, h, and j" are typically management related (organizing, planning, guiding, etc) only. With regard to the initiatives itemized in Table 3, the following was observed:

- The Business-IT alignment of most of the projects with defined and agreed business requirements was weak. The majority of the decisions originated from within the IT Department and were in most cases launched retroactively to resolve audit issue findings. So information related to the internal process perspective triggered these initiatives.
- No detailed project plans were created and no clear timelines and deliverables defined, basically because of the lack of a mature project management organization. As a result initiatives 8 to 12 failed.

Process Performance

Although process performance has not been measured by means of a Balanced Scorecard, as the finance, customer and learning & growth perspectives were not included in the performance assessment, conclusions can be made based on the internal/business process perspective. Of the ISO/IEC 17799 related activities, Table 6 specifies whether changes in performance of the information security process have been as found as described in the previous sections.

Similarly using the Shafer and Byrd (2000) framework, Table 7 shows the following changes in process performance:

Table 7. Changes in process performance, due to usage of the Information Security Management standard

Area	Case Study IV (ISO/IEC 17799)
Improved quality	Positive: a clearly improved overall information security risk profile
Reduced costs	Positive: More effective mitigation; Proactive risk mitigation
Increased flexibility	No changes found in this area
Improved customer satisfaction	No change – slight improvements regarding security awareness and understanding of staff
Overall improvements in operations	Positive, includes: Better Vulnerability Management; Enhanced Risk Assessments; Fewer Security Incidents; Better Audit Point Resolution; Security Awareness; Better Policy Deviations management; Enhanced Regulatory Compliance

One can conclude that all TRM initiated activities resulted in enhanced process performance of the information security function, although no financial analysis and reporting on the impact of these initiatives was carried out. Only a baseline measurement for the Security Awareness initiative was available, therefore, no direct changes in process performance could be determined.

ISO/IEC 17799 related activities not covered by any of the aforementioned initiatives showed no improvements, with the exception of Regulatory Compliance. In other words, the direct positive effects of using the standard did not have an (immediate) effect on other business support activities. One of the explanations may be that these activities are owned by other parts of the organization that did not change their supporting processes, nor were they directly involved in the implementation activities or provided input for the initiatives.

Performance Measurement & Analysis

The measurement and analysis of process performance was incomplete as only the internal perspective of the BSC was captured. Other perspectives were not determined by the organization nor were targets or Key Performance Indicators (KPIs) defined. In fact, facilitating process performance measurements were not part of the deliverables of any of the implemented initiatives and these had to be sourced from other systems later on. In sum, the whole process of implementing and executing process performance measurements and analysis was considered as ineffective.

Governance of Standard

With reference to the IT standards governance framework based on Weill and Ross (2005) (see Chapter 8, Table 9), the following conclusions can be drawn from this case study (Table 8).

For most of the TRM initiatives the governance was as follows: centralized implementation and coordination (reporting & assessment to ensure coordinated follow-up) and decentralized execution (resolution to ensure close contact with the customer). This structure was chosen because of the geographically dispersed nature of the Strategic Business Unit. An exception was decentralized management of security incidents, as this activity did not evolve to the desired centralized state. Due to the lack of alignment within the IT departments, regarding ownership of the incident management process, this did not suc-

Table 8. Conclusions related to IT standard governance

Decision Area	IT Standard Issue	Conclusions drawn from this case study
IT principles	What are desirable IT Standards?	The desirability of IT standards depends on, among other things, how IT services are being delivered. Outsourced IT environments require other IT principles than non-outsourced environments. In the case company, management of IT standards is left to third party vendors, except for information security standards (both products and processes) that are fully managed by the company itself.
IT architecture	Which technical capabilities should be standardized enterprisewide to support IT efficiencies and facilitate process standardization and integration? Which activities must be standardized enterprisewide to support data integration?	The level of autonomy of business units is another important factor that determines the reach and range of usage of IT standards, which has been recognized by Weill and Ross (2004). In the case company, business unit synergy is now an important driver, so information security standards (for example for encryption and dual factor authentication) are rolled out company wide.
IT infrastructure	Which infrastructure services should be implemented enterprisewide?	The following services have been implemented enterprise wide: vulnerability management and risk assessments. Security incident management unintentionally kept a service provided locally. Access control and dual factor authentication were to be implemented enterprisewide as well, but these initiatives did not work out at all.
Business application needs	How can business needs be addressed within architectural standards? When does a business need justify an exception to a standard?	Requirements come mainly from regulatory pressures, like those of the Sarbanes-Oxley Act regarding ownership of information systems and auditibility of activities on information systems. In principle, all policy exceptions have to be justified in this company. Justification should be based on Business rationale or legal/regulatory constraints.
Prioritization and investment decisions	What is the relative importance of enterprisewide versus business unit investments? Do actual investment practices reflect their relative importance?	There has been a shift from Business Unit specific investment for information security standards towards an enterprise wide approach, mainly to promote synergies and to allow economies of scale. In this case study it was only possible to check the internal / business process performance. This was positive on average, as shown in Table 6. However, there was a lack of alignment between business and IT (regarding launched initiatives and business requirements) which potentially impacted negatively on prioritization and investment decisions. Furthermore, these were made based on incomplete measurements (just one perspective of the BSC).

Table 9. Details on the ISO/IEC 17799 related activities

ISO/IEC 17799 related activity	Change in process performance	Measurement unit
Vulnerability Management	Positive (direct measurements)	% of hosts with critical vulnerabilities
Risk Assessments	Positive (direct measurements)	Risk mitigation figures
Security Incidents	Positive (direct measurements)	Number of incidents
Audit Point Resolution	Positive (direct measurements)	Number of open points
Security Awareness	Positive (indirect measurements)	Number of correct answers
Policy Deviations	Positive (direct measurements)	Number of deviations
Security Officer Operating Prototype	Positive (direct measurements)	Various KCIs

Table 10. Comparison ISO/IEC 17799:2000 and ISO/IEC 17799:2005 (ISO/IEC 17799, 2000, 2005)

ISO/IEC 17799:2000	ISO/IEC 17799:2005
1. Security Policy • Information Security Policy	1. Security Policy • Information Security Policy
2. Organizational security • Information security infrastructure • Security of third party access • Outsourcing	2. Organizing information security • Internal organization • External parties
3. Asset classification and control • Accountability for assets • Information classification	3. Asset Management • Responsibility for assets • Information classification
4. Personnel Security • Security in job definition and resourcing • User training • Responding to security incidents and malfunctions	4. Human resource security • Prior to employment • During employment • Termination or change of employment
5. Physical and environmental security • Secure areas • Equipment security • General controls	5. Physical and environmental security • Secure areas • Equipment security
6. Communications and operations management • Operational procedures and responsibilities • System planning and acceptance • Protection against malicious software • Housekeeping • Network management • Media handling and security • Exchange of information and software	6. Communications and operations management • Operational procedures and responsibilities • Third party service delivery management • System planning and acceptance • Protection against malicious and mobile code • Backup • Network security management • Media handling • Exchange of information • Electronic commerce service • Monitoring
7. Access control • Business requirement for access control • User access management • User responsibilities • User network control • Applications access control • Monitoring systems access and use • Mobile computing and teleworking	7. Access control • Business requirement for access control • User access management • User responsibilities • Network access control • Operating system access control • Applications and information access control • Mobile computing and networking
8. Systems development & maintenance • Security requirements of system • Security in applications systems • Cryptographic controls • Security of system files • Security in development and support services	8. Information systems acquisition, development and maintenance • Security requirements in information system • Correct processing in applications • Cryptographic controls • Security of system files • Security in development and support services • Technical vulnerability management
9. Business continuity management • Aspects of business continuity management	9. Business continuity management • Information security aspects of business continuity management
10. Compliance • Compliance with legal requirements • Review of security policy and technical compliance • System audit considerations	10. Compliance • Compliance with legal requirements • Compliance with security policy and standards • Information systems audit considerations
	11. Information Security Incident Management • Reporting information security events and weaknesses • Management of information security incidents and improvements

ceed. Another issue was found between TRM and several supporting departments in the use phase of the standard as the supporting processes could not interconnect (c.f. RSA, ORAP, Financial Losses).

A lack of alignment between TRM and the Business was also found for business requirements. Almost all initiatives (Table 3) originated from IT without any direct involvement from the business side. These initiatives could therefore be typified as originating from an IT monarchy (decisions to launch remediation initiatives were made by IT, based on risk mitigation perspective) except for the risk assessments. In these assessments the Business had ultimate end-decision rights & accountability of the outcome. Given this analysis the governance of this standard is typified as ineffective overall.

Management of Standard

When we refer to planning, organizing, directing and controlling this information security standard the following can be concluded. In the implementation phase significant deficiencies were observed with regard to project management of components of this standard (Table 3). Among the main problems were: no timelines or clear deliverables specified; too wide scope; insufficient or not approved budget; lack of skilled resources. Furthermore, no overall program manager was appointed who could have mitigated some of these deficiencies. As a result 5 out of 12 initiatives failed to deliver, so as far as management is concerned during the implementation of the standard, it is typified as in effective.

No targets on process performance indicators were set to allow better management in the use phase of the standard. However, by and large, management of this standard during its usage was effective (exemplified by the results in vulnerability management, risk assessments, and audit point resolution) as discussed in the section on direct effects of the standards.

Propositions

The propositions of the enhanced conceptual model applied to this case show us the following:

Proposition 1: *An effective (ineffective) IT standard selection process, positively (negatively) influences the implementation of these standards.* – The selection process was not part of the case study because ISO/IEC 17799 had already been chosen as the standard to be used in the company. The company selected this globally accepted international standard, so the outcome of that (out of scope) selection process was at least effective. On the other hand, the selection of the TRM initiatives that are basically sub-sets of ISO/IEC 17799, was largely an IT activity only. This process is considered as ineffective because direct input from the Business was lacking and other stakeholders (like service departments) were not involved either. Initiatives that required cooperation between TRM and other IT services departments were only partially implemented or failed altogether (#3, #10 and #11, Table 3). From this viewpoint it is concluded that Proposition 1 is supported by this case as the ineffective selection process negatively influenced the implementation of the standard in the company.

Proposition 2: *Effective (ineffective) governance and/or management of appropriate IT standards, positively (negatively) influences the implementation of these standards.* – In 0 it was described that 5 of 12 of the initiatives failed to be implemented. Implementation was negatively impacted by lack of proper project management. The lack of clear discussion rights and alignment between TRM on the one hand, and other supporting departments and the Business on the other hand had a negative effect on the implementation of the standard too. So in the implementation phase, governance of the standard was ineffective which was also the case for the failed initiatives (based on the discussion on governance and management of the standard). As the model suggests, ineffective governance and/or management negatively influenced the implementation of the standard. In addition, for those initiatives that were implemented successfully, a distinguishing factor was better project management (whereas governance made no difference). Therefore, Proposition 2 is supported by this case, including the 'and/or' of governance & management.

Proposition 3: *Effective (ineffective) governance and/or management of appropriate IT standards, positively (negatively) influences the use of these standards.* – Analysis of the use phase of the standard showed ineffective governance. An example was unclear ownership of the incident management process between the IT departments. Because of this, the aim to standardize and centralize the security incident management process failed and this function stayed decentralized. In the use phase the standard was managed effectively. Although 5 of 12 initiatives did not deliver (so these are not touched by this proposition), the remaining ones were used successfully. So, a negative influence of governance and, generally speaking, a positive influence of management were found when the standard was used, so Proposition 3 is supported by this case.

Proposition 4: *Effective (ineffective) use of appropriate IT standards, positively (negatively) influences process performance.* It was determined that usage of the ISO/IEC 17799 standard resulted in enhanced process performance of the information security function (Table 6, Table 7). Results of the implemented TRM activities showed positive changes in the risk profile, which is a reflection of enhanced process performance. Although no targets with respect to (key) process performance indicators were defined (see recommendations), based on the described results in this case study Proposition 4 is supported.

Referring to Table 5, items i) incident management process and j) measurement system, although ineffectively used because of respectively the lacking of an end-to-end process and limited measurement scope, this did not negatively influence process performance. In general one can argue that ineffective use of appropriate IT standards does not invariably lead to negative side effects on process performance, simply because the standard is not used as it should. So, Proposition 4 can be even further refined in: *Effective (ineffective) use of appropriate IT standards, positively influences (does not influence or negatively influences) process performance.*

Proposition 5: *A high (low) process performance due to the applied IT standards, does not lead (leads) to changes in the way these standards are governed and/or managed.* – In this case study the internal perspective of the process performance was available only, so potential decisions to change governance and management were based on a limited scope and number of measurements. As far as the internal perspective is concerned an increase in process performance was found and no changes in governance and management were carried out. So as far as data are available, Proposition 5 is supported.

Proposition 6: *Effective (ineffective) governance and/or management of appropriate IT standards, positively (negatively) influences the IT standard selection process.* – The selection process was not part of the case study as ISO/IEC 17799 had already been chosen as the standard to be used in the company. However, selection of the initiatives (i.e. subsets of this standard) listed in Table 3, was carried out solely by IT without direct Business input and involvement. With governance of the standard considered as ineffective, Proposition 6 is supported.

CONCLUSIONS

Case Conclusions

First and foremost, the Corporate IT standardization Management Framework (i.e. the enhanced conceptual model) as presented in Chapter 8, has passed its first test successfully, as the empirical results in the case study were consistent with the proposed behavior. All propositions were supported, albeit the process of standard selection (concerning Propositions 1 and 6) was limited to the TRM initiatives. Based on the insights from the three earlier in-depth case studies the original conceptual model (Chapter 4) was extended by adding management and governance constructs. Also application of standards was also split into implementation and use of standards. In this model management and governance of company IT standards not only relate to the implementation phase (i.e. project management) as it also includes setting the standards and ensuring ongoing improvements. These additions proved to be crucial in describing and explaining the effects of and the relationship between selection, implementation and usage of the ISO/IEC 17799 standard on process performance. Although the additional constructs of the conceptual model proved to be a significant improvement compared to the initial model, further case study research is necessary to determine variables and formulate and test hypotheses related to these variables. These could be validated through a large-scale survey on company standardization of IT products and processes. A further enhancement could be to model effects of organizational culture more explicitly. As part of another research stream, one could also focus more on how the information security activities took place.

Secondly, this case study contributes to two domains. It adds empirical evidence to the scarce literature on the effects of IT standards for organizational processes and adds to the very few Information Security Management research studies as well. It was shown that even with only limited effective implementation and use of an information security management standard, positive effects can be achieved. Six out of seven TRM initiated activities resulted in directly enhanced process performance of the information security process (Table 9). Only a baseline measurement for the Security Awareness initiative was available, therefore, direct changes in process performance could not be determined.

MANAGERIAL IMPLICATIONS

This case study shows the potential of an Information Security Process standard and how, if implemented in a consistent manner with the support of Senior Management, it can result in improvements of the information security process and thus in an improved risk profile. A number of initiatives were not implemented successfully, mainly because of deficiencies in project management. A key return on the use of ISO/IEC 17799 was that the Business were made aware of the true level of risk and were able to make decisions based on fact and not on fiction, which resulted in finances being made available to address risks which was a new development. The study also demonstrates what is achievable with a limited budget (1% of total IT annual expenditure) when individual and managerial commitment is in place. Those initiatives that really added value in improving the risk profile were implemented. The fact that ISO/IEC 17799 specifies the 'what' and not the 'how' of setting up practices for information security management was an advantage as this allowed maximum flexibility for the organization. Although this initiative was internally focussed, the implemented measures can be used as a head start to get certified for the information security management standard BS 7799 - Part 2, if the company wants to do so.

At a more general level, business benefits from using the information security management standard include: a) requirements from regulators (e.g. FED) to improve the risk profile were satisfied; b) Business Management became more aware of the real and not the perceived information security risks through, for example, information risk assessments of projects and vulnerability management of the IT infrastructure; c) this consequently allowed targeted investment decisions in the information security domain.

This case study allows managers to be fully aware of the potential of governance and management in the implementation and usage of company standards. Managers should be aware of the impact of allocation of decision rights and the setting of accountabilities related to company standardization. Specific recommendations regarding this case study are to pay special attention to 1) Governance and management of the company standard; 2) process performance measurements to provide effects in detail of the usage of the company standard.

As far as this case company is concerned, recommendations for the information security function include:

Ad1) to involve the Business more when initiating information security activities and to make sure that these are communicated by senior IT management to the Business. As an example, during the Security Awareness initiative, an IT duopoly could have been used (Weill and Ross, 2005) to make this activity more effective. The information security business requirements should have been better assessed and there should have also been an improved prioritization of initiatives. At this moment these decisions areas are considered to be an IT Monarchy. The lack of alignment between TRM and other parts of the organization (that perform e.g. RSAs, ORAPs and Financial Losses) should be addressed as well. Another important element is project management which should be further professionalized, as this was lacking during the implementation of sections (i.e. the initiatives) of the standard.

Ad 2) The monitoring of the effects of these initiatives should be extended, especially since only the internal/business process perspective was available. Therefore it is recommended to develop the financial perspective of the BSC by, for instance, quantification of the benefits of resolving critical vulnerabilities in the infrastructure. The introduction of the customer perspective would be beneficial too as this creates a better alignment between the business departments and the Information Security department.

Last but not least targets for KPIs should be agreed upon to effectively manage the information risk profile. A further refinement of analysis can be added to perform quantification of costs per critical vulnerability. Whilst, due to time constraints, this was not undertaken as part of this study it is recommended that such a quantification of cost is completed. An attempt has been made to quantify the investments using the ROSI method (Cavusoglu, 2004). It turned out that ROSI could not be used effectively because of its inherently large uncertainty of anticipated benefits or losses. Future research should be targeted to test these findings by investigation of the implementation of ISO/IEC 17799 in other organizations.

REFERENCES

Backhouse, J., Carol Hsu, C., & Silva, L. (2006). Circuits of Power in creating de jure Standards: Shaping an International Information Systems Security Standard. *Management Information Systems Quarterly*, *30*(Special Issue), 413–438.

Cavusoglu, H., Mishra, B., & Raghunathan, S. (2004). A model for evaluating IT security investments. *Communications of the ACM, 47*(7), 87–92. doi:10.1145/1005817.1005828

COBIT. (2000). *Cobit Executive Summary*. IL, USA: Information Systems Audit and Control Foundation.

Coffey, T., & Saidha, P. (1996). Non-repudiation with Mandatory Proof of Receipt. *Computer Communication Review, 26*(1), 6–17. doi:10.1145/232335.232338

Höne, K., & Eloff, J. H. P. (2002). Information security policy what do international information security standards say? *Computers & Security, 21*(5). doi:10.1016/S0167-4048(02)00504-7

ISACA. (2005). *Information Security Harmonisation*. IL, USA: Classification of Global Guidance, Information Systems Audit and Control Association.

ISACF. (2001). *Information security governance*. IL, USA: Guidance for Boards of Directors and Executive Management, Information Systems Audit and Control Foundation.

ISF. (2001). Information Security Standards. Positioning the Forum's Standard of Good Practice, Information Security Forum, London, UK, September 2001.

ISO/IEC 17799:2000(E) (2000). *Information technology — Security techniques — Code of practice for information security management* (1st ed.). International Organization for Standardization and International Electrotechnical Commission, Geneva, Switzerland.

ISO/IEC 17799:2005(E). (2005). *Information technology — Security techniques — Code of practice for information security management* (2nd ed.). International Organization for Standardization and International Electrotechnical Commission, Geneva, Switzerland.

ITGI. (2001). *Information Security Governance: Guidance for Boards of Directors and Executive Management*. IL, USA: IT Governance Institute - Information Systems Audit and Control Foundation.

Kotulic, A. G., & Clark, J. G. (2004). Why There Aren't More Information Security Research Studies. *Information & Management, 41*(5), 597–607. doi:10.1016/j.im.2003.08.001

Shafer, S. M., & Byrd, T. A. (2000). A framework for measuring the efficiency of organizational investments in information technology using data envelopment analysis. *Omega, 28*, 125–141. doi:10.1016/S0305-0483(99)00039-0

Sinclaire, J. K. (2005). Current Research in Information Security and Privacy. In *Proceedings of the 2005 Southern Association of Information Systems Conference*.

Siponen, M., & Stucke, C. (2006). Effective Anti-Spam Strategies in Companies: An International Study. In *Proceedings of the 39th Hawaii International Conference on System Sciences.*

Spears, J. L., & Cole, R. J. (2006). A Preliminary Investigation of the Impact of the Sarbanes-Oxley Act on Information Security. In *Proceedings of the 39th Hawaii International Conference on System Sciences.*

Weill, P., & Ross, J. (2005). A Matrixed Approach to Designing IT Governance. *MIT. Sloan Management Review, 46*(2), 26–34.

ENDNOTES

1 Authentication: The act of verifying the identity of a user and the user's eligibility to access computerized information. Authentication is designed to protect against fraudulent logon activity (COBIT 4, p. 191)

2 Non-repudiation: Non-repudiation allows an exchange of data between two principals in such a manner that the principals cannot subsequently deny their participation in the exchange (Coffey and Saidha, 1996)

3 Develops a range of products, such as IP Security Protocol (ipsec), Secure Shell (ssh) and Standard/ Multipurpose Internet Mail Extensions (S/MIME) for e-mail security and XML digital signatures that became de-facto standards.

4 Publishes common specifications for the web, such as HTML and XML.

5 A strong argument against this perceived deficiency has already been discussed in Chapter 6 in relation to the process standard CMM regarding the maturity of software development. Precisely because such standards deal with 'What' and not 'How' these provide flexibility of implementation and use within organizations.

6 http://www.gao.gov

7 http://www.bis.org/publ/bcbsca.htm

8 "This standard gives recommendations for information security management for use by those who are responsible for initiating, implementing or maintaining security in their organization. It is intended to provide a common basis for developing organizational security standards and effective security management practice and to provide confidence in inter-organizational dealings. Recommendations from this standard should be selected and used in accordance with applicable laws and regulations.", ISO/IEC 17799:2000, p. 1.

9 An overview of the development of this information security management standard, from the point of view of political persuasion and mobilization, is provided by Backhouse et al. (2006).

10 BS 7799 - Part 2:2002 became an international standard in 2005 with reference number ISO/IEC 27001: 2005

11 Because of the introduction of ISO/IEC 27001:2005, ISO/IEC 17799:2005 has been renamed into ISO/IEC 27002: 2005

12 The case company choose the term Technology Risk Management which echo's an "IT monarchism", although in practise this also included non-technological areas. Therefore, Information Risk Management or just Information Security Management would have been more appropriate.
13.*) Denotes joint initiative with other IT departments

14 Internal threat: any (potential) incident that originates from inside the physical or logical premises of the organization.

15 External threat: any (potential) incident that originates from outside the physical or logical premises of the organization.

16 **Red:** No or limited implementation of control (less than 15%)
Yellow: Control implemented to some extend or in some situations (between 15 - 40%)
Amber: Control implemented about half-way or in about half of the situations (between 40 - 65%)
Light green: Control implemented for the greater part or in most situations (between 65 - 90%)
Green: Control (almost) fully implemented or in (almost) all situations (more than 90%)
White: No information available

[17] The valuation (in terms of Poor, Average, Good) of the success factors proposed by ISO was based on the case study material and the observations by the researcher.

Section 7
Conclusions, Discussion and Recommendations

In this section a final discussion will be presented following four case studies that have been carried out with respect to company IT standards using an initial and an enhanced conceptual model. The initial model focused on the control of using IT standards whereas the enhanced version incorporated selection and implementation, besides their usage. Furthermore, control was modified into management and governance with the objective of focusing on opportunities to influence process performance to realize intended business benefits.

Chapter 10
Conclusions, Discussion, Recommendations

This chapter starts with reiterating the research questions as expressed in Chapter 1. The main research question is as follows:

How can organizations realize intended business benefits from company IT standardization?

With the following detailed questions:

1. What is a company IT standardization process and which distinguishable components does it encompass?
2. How can business effects of IT standards be measured?
3. How do company IT standards affect business performance?
4. What are the components of a company IT standardization management framework?[1]
5. How do governance and management of company IT standardization contribute to the realization of intended business benefits?

In this chapter a final discussion will be presented following four case studies that have been carried out with respect to company IT standards using an initial and an enhanced conceptual model. The

DOI: 10.4018/978-1-61520-759-6.ch010

initial model focussed on the control of using IT standards whereas the enhanced version incorporated selection and implementation, besides their usage. Furthermore, control was modified into management and governance with the objective of focussing on opportunities to influence process performance to realize intended business benefits.

In the next sections the business benefits identified in the case studies will be discussed, as well as whether these hold in a more general sense also. The structure of this chapter is as follows. First a summary and the conclusions of this research will be provided. Than, the contributions to theory and practice will be discussed including the generalizability of the findings and the limitations of this research. This chapter is concluded with recommendations for further research.

LOOKING BACK

This research has focused on company IT standards that facilitate business processes in large companies. The core of this research has been to investigate how an organization can realize intended business benefits from company IT standardization. The focus has, therefore been on 1) investigating the components of the company IT standardization process, 2) providing insight into the effects of company IT product and process standards on process performance, and 3) providing insight into the factors affecting performance of these processes when utilizing such standards.

From the literature review and a pilot case study an initial conceptual model has been derived, which includes the constructs[2] *'Process of Standard Selection'*, 'Application of Standard', 'Control (on usage) of Standard' and *'Process Performance'*. Subsequently this model was tested using three in-depth case studies related to Client Server, Software Development and company ERP/HR standards. Lessons learned from these three case studies showed that a more detailed model would add value to the descriptive and explanatory nature of this research topic. To that end, the construct 'Application of Standard' was split into *'Implementation of Standard'* and *'Use of Standard'*. In addition, 'Control of Standard' was differentiated into the two constructs *'Governance* and *Management* (of Selection, Implementation and Use) *of Standard'*. Subsequently a fourth in-depth case study was carried out to test the extended model. Key characteristics of these case studies are itemized in Table 1.

Based on the initial and extended conceptual models, propositions have been formulated describing the relations between these constructs. The initial model has been tested in three case studies: Client Server, Software Development, and HRM company standards. The extended model has been tested in a case study regarding an Information Security Management standard.

The *Client Server* case study described the complete cycle of standard selection, implementation and usage. The case concerned a set of hardware and software products that were selected to be the preferred

Table 1. Key characteristics of the four case studies

Case Study	Type of Standard	Range
Client Server	Product	Business Unit
Software Development	Process	Business Unit
HRM	Product, Data and Process (ERP)	Enterprise
Information Security Management	Process	Business Unit

assortment. So this set was defined as the company C/S standard to be used. It was described how that standard remained up-to-date and aligned with Business requirements. Key business benefits of this standard were a reduction in costs per workstation with 50% and at the same time an improvement of the quality of IT service delivery.

The *Software Development* case study described how the usage of a combination of two process standards (CMM & DSDM) resulted in a significant drop of the costs of developing software by 20%. These process standards were implemented accompanied by an organizational change process, which proved to be important to ensure the organization adopted these standards. In spite of this, the IT department was not able to fully exploit the potential of these standards. Because it concerned process standards, it affected the way staff and management worked, and making it a success was found to be more difficult than in the product standard case.

The *HRM* case study described the implementation of an ERP HR suite that was selected as company standard. This included standardization of data (both syntax and semantics) which is known to be very complicated (Boh and Yellin, 2007). The absence of implementation guidelines (i.e. a standard way of implementation) and optional features of a lot of elements of the standard did not help to make it a success either. In this case study the effects of ineffective allocation of decision rights and accountability became obvious. Only when this was changed the project progressed as originally anticipated.

The *Information Security* case study described the positive effects of using an information security management standard on the risk profile satisfying internal and external requirements. In this case study it was discussed how changes in governance and management of the standard could have resulted in potentially even better process performance of the information security function. This included Business-IT alignment, project management, and performance monitoring. Because collaboration with and input from the Business was only marginal, the business benefits of the implemented measures, though substantial, remained sub-optimal.

CONCLUSIONS

The aim of this book is to provide insight into how organizations can realize intended business benefits from company IT standardization. Hence detailed research questions have been formulated that will guide us though this section. Based on the literature review, the pilot case study, the conceptual model, the four in-depth case studies and the cross case analysis, the following conclusions can be drawn.

Selection, Implementation and Use

Q1. What is a company IT standardization process and which distinguishable components does it encompass?

A company IT standardization process is a process that is carried out by an organization with the objective of providing specifications for an IT product or process (which may include the accompanying data used in that process) to be repeatedly and consistently used in that company. The components of this process are the *selection* "the way the company IT standard is chosen", the *implementation* "the way the company IT standard is put into operation" and the *use* "the way the company IT standard is operated".

With respect to the construct *Process of Standard Selection*, an important variable is the level of involvement and cooperation between Business and IT. Although business drivers for standardization such as cost reduction and quality improvement may be clear, the absence of proper business alignment can counteract the potential benefits of company standards.

With respect to the construct *Implementation of Standard*, obviously the quality of project management plays an important role. But it is equally important, especially for standards that are being implemented across organizational units (see *HRM* case study), to ensure a prescribed set and/or standard way of implementation is pursued. Failure to do so could result in incompatible instances of the standard, severely diminishing its benefits.

With respect to the construct *Use of Standard*, there are several important elements that determine whether a company standard is being used effectively. Among the more important ones are: 1) processes and procedures that support the usage of the standard, such as the way exceptions are dealt with and whether these are integrated in the existing standard; 2) the type of standard, as process standards typically have more impact on the way staff work than product and data standards have; 3) the level of Management support of the standard from both IT and Business and the enforcement by the IT organization. For company IT standards with an enterprise wide reach, efficient usage becomes even more challenging, as what is perceived as beneficial by one unit does not necessarily hold good for another organizational unit.

A further important element in this respect is the relationship between the selection, implementation and usage of IT standards in a company. The propositions of the initial conceptual model and those of the extended model provide insight into this relationship. As far as the initial model is concerned there was a positive relationship found between effectiveness in selection on the one hand and implementation and usage on the other hand. Involving the proper stakeholders, following a stakeholder analysis, contributes greatly to the effectiveness in standard selection. The positive relationship between effective implementation and usage was found as well using the Corporate IT Standardization Framework (in cases I and III). An important observation is, especially when implementing and using process standards, that one could not change the way staff was working without giving careful attention to changes in behavior as well (cases II and III). So, an organizational change process accompanying the implementation of company IT process standards boosts its effectiveness. Another important observation was that the implementation sequence a) product, process vs. b) process, product impacts on the usage. In other words, to first agree on process standards, and only then on the supporting product standards pays off.

Variables that contribute to the effectiveness of company IT standardization related to these three constructs include: 1) the level of endorsement by Business and IT management; 2) the level of prescription and enforcement of related processes and procedures[3]; 3) the level of collaboration between Business and IT. As part of the second item, so-called implementation standards are of importance. It constitutes a detailed description of how to implement a chosen company standard in order to prevent incompatible versions of the same standard. Such activities should be monitored by a central authority.

The case studies showed that business benefits were accomplished by using the company IT standards and that the three components are essential elements in the process of company IT standardization. Additionally, the case studies also showed that two other components are essential to accomplish intended business benefits from company IT standardization: its respective governance and management that constitute the management framework.

Measuring Business Effects

Q2. How can business effects of IT standards be measured?

With respect to the construct *Process Performance*, to directly assess the business effects of IT on the performance of a firm seems to be an unreasonable abstraction as outcomes are in most cases visible as second or third order effects only (Weill & Broadbent, 1998). The effects of IT (including those of IT standards) are, therefore, best recognized at the process level of a firm (Ray et al., 2005).

Several approaches to determine process performance were considered on its applicability, such as the Performance Pyramid, and the Performance Prism. Each technique has its strengths and weaknesses and there is no overall best and generally accepted method available. The Balanced Scorecard (BSC) tool was chosen (Kaplan and Norton, 1992), because it uses a combination of traditional financial evaluation techniques (the financial perspective) and metrics aligned with the company business aims and strategy (customer, internal and learning & growth perspectives). Furthermore, the BSC is a well-known and widely accepted tool in management science and practice. Although its core application is that of a strategic management tool, it offers a relatively practical way to measure process performance as well.

Process Performance

Q3. How do company IT standards affect business performance?

Effects have been measured at the process level. Process performance has been assessed from the four BSC perspectives per case study and the following benefits (based on the four case studies) were found:

- **Financial perspective:** costs of IT development and support decreased;
- **Customer perspective:** customer satisfaction increased when using IT standards, but this was dependent on the level of business participation;
- **Internal perspective:** quality and flexibility increased whereas the overall application of IT standards was constrained by country specific regulations;
- **Learning & growth perspective:** IT process and product standards were integrated as little as possible to ease change management and allow straightforward migration to rivaling processes and products to minimize potential vendor lock-ins.

Exceptions from the BSC perspectives were related to: a) financial: higher than expected implementation costs because of deficiencies in project management b) customer: occasionally burdens of standard use on end-users; c) internal: level of restrictions (limitation on variety) on the IT company standard, d) learning & growth: employability issues; one size fits all issues. Essential elements of adequate governance are involvement and alignment of all stakeholders and assigning ownership of the standard or elements within that standard. For management these include planning in the selection and implementation phase and exception handling in the operational phase of the company IT standard.

Correct and complete measurements of the process performance turned out to be vital to draw conclusions and make correct decisions of how to apply these standards. Cross-case analysis showed that reselection of standards is not necessarily based on process performance outcomes but could be triggered by governance and management of the company IT standards. Furthermore, in spite of popular beliefs, no decrease in flexibility was found. With the exception of the fourth case study, an increase in flexibility was found at the organizational, process and technical level. As the potential risk of being locked-into a company standard could significantly influence process performance, this aspect will be discussed in the next section.

Lock-in Effects

In all four cases the case company chose just one company IT standard so we will have a closer look at (vendor) lock-in effects into these process and product standards. If users have committed themselves to using a standard, they tend to stick with it. When better standards arrive in the market place, users could face migration issues. Changes may require large switching costs that effectively hampers progress, as users are likely to maintain the current and less favorable standard. Using two competing company IT standards simultaneously does not seem to be an economically viable option as this would basically double all related costs to the standard (implementation, training, license, support, etc.) and might cause interoperability issues.

Which lock-in risks and potential migration issues have been encountered in the four case studies when using just a single standard? What does it mean: 1) being tied to a single manufacturer or supplier and; 2) choosing a product that is potentially incompatible with other standards. In the first case, the C/S environment, the Business Unit decided to use the de facto standards for hardware and software of "WINTEL". They accepted lock-in into this technology as this risk was considered low because of the huge installed base worldwide, i.e. market dominance in both the professional and personal domains. The advantages of using this de facto standard, such as new product development by third party vendors that comply with "Wintel", far outweighed its disadvantages, such as future migration issues.

In the software development case the chosen company IT process standards DSDM and CMM are supplier independent with a relatively large market acceptance. This should offer guarantees to a quantitatively and qualitatively high supply as far as professional expertise is concerned. Furthermore, the organization could influence future developments of the DSDM standard by participating in further development of the standard. Hence, lock-in effects were considered low to medium.

In the third case the ERP HR suite was selected as company IT standard based on its "Best-in-Class" rating but being a propriety product the risk of lock-in is real. However, selecting any alternative product will result in the same problem. Furthermore the ERP HR suite currently being used by the case company will be migrated in the future by its new owner to a new platform, mitigating migration issues. Because the product has a large installed base worldwide, supplier lock-in was not considered as a high risk. For example the case company would be able to bargain and obtain lower prices for implementation and support.

In the fourth and final case the international standard ISO/IEC 17799 was chosen, the reason being that it has broad acceptance in the information security profession because of its perceived usefulness. This information security management standard consists of a number of best practices and, by definition, one is not tied very strongly to this standard as competing ones have more or less the same set of best practice ingredients. Furthermore, again because of its large installed base it offers guarantees regarding quality of contractors so that future migration and lock-in risks are considered as low.

The overarching tactic in the adoption of the standards by the case company is that of risk avoidance since the company chooses proven and well-established standards.

Difference Between IT Process and Product Company Standards

Two key differences were found between IT process and product standards. First of all the speed at which product standards change and thus have to be reselected is higher than that for process standards. This has consequences for the selection process and its subsequent activities. So, in general, product standards require more attention in this respect than process standards. Secondly, as process standards typically change the way staff works, more consideration should be paid to the soft-side (like company politics and other intangibles) when dealing with process standards as compared to product standards. It was also found that aligning all stakeholders to standardized data semantics (as part of processes), a tremendous effort is required. In company standardization, this is one of the most difficult activities to complete successfully which was also found by Boh and Yellin (2007). A third difference between process and product standards manifests itself in the implementation sequence: first one has to focus on process standards, then on product ones.

Management Framework

Q4. What are the components of a company IT standardization management framework?

There are two components that constitute the company IT standardization management framework, which are governance and management of the company IT standards.

The construct *Governance of Standard*, has been defined from the viewpoint of Weill and Ross (2004), related to decision rights specification and accountability. The elements of governance are to encourage desirable behavior in the selection, implementation and usage of IT standards within an organization. It deals with the capabilities and activities which should be standardized enterprise wide to support IT efficiencies, data integration and facilitating process standardization and integration, and which ones should be kept local. Another important aspect of this governance is whether to centralize or decentralize selection and implementation activities.

The construct *Managementof Standard,* has been defined from the viewpoint of decision-making related to planning, organizing, controlling, and directing the selection, implementation and usage of IT standards within an organization. As implementation of IT standards is typically carried out in projects, management of IT standards in this phase relates to Project Management, whereas in the operational phase (usage) this activity is related to IT Service Management. The selection of IT standards can be part of either of these two management activities.

The company IT standardization management framework consists of the Governance and Management constructs that pertain to propositions 2, 3, 6 (Chapter 8), whereas propositions 1, 4, 5 relate to selection, implementation, use and process performance, complementing the remainder of the framework. The propositions 1,4 and 5 are an integral part of the extended conceptual model.

The extended conceptual model, with its formative constructs, variables and propositions was tested and proved to be successful in describing and explaining effects of IT products and processes to be used as standards in a company. The six propositions of the extended conceptual model have been applied successfully to all four case studies and are listed in Table 2.

Table 2. Overall assessment of the cases using the extended conceptual model[4]

Proposition No	Supported by Case Study I	Supported by Case Study II	Supported by Case Study III	Supported by Case Study IV	Cases 1..4 Overall
P1 An effective (ineffective) IT standard selection process, positively (negatively) influences the implementation of these standards.	Yes	Yes	Yes	Yes	Yes
P2 Effective (ineffective) governance and/or management of appropriate IT standards, positively (negatively) influences the implementation of these standards.	Yes	Yes	Yes	Yes	Yes
P3 Effective (ineffective) governance and/or management of appropriate IT standards, positively (negatively) influences the use of these standards.	Yes	Yes	Yes	Yes	Yes
P4 Effective (ineffective) use of appropriate IT standards, positively influences (does not influence or negatively influences) process performance.	Yes	Yes	Yes	Yes	Yes
P5 A high (low) business process performance due to the applied IT standards, does not lead (leads) to changes in the way these standards are governed and/or managed.	Yes	Yes	Yes	Yes	Yes
P6 Effective (ineffective) governance and/or management of appropriate IT standards, positively (negatively) influences the IT standard selection process.	Yes	Yes	Yes	Yes	Yes

Influence of Governance and Management

Q5. How do governance and management of company IT standardization contribute to the realization of intended business benefits?

The four case studies revealed that there are two dominant moderators of the constructs selection, implementation and usage of IT standards: management and governance. The extended model relates management and governance of standards to the constructs as discussed in this chapter at research question Q1. With management and governance moderating these constructs, this allows controlling process performance and thus contributing to the realization of intended business benefits. The cross-case analysis showed that ineffective selection could be compensated for by effective control to improve process performance, as in two cases the Process Performance was rated 'High' in spite of a 'Low' rating for selection. This was worked out in more detail in the fourth case study, which showed ineffective governance could be compensated with effective management. The reverse scenario was not found in the case studies. Other effects that influence selection, implementation and usage of company IT standards and thus indirectly process performance are:

As far as governance is concerned:

- The extent to which Business and IT were involved
- The extent of Business and IT alignment
- The level of agreed ownership of the standard and/or entities within this standard.

With respect to management, these include:

- The level of consideration paid to the business model and business drivers
- The level of endorsement by senior management
- The extent to which exception handling is carried out
- The level of restrictiveness of the standard

What is the Optimal Level of Standardization?

The optimal level of company IT standardization can not be decided upon unequivocally as this depends on the type of company and its business. We have seen that IT governance, including that of company IT standards, deals with which capabilities and activities should be standardized enterprise-wide and which ones should be specific to a Business Unit (Chapter 8). Standardization can be carried out in several areas with an increasing level of difficulty: 1) technology, to generate economies of scale with shared services; 2) data – to facilitate process integration; 3) processes – to facilitate business application integration across the enterprise.

In Chapter 2 it was discussed that the demand for synergies (in the areas of technology, data and processes) typically depends on the value disciplines of a company. This was also found in the Pilot case study (Chapter 4). Product leadership only requires technology synergies, customer intimate firms also seek shared data whereas enterprises pursuing operational excellence engage in standardization in all three areas. Enterprises promoting business unit autonomy usually focus on shared technology and data only. The shared infrastructure and data provide the base for all other applications that are needed to support the business processes (see also Chapter 1, Figure 1). Weill and Ross (2004) argue that the distinction between infrastructure standardization on the one hand and business specific applications on the other hand, allows enterprises to profit from economies of scale while retaining flexibility. On the other hand, enterprises seeking more synergies between the business units gradually work towards data and process standardization as well.

In sum, diversified businesses usually have fewer needs for enterprise-wide standardization and this could be limited to a shared infrastructure that facilitates common objectives such as procurement and information security. When we cross-reference this with the results from the case studies the pattern emerges as specified in Table 3.

Case 3 is a typical one of business application integration across the enterprise, which was shown to be the most difficult one to accomplish indeed. Cases 2 and 4 concerned a process standardization initiative that did not directly involve technology, whereas case 1 was a typical one related to accomplishing economies of scale albeit limited to a single BU. The conclusion can be drawn that all four initiatives

Table 3. Areas of standardization in relation to the four case studies

Case study	Technology	Data	Processes	Range
1. C/S environment	Yes	No	No	BU
2. Software development	N/A	N/A	Yes	BU
3. HRM	Yes	Yes	Yes	Enterprise
4. Information Security Management	N/A	N/A	Yes	BU

could potentially have been implemented with an enterprise-wide range, however, all Business Units had the authority to act autonomously and did not leap at this opportunity.

Overall Conclusion

Main research question. How can organizations realize intended business benefits from company IT standardization?

The primary value offered by IT standards is to improve business performance that, either directly or indirectly, results in business benefits. Examples of intended business benefits are: 1) to cut costs of development and support of the IT infrastructure; 2) to improve customer satisfaction with the IT services offered; 3) to facilitate interoperability and quality of the information systems both intra- and inter-company; 4) to increase scalability and adaptability of IT systems.

In order to achieve the intended benefits from company IT standardization, it is essential a number of steps are taken. Foremost, determine what is to be standardized enterprise wide and what should remain specific to local needs. Then, based on the intended business benefits, determine which data from business processes (KPIs) have to be measured and ensure you gather the data one way or the other. Subsequently baseline these measurements to make comparisons at a later stage possible. Realization of expected business benefits is conditional to the way governance and management on selection, implementation and usage of company IT standards are carried out. At research question Q5 the influences of governance and management have been described, which resulted in an overall improvement as seen from a process performance perspective in the four case studies (research question Q3).

Based on the empirical evidence from the case studies, a comprehensive company IT standardization framework was developed that includes governance and management of the standards. This framework turned out to be elementary in describing and explaining changes in process performance as a result of applying such standards. Governance of company IT standards concerns the specification of decision rights and an accountability framework to encourage desirable behavior. Management of company IT standards concerns the decision-making efforts associated with planning, organizing, controlling, and directing. Both governance and management relate to the selection, implementation and usage of company IT standards and contribute to the realization of intended business benefits.

As far as governance is concerned, key factors for effective selection, implementation and usage of company IT standards and ultimately the intended business benefits are ownership and accountability. Ownership of the company standard should reside at the functional domain (such as IT, HR and Finance). These domain owners are accountable for the contents of the standard and make certain it reflects present-day business needs. Governance of the company IT standards should be an integral part of the overall IT governance of the company, as IT standards set specifications for (part of) the overall IT infrastructure (Weill and Broadbent, 1998; Weill and Ross, 2004). Paramount in the governance of the company standards is that the correct stakeholders should be involved from both Business and (local) IT in the decision, implementation and use of company standards and that ownership has been assigned to the domain owners. Besides participation of the IT department in all cases, for Case 1 this included Business Management as regards the functionality to be offered in de Client Server standards and for Case 2 this was related to the way in which the Business was involved when setting up the software development process standard. For Case 3 this concerned the HR Business when setting the company standard, whereas in Case 4 again Business Management was involved in setting the priority of risk profile improvements activities. It was shown in the case studies that, apart from the management of the company standards, the effectiveness of the company standards also depended on how these stakeholders were involved in this governance process.

Key contributors to effective management of company IT standards include endorsement by Senior Management and the way exceptions are being handled and thus how business requirements and the company standards remain aligned. A final question should be answered in this respect: "who" manages the selection, implementation and use of the company standards and "where" in the organization should this be carried out? From the case studies it was found that the departments that managed the company standards were closely linked to the domain where the standards were being used, because of the required knowledge of and inherent interest in the subject matter. For Case 1 this concerned the IT infrastructure, for Case 2 this was IT software development, for Case 3 this related to the HR domain and for Case 4 this was the information security. In the case company, ownership of the company standard was scattered around IT architecture and strategy groups in the Business Units (Cases 1, 2 end 4) and in the HR case ownership resided at the project organization that would hand over the standards to the Global HR Business. So in this case company, management of company standards was not structured into a single organizational entity (i.e. centralized). To prevent isolated and incompatible solutions and ensure cross-departmental cooperation, the management of the company standards should be structured in a dedicated group for all functional domains that engage in company standardization. The reasons and current tendency to centralize was also discussed in Chapter 8. In combination with the governance described above this should result in enhanced performance and the anticipated business benefits.

The overall conclusion is that company IT standards can positively affect process performance and thus provide Business benefits, provided adequate governance and management of selection, implementation and usage is set-up as described in the preceding pages. In addition it should be recognized that the level of enterprise-wide company standardization depends on the level of diversification of the Businesses (i.e. the more diversification, the less the need for enterprise-wide company standardization).

DISCUSSION

Contributions to Theory

While in academic research the effects of project management and ERP implementations on the success or failure of IS have been explored extensively, no studies to date directly addressed the success factors for effective and efficient selection, implementing and usage of company IT standards on process performance. This book, therefore, contributes to IS literature in several ways.

The first contribution relates to the fact that only very limited research has been done on company IT standards, which holds especially for the empirical effects of using such standards. From the little theory that exists on business effects of company IT standards, combined with a pilot case study, an initial conceptual model was developed. Subsequently, by testing this model using in-depth case study research, followed by analytic generalization in Chapter 8, an extended conceptual model has been developed which consists of constructs and variables that affect process performance. This enhanced model was also tested successfully and some improvements were added as a result of a fourth case study.

The second contribution relates to the business benefits from company IT standards. The case studies showed that with company IT standardization overall improvements in process performance were achieved. For all case studies detailed results were discussed on how process performance was affected as a result of these standards. The overall results from a process performance perspective were provided when discussing research question Q3.

The third contribution of this study, and covering the main research question, relates to the empirical evidence on how to realize intended business benefits from company IT standardization. This book showed how governance and management of company IT standards, moderating selection, implementation and usage, affects process performance and thus contributes greatly to accomplish intended business benefits. To the best of our knowledge the Corporate IT Standardization Management Framework, relating selection, implementation and use of standards to process performance and moderated by governance and management did not exist until now.

Generalizability and Limitations

FINCORP has been used to complement the existing theory base on company IT standardization by means of a pilot case study in order to arrive at an initial conceptual model. Subsequently, in this financial services company in-depth case studies have been carried out because detailed data could be used to test this model and further refine the conceptual model. Although the case studies have been carried out within Business Units of FINCORP only, the diversity of these units offered enough variability to test the conceptual model and subsequently refine it. A key methodological question that should be answered in any research is that of external validity, also known as generalizability. This research examined multiple cases using the same semi-structured questionnaire (i.e. replication logic), thereby paving the way for analytic generalization. With this analytic generalization the previously developed theory (i.e. the conceptual model) was used as a template against which the empirical results of the case studies could be tested. The initial and extended conceptual models were applied successfully using four case studies, thereby increasing confidence in the theory.

With respect to the general applicability of the extended conceptual model and the conclusions on how to accomplish intended business benefits in particular, the following should be taken into consideration. The domain of this theory constitutes IT standardization in companies for supporting processes. Referring to existing literature in the IS domain, on which the conceptual model is partly based, the conclusions drawn in this chapter can be regarded as an extension of the existing knowledge. Already in the late eighties Cargill (1989) addressed control aspects of IT standards in a general sense. Weill and Broadbent (1998) contributed to this area as well. Kayworth and Sambamurthy (2000) and Hanseth and Braa (2001) investigated this aspect for IT infrastructure standards, whereas Rada and Craparo (2001) did the same for software development standards. The organizational set-up influenced the effectiveness of such standards. In addition, literature on IT architecture by Ross (2003) and literature on IT governance by Weill and Ross (2004) were taken into account when creating the extended conceptual model. Thus the investigated area of research relating to IT company standards can be partly explained with existing literature as well. It is therefore anticipated that the conclusions of this research are valid in the larger setting of enterprises using company IT product and process standards to support business processes. So, the developed theory in this research is limited to product and process standards that are utilized in support processes (IT, HR, Finance, Operations, etc) in medium-sized to large organizations. More case study research needs be carried out (i.e. replication) to further test the theory in order to improve confidence in the robustness of the theory. While the domain of this study is limited to company IT standards for supporting processes, it may have the potential to be applicable to non IT standards as well, as one could argue that it is also relevant in the area of management and governance of selection, implementation and use. Further research is required to substantiate this claim.

Another important consideration in this respect is that the standards considered in this research are related to support processes (back office) only and not to primary business processes (front office). Hence, whether the findings also hold good for standards used in this latter category also requires further research. At what level standardization of products and processes, if at all, should take place at the front office remains unaddressed and probably requires an extension of the conceptual model that includes aspects such as requirements from clients. In addition, exogenous factors such as industry pressures could be included explicitly in an expanded model as well (see Chapter 8, Figure 3).

Contributions to Practice

The contributions of this research to organizations first of all show that with the application of IT product and/or process standards, considerable improvements on process performance can be gained. Significant positive effects were found at the financial, customer, internal and learning & growth perspectives. In other words, organizations can gain business benefits from IT standards.

Furthermore this research provides an insight into significant aspects affecting process performance as a result of company IT standards. It provides insight to the industry about how company IT standards affect business processes and provides examples or even guidance on how to govern and manage such standards in practice. The application of the Balanced Scorecard turned out to be a practical tool to assess the impact of the standards on process performance.

It allows managers to be fully aware of the potential of governance and management of company standards. Managers should be aware of the impact of allocation of decision rights and the setting of accountabilities related to company standardization. The implications of this research to organizations refer to the decision making process by organizations with regard to selection, implementation and usage. Companies may wish to reconsider the way they are currently dealing with company IT standards.

LOOKING AHEAD

There are a number of areas where further research is required, both from a scientific and practical point of view.

With regard to the theoretical contribution, although the domain of the theory is relatively broad (company IT standardization and IT standards that support business processes), the population used to test the theory was rather small (four case studies have been carried out in a single company in the financial services sector). Further research should include other companies, possibly from other areas such as manufacturing, which will add to the robustness and trustworthiness of the theory, and allows analyzing potential cross-industry similarities and differences. Company standards other than the IT domain could also be included which might lead to an extension of the domain of the theory.

Although this research has presented a way to affect process performance as a result of company IT standards, further research is necessary to determine the way each of the variables affect the constructs by formulating and testing hypotheses related to these variables. The feedback loops, representing the dynamic character of the conceptual model, should also be analyzed in more detail to understand the specific situations and characteristics triggering the decisions to initiate changes to selection implementation and usage of company IT standards. In particular the dichotomy of governance and management and its mutual moderating effects on selection, implementation and use should be further investigated. To further zoom in similarities and differences between product and process standards is another direction that would add value to this research topic.

It is therefore recommended that the extended conceptual model is applied to a larger number of (longitudinal) case studies in the IT domain in other companies. Subsequently survey research could be carried out to further validate the theory. Then the applicability of the model for support functions outside the IT domain should be investigated. Possibly other variables are of interest in these domains. Investigating the impact of company IT standardization and how to accomplish its intended business benefits when dealing with primary business processes is also a topic for future research as additional constructs may be required. These further studies would allow generalizing the theory to include several domains and even apply across industry sectors.

With regard to the practical point of view it is recommended applying the extended conceptual model to enterprises in other industry sectors, such as telecommunications, oil and gas, computer services, manufacturing and the public sector as well. It is anticipated that, since such companies have similar supporting processes, standardization of both products and processes used to support their core business processes would add value as demonstrated in this research.

REFERENCES

Boh, W. F., & Yellin, D. (2007). Using Enterprise Architecture Standards in Managing Information Technology. *Journal of Management Information Systems*, *23*(3), 163–207. doi:10.2753/MIS0742-1222230307

Cargill, C. F. (1989). *Information Technology Standardization: Theory, Process, and Organizations*. Bedford, MA: Digital Press.

Hanseth, O., & Braa, K. (2001). Hunting for the treasure at the end of the Rainbow: Standardizing Corporate IT Infrastructure. *Computer Supported Cooperative Work*, *10*, 261–292. doi:10.1023/A:1012637309336

Kaplan, R. S., & Norton, D. P. (1992). The Balanced Scorecard - Measures that Drive Performance. *Harvard Business Review*, *70*(1), 71–79.

Kayworth, T., & Sambamurthy, V. (2000). Facilitating localized exploitation and enterprise-wide integration in the use of IT infrastructures: The role of PC/LAN infrastructure standard. *The Data Base for Advances in Information Systems*, *31*(4), 54–81.

Rada, R., & Craparo, J. S. (2001). Standardizing Management of Software Engineering Projects, *Knowledge, Technology, & Policy*, *14*(2), 67–77.

Ray, G., Muhanna, W. A., & Barney, J. B. (2005). Information Technology and the Performance of the Customer Service Process: A Resource-Based Analysis. *Management Information Systems Quarterly*, *29*(4).

Ross, J. W. (2003). Strategic IT architecture competency. *MIS Quarterly Executive*, *2*(1), 31–43.

Weill, P., & Broadbent, M. (1998). *Leveraging the new Infrastructure. How Market Leaders Capitalize on Information Technology*. Boston, MA: Harvard Business School Press.

Weill, P., & Ross, J. (2004). *IT Governance - How Top Performers Manage IT Decision Rights for Superior Results*. Boston, MA: Harvard Business School Press.

ENDNOTES

1 Following Chapter 8, 'control on the usage' of IT standards was modified into 'governance and management of selection, implementation and application' of IT standards. The original corresponding sub-question: *"How can the intended application of IT standardization be assured?"* was, therefore, changed into *"What are components of a company IT standardization framework?"*. Moreover a fifth research question was added which reflects the new insights on ways to accomplish intended business benefits from company IT standardization.

2 Retained and renewed constructs are denoted in *Italics*.

3 We have seen that at the case company, failure to prescribe and enforce company IT standards by management effectively made some standardization efforts fruitless.

4 Governance and management of IT standards are considered as adequate when business process performance targets are met.

Summary

RESEARCH QUESTIONS
Main question: How can organizations realize intended business benefits from company IT standardization?
Detailed questions: 1. What is a company IT standardization process and which distinguishable components does it encompass? 2. How can business effects of IT standards be measured? 3. How do company IT standards affect business performance? 4. What are the components of a company IT standardization management framework? 5. How do governance and management of company IT standardization contribute to the realization of intended business benefits?

This research is one of the first attempts to chart the unexplored terrain of company IT standardization and its business benefits. In this research, a *company IT standard* is defined as "*The specification of an IT process or IT product to be repeatedly and consistently used in the company*". IT process standards concern, but are not limited to, standards for quality improvement of processes and services, IT governance, IT service management, and project management. IT product standards include standards for interoperability, safety and quality. The primary value offered by company IT standards is to improve business performance and in that way accomplish business benefits. Examples of intended business benefits are: 1) to cut development and support costs of the IT infrastructure; 2) to improve customer satisfaction with the IT services offered; 3) to facilitate interoperability and quality of the information systems both within and between companies; 4) to increase scalability and adaptability of IT systems.

The core of this research is to investigate how organizations can realize intended business benefits [Main question] from company IT standardization. A few exceptions apart, academic literature on how company IT standards impact on business performance is notably absent. Current literature on IT standardization and standards focuses mainly on the effects of IT standards at a macro economic scale and the standardization processes carried out in industry by consortia and international standard setting organizations. To fill in this gap, an initial conceptual model was created based on the little literature available in the field of company IT standardization. The model was complemented with insights gained from a pilot case study. Subsequently in-depth case study research was carried out to test this model.

A company IT standardization process is a process that is carried out by an organization with the objective of providing specifications for an IT product or process to be repeatedly and consistently used in that company. This process consists of three distinguishable components [Detailed question 1]: selection, implementation and usage. In the case studies, issues regarding selection, implementation and use of company IT standards are discussed in detail. Rather than choosing processes and products on a project-by-project basis, in the *selection* phase the focus is on due consideration of IT products and processes. It is shown that the effectiveness of the resulting company IT standard depends on a number of factors in this selection process. This includes the level of alignment between the Business and IT departments and the level of consideration paid to the business model and business drivers. In the *implementation* phase, the quality of project management obviously plays an important role. Of an equal importance, especially for standards being implemented across organizational units, is that the department that manages the company IT standards should ensure that a prescribed set of products and/or standard way of implementation is pursued. Failure to comply herewith could result in incompatible instances of the company IT standard, severely mitigating its benefits. In the *usage* phase, there are several important elements that determine whether a company IT standard is being used effectively. Among the more important ones are: 1) processes and procedures that support the usage of the standard, including the way in which exceptions are being handled and whether these exceptions are integrated into the existing standard; 2) whether it concerns a process or product standard because of differences between these types, as the first one typically has more impact on the way staff work than the latter; 3) the level of IT and Business Management support of the standard and the enforcement in and by the organization.

Business effects of company IT standards were measured from the four Balanced Scorecard perspectives [Detailed question 2] as this method includes financial as well as non financial elements and is widely accepted in both the academic and professional world. The cases provide evidence that an appropriate application of company IT standards improves business performance [Detailed question 3]. As an effect, we found significant positive effects at the Financial, Customer, Internal and Learning & Growth perspectives: 1) costs of IT development and support decreased and the standardization initiatives resulted in staff redundancies; 2) customer satisfaction increased; 3) quality improvements were realized (such as fewer errors, increased stability and maintainability; improved security and data consistency); 4) IT process and product standards were implemented so that interdependencies between the standards were kept to a minimum (modularity principle) to ease change management. This would allow straightforward migration to rivaling standards which minimizes the potential danger of vendor lock-ins.

Based on the empirical evidence from the case studies, a comprehensive company IT standardization management framework [Detailed question 4] was developed that includes governance and management of the standards. This framework turned out to be elementary in describing and explaining changes in business performance as a result of applying such standards. Governance of company IT standards concerns the specification of decision rights and an accountability framework to encourage desirable behavior. Management of company IT standards concerns the decision-making efforts associated with planning, organizing, directing and controlling, the selection, implementation and use such standards. Both governance and management relate to the selection, implementation and usage of company IT standards and contribute to the realization of intended business benefits [(Detailed question 5)]. As far as governance is concerned, the main elements that influence selection, implementation and usage of company IT standards and hence process performance are: 1) the extent to which Business and IT departments were involved and aligned; 2) the level of agreed ownership of the standard and/or entities within this standard. With respect to management of company IT standards, the main elements include: 1) the level of consideration paid to the business model and business drivers; 2) the level of endorsement by senior management; 3) the extent to which exception handling is carried out effectively and efficiently.

This research concerns company standards in the IT domain in support processes only. FINCORP has been used as the case company to test the conceptual model that proved to be successful in answering the research questions. The scope of the conceptual model, which focuses on how to benefit from company standardization, is restricted to IT company standards. It is anticipated that the results discussed in this research are also relevant to other medium to large organizations that use company product and process standards in support processes (e.g. IT, HR, Finance, Operations). Recommendations for future research include: 1) to test the conceptual model in similar companies in the IT domain, 2) to evaluate the applicability of the conceptual model for support functions outside the IT domain; 3) to investigate similarities and differences between primary business processes and support processes. These recommendations would allow generalizing the conclusions to specific industry sectors or even across industries.

The contributions of this research to large organizations show first of all that business benefits can be achieved by applying IT product and/or process standards, as considerable improvements in process performance were accomplished. It provides insight in how company IT standards affect business processes and it shows how to govern and manage such standards in practice. The implications of this research to organizations refer to the design of and decision making process by organizations with regard to selection, implementation and usage of standards. Companies may wish to reconsider the way they are currently dealing with company IT standards.

Appendix I
Case Study Questionnaire

The interviews carried out during the case studies are based on the following questionnaire which is divided into three sections, each covering an aspect of company IT standardization (section, application, control and performance) that relate to the initial conceptual model (Figure 3, Chapter 3).

The aim of this questionnaire is to determine how to "Realize Business Benefits from Company IT Standardization".

Instruction: Please complete the questions in their original order. The results will remain anonymous. There are no incorrect answers!

Section I: Questions on company IT standard selection and control

Fifteen states of affairs are given. *Please select the answer that describes best your organization.* (Only 1 answer possible).

1) The attention paid to the Business model, when determining standards is:

None: Little: Moderate: Great: Extensive:

2) The attention paid of the Business drivers, when determining standards is:

None: Little: Moderate: Great: Extensive:

3) When determining standards, the level of Business involvement is:

None: Little: Moderate: Great: Extensive:

4) When determining standards, the level of IT Engineering involvement is:

None: Little: Moderate: Great: Extensive:

5) When determining standards, the level of IT Operations involvement is:

None: Little: Moderate: Great: Extensive:

6) The level of understanding and openness (alignment) between Business and IT is:

None: Little: Moderate: Great: Extensive:

7) Business Management knowledge on standards is:

None: Little: Moderate: Great: Extensive:

8) IT Management knowledge on standards is:

None: Little: Moderate: Great: Extensive:

9) The level of standard endorsement/support by Business and IT management is:

None: Little: Moderate: Great: Extensive:

10) The level of standard prescription is:

None: Little: Moderate: Great: Extensive:

11) The level of standard enforcing is:

None: Little: Moderate: Great: Extensive:

12) The level of standard awareness at the Business is:

None: Little: Moderate: Great: Extensive:

13) The level of standard awareness at IT is:

None: Little: Moderate: Great: Extensive:

14) The choice of 'flavors' within a standard is:

None: Little: Moderate: Great: Extensive:

15) Reusability of standardized modules is:

None: Little: Moderate: Great: Extensive:

Section II A: Open questions on the IT standard selection process

Is there a formal process and organization to decide which IT product or process will become the company standard?
Answer indication: how formal is process and/or organizational set-up.

How is the balance of power between Business, IT Development and IT Support when selecting IT standards?
Answer indication: from no involvement to active participation between all parties.

What are the drivers to standardize, if any?
Answer indication: quality, costs, etc.

Are the standards more technically or managerially focussed?
Answer indication: technically (e.g. performance); managerial (e.g. costs).

Section II B: Open questions on the *application* of IT standards

What is the type of standard in this case study?
Answer indication: process standard or product standard; is this an interface standard.

What is the *reach* of the standard?
Answer indication: From a single department to the whole enterprise.

What is the origin of the standard?
Answer indication: De facto; Consensus; De jure (by law).

What is the maturity of the standard?
Answer indication: Emerging; Established; Fading.

Do the company standards cover the full *range* of IT?
Answer indication: from a singe application to whole technical infrastructure.

How would you describe the general attitude of both Business and IT management towards the usage of IT standards?
Answer indication: opposite, indifferent, supportive.

Section II C: Open questions on the *control* of the IT standard

How and at which level takes standard endorsement/support place?
Answer indication: Organizational level; management commitment.

How prescriptive are the IT standards?
Answer indication: from recommended to mandatory.

In which way is it possible to divert from the IT standards when Business requirements deem so?
Answer indication: consideration of Business opportunities in case of deviations.

How would you describe the quality level of control processes and procedures during application of the IT standards?
Answer indication: from low ad-hoc to high quality effective and efficient.

Are the standards more or less restrictive in comparison to typical other firms and are these perceived as sufficient by the Business?
Answer indication: possibility to choose from certain 'flavors' (e.g. UNIX® operating systems Sun OS and/or HP-UX).

Section II D: Open questions on *business performance* as a result of IT standards

How do IT standards influence the capabilities of your Business Unit?
Answer indication: think in terms of quality, quantity and costs.

Did end-user satisfaction on IT delivery and support change when IT standards were introduced? And what about client satisfaction?
Answer indication: is one content or are there complains (specify type of approvals or complains).

In which way did IT standardization affect the profitability of your Business Unit?
Answer indication: asses the usage of IT standards related to economic profit and value.

To what extend did the efficiency of your Business Unit change when standards were introduced?
Answer indication: think in terms of number of staff, problem solving, duration of projects.

Did you observe any changes in "down-time" of IT systems after introduction of IT standards?
Answer indication: asses the usage of IT standards related to application availability and capacity.

Is standardization generally perceived as inhibitor or enabler when rapid business changes are necessary?
Answer indication: asses the usage of IT standards related to Business model drivers and opportunities.

What were the effects of using standards on adaptability and expandability of IT systems?
Answer indication: asses the usage of IT standards related to flexibility of the systems.

How was the application functionality affected when IT standards were introduced? Was this a positive or a negative effect?
Answer indication: asses the usage of IT standards related to the functionality of the applications that you now use.

Section III: Some business effects of IT standards

In this section of the questionnaire we ask you to grade the effects on business performance due to IT standardization. (Only 1 answer possible).

-2: Strongly Negative   -1: Negative   0: None   1: Positive   2: Strongly Positive

	-2	-1	0	1	2	N/A	Specify value if known
Throughput time requests							
Service Quality							
Time to support							
Cost to develop							
Availability							
Time to develop							
Risk							
Compatibility							
Client satisfaction							
Staff motivation							
Adaptability							
Time to market							
Modularity							
Costs to support							
Scalability							
Innovativeness							
ROI							
Perceived complexity							
Economic Value-added							
Robustness							
Error and rework rates							
On-time service delivery							
Do you recognize other effects? <please specify>							

<table>
<tr><td colspan="2">Section IV: Some general questions</td></tr>
<tr><td colspan="2">Please select the appropriate answer to these descriptive questions (1 answer possible).</td></tr>
<tr><td>1) What type of business are you in?

a) Consumer banking
b) Private banking
c) Investment banking
d) Asset management
e) Other</td><td>2) What is the size of your company?

a) Less than 100 FTE
b) Between 100 and 300 FTE
c) Between 300 and 1,000 FTE
d) Between 1,000 and 3,000 FTE
e) Between 3,000 and 10,000 FTE
f) More than 10,000 FTE</td></tr>
<tr><td>3) What is your company's focus?

a) Regional
b) National
c) Several countries
d) Global</td><td>4) How do you use computers?

a) IT Developer
b) IT Supporter
c) End User</td></tr>
<tr><td>5) What is your computer experience?

a) Less 1 year
b) Between 1 and 3 years
c) Between 3 and 10 years
d) 10 years and more</td><td>6) How often do you use computers?

a) About once a week or less
b) Between 1 and 3 days a week
c) About once a day
d) Several times a day</td></tr>
<tr><td>7) What is your age?

a) Below 25
b) Between 25 and 34
c) Between 35 and 44
d) Between 45 and 54
e) 55 or older</td><td>8) What is your gender?

a) Female
b) Male</td></tr>
</table>

Thank you very much for your time and effort!

Appendix II
List of Interviewees

Table 1. List of interviewees for the pilot case study

Interview number	Role Interviewee	Interview Date	Interview Type	Taped
I	Head of Group IT	18/07/2001	Unstructured	No
II	IT Architect WCS	03/04/2002	Unstructured	No
III	Project Manager eTrust PC/AM	09/04/2002	Unstructured	No
IV	Head of Group IT Architecture and Standards & Head of Group IT Strategy	16/05/2002	Unstructured	No
V	Head of IT Architecture WCS	28/05/2002	Unstructured	No
VI	Head of Group Administrative Organization and CAT/CART.	30/05/2002	Unstructured	No

Table 2. List of interviewees for C/S case study

Interview number	Role Interviewee	Interview Date	Interview Type	Taped
I	Project member implementation C/S standard	04/02/2003	Unstructured	No
II	Project lead implementation C/S standard	26/02/2003	Unstructured	No
III	Staff member Corporate ICT	13/05/2003	Unstructured	No
IIa	Project lead implementation	13/05/2003	Semi-structured	No
IV	Product manager C/S standard	12/11/2003	Unstructured	No
V	ICT architect C/S standard	23/02/2004	Semi-structured	Yes
IVa	Product manager C/S standard	25/02/2004	Semi-structured	Yes
VI	Product coordinator C/S standard	10/03/2004	Unstructured	Yes

Table 3. List of interviewees for Inspiration case study

Interview number	Role Interviewee	Interview Date	Interview Type	Taped
I	Program manager Inspiration	18/11/2002	Unstructured	No
II	Program manager Inspiration	10/09/2003	Unstructured	No
III	DSDM coach	23/09/2004	Semi-structured	No
IV	Project lead - DSDM	17/11/2004	Semi-structured	Yes
V	Project lead - CMM	06/12/2004	Semi-structured	Yes
VI	Head Project Office ICT	20/12/2004	Unstructured	Yes
VII	CMM coach	30/01/2007	Semi-structured	Yes
VIII	CMM coach	05/02/2007	Semi-structured	Yes

Table 4. List of interviewees for CHRISP case study

Interview number	Role Interviewee	Interview Date	Interview Type	Taped
I	Program manager	16/02/2005	Semi-structured	Yes
II	Process work stream lead	24/03/2005	Unstructured	Yes
III	Financial management Officer	21/04/2005	Semi-structured	Yes
IV	Data Warehouse team lead	25/04/2005	Unstructured	Yes
V	Marketing & Sales CHRISP	02/05/2005	Unstructured	Yes
VI	Customer Support & IT Infrastructure	18/05/2005	Unstructured	No
VII	Data Warehouse team lead	12/12/2005	Unstructured	Yes

About the Author

Robert M. van Wessel holds a Master in Electrical Engineering from Twente University and an PhD in Business Administration from Tilburg University (Department of Information Systems and Management). Robert's research interests relate to the interaction and alignment of Business & Information Technology and include Business Performance and the Value of IT, Portfolio Management, IT Governance, Information Security Management and IT Standardization & Standards. Robert has a broad expertise on the practical application of IT, ranging from data modeling to IT Service Management. Robert is currently Business Architect at a financial services enterprise and founder of ApexIS, a firm providing consultancy services to companies in his areas of research.

Index

A

academic literature 261
application rationalization 182, 208
application rationalization phase 182
appropriate level 35
axiomatic 35

B

balanced scorecard (BSC) 88, 94, 96, 101, 124, 162, 170, 176, 221, 229, 233, 249
Balanced Scorecard (BSC) approach 56
Balanced Scorecard (BSC) tool 249
balanced scorecard framework 184
balanced scorecard method 50, 56, 57, 58, 59, 73, 74, 75, 135, 136, 152, 160
bandwagon effect 14
benchmark recommendations long term (BREL) 135, 136
benchmark short term (BMST) 135, 136
Best-in-Class rating 165, 172
BPR program 134
browser-based access 114
BSC approach 95
BU autonomy 34
business IT alignment 1, 82, 85, 87, 92, 173
business performance 2, 3, 4, 5, 7, 50, 52, 54, 56, 57, 58, 70, 133, 158, 159
business performance, effectiveness of 2
business processes 3, 6, 50, 51, 53, 54, 55, 59, 60, 61, 63, 64, 66
business processes, competitiveness of 13
business processes, quality of 13
business process integration 163
business process performance 4, 5, 78, 80, 87, 88, 98, 101
business process redesign 51, 72
business process reengineering (BPR) 51, 134
Business Technology Policy Board (BTPB) 82
business unit 113, 114, 115, 116, 117, 120, 121, 123, 124, 125, 126, 127, 130

C

capability maturity model (CMM) 30, 133, 135, 136, 137, 142, 143, 144, 145, 146, 147, 148, 149, 150, 151, 152, 153, 154, 155, 156, 157, 158, 159, 160, 161, 183, 185, 186, 188, 189, 192, 194, 195, 196, 198, 209, 247, 250
Central Quality Officer (CQO) 147, 155
Change Management 115
client server 246, 247
client/server (C/S) standardization project 182
client/server (C/S) standards 113, 115, 116, 117, 118, 119, 120, 122, 123, 124, 126, 127, 128, 129, 130, 132
CMM quality management system 136, 143, 158
collaboration 91, 93, 94, 123
common human resources information system program (CHRISP) 162, 164, 166, 167, 168, 169, 170, 173, 174, 176
communication protocol 92
company IT standards 245, 246, 248, 249, 250, 251, 252, 253, 254, 255, 256, 257, 258, 259
compatibility 14, 24, 25, 30, 32, 39, 41, 42, 43, 44, 47, 49
component-based development (CBD) 83

conceptual model 78, 79, 85, 86, 87, 88, 90, 92, 93, 96, 97, 98, 100, 101, 102, 104, 116, 119, 120, 128, 129, 130, 162, 175, 178, 245, 246, 247, 248, 251, 255, 256, 257, 258
Configuration & Change Managers (CCM) 147
control objectives for information and related technology (COBIT) 218, 219, 241, 242
corporate architecture review team (CART) 80, 81, 83, 84, 85
corporate architecture team (CAT) 80, 81, 83, 84, 85, 120
Corporate Clients 115
corporate IT standardization 79
corporate IT standardization management framework 182, 207
corporate procurement database 51
Corporate Sales 115
corporate standards and policies committee (CSPC) 80, 81, 85
costs-effective deployment 30
cross-case process performance 184
C/S hardware 183
customer intimacy 30
Customer perspective 249

D

Dashboard 135, 136, 142, 149, 152
data consistency 261
data elements 171, 173, 174, 176, 177, 179
data integration 251
data structures 37
de facto 17, 18, 19, 20, 23, 26, 27, 39, 49
demanding customers 1
design-oriented research 7
Design-oriented research 7
desktop environments 112, 114, 121, 124, 128
desktop environments, back-end 112, 114, 119, 127, 182
desktop environments, front-end 112, 127, 182
Dvorak Simplified Keyboard 14
dynamic system development method (DSDM) 133, 135, 136, 137, 138, 139, 140, 141, 142, 143, 188, 189, 192, 193, 194, 195, 196, 198, 199, 209, 247, 250

E

economic research 41
economic value 15
economies of scale 13, 26, 28, 34, 37, 38, 41, 79, 96
economies of scope 14
EDI systems 54
effectiveness 13, 30, 35
efficiency 13, 24, 26, 27, 36, 37, 38
EFQM2 management model 55
EITAF model 83
emergency password process 221
end-user 168, 170
enterprise architecture 34, 37, 41
Enterprise Architecture (EA) 203
Enterprise Information Technology Architecture Framework (EITAF) 83
enterprise IT architecture 33
enterprise resource planning (ERP) 162, 163, 164, 165, 166, 168, 172, 178, 179, 180, 246, 247, 250, 255
enterprise resource planning (ERP) systems 51, 72
enterprise-wide range 254
ERP HR modules 162
ERP HR suite 183
ERP systems 162, 163, 164, 179
ERP technologies 162
ERP usage 163
European Foundation for Quality Management 57, 76
Extensible Markup Language XML 31
externality 14

F

Financial Information Exchange (FIX) 40, 70
Financial Information Exchange (FIX) standard 70
financial performance 50, 54, 56
financial services 3, 4, 7
FINCORP 3, 5, 7, 79, 80, 81, 102, 112, 117, 127, 134, 138, 160, 161, 162, 164, 170
flexibility 1, 2, 3, 5, 8, 34, 35, 37, 38, 39, 120, 121, 123, 125, 127, 128, 130, 131, 182, 188, 194, 197, 198, 204, 205, 208

free rider problem 14
free seating 113, 114, 124, 126, 132
Full Expertise Teams (FET) 136
fundamental research 3, 5

G

gateways 79
global economy 16
global HR information system 169, 170, 178
globalization 1
global role description 170
Group Shared Services (GSS) 168
GSM standard 14

H

hardware-related 127
HLAM 221, 223
HP desktop 120
HP server 120
HR administration 165, 171
HR business 172, 173, 174, 176, 178, 183, 254, 255
HR business model 172
HR community 170
HR costs 170, 177
HR data 164, 166, 169, 170, 173, 174, 176, 177, 178, 179
HR information system 169, 170, 171, 172, 174, 178
HR IS infrastructure 171
HR IS standard 166, 168, 169, 172, 173, 174, 175, 176, 177, 178
HR IS Standard 171
HR organization 165, 174, 179
HR processes 183, 184, 190, 198, 199, 209, 210
HR-processes 166, 167, 168, 173
HR ratio 170, 175
HR risks 116
HR staff 170, 171, 172, 175, 178
HRTP phase 176
human resources (HR) 164, 183, 184, 186, 188, 189, 190, 191, 194, 195, 198, 199, 209, 210, 213
human resources management (HRM) 246, 247, 248, 253
Human Resources Transformation Program (HRTP) 168

I

IFX 31
incremental approach 51
information security 217, 218, 219, 220, 221, 223, 225, 229, 232, 234, 236, 239, 240, 241, 242, 246, 247, 253
information security management (ISM) standards 217, 218, 219, 239, 240, 242
information security management standard 246
information security standards 218, 235, 241
information systems 162, 165, 171
information technologies 3
information technology (IT) 1, 2, 3, 4, 5, 6, 7, 8, 9, 10
infrastructure standards 35
INSPIRATION BPR program 134, 135, 136, 137, 145, 146, 147, 148, 149, 150, 151, 152, 153, 154, 155, 159, 160, 161
installed base 14, 49
intellectual property rights 18, 22
internal-business-process 124
Internal perspective 249
internal rate of return (IRR) 59, 94
international community 21
International Financial Reporting Standard (IFRS) 24
International Organization for Standardization (ISO) 12, 15, 16, 20, 21, 22, 23, 24, 39, 44, 48
International Telecommunication Union (ITU) 12
Internet engineering task force (IETF) 218
Internet Engineering Task Force (IETF) 21
interoperability 1, 79, 80, 85, 98, 99, 100, 103
interoperability software 79
IS domain 3
IS literature 164
ISO/IEC 17799 standard 217, 218, 219, 220, 221, 222, 223, 224, 225, 226, 227, 229, 230, 231, 232, 233, 234, 235, 236, 237, 238, 239, 240, 241, 242
IS product standardization 162
IS standard control 179

IS standardization community 163
IS standards control 179
IT architecture 201, 203
IT budget 221
IT business 52, 53, 55
IT cooperation 140
IT delivery 113, 123, 125
IT department 80, 85, 86, 93, 94, 101, 114, 117, 120, 121, 122
IT development 1, 83, 97, 99, 249
IT Development organization 134, 135
IT domain 262
IT duopoly 201
IT engineering department 113
IT environment 112, 114, 116, 117, 118, 120, 124, 125, 126, 127, 128, 130, 199
IT governance 199, 200, 201, 202, 205, 206
IT infrastructure 1, 2, 63, 65, 66, 70, 84, 93, 97, 99, 103, 104, 110, 221, 225, 226, 235, 240, 254, 255, 256
IT investments 50, 51, 54, 57, 59, 60, 162, 202, 205
IT investments, business contribution of 78
IT maintainability 33, 112
IT management 221, 240
IT management processes 30
IT managers 199
IT-monarchism 81
IT monarchy 201
IT participation 202
IT principles 201
IT process 248, 249, 250, 251, 260, 261
IT product 246, 247, 256, 257, 260, 261, 262
IT products 113, 116, 118, 122
IT product standardization policy 80
IT services 221, 235, 237, 261
IT standard 162, 176, 177, 247, 249, 250, 252, 260, 261
IT standardization 78, 79, 80, 81, 82, 85, 91, 93, 95, 97, 245, 246, 247, 248, 251, 252, 253, 254, 256, 257, 258, 259, 260, 261
IT standards 50, 52, 54, 55, 56, 60, 61, 62, 66, 70, 71, 78, 80, 197, 177, 198, 200, 201, 202, 203, 205, 206, 207, 208, 209, 211, 212, 245, 246, 248, 249, 250, 251, 252, 253, 254, 255, 256, 257, 258, 259
IT standards, company 3, 4, 6, 7
IT support organization 116, 117
IT systems 1, 219, 225, 254
IT technology standardization 33
IT usage 91, 93, 95, 97
IT value 50, 51, 54, 72
IT value articles 54

J

Java Virtual Machines 114
Journal of Management Information Systems 12, 43
JVM version 122

K

Key Control Indicators (KCIs) 229
Key Performance Indicators (KPIs) 95
Key Process Areas (KPA's) 143

L

laissez faire 34
LAN environment 127
Local Firm 53
logical nodes 114
long-lasting solution 39

M

macro-economic level 41
macro economic scale 261
management framework 245, 248, 251
management knowledge 172
Managementof Standard 251
management processes 51, 61
Method/1 waterfall approach 134, 160
methodology 51
middleware 79, 82, 110
mobile telecommunication 14
modular architecture stage 33
modularization 2

N

net present value (NPV) 59, 94
network designers 21
network effects 13, 14, 37
network effects, direct 13

network effects, indirect 14
network externalities 38, 48
non-conformities 35
non-financial benefits 162

O

OFX 31
operational excellence 30, 31, 41
operational processes 51
Oracle® 163
organizational adoption 3
organizational context 92, 93
organizational culture 163
organizational efficiency 163
organizational leaning 37
organizational-level acceptance 31
organizational performance 51, 52, 53, 54, 56, 73
organizational project 136
organizational relationships 34
organizational resources 53

P

path dependency 14, 37
payback period (PP) 59
PC-LAN infrastructure responsiveness 35
PC-LAN infrastructure standards 35
PC manufacturer/assembler 55
PeopleSoft 165, 166, 167, 168, 169, 170, 171, 172, 173, 180
PeopleSoft® 162
Performance Prism 249
policy, standard and procedures (PSPs) 80, 81
portability 54
present-day business needs 254
Process Improvement Managers (PIM) 147
Process Improvement Plans (PIP) 147
process-level measures 52
process-oriented perspective 70
process performance 50, 52, 53, 54, 55, 56, 60, 61, 70, 71, 246, 247, 249, 250, 251, 252, 254, 255, 256, 257, 259
process standardization 133, 159
process standards 133, 137, 147, 183, 185, 190, 191, 194, 196, 197, 246, 247, 248, 250, 251, 256, 257, 258
product leadership 30
professional attitude (PA) 135, 136, 137, 151, 161
professionalize project management (PPM) 135, 136
Project Management 251
Project Quality Assurance Leaders (PQALs) 147
project scope 221
Publicly Available Specifications (PAS) 22

Q

quality standards 133, 143
QWERTY keyboard 14
QWERTY keyboard layout 14

R

rationalized data architecture stage 33
regulatory requirements 1
research context 55, 59, 70
research project 4
Resource-based view 52
return on investment (ROI) 59, 94, 164, 174
re-usability 1
revolutionary approach 51
role based access control 221, 223

S

SAP® 163
scalability 13
Secure Socket Layer 168
security objective 217
security officer standard operating model (SOM) 221, 222, 223, 224, 225, 226, 229, 233
security policy 217, 219, 223, 228, 232, 236, 241
server-based computing 113, 121
service level agreement (SLA) 113, 115
shared infrastructure 112
single sign on 221
software development 133, 134, 135, 136, 137, 138, 141, 142, 143, 144, 145, 146, 147, 150, 152, 153, 154, 155, 156, 157, 158, 159, 161, 246, 247

software quality standards 133
software rationalization 182
SOMA method 134
SSL Protocol 168
Standard Graphic Markup Language (SGML) 20
standardization 1, 2, 3, 4, 5, 6, 7, 10, 12, 13, 14, 15, 16, 48, 78, 79, 80, 81, 82, 83, 85, 86, 87, 91, 92, 93, 95, 97, 98, 99, 100, 103, 104, 105, 108, 159, 162, 163, 166, 168, 169, 170, 172, 173, 174, 175, 176, 177, 179, 180
standardization procedures 133, 136, 145, 155
standardization processes 133
standardization projects 182, 191, 198
standardized technology architecture stage 33, 112
standards 12, 13, 14, 15, 16, 17, 18, 19, 20, 21, 22, 23, 93, 94, 95, 96, 97, 98, 99, 100, 101, 205, 102, 103, 104, 106, 108, 110, 112, 113, 116, 117, 118, 119, 120, 121, 122, 123, 127, 128, 129, 197, 198, 199, 200, 130, 201, 202, 203, 205, 206, 207, 208, 209, 210, 211, 212, 213, 214
standards application 78
standards control 78
standard software 183
strategic business unit (SBU) 79, 81, 82, 85, 102
Strategic Fit 59
strategic management tool 56, 57, 58
supply chain 2
switching costs 13, 14, 15, 28, 37, 39, 42, 44
systems-related objectives 51

T

technological maturity 18
Technology Acceptance Model (TAM) 31
Technology-Organization-Environment (TOE) 31
Technology-Organization-Environment (TOE) framework 31
technology risk accreditation process (TRAP) 221
technology risk management (TRM) 221, 223, 233, 234, 237, 238, 239, 240
Technology Risk Management (TRM) 221
telecommunication networks 19, 51
testability 54
theoretical body of knowledge 7
theory of organizational behavior 34
TOE framework 31
total cost of ownership (TCO) 113, 119, 131
transaction performance 50
two factor authentication 221, 223

U

UNIX 83
user data 114, 115
user-focused solution 136
user-orientation 95
user-requirement driven 27

V

variable costs 13
vendor packages 112
Video Home System (VHS™) 17
virtual corporations 2, 8
Vulnerability Management 221, 222, 223, 224, 233, 234, 235

W

web based applications 51
web-browsers 114
Web-servers 114, 168
WebSphere® 114, 125
WINTEL platform 115